Sustainable Design Basics

Sustainable Design Basics

Sharon B. Jaffe

Rob Fleming

Mark Karlen

Saglinda H. Roberts

WILEY

For general information about our other products and services, please contact our Customer Care Department within the United States at (800) 762–2974, outside the United States at (317) 572–3993 or fax (317) 572–4002.

Wiley publishes in a variety of print and electronic formats and by print-on-demand. Some material included with standard print versions of this book may not be included in e-books or in print-on-demand. If this book refers to media such as a CD or DVD that is not included in the version you purchased, you may download this material at http://booksupport.wiley.com. For more information about Wiley products, visit www.wiley.com.

Cover design: Wiley
Cover Illustrations: Sharon B. Jaffe

This book is printed on acid-free paper.

Library of Congress Cataloging-in-Publication Data
Names: Karlen, Mark, author. | Jaffe, Sharon B., 1958- author. |
   Fleming, Rob (Robert Michael), author. | Roberts, Saglinda, author.
Title: Sustainable design basics / Mark Karlen, Ph.D., AIA, NCIDQ;
   Sharon B. Jaffe, LEED AP ID + C, IIDA, NCIDQ; Rob Fleming, AIA, LEED AP BD+C;
   Saglinda H. Roberts, ASID, CID, LEED Green Associate.
Description: Hoboken, New Jersey : Wiley, [2020] | Includes index.
Identifiers: LCCN 2019027145 (print) | LCCN 2019027146 (ebook) |
   ISBN 9781119443735 (paperback) | ISBN 9781119443803 (adobe pdf) |
   ISBN 9781119443841 (epub)
Subjects: LCSH: Sustainable design—Textbooks.
Classification: LCC NK1520 K37. 2020 (print) | LCC NK1520 (ebook) | DDC
   745.4—dc23
LC record available at https://lccn.loc.gov/2019027145
LC ebook record available at https://lccn.loc.gov/2019027146

Printed in the United States of America

V10017230_012820

Dedication

To my husband, my fellow adventurer, with whom I discovered everything is related to everything, and nature's delicate balance is both thrilling and vulnerable. No one can do everything, but everyone can do something; and I can make a start.

Sharon Jaffe

To my family, friends, and colleagues who endured a seemingly never-ending period of intense distraction, and to my co-writers, who endured my amazing ability to procrastinate. "Why do something today when it can be done next year"

Rob Fleming

To my wife for graciously accepting my too frequent distractions created by my writing tasks, and to my students and co-authors who are always a source of inspiration.

Mark Karlen

To my family, friends and colleagues thank you for your wisdom inspiration and support, and never being tired of hearing "I'm sorry, I can't, I have to work." The built environment can be a powerful force for restoration at every level and it is my hope that this book will take us one step closer.

Saglinda Roberts

Contents

Acknowledgments

Much like the sustainable design process, this textbook, *Sustainable Design Basics*, and the new methodology it presents is the result of collaborative efforts. We are grateful for the knowledge, insight, talent, and time of all of those who contributed to this process. Special thanks and acknowledgment are due to the following:

Thomas Jefferson University. The methodology presented is in large part a response to, and developed for, the use in master's in sustainable design studio courses at the university.

Our students in the master's in sustainable design program at Thomas Jefferson University whose honest and detailed feedback on the SDB methodology, even when less than favorable, helped us evaluate, revise, and refine the methodology presented in this text. Particular thanks to Abhiri Khisty, Jaspreet (JP) Bullar, Surabhi Khanderia, Rupali Gadagkar, and Shane Clark for their consistent work and positive spirit, Arpita Ganti for her enthusiasm and early SketchUp work and Keaghan Caldwell for his amazing design, SketchUp and Sefaira work. An extra thank you to master's in sustainable design staff members Savannah Nierintz, and especially Laura Parisi, who was an absolute rock star during her time at the university and in her work to support this book!

Teaching colleagues at Thomas Jefferson University have provided insight and support.

Rebecca Parish, who produced SDB Revit and AutoCAD drawings.

Jeff Zarnoch, who has been consistently supportive.

James Query, who helped us with topography contours.

Frank Sherman, who, with his class, employed the SDB methodology and provided insightful feedback.

We have received great support from our professional colleagues including:

Lois Brink of The Big SandBox, who provided invaluable site design advice.

Re:Vision Architecture, who provided insightful examples of project guiding principles.

Alkesh Taylor and Stephen Miller from Kitchen Associates, who provided an understanding of the demonstration project building active HVAC requirements.

Early readers of this textbook deserve special thanks. Hannah Rose Mamary, Celia Mamary, Rita Jaffe, and Carolyn Card Sutton each waded through various versions of this textbook providing insightful observations, suggestions, and edits that improved the overall readability, continuity, and structure.

Kim Conway Wilson, whose clear-eyed graphic appraisal and illustration skills helped focus and simplify the presentation of complex concepts and images.

The team at Wiley publishing saw the value in expanding the successful Basics franchise, from Space Planning Basics, and Lighting Design Basics, into the area of Sustainable Design. Amanda Shettleton, Margaret Cummins, Kalli Schultea, Amy Odum, and the vast support a project of this scale requires, we offer our gratitude and thanks for supporting us through the process.

Deficiencies, errors, or ambiguities found in this text, (as surely, we have missed one or two) are the responsibilities of the authors.

About the Authors

Sharon B Jaffe, LEED AP ID + C, IIDA, NCIDQ. Designer, educator, and sustainable re-developer specializing in the collaborative development of environmentally sustainable environments. She currently teaches at Thomas Jefferson University in Philadelphia.

Rob Fleming, AIA, LEED AP BD+C. Rob Fleming has been teaching, researching, advocating, and practicing sustainability for over 20 years in pursuit of a deeper and more meaningful understanding of sustainability. He is the founding director of and a professor in the master's in sustainable design program at Thomas Jefferson University.

Mark Karlen, Ph.D., AIA, NCIDQ Mark Karlen has been practicing, teaching, and writing about interior design and architecture for several decades. He has chaired interior architecture programs at the University of Cincinnati and Pratt Institute.

Saglinda H Roberts, IIDA, CID NJ, NCIDQ, LEED Green Associate. Saglinda Roberts is currently an Assistant Professor at Chatham University. She is the founder of a consulting firm which focuses on restorative and holistic sustainable design. She has over 30 years of extensive design experience and has won numerous local and AIA design awards. Passionate about architecture and its ability to transform lives, Saglinda has published several articles on the future of integral sustainable design and presented her research internationally.

About the Companion Website

Don't forget to visit the companion website for this book:
www.wiley.com/go/jaffesustainable.

The companion website to this book has a variety of tools, matrices, templates, SketchUp and AutoCAD files not found in the printed text, as well as:

- PowerPoint files with simple slides that review the materials addressed in the book.
- Narrated videos that review and augment concepts presented in the text.
- Simulation and validation assignments which require energy modeling software.

1

Why, How, Who, and What

Sustainability does not fit nicely under a single heading; it does not belong to a specific academic discipline or school subject. Nor is it the domain of any one sector—environment, education, business, or government. The quest to increase global sustainability involves many aspects of culture and a variety of disciplines that affect the world's ecology, economics, ethics, and education. Sustainability is an issue beyond a given lifetime or location. It is everybody's business and involves all aspects of how one lives in the modern world.

WHY USE THIS BOOK

This text is a basic primer focused on the design process for the sustainable built environment.

Buildings that are sustainably constructed and maintained contribute to the repair of the global ecosystem throughout their entire life cycle, while protecting the health and increasing the productivity of building occupants. The design of sustainable buildings requires that the architectural design process evolve into a new framework that promotes a transformation of the built environment globally. This framework must address the local context and apply to the full life cycle of the building.

Sustainable buildings are resilient buildings, mitigating damage to the environment and capable of adaptation. They are designed for longevity with low embodied energy requirements. Resilience requires a holistic approach to sustainability that extends to both lifestyle and the community beyond the buildings themselves.

Sustainable Design Basics presents design strategies that leverage renewable natural resources and innovative construction techniques to incorporate systems that conserve energy and resources. However, this book is more than a collection of sustainable strategies. *Sustainable Design Basics* is a methodology.

HOW TO USE THIS BOOK

This text is an instructional tool that presents both basic technical information and sustainability strategies required for sustainability, and a methodology to facilitate the collection, analysis, and evaluation required to approach a sustainable building project.

Sustainable design is inherently a complicated process. It requires an understanding of influencing factors far beyond client preferences, program requirements, and construction methods. For the architect or designer first approaching sustainable building design, it can be overwhelming.

For this reason, *Sustainable Design Basics* (SDB) has simplified the process to its most basic design steps. SDB introduces a step-by-step methodology with a series of matrices and worksheets as decision-making tools, as well as a demonstration project that illustrates each step. The SDB methodology is a working tool intended for use in the design process, not merely a text to be read for information. While an individual learner may use the SDB methodology, it was conceived and is intended for use in a conventional studio classroom setting.

WHO SHOULD USE THIS BOOK

As a basics book, in the tradition of *Space Planning Basics* by Mark Karlen and Rob Fleming and *Lighting Design Basics* by Mark Karlen, Christina Spangler, and James R. Benya, *Sustainable Design Basics* is directed primarily to intermediate-level (sophomore or junior levels in a baccalaureate or first professional degree program) interior architecture, interior design, and architecture students. These previous "Basics" books are the inspiration for a precise, easily accessible methodology to address sustainable design. However, this particular subject matter asks a lot of the reader. Sustainable design is a far-reaching subject that touches every aspect of design and deals with a wide range of design variables. It is a challenging subject. In breaking down the topic to address basics, a few readers may find some topics too simple and other topics too complicated. Hopefully, the bulk of the text addresses the subject material with an easily accessible, informative, and applicable approach.

One of the critical aspects of sustainability is the interrelated nature of global society. That is true for the environment, marketplaces, and education. Readers may come to this text from all parts of the world. With that understanding, the language of this book is direct and straightforward. Complex matters are broken down to smaller basic concepts to avoid, where possible, multilayered, complex theory. The authors are based in the United States, yet the sustainable design principles and practices in this book have global application. Locations in the United States may dominate the examples and exercises, but the choice of specific site locations was a result of limited time to address an ambitious scope of challenging material and not an effort to exclude other people or countries.

WHAT ARE THE PARAMETERS OF THIS BOOK

The primary focus of *Sustainable Design Basics* is design, not technology nor terminology. Specifically, the focus is limited to interior architecture, interior design, and architecture. The methodology described applies to both new construction and to renovation of existing buildings. For clarity, this text limits the number of variables with a focus on new construction variables, although renovation and building reuse are vital elements of a sustainable built environment. However, each existing building has unique characteristics of construction, materials, and existing systems, beyond what a basics text can competently address.

A site for a building is a complex and worthy topic for sustainable design exploration. Limited by time and textbook length, in-depth exploration of the landscape and the complexities and challenges presented to sustainable designers are beyond the scope of this book.

ORGANIZATION

Sustainable Design Basics is a step by step, how-to methodology. Sadly, books are by default linear. There is not a "spiraling" option for information in print. While the text flows in a direct linear sequence of information, understand that sustainable design is not a linear process. The sustainable design process is integrated and iterative, frequently looping back to revisit preceding design decisions.

EXERCISES

The concepts and strategies included in this text have direct application to interior design, interior architecture, and architecture. The exercises that accompany the text follow the step-by-step methodology allowing the reader to do work independently to develop sustainable design skills through project-based learning. A set of undeveloped sites and building "shells" in a variety of geographic locations in the United States provided for exercise project locations each have different geological, climatic, and cultural contexts. Completing assignments on different sites allows the exploration of the sense of "place" as a fundamental design influence, inspiring different design ideas. A variety of clients, users, and contexts ranging from rural to urban are provided as exercise variables. The study of hundreds of projects is possible by mixing and matching exercise variables. Projects can be explored in the studio classroom setting or independently.

Users of this text are expected to possess basic knowledge of design, drafting, and planning skills. Many of the exercises require the ability to open and print AutoCAD files or to download and print PDF files. Some of the exercises in Chapter 15 require software. There are also exercises that can be completed, with some variation, without software. Additional software information is available in the appendix and the companion website.

COMPANION WEBSITE

A companion website to this book (www.wiley.com/go/jaffesustainable) has a variety of tools, matrices, templates, SketchUp, and AutoCAD files not found in the printed text, as well as:

- PowerPoint files with simple slides that review the materials addressed in the book
- Narrated videos that review and augment concepts presented in the text
- Simulation and validation assignments which require energy modeling software

2

Mindset

At the most basic level, designers of the built environment create the spaces and places that provide shelter from the elements, and thermal comfort while creating the surroundings of life. The quality of life is dependent upon the work designers, builders, engineers, and architects accomplish daily. It takes a lot of material and energy to construct and operate the buildings, interiors, and landscapes of the world. The use of these materials and energy sources affect the larger environment that humans rely on for fresh air, clean water, light, energy, and food. Such *ecosystem services* are fundamental to the continuance of civilization into the future. In other words, if society wastes energy and materials, if society carelessly releases pollution into the air and water, if humanity drives animals to extinction and forever alters the climate to produce uninhabitable conditions, humanity threatens its existence.

Put bluntly, the current pattern of life on earth is unsustainable.

The current distressed state of the planet is a direct result of how people think. Changing how individuals think can change the direction of society's thinking. With a mindset change, one can begin to imagine a sustainable future. This chapter deals directly with the "why" of sustainable design and the essential mindset for a capable, sustainable designer. Included in this chapter are significant historical events, prominent people, and notable frameworks that support an understanding of sustainability and sustainable design. The remainder of the book is the "what" and "how" of sustainable design, and the step-by-step methodology used to achieve a sustainable design project.

First, before delving into the methodology, a bit of historical context is appropriate, a brief journey through history that reveals our changing relationship with nature.

Sustainable design focuses on stabilizing the planet, cleaning the water and air, conserving energy resources, expanding renewable energy sources, preserving biodiversity, and using materials wisely: all to save the planet. If the planet is "saved," humanity is "saved." Society may persist in the future—hence the word "sustainable." However, it is not that simple. An overall holistic approach to sustainability must address the many economic, social, and aesthetic dimensions of human existence. Sustainable design is more than just the environment.

Sustainable design is a holistic *practice*. Physical objects, the built environment, and services are designed by responding to the goals and principles of sustainability as viewed from multiple perspectives across space and time. The triple bottom line is a phrase that expresses key concerns of sustainability:

- Social equity
- Economic prosperity
- Ecological protection

A fourth sustainability value, beauty, is added to make sustainable buildings more meaningful and more satisfying.

THE HOLOCENE AND THE AGE OF AGRICULTURE

To see the big picture and understand the threats the world faces, one must look back 12,000 years to the end of the last ice age. Earth entered what is called an interglacial, a period between ice ages when the planet was very warm. The most recent interglacial is called the Holocene. This period of warmth is rare and valuable. The Holocene set the stage for the Age of Agriculture, a population boom, and civilization as it is known today.

A few key points to remember:

1. The climate today is a rarity in the context of the four-billion-year history of the planet.
2. Humans have emerged as the dominant species on the planet primarily due to the advantageous conditions of the Holocene.
3. Humans have assumed it is a right to dominate other species and less powerful and less technologically advanced humans in the pursuit of power and resources.

THE INDUSTRIAL REVOLUTION AND THE ENVIRONMENT

As the agricultural age progressed, humanity continued to benefit from a warm climate and seemingly infinite natural resources. Technological advances continued to advance humanity's dominion over the environment. It was also a time when the drive for power, profit, and comfort led to the oppression of millions of people through slavery and indefinable levels of environmental destruction. Humanity's consciousness evolved, leading to great scientific discoveries, insight into how the universe works, and critical social innovations such as labor laws, public education, and democracy.

The seeds of today's environmental and social problems originated during this fantastic time of human achievement. The Western industrial revolution saw the introduction of efficient engines to power industrial production and generate electricity. Industry was powered mainly by coal resulting in air tinged by coal smoke casting a pall across European industrial cities. The pollution of the air with coal smoke became the primary environmental concern in London. In response, the early nineteenth century saw the rise of Romanticism with an emphasis on nature and natural beauty. By the late nineteenth century, the first European nongovernmental environmental organizations (NGOs) came into being in London, focused on mitigating air pollution. In North America, John Muir, an early environmentalist, urged the government to create a national park to preserve the natural beauty of the Yosemite Valley. The industrial society sparked increasing environmental and social concerns during the Enlightenment and Romantic movements.

The industrial revolution ended in what is called the "great acceleration." This was a period during the twentieth century of rapidly increasing negative impact on the earth's environment and systems from human activity, consumption of natural resources, and the unintended results of technological progress. "Progress" is a two-sided coin. The post–World War II boom led humanity to previously unequaled technical achievements and unprecedented population growth, yet the presumption of inexhaustible natural resources resulted in undisputable environmental destruction.

ENVIRONMENTALISM AND THE AGE OF INFORMATION

1960s

By the 1960s some individuals started to understand that the environment was in trouble. Humanity's very existence was at risk. The world started to study the environment in many ways, purposefully using scientific methods to prove that there was, in fact, a problem. This understanding was the beginning of environmentalism. The American marine biologist, writer, and ecologist Rachel Carson wrote a book called *Silent Spring*, which documented the negative impacts of pesticides on the general ecology. She observed that spraying poisonous insecticides that killed crop-damaging bugs also killed the birds that ate the bugs. No birds left to sing prompted the title, "silent spring." Rachel Carson's work called for a change in how the world viewed nature and its ecosystems. Her work, along with many others, led to the birth of the environmentalist movement.

The American civil rights movement, begun in the mid-1950s and building through the 1960s, heralded a new era of progressive thinking about the global condition of humanity and how social equity in society impacts sustainability. Around the same time a Scottish landscape architect named Ian McHarg wrote a book called *Design with Nature*, in which he outlined how designers can improve the environment using natural systems through ecological planning. The relationship between urban and natural environments can be synergistic and regenerative when the holistic, living nature of the earth's systems and humanity's impact on it are understood. Such understanding can be used to adapt human patterns and process into integrated ecosystems. McHarg's design approach promoted incorporating the natural world into design projects functionally and aesthetically. He showed that the natural world can, and should, act as a partner and co-designer in the design process.

McHarg also taught people to think about how the environment of a specific place and time influence their experiences and how broad environmental context influences the design of the built environment. He asserted that projects could and should look different in places with different climates, cultures and geographies.

1970s

The 1970s saw the beginning of a response to environmental concerns. Laws were passed to protect the air, water, and endangered species in the United States. The Environmental Protection Agency (EPA) was founded to fight pollution. E.F. Schumacher, a British economist, examined the economic world, determining that the modern economy was unsustainable with natural resources managed as expendable income rather than nonrenewable capital. Schumacher presented a philosophy based on the appreciation of human needs and limitations in his book *Small Is Beautiful: A Study of Economics as if People Mattered.*

The 1970s also saw the beginning of the growing public awareness that energy sources such as oil, gas, and coal were limited and that these fossil fuels were a significant culprit in polluting the air and causing climate change. The release of carbon dioxide, methane, and other gases as a result of burning fossil fuel created a thicker than usual layer of greenhouse gases around the planet. Greenhouse gases trap more heat inside the earth's atmosphere, causing temperatures to rise higher than typical expectations.

1980s

Deindustrialization in the American Midwest resulted in the relocation of much of the industrial manufacturing and its accompanying pollution to China and India.

1987

The United Nations formed the Brundtland Commission in 1987 to address the now obvious need for a new model of development, one that would protect the environment and support a more equitable society, a new way forward that would remediate the negative impacts of the Industrial Revolution and conceive of a new way to think about progress. The commission produced a report, *Our Common Future*, which suggested a new spirit of cooperation. This report expressed the belief that the success or failure of civilization and the planet is a shared goal and responsibility of all nations.

The Brundtland Commission proposed a formal definition of sustainable development. "Sustainable development is development that meets the needs of the current generation without compromising the needs of future generations to meet their own needs."[1]

This definition clearly articulates indigenous wisdom and traditional knowledge too often ignored in the name of progress: Humankind must care for the earth as stewards for future generations. The document demands long-term thinking even when making short-term decisions, such as designing a building.

---

[1] World Commission on Environment and Development, *Our Common Future* (New York and London: Oxford University Press, 1987), p. 43.

1990s

By the early 1990s sustainability began to take more definitive shape as people like John Elkington developed new frameworks like the "triple bottom line" for thinking about sustainability, referencing society, environment, and economy as the more alliterative "people, planet, and profit."

Figure 2.0 diagrams the triple bottom line sustainability framework as outlined by John Elkington. The three overlapping sustainability concerns—society, environment, and economy—are only fully realized when all three concerns are addressed.

Triple bottom line framework provides an expansive accountability method by which people and organizations can evaluate performance beyond the immediate and direct financial bottom line or profit. Profit, the traditional bottom line for many years, has not accounted for the true project costs. To be sustainable, decisions made by organizations must meet environmental and social bottom lines, not just the economic bottom line. Equal consideration of all three goals by aligning business

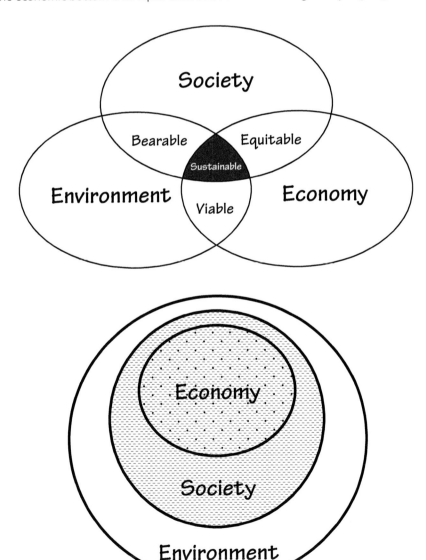

Figure 2.0 John Elkington's triple bottom line framework
Source: Rob Fleming

Figure 2.1 Nested triple bottom line diagram
Source: Wikipedia; redrawn by Rob Fleming

thinking with social and environmental considerations achieves greater value, by establishing a clearer pathway toward a sustainable future.

The framework of the triple bottom line makes a few assumptions that raise questions. Are all three sectors—the economy, society, and environment—always of equal weight? Can individual sectors be compartmentalized to operate with autonomy? How does an accounting framework deal with the invaluable, irreplaceable aspects of natural resources? While the accountants and politicians may prioritize the economy, it is the environment that is the limiting factor. Consider that the economy exists as a construct of society. Society, human beings, cannot exist without the environment. The nested circles of sustainability in Figure 2.1 better reflect the relationship of the economy as a subset of society and the dependence of society on the environment.

1993

In 1993 the design community formally entered into the sustainability movement. Four significant events occurred that fundamentally shaped sustainable design:

1. William McDonough wrote *Design, Ecology, Ethics and the Making of Things*, commonly known as the Centennial Sermon, which charged the design community to pursue design as an environmental imperative, leading to an ethical foundation for design rather than the more conventional aesthetically driven creative process.
2. Hillary and Bill Clinton "greened" the White House by adding solar panels to the roof and by using "green" practices in the restoration of the building.
3. Susan Maxman became the first female president of the American Institute of Architects, championing sustainability as her platform during the election.
4. The United States Green Building Council was formed in 1993 and developed the LEED Rating System. LEED stands for Leadership in Energy and Environmental Design. This framework for green buildings is used by thousands of designers, engineers, and clients to achieve projects that minimized environmental damage and increased energy efficiency of projects.

The race toward a sustainable future was accelerating and most Fortune 500 companies, eager to become stewards of the environment, incorporated LEED metrics for green buildings as part of their triple bottom line initiatives. By 2005 thousands of green buildings were constructed all over the world. The green design movement was a success.

2005

In 2005, another series of events occurred signaling society that "greening" was not enough. The environmental problems were bigger and more threatening than previously imagined. The sustaining warm climate of the Holocene had now become hotter, so much so that environmental conditions were changing in dramatic ways. It is not good practice to say that one environmental disaster or another is the result of climate change, but over time, a correlation was starting to become clear: global warming was altering the climate in ways that were not beneficial to humankind.

Hurricanes Katrina and Rita destroyed much of New Orleans in Louisiana, demonstrating that the new types of storms would be bigger and more devastating than ever. The city's infrastructure could not adequately respond to the extensive and widespread damage. As often happens, those most vulnerable, living in economically disadvantaged areas of New Orleans, suffered disproportionately relative to populations with more significant financial resources and living on the high ground of the city.

In 2005 gas prices hit all-time highs in the U.S., causing people to think more deeply about limited fossil fuel reserves, long-term adverse life-cycle effects, the wasteful use of energy, and the resulting harm to the environment.

2006

Al Gore's book *An Inconvenient Truth* was released and further embedded in the collected psyche of society the link between carbon dioxide emissions and climate change.

2012

Unpredictable weather has become an ongoing, inevitable occurrence. Rising temperatures and disastrous weather-related events left little doubt that the effects of global warming were *not* temporary. Hurricane Sandy and droughts in California further affirmed that reality. The BP oil spill illustrated the dangers of drilling for oil far out to sea; it killed 11 people and inflicted extensive and long-lasting environmental destruction upon the Gulf of Mexico. However, at the same time, the renewable energy movement had reached full steam with installations of wind and solar farms on the rise.

2017

The year 2017 saw further evidence of extreme climate change in the form of a series of cataclysmic hurricanes—Harvey, Jose, Maria, Irma, and Ophelia—that wrought destruction and caused massive upheaval. These hurricanes, along with a shrinking Arctic ice cap, sea level rise, and record high global temperatures, bring us to today's unsustainable conditions.

REALIZATIONS OF THE HISTORIC SUSTAINABILITY EVENTS TIMELINE

Today there is a growing realization that the earth is under threat. Changes in climate, the temperature rise, and polluted oceans all indicate that a "business as usual" approach to solving these problems will not work. Humanity's thinking must change. A famous quote often attributed to Albert Einstein, "We cannot solve problems by using the same kind of thinking we used when we created them," is more appropriate than ever.

The mindset of each person, each community, each country, and the world must change. Sustainable design offers a pathway to think and act differently. This framework for design is compelling, as well as very complex. Sustainable design is about interconnection, interdependence, integration, and whole systems thinking.

John Muir famously wrote, "When we try to pick out anything by itself, we find it hitched to everything else in the Universe." Individual "things" (plants, people, communities, watersheds, economies) can't be fully understood apart from their larger systems. It is vital to think of relationships, connectedness, and context. Systems thinking recognizes that the interrelationships are as important as the individual components themselves. When looking at the whole, systems thinking shifts emphasis from objects to relationships, from structures to process, and from contents to cyclical patterns. In systems thinking, cause and effect focuses on cyclical rather than linear processes and implies an interdependence of objects and their attributes.

In this book, *Sustainable Design Basics,* this way of thinking is called "holistic." There are "systems" within larger systems. A building sits on the site, the site within the neighborhood, and the neighborhood is a part of the city. The city is within the region and so on. For example, in the ecosystem, air, water, plants, and animals all work together to function. Remove any one element, and the overall system will struggle to survive, and perhaps will even perish. Holistic thinking forms the cornerstone of sustainable design. Without a holistic approach, the built environment's negative impact on the climate will continue. In architecture and design, this holistic approach is called "whole building design, integrated design, or integrative design." These terms are often used interchangeably to reference cyclical thinking. A linear mindset follows a direct progression, ordering steps as experienced as unique and separate elements, as diagramed in Figure 2.2. Contrast that with cyclical or holistic thinking diagramed in Figure 2.3, indicating the interrelated and cyclical relationship of the sustainable built environment, renewable natural resources, and clear air, energy, and water. Sustainable buildings go beyond addressing a specific building for a specific client. Sustainable design sees each project as connected with the larger environment.

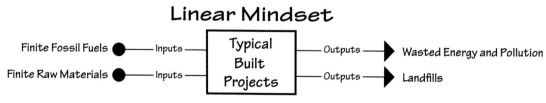

Figure 2.2 A linear mindset
Source: Rob Fleming

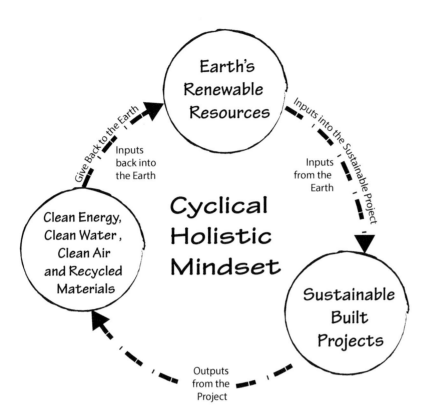

Figure 2.3 Cyclical, holistic mindset
Source: Rob Fleming

THINKING AND SEEING FROM MULTIPLE PERSPECTIVES

Sustainable design is a complex process that integrates many disciplines and viewpoints. One team member will have different priorities for a project than another. One design strategy will leverage specific resources differently than the next. Contradictions are an everyday reality in the sustainable design process. To effectively evaluate and determine the appropriate steps in the sustainable design process, it is necessary to address broad issues that move beyond technology and numeric metrics. The *Sustainable Design Basics* matrix system organizes each aspect of a project through the four perspectives of performance, systems, culture, and experience, to balance the tangible and intangible concerns of a project. These *four perspectives* group varied design directives to help evaluate both objective and subjective aspects of a project and identify synergies between them.

INTEGRAL SUSTAINABLE DESIGN

Integral sustainable design requires the design of buildings with the understanding that sustainability is more than just energy performance and high performing technology. Figure 2.4 presents two diagrams that organize thinking to include both the objective point of view (performance and systems) and the subjective points of view (experience and culture). It is essential to think holistically and consider performance and systems as equals with experience and culture. The two rows each represent individual and collective points of view. All four perspectives are considered simultaneously in the sustainable design process. The perspectives are evaluated looking inward and looking outward.

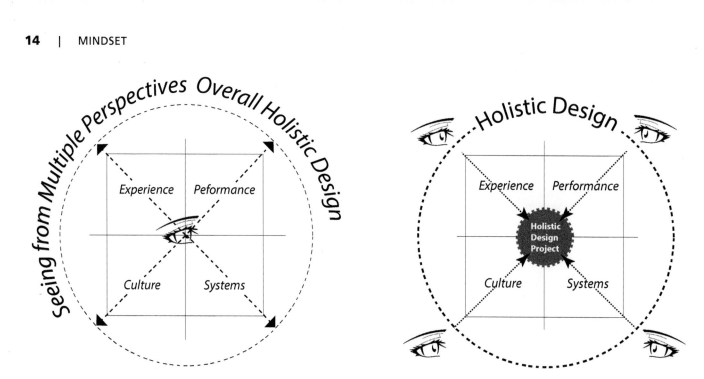

Figure 2.4 Four perspectives: holistic design, looking outward, and looking inward
Source: Rob Fleming

THE FOUR PERSPECTIVES OF INTEGRAL SUSTAINABLE DESIGN

Performance

Performance is the perspective that addresses the measurable and describable aspects of the project. It is the quadrant most associated with sustainable design because it deals directly with energy efficiency and reducing the environmental destruction resulting from fossil fuel consumption. In this book, performance metrics such as energy use intensity (EUI), which is the measure of energy use in a building, and the daylight factor, which is a measure of daylighting in a building, are thoroughly discussed.

The performance quadrant deals with amounts of things, and any other readily measurable, observable traits. These include facts and statistics, both analytical and logical. Performance is about building characteristics and functional requirements, all of which can be weighed and measured to assess results.

Systems

The systems perspective relates to performance in that both are measurable and describable. The systems perspective has an additional trait of interaction. Systems are dynamic, always changing, with hundreds or even thousands of different interactions. Ecology is a system, as is a car engine. One is natural and one is human-made, but they are both systems. These systems are closely associated with sustainable building design:

- Life cycle systems is consideration of the environmental impact of a product, material, or process, throughout its existence from "cradle to cradle." The process of extracting, manufacturing, transporting, using, disposing, and reuse of materials all impact the lifecycle of buildings.

- Passive systems, commonly referred to as "strategies," include shading, orientation, natural ventilation, and daylighting. Passive systems do not require an external power source to function.
- Active systems use *technologies* such as heating, ventilation, air-conditioning, plumbing, and transportation, all which require some external power source.
- Living systems work with biological sciences and nature to support and create the built environment. Green roofs, living walls, living machines, even the natural percolation of stormwater through the earth soil help buildings and sites become more ecologically sustainable.
- Human systems include all the social organizations, policies, and procedures that govern how humans relate to each other and their buildings.

When all of the systems are considered and optimized to work together, building performance is enhanced, leading to measurable energy savings and environmental improvement.

Culture

The culture perspective addresses the intangible aspects of human behavior in groups. Shared values, shared beliefs, religious rituals, local history, cultural heritage, traditions, and norms are all examples or elements of the culture perspective. The vernacular of local architecture and materials is part of the local history and cultural heritage. Material and form have established traditions that are an outgrowth of the local context, materials, and climate. It is essential to understand the principles and materials incorporated into the vernacular and traditional architecture and how they may apply to current architecture and development.

Worldview is the framework that shapes an individual's or societal perception, interpretation, and interaction with the world; it is a vital aspect of the cultural perspective. Worldview defines how society views nature and how people treat each other. The fight for equality in society is endless. It is an ongoing fight for equity in social standing equal pay and treatment of women, better opportunities for people of color, and economic equity in general – the fight for equality parallels and influences the environmental movement. Equity and environmentalism cannot be separated, nor should they be. Empathy is at the core of both environmentalism and equity. The ability to assume the perspective of another person, animal, or nature itself, and begin to operate out of their perspective, is empathy and is the basis of holistic design. Advocate for all, as all deserve equality. Ultimately, a holistic empathetic model of sustainability serves the environment and humanity.

Experience

What about the perspective of architects and designers, the makers of space and places? What role does aesthetics play in the process? What does aesthetics influence in the sustainable design process? Well, in a word, *everything*. A green building may help "save the planet" but if it is not desirable for people to use, maintain, and love, odds are it will not last very long. Buildings and structures that survive through time, despite the significant and historical upheaval, are buildings that are loved. Buildings that are loved are renovated time and time again. That is a form of sustainability. The energy required to extract, manufacture, transport, and construct the original building is saved over and over again as the building is reused instead of demolished. Adaptive reuse and historic preservation of the built environment are vital to sustainable design. Traditional building forms that survive over time tend to be aesthetically pleasing. Beauty itself is an attraction. Nature uses beauty as an attractor to encourage reproduction to sustain the species. Designers strive to make cities, landscapes, buildings, interiors, and products beautiful because beauty makes them viable, desired, even cherished. Designers hope their buildings and designs will be perpetuated through time, reimagined, restored, renovated, and reused.

One of the essential elements of holistic thinking is the ability to think across time and design with empathy. Unwittingly, designers may make decisions that work well in the short term, only to later find the decision leads to environmental problems. Thinking about how a building looks instead of thinking about the life of the building over time may have a negative environmental impact as a consequence. The diagram in Figure 2.5 represents the understanding and influence of time in holistic thinking. Holistic thinking requires one to think across time to learn from the past and consider the future while making decisions for the present.

Careful analysis and selection of building materials can help to limit damage to the environment. Using local building materials limits the negative impact on the planet from the consumption of fossil fuel and the harmful byproducts produced when transporting building materials. Setting ambitious energy and water conservation and efficiency goals are evidence of considerations for generations to come. These goals ask the designer to think about each project's unique situation and careful conservation of precious resources and the reduction of air pollution levels, which are acts of compassion that will benefit the future. It is vital to integrate the context of the future into building design decisions.

LEARNING FROM THE PAST: GENERAL RULES

The past has enormous value and can teach designers a lot about sustainable design. The world today is not the first civilization to think about sustainable design. Before the advent of fossil fuels and electricity, designers used "sustainable" strategies, similar to those previously listed, out of necessity, to make buildings as comfortable as possible. The cliff dwellings of Native Americans are an excellent example of passive solar design: allowing the warm winter sun, low in the sky, to heat the building, while the cliff provided shade from the hot summer sun high in the sky. The cliff dwellings are just one of many examples of indigenous intelligent design and guidelines that apply to sustainable design. Adages, or truisms, often serve as the starting points for sustainable design projects because they are universal, fundamental, and effective in meeting sustainability goals.

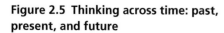
Figure 2.5 Thinking across time: past, present, and future
Source: Rob Fleming

Many examples remind us that there is a lot to learn from historical and vernacular structures about sustainable strategies. Ancient Chinese villages were built to maximize the sun path. Openings on the southern exposure of individual buildings were positioned to allow solar gain in the winter and shading in the summer. Middle Eastern mud structures with thick walls, small openings, and shaded courtyards were ideally suited for their climate. Master builders through time, such as Vitruvius during the first century BCE in Rome, Leonardo da Vinci in fifteenth-century Florence, Palladio in sixteenth-century Venice, and Thomas Jefferson in eighteenth-century Virginia all designed buildings to work with the environment. Each of these designer builders looked for that perfect balance between reason and beauty that results in sustainable design. Analyzing vernacular architecture practices of a specific climate and geography is an excellent place to begin investigating viable, sustainable strategies.

SPACE AND SCALE

In the same way that one thinks across time, one can also think across scales. The catchphrase "Think Globally, Act Locally" is a wonderful axiom for designers. It urges the consideration of global effects of each design decision. Figure 2.6 diagrams the relationship between local buildings and global impact. Designers must think holistically to understand that the systems designed in a building are "nested" within more extensive systems of the site, neighborhood, city, and beyond. Consider that buildings are responsible for large amounts of CO_2 emissions. The impact of CO_2 and other greenhouse gases on the environment was mentioned earlier in this chapter. Sustainable design offers an opportunity to begin to reverse the damage to global systems created by local buildings.

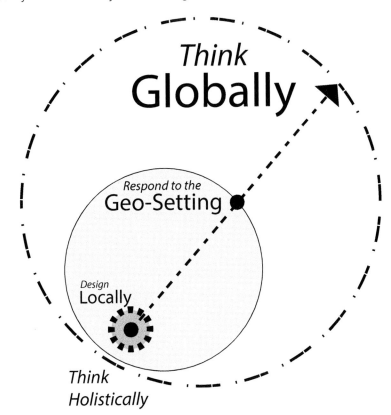

Figure 2.6 Think across scales

Source: Rob Fleming

THE INTEGRATIVE DESIGN PROCESS

The integrative design process, or holistic design approach, values the contribution of stakeholders, who are the people affected by the design project, including the client, and the people in the neighborhood where the building is located. Each group has a different point of view or position relative to the project design. The various professionals on the design team are also stakeholders. The engineer may prioritize the performance and systems of the project. The landscape architect may focus on the ecological systems of the site, and what kinds of vegetation will thrive in the microclimate. The interior designer may consider the flow of space in that the experience of the building occupants is their predominant concern. Sustainable design values and requires that all of the stakeholders' concerns be addressed.

Integrated building design is, at its heart, a collaborative multidiscipline design process. It is a manifestation of social equity, and it begins at the very start of a project through occupancy and beyond. Each design decision is explored from varied viewpoints from the earliest conceptualization throughout the design process. The various design and construction disciplines of the integrated design team, with the input of all the stakeholder participants, evaluate the developing design for cost, quality-of-life, future flexibility, efficiency, overall environmental impact, operational function, productivity, and creativity. Figure 2.7 illustrates the equal input positions of the integrated design team. Unlike the traditional linear development and architecture process, integrated design team members are all participants from the earliest stages of conceptualization throughout the design process.

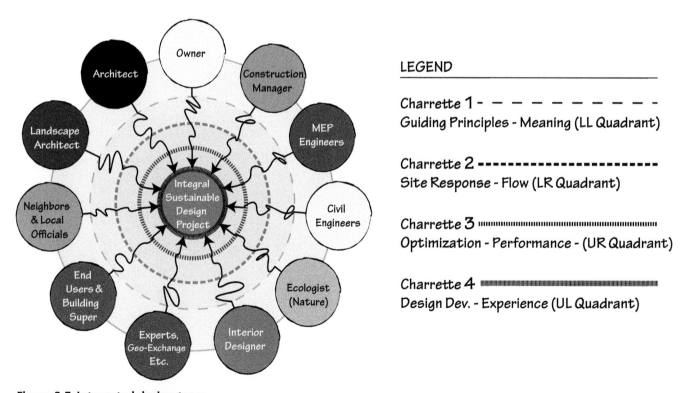

LEGEND

Charrette 1 - – – – – – – – – -
Guiding Principles - Meaning (LL Quadrant)

Charrette 2 --------------------------
Site Response - Flow (LR Quadrant)

Charrette 3
Optimization - Performance - (UR Quadrant)

Charrette 4
Design Dev. - Experience (UL Quadrant)

Figure 2.7 Integrated design team
Source: Rob Fleming

Rating Systems

The building and construction industries continue to evolve and develop new rating systems, such as the Living Building Challenge (LBC), Passive House, and the Well Building Standard emerging to tackle sustainable design from different approaches and priorities. LBC applies an ambitious holistic framework that includes regeneration of the natural environment as one of its goals. Passive House is energy conservation and efficiency-focused as a means to drastically reduce CO_2 emissions, and by extension, fight climate change. The Well Building Standard concentrates on human health as an outcome of green building design. All of these green building rating systems along with LEED and other standards and rating systems exist for the simple reason that sustainable design is a complex and challenging process. Green building rating systems help the client, and the design team align the design thinking around specific goals and metrics that will reach a specific level of energy and environmental performance.

This book does not use a specific rating system. *Sustainable Design Basics* is about teaching a methodology, a process. The *SDB* process can be used to meet the standards of any of the rating systems. But sustainability is more vital, more fundamental, and ultimately more important than any specific rating system. Rating systems change over time, but the mindset that inspires these rating systems is the mindset that is defined in this book. The methodology set out in *Sustainable Design Basics* can produce the type of sustainable projects necessary for resource conservation, environmental regeneration, and community resilience, with or without a specific rating system.

The focus of *Sustainable Design Basics* is the built environment. Others are working on sustainable food systems, eco-friendly products, green infrastructure, new business models, and new software packages, all aimed at changing the course of civilization toward a sustainable future. It is vital to change the world's thinking, methods, and products to restore the planet earth to a point where it can sustain humanity as a species into the future.

3

Step 1: Context

Step 4
**Design
Resolution**

4A Design Synthesis
4B Final Design Validation
4C Presenting the Project

Step 3
Design

3A Preliminary Design
3B Passive Design
3C Building Envelope
3D Green Materials
  * Beyond the Basics

Step 2
...nning

2B ... Case Studies
2C
2D S... ...nships

Step 1
Context

1A Project Information
1B Guiding Principles
1C Macro / Micro Context
1D Site Inventory & Analysis

Figure 3.0 *Sustainable Design Basics*, **step 1**
Source: Sharon B. Jaffe

THE SUSTAINABLE DESIGN BASICS METHODOLOGY: AN OVERVIEW

Sustainable design is about transforming how people think, how they design, how they build, and how they maintain the built environment.

Sustainable design decisions extend beyond functional, spatial, and aesthetic criteria to consider the impact to the environment and the local community. Sustainable design requires designers to think beyond the building itself, and consider the influence and inspiration a project brings to the broader community and societal concerns. There is a lot to think about in order to design sustainably and holistically. Many things not previously considered warrant close examination.

A significant change to the built environment requires the integration and application of new principles to the traditional systems of architecture and development to facilitate the evolution of outdated conventional thinking to a holistic sustainable approach.

Where to begin?

Methodology and Planning

Transformation is not easy. Requirements for sustainable buildings have expanded to encompass increasingly complex performance criteria, life cycle, cultural influences, and economic implications. A holistic approach to sustainable building design requires the analysis of a great deal of information. A precise methodology is needed to organize volumes of information, both objective and subjective, in a manner that enables analysis and evaluation of the information relative to stated project principles and goals. The sustainable design methodology described in this textbook may seem very different from other textbooks. Sustainable design decisions are not autonomous. Each decision will impact and may direct, the next decision. Understanding the interdependent nature of a building and site as an integrated system is fundamental.

Interdependence and interaction are inherent in a global society. Everything is related to everything else. Sustainable design is multidimensional. Optimal sustainability can be achieved by designs that integrate an understanding of the varied aspects of a project as wide-ranging and intimately connected globally.

Overall goals of sustainable design
- Reduce consumption of natural resources: energy, materials, water
- Preserve environmental quality, ecological systems, and habitat
- Minimize waste
- Support a healthy environment
- Create spaces that support occupant health and well-being
- Create spaces that support local historical and cultural connections
- Create adaptable and resilient spaces
- Create inclusive and equitably distributed space

Sustainable Design Basics (SDB) distills the complicated process into a clear step by step methodology comprised of 4 basic steps:

- Step 1 - Context
- Step 2 - Pre-planning
- Step 3 - Design
- Step 4 - Final validation and presentation

Tools of the SDB Step by Step Methodology: The Matrix

Sustainable Design Basics present a methodology to support a holistic approach to sustainable design. In addition to traditional pre-planning research, design methods, and techniques, matrices are used to organize, prioritize, analyze, and evaluate critical tangible and intangible information, key design concerns, the stated goals of the design project being undertaken, and strategies used in the sustainable design process.

The SDB matrices are tables created with columns and rows that contain a customized collection of instructions and questions to be completed with data, research, files, and other materials to inform the design directives and strategies of the sustainable design process. As discussed in the previous chapter, sustainability is about much more than saving energy or protecting the environment. Sustainability is a holistic philosophy that acknowledges the interrelated symbiotic relationships between the natural environment, the built environment, and the people who inhabit the world. Throughout the sustainable design process, the four perspectives—performance, systems, culture, and experience— distill and organize key intangible and tangible elements that may influence design decisions. Because the activities of the sustainable design process often take place over time, the matrix may need to be accessed multiple times as additional information is gathered informing design decisions.

STEP 1: CONTEXT

A sustainable building design project begins by understanding the project's context at various scales, over time and through a variety of perspectives. This first phase of a project requires a great deal of information gathering through observation, inquiry, and research to identify factors and reveal challenges and opportunities. Once identified and understood, challenges can be effectively addressed and opportunities leveraged for a successful project. Careful documentation and organization of the gathered information early on is key to easy retrieval later in pre-planning and design phases of the project.

Context refers to the external elements of, and surrounding, a specific project location. Context influences both physical and nonphysical design. Roads, buildings, and land contours are examples of physical elements. Local culture, political, and financial constraints are examples of nonphysical elements. Examining context through the perspectives of performance, systems, culture, and experience ensures identification and holistic examination of assets and resources.

Time and Scale Context

Context exists at both macro (larger, regional and global) and micro (smaller and local) scales and acknowledges the impact of global issues on the conditions surrounding and inhabiting a specific site. Understanding historical conditions, disasters, and disruptions, as well as the current context, will prepare a project for change that may happen in the future. Context can change over time. A design that anticipates and prepares for inevitable change adds resilience to a sustainable building project.

Physical Context

Sustainable, restorative, and regenerative efforts all begin within the framework of what exists. The topography of a site, along with changes in grade or level, are key factors in determining the position of the building on the site. Working with the existing topography greatly reduces the need to disrupt the existing grade, soil, vegetation, and wildlife. Designing in harmony with the climate, topography, flora, and fauna, and understanding how water and air move on and through the site, minimizes erosion and disruption of the natural plant life. A design that responds to and utilizes the existing site topography effectively avoids many initial site construction expenses and avoids complicated constructed drainage systems.

Philosophical Context

Sustainability embraces an integrated, holistic approach to design that acknowledges the fundamental, interconnected nature of the world. An efficient building in harmony and balance with both the natural and nearby built environments benefits both the building occupants and the surrounding community.

STEP 1A: PROJECT INFORMATION

A clear understanding of the client, the client's goals and project intent, functional requirements, physical parameters of the site including macroclimate and microclimate, local zoning, codes, and other regulations are all essential from the very start of a project.

Who Is the Client? What Are the Client's Priorities?

A client is the person or organization for whom the designer is working. The client may be the end user or the landlord. Clients may or may not be committed to sustainability as an ethos but will typically have a keen interest in sustainable strategies that reduce operational and maintenance costs. While most clients are budget-conscious regarding initial development and construction costs, they may be unaware of the life-cycle costs. A designer often takes on the role of educator and advocate for sustainable measures. Clients may be unaware of specific environmental costs or they may evaluate financial investment based only on initial capital expense. Sustainable strategies may provide both environmental and long-term financial benefits that clients might well embrace once they are fully informed. There is a growing realization that individuals impact the environment and the environment affects the individual. A healthier sustainable environment may positively affect business productivity.

Employees and clients have begun to see and act on sustainability issues on a personal level. Businesses that have begun to acknowledge many practices undertaken in the interest of sustainability have increased productivity and employee satisfaction. Employees and clients are more engaged and have begun to clearly articulate a preference for business practices that align with personal values.

Owner/End User: Typically, end users have a keen interest in sustainable strategies that impact ongoing operational costs as well as initial development and construction costs. Life-cycle costs, the cost of a material from extraction through the end of its useful life, may also be meaningful to a client. End users may not be aware of life-cycle financial costs and environmental impact of material choices. A less expensive capital cost may have increased operational costs. It is important for designers to understand and educate their clients on the financial and environmental costs. These explanations have resonance with end-user clients.

Investor: An investor client builds on speculation, often before a tenant is identified, with the expectation of renting space during, or after, construction. The shell of the building is built with the interior lobby and support spaces fully finished. Generally, tenant space is left in a rough, unfinished state to be built out to suit individual tenant requirements and preferences. Tenants are attracted to spaces with a high level of energy efficiency. Building resilience allows a structure to accommodate a variety of tenant types and meet future modifications as tenants come and go, thereby minimizing intensive, costly design changes. Building owners and tenants are beginning to plan for unforeseen events such as natural disaster or infrastructure failure. Marketability and future resilience are motivating factors for investor clients.

Tenant: A tenant occupies a building that is owned by a landlord. While the tenants do not own the physical building, they may be financially responsible for making changes to the building shell that are necessary to conduct business. Generally, tenants pay all utilities and are very interested in sustainable strategies that reduce operating expenses. Existing space, structure, systems, and other building restrictions may limit building modifications. Before the design process begins, it is important to understand all limitations of an existing building to determine what sustainable features can be employed.

Client Motivation

The Mission-Driven Client

An organization that has a mission at its core strives to integrate that mission into all aspects of the organization, from day-to-day activities to the buildings and structures in which they operate. For mission-driven clients, a sustainable building design is an extension of that organization's purpose, especially when the client expects to be the building occupant.

The Return on Investment (ROI) Client

Social and environmental factors have an impact on the value of a real estate property. Tenants are often seeking occupancy of certified "green" buildings. Demand is rising for buildings that address an organization's and its workers' environmental and social concerns relating to energy, water, waste, sourcing of construction materials, and ongoing material needs. High indoor air quality, occupant comfort, and access to public or alternative means of transportation are requirements for Class A office space. Superior building system performance and increased environmental quality are demonstrable selling points when building speculatively before identifying a specific end user or tenant. Resilience is another motivating factor. Building owners are beginning to plan for unexpected natural events and/or tenant requirements.

The Tenant Client

This client may or may not be committed to sustainability as an ethos but will typically have a keen interest in sustainable strategies that reduce operational and maintenance costs. While the end user or occupant may be budget-conscious regarding initial development and construction costs, life-cycle explanations will have resonance.

Client Intention and Expectation

The program, or owner project requirements (OPR), details requirements and functional expectations for the project and may include sustainability goals for energy, water, indoor environmental quality, occupant health and wellness, and general durability to successfully meet an owner's requirements. A program is developed as part of the project planning process by and with input from the client, owner, end user, contractor, and stakeholders, wherever possible. Ultimately, final approval from the owner or owner's representative is required. The program establishes baseline criteria for facility function and guidance for all design, performance, and operational decisions. It includes:

- Project description
- Project objectives
- Functional use
- Spatial requirements and adjacencies
- Access requirements
- Equipment and mechanical needs
- Quality of materials
- Occupancy requirements
- Special indoor environmental quality requirements
- Building rating systems and performance criteria
- Construction considerations
- Budget considerations and limitations

STEP 1B: GUIDING PRINCIPLES

Guiding principles serve as both a foundation and a yardstick that enhance and support the building program information, best practices, and other standards that define project goals. The Oxford dictionary defines a principle as a "fundamental truth" that serves as the foundation for a system of belief, behavior, or a chain of reasoning. Guiding principles allow an organization to express its "fundamental truth" through the design process and the resulting built structure. Established and prioritized with the client and project stakeholders early in the pre-planning process, guiding principles can be thought of as the basic ground rules governing all design decisions. It is appropriate for guiding principles to be aspirational and inspirational, big idea statements that reflect and communicate the client's and the project's purpose.

Useful guiding principles are broad enough to be flexible, yet specific enough to be actionable. An example of a weak guiding principle for a design project is "End world hunger." It is too broad and not actionable by the design team. An example of a good guiding principle might be "Celebrate the rich cultural heritage of the site." It is both broad and actionable. "Provide adequate storage space for all building occupants" is an example of a guiding principle that is too specific. While "adequate storage space for all occupants" is not a guiding principle; it is a reasonable desire and a specific requirement of the design program.

Organize guiding principles around the four perspectives identified in Chapter 2:

1. **Performance:** Principles that help frame high performance (function and energy) to support the planet in becoming healthier through design
2. **Systems:** Principles relevant to ecological systems and technology integration
3. **Culture:** Principles that promote a shared sense of community and an equitable ethos in the project
4. **Experience:** Principles that motivate the design team to pursue beauty as expressed through design

Guiding principles are communicated in simple, powerful, clear, aspirational, or inspirational short statements. As an example, here is a set of guiding principles from a project recently completed for the Lancaster County Conservancy by Re:Vision Architecture, Philadelphia.

Performance perspective
- Create the healthiest environment imaginable at the urban forest center.

Systems perspective
- Instill an environmental ethic through a safe and fun interactive experience with nature.
- Be the best example of integrated, holistic sustainability through land conservation, restoration, preservation, and green building (Living Building Challenge Project).

Culture perspective
- Educate and inspire about nature, stewardship, land protection, and sustainable design through the building, site, program and process.
- Connect the community and the conservancy.

Experience perspective
- Infuse a sense of beauty into every decision.

Notice that all the principles start with an action verb. Action is an important characteristic of a guiding principle because the process of design is an action. Also notice that the guiding principles are broad in nature but specific enough to help the design team make decisions, and to evaluate and validate the design throughout the process and at project completion. Guiding principles keep the design team focused, and they also serve throughout the design project as a measure to safeguard the original intent of the design. From the beginning of a project to completion and post-occupation, in the SDB methodology, guiding principles are used to assess the relative success of a design. Figure 3.1 is a reduced form of the guiding principles matrix.

Completing the Guiding Principles Matrix

The purpose of the guiding principles matrix (Table 3.1) and the other matrices in the *Sustainable Design Basics* methodology is to guide the early project process through the collection, organization, analysis, and synthesis of varied information required to design a sustainable project effectively. The information, analysis, and evaluation for each step of the process may take some time. Therefore, a specific matrix may need to be accessed multiple times during the design process. See the demonstration project in later chapters for additional information and specific descriptions of how this and other matrices are completed.

STEP 1C: MACRO CONTEXT AND MICRO CONTEXT

Planet earth is one interconnected system. The interrelationship of the oceans, the land, the atmosphere, and life on earth are dynamic, and the socioeconomic world is rapidly creating an interconnected global community. What affects the environment, economy, and society in one place will eventually have an impact on the earth and the global environment.

Context, in its many forms, both constrains and expands sustainable design. Significant forms of context include ecological, physical, cultural, sociological, and technological. In sustainable design, it is vital to understand context and its potential impact on the immediate site, the surrounding community, and beyond.

TABLE 3.1 GUIDING PRINCIPLES MATRIX/BLANK

Guiding Principles Matrix					
	Objective/Tangible Aspects		Subjective/Intangible Aspects		
The Four Perspectives	**Performance**	**Systems**	**Culture**		**Experience**
Guiding Principle	*Stated overarching performance principle*	*Stated overarching ecological principle*	*Stated overarching principle*	*Stated overarching culture principle*	*Stated overarching experiential principle*
Reflections					

Sustainable Design Basics: A methodology for the schematic design of sustainable buildings

Source: Sharon B. Jaffe

Macro Context

Macro context examines large-scale conditions, conditions that are influenced by, or have influence on, global events. Most building projects are built within an existing framework: on a particular continent, in a specific region, in a certain state and climate. A building may be located on an urban street, in a suburban neighborhood, or a rural area. Such macro context contributes to the specific conditions of the project environment. Macro context has implications for analysis and evaluation of project information that influences the design of a sustainable building. It is important to acknowledge and address how a single specific project will produce ramifications for a neighborhood, city, or even the global ecosystem. Every building is part of a "whole," and the macro context is focused on looking at all of the parts in relation to the "whole" and the "whole" in relation of its parts.

Sustainable design looks to understand concerns at the **global** and **regional** scales, or the **macro context**, to take steps with each sustainable project to address the issues, not only to avoid adding to the problem, but through each new project to contribute to a healthier, sustainable future.

Micro Context

Micro context looks at the small-scale elements and details of a particular site. Building design is placemaking. The relationship between a building with its surroundings is instructive, and understanding the surrounding built environment is vital to a well-designed project. Are there views or landscape features to be highlighted? What is the building and architectural vocabulary of the surrounding area: size, form, materials, and aesthetics?

Respect the community context of each project. The design of a building within an existing community affects the social construct of a project and the community.

A previously occupied site will have a history and the history of a site is all part of the micro context. Document the historical context, character, and significant points of interest in the surrounding area. Understanding the history of the client/ organization/end user, the surrounding community, and the local site, allows a project to be designed to serve the client while contributing to the overall community.

Compared to **macro context**, the issues of **micro context** are very specific and have immediate impact on the operational efficiencies of a building, the building site, and the environment surrounding the site. *Sustainable Design Basics* uses the resources of the specific project site as well as the resource focus of the **micro context.** Each specific location has opportunities inherent in its geographic, ecologic, and societal factors. Determining which sustainable design strategies are best suited for the specific project's energy, water, air, and cultural goals is apparent when available resources have been appropriately inventoried and assessed correctly.

Geosetting

Geosetting is an umbrella term used to describe physical properties of the area surrounding a building site that has applications at the macro- and microscale. Geosetting includes:

- Geographic setting or location
- Climate
  - Macroclimate
  - Microclimate
- Settlement patterns
- Site context
  - Characteristics of the surrounding built environment: topography, ecological type, water
  - Characteristics of the local community

The geographic setting and location of a site are key factors influencing the design of the site and the building. The geographic setting informs the designer of a great many specific factors such as climate, solar orientation, wind direction, rainfall, flooding, and other less obvious influences on appropriate building technology and materials.

Climate is one of the first and most important environmental factors to be understood before designing a building and its site.

Macroclimate

The macroclimate indicates the general climate severity: temperature swings, typical wind speed, annual totals of solar radiation, and driving rain index, which relate to the thermal conductivity of external surfaces. Global climate influences the built environment. The built environment influences human choices, which in turn affect health and the global climate. As previously noted in Chapter 2, "Mindset," cause and effect are cyclical, holistic, and interrelated. Global climate conditions and trends will continue to impact ecology and influence infrastructure development, as the effects of changing global climate on resources, biodiversity, and population health are better understood.

Microclimate

Microclimate references the historical weather conditions and environmental influences such as sun angle, the direction of breezes, site contours, and habitat specific to the building site. The microclimate of a building site can vary from the overall regional climate in ways that will influence the building's interaction with the site. To understand the microclimate, it is necessary to account for air movement directed by surrounding slopes, which may alter regional prevailing winds, and specific solar conditions. Shade from adjacent built or natural structure might also alter microclimate. These conditions are significant and guide the position and orientation of the building on the site, its relationship to the surrounding community, as well as the choice of sustainable strategies that will be most effective.

Consider the impact of the microclimate on the site, community, and surroundings. Is the site located in a high wind path? Do cars from traffic accidents end up on the corner of the site every ice storm? Evaluate any features, natural or human-made, that would change or influence the general historical climate data. For example, do tall buildings substantially shade the subject site or redirect predominate wind paths? Microclimate can differ from one side of the building to another, in significant ways due to the hyperlocal impact of immediate surroundings on solar access, wind, temperature, and humidity.

Settlement Patterns

Buildings are grouped together in settlement patterns. Local landscape, farming needs, the availability of material, welfare, and social interaction all influenced the location and formation of early rural settlements. The original landowner and de facto planner may have determined early urban settlement patterns. Philadelphia is a good example. William Penn was an English real estate developer who founded the English colony of Pennsylvania in North America. As the owner and ruler of the English colony, Penn established the settlement pattern of Philadelphia. Penn organized Philadelphia on a rectilinear grid of streets around a center square that stretched between two rivers that served as boundaries. The grid organization guided construction in Philadelphia as the city grew. As the settlement pattern of an important early urban environment, Philadelphia influenced settlement patterns throughout North America.

In order to refer to common characteristics relevant to the built environment, urban planners developed classifications of settlement patterns that denote general, common settlement characteristics: urban, suburban, and rural. Table 3.2 summarizes these characteristics. *Sustainable Design Basics* addresses sustainable design in rural, suburban, and urban settlement patterns.

Site Context

Where a project is located and developed determines the site context. Building size and construction parameters are governed by regulation, as well as contextual relationships relative to history, architectural aesthetic, geography, and connection of the site/building to its physical and community surroundings.

Sustainable design requires inventory and analysis of the site context from objective and subjective points of view in order to better implement appropriate sustainable strategies. Analyzing a site from all four perspectives identifies the broad spectrum of site and community resources and opportunities to be leveraged in the design process.

Site selection is undertaken before the actual design of the sustainable building by the client/owner, select business, real estate consultants, and project team. The site selection process involves a detailed evaluation that includes broad business criteria and sustainable design concerns.

TABLE 3.2 SETTLEMENT PATTERN CHARACTERISTICS AND IMPLICATIONS

Settlement Pattern	Definition	Characteristics	Infrastructure
RURAL	Underdeveloped land or farmland	Sparse scattered development Farm land Low population density	Limited infrastructure, (roads and public utilities) No public transit
SUBURBAN	A lower density built environment Predominantly residential mixed-use development that supplies workforce housing for nearby urban areas	Single-family homes A higher percentage of green-space than urban areas Less dense population than cities	Infrastructure is variable Generally good roads Public transit is variable Car-centric
URBAN	Commercial, industrial, and cultural center for surrounding areas	Dense development Multi-story buildings Majority nonagricultural workers Limited green space High density population	Established infrastructure of public utilities, sanitation, roads, bridges, railways Public transit available High level of regulatory oversight for all development

Source: Sharon B. Jaffe

Sustainability advocates are concerned with the conservation of natural resources. Understanding existing and historic site conditions can provide opportunities for restoration of a degraded site while supporting sustainable building strategies.

It is an accepted fact that land is a limited commodity. Previous undeveloped lands, generally parks or agricultural lands, are critical in the natural process of stormwater management, preserving biodiversity and healthy ecology.

There are a few site types that support the preservation of open green space; for instance, an existing structure that can be retrofitted for a new occupant or use can be a cost-effective approach. The reuse of an existing building has the virtue of reducing the need to use raw materials. It has been said that "the greenest building is the one already standing," giving great value to historic preservation and adaptive reuse of existing buildings. When an existing building is reused, rehabilitated, or renovated, the embodied energy already invested in the materials and labor in the original building is preserved and reduces material added to landfills. Renovation of an existing building and/or site may require additional time planning and expense to utilize positive aspects and abate previous unfavorable conditions, but the ease of utilizing a building and operations with existing ties to the community, neighborhood, and existing public transit and infrastructure may be cost effective in the long run.

Site selection for sustainability also requires sensitivity to the increased economic concerns, the site should:

• Reduce the consumption of resources
• Address societal concerns relative to environmental, community, and human health.

Land for building sites is broadly categorized as grayfield, brownfield, or greenfield:

A *grayfield*, a site that had previously been developed, but is outdated or outclassed in its current state. Often found in urban areas as infill sites, a grayfield redeveloped with the right kind of use has the potential to provide new vitality and support to an existing community. Grayfields utilize existing infrastructure and typically do not require remediation of environmental contamination. Reuse of previously developed land reduces pressure to develop and supports the preservation and conservation of previously undeveloped land.

A *brownfield* is a site previously developed for industrial or commercial use and possibly affected by environmental contamination requiring remediation. Cleaning up, restoring, and redeveloping a brownfield can be an essential step in economic redevelopment, revitalizing communities that have been devastated by ecological contamination. Specialized grants, loans, and other funding sources are available for brownfield redevelopment. Brownfield remediation contributes to environmental health, economic opportunity, and other public benefits.

A *greenfield* is a previously undeveloped site. When a new building on a previously undeveloped site is appropriate, impact on the local and global environments must be considered. Sustainable building practices and selection of site require sensitivity to increased environmental and economic concerns, the need to reduce the consumption of resources, and the desire to address societal concerns relative to environmental, community, and human health. Greenfield development should minimize the impact on the ecosystem by minimizing the building footprint and restoring ecosystems disturbed by new construction.

Setting/Geography

The immediate surroundings of a site, and the buildings on that site, effectively alter local weather patterns. Dense building or a grove of trees will impact prevailing breezes; tall buildings nearby may limit solar exposure and opportunities for daylighting. A highly developed area with a high level of impervious surface may impact stormwater runoff patterns with potential for site erosion.

The geographic setting of a site provides varied opportunities for sustainable actions. A site easily accessible by public transit, bicycle paths, and pedestrian walkways encourages community interaction. A transit adjacent site reduces the need for building occupants and visitors to travel by personal automobile. Less driving resulting in less pollution is better for the overall environment, reducing traffic, which is better for the local community and reduces the demand for parking on site, which may allow greater flexibility in site design. Inviting bicycle paths and pedestrian walkways with connections to transit encourages residents and workers to bike and walk more. People walking and biking to work are participants in community life, even if only through observing the surroundings.

Topography and the underlying geology influence the development of sustainable buildings. Geological information provides an understanding of soil, groundwater, and local mineral conditions and characteristics. Topographic challenges and opportunities impact the ability to minimize runoff, erosion, and groundwater contamination. Topographic features such as hills, valleys, plains, creeks, and other natural and constructed features may affect access to sun, breezes, and view, which in turn influence building location and orientation.

Infrastructure

Access and proximity to existing infrastructure, such as public transit, roads, communication technologies, sanitation, electrical power, water, and sewer, support the day-to-day functions and economic growth of our communities. Operation of our infrastructure in ways that support our local microeconomies and do not negatively impact our ecological systems, society, and economy is key to our sustainable future. That means incorporating sustainable principles, such as the use of renewable fuel sources, to mitigate negative impact on ecosystems. Restoration procedures following construction, energy efficiency, resource neutral operations, and maintenance meet user needs and preferences while carefully growing the infrastructure systems for maximum effectiveness.

Population and Community

"People, planet, and profit" is a phrase often referenced as the triple bottom line. The phrase invokes the overlapping concerns of sustainability. "People" is commonly interpreted to represent an equitable society. How is the equity aspect, a broad high-minded concept, relevant to the development of a new building?

Neighborhood character and community are influenced by the arrangement of the land and its diverse use, as well as structures, buildings, roadway, walkways, and green space within their defined geographic settings. Designing community-friendly and accessible space that preserves access to desirable community amenities such as green space, view corridors, and recreation spaces contributes to social equity and the livable nature of a community. Understanding the social context of the surrounding community facilitates green building concepts that integrate the building and site into the community with the goal of improving the overall quality of life, minimizing strain on the local infrastructure, and maximizing public/private synergies.

The best way to know a community is to be involved with the community. In the world of community development, meetings with the project stakeholders (called a charrette) to learn the community wants and needs are hosted by the design team. In an academic environment, research is conducted to establish social, demographic, economic, and other pertinent data, from which the community wants and needs are deduced.

Building Typology

Building typology is the classification and correlation of traits and characteristics of a building. Typology is used to identify common characteristics, typically physical, that align with specific functional requirements for a specific building use or type. Functional characteristics may include relationships of building to building, building to street, and building configuration. Establishing a building's typology allows the designer to consider the general requirements of a typical program, traditional structure and form, site requirements, and access.

Urban planning and architecture use typology classifications to imply and reflect the typical physical characteristics tied to building function, form, and setting. The intended function highly influences building design and construction. Healthcare facilities have very different operational and spatial needs than those of an office building, a school, or an industrial production facility. Each building type has specific attributes and requirements, including but not limited to types and size of spaces, light requirements, special ventilation, public/private access, standards, technologies, communications, safety, and security concerns.

Typology impacts:

- Order of spaces: Use requirements
- Construction: Code and best practices demand different construction material and techniques
- Structure: Efficient and effective structural requirements, materials, and structural grid
- Occupant quantity: The concentrations of workers in a single building impacts the buildings relationship to the site and the broader community.

STEP 1D: SITE INVENTORY AND ANALYSIS

Site inventory and analysis is one of the most important and also one of the most challenging steps in the sustainable design process. Before a designer begins drawing building shapes and plans, it is important to understand the opportunities and challenges of the building site, especially when making decisions about building location, orientation, shape, plan, and massing.

The Elements of Site Inventory

Physical, biological, and cultural attributes of the site influence building design. To maximize available natural and human-made resources, and benefit from inherent opportunities, a complete and thorough site assessment is essential during the pre-planning research and design analysis process. Significant physical, biological, ecological, social, and cultural attributes are inventoried and the property's legal description, zoning, code, and other regulatory requirements documented. Research and documentation of the broader context of the environment and the community surrounding the site will provide vital insights into other conditions that may be influences. A crucial task in the SDB methodology, the site inventory provides the basis for quantitative and qualitative interpretation.

Macroclimate

Climate is one of the most variable, and arguably the most important, environmental factors influencing building location, orientation, and design. Climate is different from the weather in that climate refers to the average weather patterns over a period of many years. The primary factors of climate are temperature, air movement, and moisture determined by latitude, altitude, and terrain. These conditions directly impact the thermal comfort of humans and the energy usage required to maintain thermal comfort. Building design strategies specific to macroclimate influence building adaption and resilience. A building design that will provide appropriate thermal comfort for occupants in the face of future climate change requires a good understanding of the climate and sustainable strategies, as well as a good measure of inventiveness.

Macroclimate considerations include:

- Temperature
- Humidity
- Precipitation
- Wind
- Sun and clouds

There are multiple climate classification systems. For instance, the United States Department of Energy has issued a guide to U.S. climates zone, and the state of California has its own specific guidelines. The Koppen-Geiger Classification is widely used internationally; it is a system of five broad categories with additional subcategories to refine climate descriptions.

The definition of the different climates zones is based on the following:

- Global latitude
- Temperature
- Precipitation
- Humidity

Climate classifications used in this textbook are distilled and simplified Koppen-Geiger Classifications, as summarized in Table 3.3. *Subcategory* refers to specific climates within the broader climate. For example, in a dry climate, there are arid and semiarid sub-climates. *Characteristics* include average precipitation and temperatures in a climate zone. *Implication* refers to the kind of design challenges and opportunities faced in each climate zone. Cloudy weather or intense sun are examples of implications. *Representative locations* are major cities that are located in the climate zones. *Building form expression* outlines the standard building design practices that historically have proven effective in response to the specific climate zone elements. These expressions are inspirations to consider when designing an actual project.

Microclimate

Within a specific climate zone, the location of each specific site has unique characteristics and conditions. The climate conditions of a specific site may vary from the macroclimate of the region and will have a profound effect on building design and performance. This highly localized climate is the microclimate.

TABLE 3.3 MACRO CLIMATE ZONES CATEGORIES, CHARACTERISTICS, AND IMPLICATIONS

	Climate Group	Subcategory	Characteristic	Implication	Representative Locations	Building Form Expression
Koppen-Geiger A	Tropical	Wet (rainforest) Monsoon Wet and dry (savanna)	Consistent warm temperatures and regular rainfall. Annual rainfall over 59inches, 68- 91°F temperature	Warm moist conditions result in dense cloud cover reducing the solar efficacy	Havana, Cuba Kolkata, India Miami, FL Singapore	High ceilings, large windows shaded by exterior plantings, shutters or louvers; Fenestration for cross ventilation and thermal venting; Raised first level; Shaded porches
Koppen-Geiger B	Dry	Semi-Arid	Low precipitation High evaporation rate Extreme temperature variation	Lots of sunshine	Phoeniz, AZ Riyadh, Saudi Arabia	Minimize exposure, maximize shade; Compact urban form, Thick walls, Courtyards with fountains
Koppen-Geiger C	Mild Temperate	Mediterranean Humid Subtropical Marine	Moderate with extremes of temperature and precipitation. Typically four seasons	Unpredictable and varied weather. Building structure and systems must accommodate wide variables	Jerusalem, Israel Seattle, WA Shanghai, China Sydney, Australia Philadelphia PA New Haven CT	Maximize solar in winter, minimize solar gain in summer. Rectilinear building form on an east-west axis. Narrow floor plate to facilitate daylight and natural ventilation. High ceilings and windows positioned for cross ventilation
Koppen-Geiger D	Continental	Warm summer Cool summer Subarctic	Colder winter, shorter growing season. Extreme seasonal changes.	Harsh weather Thunderstorms and tornadoes	Only in the Northern Hemisphere. Calgary Canada; Pittsburgh, Pennsylvania; much of Scandinavia	Small, compact footprint, small windows minimize heat loss; larger windows face south maximize winter sunlight and heat gain; Sloped roofs to shed heavy snowfall; Lower interior ceiling
Koppen-Geiger E	Polar	Tundra Ice Cap	Tundra—Short summers with plentiful fauna and flora. Ice cap—extreme cold year-round; - 30F avg wind temp.	Large snow drifts can collect as high as 12 feet	Tundra—Nome, AK, Norway. Ice cap—Arctic and Arctic Circles at North and South Poles	Compact footprint, lower ceilings highly insulated, sm. window size. Optimize window opening/location for daylighting; renewable energy—biomass heating

Source: Sharon B. Jaffe

The site's microclimate is a variable condition, and an important environmental factor affecting building design. Microclimate conditions directly determine and impact the interventions required to provide a comfortable environment for building occupants. Natural resources available in the microclimate may be leveraged to achieve design efficiencies.

The elements of microclimate and their effect on building and systems design include:

- Elevation above sea level
  - Temperatures drop with an increase in elevation
- The form of the land/local terrain
  - Hills and valleys: Air movement is affected by surrounding slopes. Valley floor remains cooler longer than locations further up the slope.
  - Low areas tend to collect heavy cold air, forming fog. Fog reflects solar radiation, keeping the temperatures cooler longer.
  - Crests and ridges of hills compress wind, producing increased wind velocity
- Proximity to water
  - Large bodies of water moderate temperature
- Soil type
  - Color, composition, and water content of soil all impact heat capacity and impact the microclimate. The light color of sand reflects much of the solar radiation and increases the level of radiant heat.
- Vegetation
  - Significantly reduces air and ground temperatures by blocking the sun's rays
  - Blocks the wind, moderating the cooling effects.
  - Reduces stormwater runoff, minimizing erosion and filtering sediment of dust and other pollutants from rainwater to nearby bodies of water.
  - Improves air quality, removing carbon dioxide, smoke, dust, and other pollutants from the atmosphere.
  - Appropriately selected and located vegetation can significantly reduce noise pollution.
  - Provides necessary habitat for birds and other wildlife in an ecosystem.
- Humanmade structures
  - Shade the ground
  - Change wind flow patterns; increase pedestrian level wind
  - Effect water runoff and drainage

The site-specific microclimate provides both challenges and opportunities that greatly influence the selection of appropriate and effective sustainable strategies.

Sun

Helios to the Greeks, Sol to the Romans, Ra to the ancient Egyptians—cultures around the world have worshipped the sun as a god, perhaps appropriately so because the light, heat, and energy provided by the sun is required for existence on earth.

The sun's radiant energy is experienced through the visible sun rays that warm surfaces even on cold days. Quantity and intensity of solar radiation drive the weather,

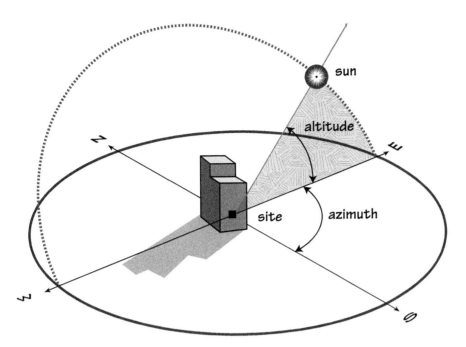

Figure 3.1 Sun position and path, altitude and azimuth
Source: Sharon B. Jaffe

influence climate and vegetation, and determine the solar energy available. The earth's shape and elliptical orbit around the sun varies the intensity of solar energy by geographic position, time of day, and season.

Sun Position and Path

Sun position and solar path relative to a building site are critical in determining orientation and massing of a building, impacting its solar energy collection potential. The utility of sustainable strategies such as daylighting, passive heating, PV energy, and natural ventilation is dependent upon the sun's position and solar path relative to a specific site. Figure 3.1 illustrates altitude and azimuth relative to the sun's path.

Sun position in the northern hemisphere: the summer sun is high in the sky traveling from east to west as it rises and sets in the northern sky. The winter sun is low in the sky and rises and sets south of the east-west path.

Solar path: The earth's movement around the sun and path determines how long a day will be and the amount of daylight available relative to any position on earth on any given day. Solar path varies throughout the day and year in a pattern we know as seasons.

Visualizing the Sun's Path

A *sun path diagram* represents the annual changes in the sun's path in the form of a diagram (Figure 3.2). The sun path diagram charts the solar *azimuth* (the angle along the horizon, or direction of the sun) and *altitude* (the elevation angle of the sun) for a specific location, longitude, and latitude at specific dates and times. Sun path charts are useful tools for determining the position of the sun at various times of year. The charts do not take into consideration the topography/land conditions.

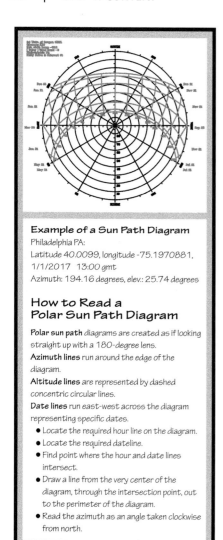

Example of a Sun Path Diagram
Philadelphia PA:
Latitude 40.0099, longitude -75.1970881,
1/1/2017 13:00 gmt
Azimuth: 194.16 degrees, elev.: 25.74 degrees

How to Read a Polar Sun Path Diagram

Polar sun path diagrams are created as if looking straight up with a 180-degree lens.
Azimuth lines run around the edge of the diagram.
Altitude lines are represented by dashed concentric circular lines.
Date lines run east-west across the diagram representing specific dates.
  • Locate the required hour line on the diagram.
  • Locate the required dateline.
  • Find point where the hour and date lines intersect.
  • Draw a line from the very center of the diagram, through the intersection point, out to the perimeter of the diagram.
  • Read the azimuth as an angle taken clockwise from north.

Sun path data is available via Solardat.uoregon.edu/Sun-ChartProgram.html
See Enlarged Sun Path Diagram in Appendix

Figure 3.2 How to read a polar solar chart

Source: Sharon B. Jaffe

If possible, visit the physical site to observe the impact of elements of nature and the built environment that will interrupt the sun's rays. Trees, foliage, fences, surrounding buildings, and other elements will block sunlight and cast a shadow. Some architectural software includes climate analysis and sun path visualization tools. See more about determining the solar path and using solar diagrams to facilitate active and passive sustainable design strategies in the appendix.

Sky Conditions

As the sun moves along the solar path, it may encounter sky conditions that block or diffuse sunlight, thereby impacting the effectiveness of sustainable solar strategies. Sky conditions are particularly important when designing for interior daylighting. Cloud cover will impact sky illumination, solar heat gain, and effective daylighting. The frequency and opacity of cloud cover must be modeled in order to ensure effective passive solar design. Information on sky conditions is available through a variety of software and websites.

Sun as a Source of Energy

Throughout centuries of human history, passive solar energy has been used to heat and light building spaces. Thousands of years ago the Chinese built to maximize winter solar gain using an east-west orientation for main streets in towns to assure south-facing exposure for buildings. Ancient Chinese village homes oriented the one opening in the building to face south, using the winter sun for supplemental heat. Ancient Egyptians used black-tiled pools to heat water during the day, then used the warmed water in a system of interior pipes to heat the building at night. Ancient Greeks used large south-facing windows to collect heat from solar radiation, and stone as thermal mass to absorb heat to warm bathhouses. Ancient Greeks also used skylights with interior mirrors to redirect sunlight into buildings.

Passive solar energy is most commonly demonstrated through passive heating and daylighting. Critical components of passive solar systems include:

• Building orientation
  Passive solar strategies are optimized when a building is oriented with an unobstructed view of the sun. Building shape and mass determines the efficiency of the building to absorb the sun's heat energy.
• Windows
  Windows facing the sun unshaded allow sunlight and the accompanying heat to enter the building. Unshaded sun exposure may be desirable during cold seasons, but windows must have exterior shading to block direct heat gain from sunlight in warm seasons.
• Thermal mass
  Thermal mass, typically brick, concrete, stone, tile, or similar materials, absorbs and stores heat when exposed to sunlight, discharging that heat when the temperature of the surrounding air is cooler than the thermal mass.

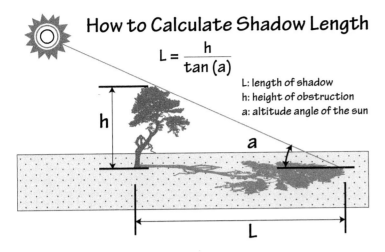

Figure 3.3 How to calculate sun shadows
Source: Sharon Jaffe

- Natural convection and radiation
  Convection is the movement of air as driven by changing temperature. Air, when warmed, expands and becomes less dense, causing the warm air to rise and transfer heat via the air movement. *Radiation* is the movement of heat from a warmer surface to a cooler surface.

Active solar energy uses technology to capture, convert, and distribute solar energy.

Solar thermal collectors collect energy from direct sunlight that is absorbed by thermal collector tubes filled with liquid. Solar heated liquid contained in tubes transfers its heat to warm water collected in a storage tank or pipes.

Solar photovoltaic panel systems use conductive materials that convert sunlight into electricity to power operations. When the more intense sunlight strikes the PV modules directly, the PV module produces more power. Sunlight interacts with the semiconductor materials in PV cells creating an electric current. PV modules are very sensitive to shade. It is crucial that PV array have clear solar access without excessive shadows from adjacent natural or built structures. Figure 3.3 describes how to calculate shadow length. Appropriate location of the PV array and mounting angle of the PV panel are critical for maximum power generation.

Photovoltaic systems can be net-metered or grid-connected systems. Grid-connected systems are tied into the utility grid and metered to credit the power generated above the required building load back to the customer; the meter runs backward. Stand-alone, off-grid systems require storage batteries to store the power above the immediate need during peak sun hours for use when sunlight is not available.

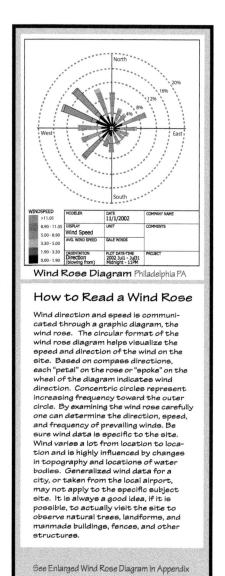

How to Read a Wind Rose

Wind direction and speed is communicated through a graphic diagram, the wind rose. The circular format of the wind rose diagram helps visualize the speed and direction of the wind on the site. Based on compass directions, each "petal" on the rose or "spoke" on the wheel of the diagram indicates wind direction. Concentric circles represent increasing frequency toward the outer circle. By examining the wind rose carefully one can determine the direction, speed, and frequency of prevailing winds. Be sure wind data is specific to the site. Wind varies a lot from location to location and is highly influenced by changes in topography and locations of water bodies. Generalized wind data for a city, or taken from the local airport, may not apply to the specific subject site. It is always a good idea, if it is possible, to actually visit the site to observe natural trees, landforms, and manmade buildings, fences, and other structures.

See Enlarged Wind Rose Diagram in Appendix

Figure 3.4 How to read a wind rose
Source: Sharon B. Jaffe

Daylighting

The power of the sun can be felt and seen through its heat and light. Sustainable buildings embrace daylight. The sunlight is free and is vital to human health and well-being and, when used in place of artificial lighting, will save energy. Daylighting is a consideration that begins early in the SDB methodology by setting goals, and determining the site, building orientation, massing, and form. By understanding the solar exposure available on the proposed building site opportunities for daylighting can be maximized. Access to daylight is a critical part of the building program and functional requirements. Make the most of the southern exposure and maximize available daylight by organizing the interior space plan to pair spatial functions with sun exposure appropriately. Control the exposure of equator-facing windows with exterior horizontal shading and use of interior light shelves to protect from unwanted direct heat gain and glare. The ability to bounce daylight through the interior will require careful space planning to avoid obstructing daylight, light-reflective material finishes, and daylight reflector systems (i.e., light shelves that reflect daylight onto the ceiling as an indirect lighting source).

Air

Wind

Prevailing winds are significant site considerations. Knowing the wind pattern at a specific site influences a building orientation, massing, and the position of its windows and doors. Natural ventilation moves air through a building without mechanical assistance. Wind direction and speed of prevailing winds are crucial considerations when designing for natural ventilation. The greatest indoor air velocity is achieved when the ventilation opening is positioned 90 degrees to the wind direction. Figure 3.4 explains how to read a wind rose to determine wind direction. Air exchange is a necessity for a healthy interior environment. An open window and breeze on a warm day supports active convective and evaporative cooling. In cold weather, a carefully positioned landscape windbreak can buffer a building from cold winds. Wind can also be a source of renewable energy.

Wind Power

Winds are caused by uneven heating of the earth's atmosphere by the sun, so at its most basic level, wind power is a form of solar energy. Topography or terrain, vegetation, and bodies of water influence wind direction and flow patterns. Wind turbines convert the movement of the wind into mechanical power used to power an electric generator that produces electricity. Wind turbines are available from single small turbines sized below 50 kilowatts for a small business to substantial 750 kilowatts utility sized turbines.

The viability of wind power is dependent on the available wind speed and quantity optimal for the wind turbine. The return on investment for wind energy can vary wildly with local costs of electricity, economies of scale, and specific site considerations. Be sure to investigate permit and zoning requirements.

Air Quality and Pollution Levels

Clean air is essential to life. Flora, fauna, and people need clean air to breathe. Even so, globally, the air is sullied every day. Construction, traffic, manufacturing gases, burning fuel, even farms add pollution to the air. Indoor air quality (IAQ) is affected by outdoor air. Human health and wellness are closely tied to both the ambient external air quality and interior building air quality. Years of life lost due to ambient air pollution exposure is substantial, particularly in urban centers. Given the nature of air pollution and the ease with which ambient air diffuses, it is essential to understand the local air quality, sources of particulate matter, gases, and other pollutants to mitigate the negative impact on people and environment, and to design buildings that do not contribute to the problem.

State and local codes incorporate industry-generated evidence-based best-practice guidelines to set limits on pollution and contaminants, in order to improve air quality. Green building rating systems set increasingly high standards for indoor air quality. Natural ventilation methods can counterintuitively reduce indoor air quality if external ambient air quality is poor. Specific and focused strategies to control air intake and air cleaning/filtration may be required, depending on the specific characteristics of ambient air at the site.

Water

Precipitation and Stormwater

Water is required to support the environment. Green building design considers interior and exterior potable water and precipitation holistically. In order to conserve water, manage wastewater and stormwater. Fresh water is a necessity for flora, fauna, and humans to thrive, yet it is an increasingly scarce resource. Buildings built with sustainability goals recognize the importance of water and its place in the ecological cycle. Conservation of potable water and management of stormwater runoff supports a healthy environment, fulfills code requirements, and reduces operational cost.

Rainwater

Harvesting rainwater has been a common practice from the earliest times of humankind. Evidence of cisterns, tanks used for storing water harvested from rainfall, have been found and traced back as far as the Neolithic age. Cisterns were one of the central features of well-designed Roman cities, and were accompanied by other water supply, drainage, and sanitation innovations.

Fresh or potable water usage can be conserved by:

- Efficient use of water
- Selecting materials requiring limited water in the production process
- Use of no- or low-flow plumbing fixtures

Figure 3.5 How to calculate plumbing fixture water usage
Source: Sharon B. Jaffe

How to Estimate Daily Water Usage

Daily use (gal/day) =
Average number of daily occupants × 8 (gal/person)
High estimated daily use (gal/day) =
Average number of daily occupants × 12 (gal/person)

- Use of aerators or thermostatic mixer taps
- Maintenance to prevent leaks
- Reclamation of graywater (wastewater discharged from sinks, bathtubs, showers, and clothes washers) for appropriate uses (i.e., irrigation, flushing sanitary fixtures)
- Harvesting rainwater for irrigation and other uses not requiring potable water

Rainwater can be easily harvested and used to accomplish important sustainability goals. Rainwater harvesting does at least two great things:

- Reduces the need for potable water (water fit for human consumption)
- Reduces stormwater runoff that can flood roads, rivers, and cause erosion

While there are reasonable concerns regarding the use of rainwater for consumption, not least of which is local code prohibitions, rainwater can be used for agriculture, landscape irrigation, and flushing toilets. Figure 3.6 provides basic formulas to calculate rainwater runoff.

- 37 percent of the water used by a typical office building in the United States is for sanitary flush fixtures.
- 22 percent of the water used by a typical office building in the United States is for irrigation.
- 13 percent of the water used by a typical office building in the United States is for kitchen/dishwashing.
- 28 percent of the water used by a typical office building in the United States is for cooling and heating.

Stormwater runoff negatively impacts the overall environment by:

- Impairing and flooding streams and rivers
- Eroding stream banks
- Damaging aquatic habitat
- Pushing pollutants into waterways

Stormwater can be managed through careful planning and use of:

- Well-located, cultivated vegetation and habitat
- Percolation: Use of permeable surfaces

How to estimate **Rainwater** runoff

Determine the collection area size.
This is usually the roof of the building, but it can include other impervious surfaces from which rainwater can be collected.

Catchment Area
Calculate a rectangular surface:
length (ft) x width (ft) = catchment area (ft^2)

Loss Factor
Accounts for evaporation and first flush. Rainfall information is available from a variety of government and NGO sources.

1" rainfall over one square foot of area = 0.6208 gallons

Loss factor – losses due to evaporation, first flush, etc. = decimal value ≤ 1.0

Collected rainwater (gallons) =
Area (sf) x **Rain** (in) x **(1- loss factor)** x **0.6208**

Figure 3.6 How to calculate rainwater runoff
Source: Sharon B. Jaffe

- Rain gardens: Strategically located and planted depressions that collect rain and stormwater runoff from impervious surfaces. Plant with vegetation with deep plant roots that are tolerant of garden flushing/flooding. Stormwater or rainwater is then slowly absorbed back into the earth, naturally filtering runoff through layers of soil, sand, gravel, and rock, removing pollutants from the runoff, avoiding much of the erosion associated with heavy rain and storm runoff.
- Cisterns and rain barrels: Collection of stormwater runoff for nonpotable water use

Storing Rainwater

Cisterns are large storage tanks, located either above or below ground, that hold rainwater to be used for the benefit of the building and/or site. Cisterns support stormwater management and collect water for reuse from roofs or other impervious surfaces. Stored water is either drained by gravity or pumped to its end-use location.

There are a few different types of cistern tanks, ranging in sizes from 600 gallons to 50,000 gallons. Evaluate available space and appropriate investment for the project.

- Surface cistern tanks can be sited on the rooftop or integrated into the site. They drain by gravity or pump.
- Subsurface cistern tanks are recommended in areas where freezing is a concern.

Cisterns should be located as close as reasonably possible to where the water will be used. The ground surface can be graded away from the cistern to minimize distribution system requirements. Cisterns must be located upslope from any form of sewage disposal facilities, septic tanks, sewer, or drain lines. Avoid locating cisterns in low-lying areas prone to flooding. Cisterns must be watertight and fabricated from a nontoxic water-safe material.

Rain Garden as Stormwater Management

A rain garden collects and stores fast-moving stormwater runoff, providing time for the stormwater to infiltrate the soil. An uncomplicated depression in the landscape, planted with hardy native vegetation that can tolerate flooding and slow water draining, can reduce urban flooding and erosion of river and stream banks. The natural filtering process of a rain garden also reduces the pollutants flowing into our waterways.

Rain gardens can be planted to facilitate natural habitat for birds, butterflies, and other beneficial insects, while providing year-round color and interest to the landscape.

Additional Strategies for Stormwater Management

Vegetative swales are essentially rain gardens that fit into the long narrow spaces between curb and sidewalk. Vegetative swales, like rain gardens, slow water draining and naturally filter stormwater, reducing the number of pollutants flowing into our waterways.

Drywells also manage stormwater runoff. Drywells are proportioned to be deeper than they are wide. Stormwater flows into a below-grade concrete chamber drywell. There the water sits, allowing time for solids to settle before the water flows through an oil-absorbent filter, then to an infiltration filter, before slowly soaking through the porous wall of the dry well into the surrounding soil.

Habitat (Flora and Fauna)

Cities can be so much more than a collection of buildings. The green space between human-built structures plays a critical role in the health of a community. Humans crave connection to nature. People are drawn outside on a beautiful spring day, happy to be sitting outside enjoying the breeze, the warmth of the sun, a spot of green, or a view of the water. It is part of the biophilic response. Integration of building design and the landscape can support sustainable building goals, and provide even more significant opportunities to support an ecosystem.

Flora (indigenous or native plants) and fauna (wildlife) are vital elements in an interdependent ecosystem. Human life is dependent on air, food, and water; much of what humans depend on to survive comes directly or indirectly from the ecosystem, supported by the earth's flora and fauna.

Building sites that utilize the surrounding landscape to support and restore local habitat are more resilient. The site and building that creates an interwoven ecosystem encourages natural biodiversity and supports a sustainable environment and vital ecosystem function. All things in an ecosystem are interdependent. Flora produce oxygen necessary to breathe. Fauna produce carbon dioxide, which flora need for the photosynthesis process that produces oxygen.

Food

Food and its quality directly impact our well-being, both physically and psychologically. Food production, processing, and transportation impact environmental and socioeconomic systems and indirectly affect human well-being.

Socially and environmentally aware societies are looking for better options to address the food system's negative impact on the environment and food security concerns. Urban agriculture and farming are a growing sector of production and delivery systems and often target food deserts (urban areas without access to healthy food) for production, distribution, and consumption of crops while providing local agriculture education and economic opportunity. Dense urban areas have begun to see empty lots, old factory sites, and rooftops used for food production in raised beds, rooftop gardens, container and vertical gardens, and hydroponic growing. The farm-to-table movement in North American restaurants and "buy local" production and direct-to-consumer distribution networks are further evidence of the growing awareness and demand for sustainable food systems.

The Senses

The traditional world, and even more intensely the world of design, is dominated by the visual. Humans are trained to see in a way that allows them to use the visual sense as an impactful tool. It is accepted historically that humans have five basic senses: touch, sight, hearing, smell, and taste. People experience the world through sensory perceptions.

The senses activate emotional responses that allow humans to connect with the world around them in a deeper, more meaningful way. Together, the senses bring a depth of subconscious understanding and emotional response to the surface with more intensity than any one sense working alone.

Multisensory design orchestrates the stimuli of an environment and its effect on human behavior. When integrating stimuli as elements into the design, context is critical. A specific sound or color associated with fun and excitement in one setting may trigger anxiety and concern in another. Sensory stimuli can help building occupants orient their emotional intelligence and intuit appropriate behaviors and actions. Ultimately sensory stimuli that nurture and support human behavior and psychological comfort result in a higher sense of well-being and positive experience of place.

Sound

Sound (acoustics and vibration) is an important element of our environment. Sounds heard in a space, whether originating inside or from outside the space, provide subtle cues. The distant sound of the 7 AM train, the rustling of children as they rise from bed, the morning chirping of birds outside one's window—all provide cues relating to time. A hushed interior space implies calm, an opportunity for focused work and introspection; a noisy space signals stimulation and activity.

Sound affects our emotional state; the distant buzz of bees or the sound of a light breeze outside can be calming, the sound of heavy rain and wind concerning. Many natural sounds have proven to have a restorative effect on our health. Exposure to natural sound increases cognitive capacity. Excessive environmental noise and vibration negatively impact human health and wellness reducing our ability to focus, increasing stress and slowing reaction time. Noisy ambient background sound interferes with the ability to learn and can interfere with building function. The complete absence of sound—sound isolation—is disturbing. The impact of sound, noise, and vibration should be assessed, and as required, plan for mitigation during the early stages of the design process.

Sources of external noise and vibration might be:

• Nearby roadway traffic
• Trains and aircraft
• Adjacent building systems and function
• Recreational activity
• Industrial machine activity

Some building uses are particularly sensitive to sound and vibration. Schools, homes, hospitals, offices, and public buildings all require a base understanding of the ambient sound and vibration. Positive ambient sound conditions may be utilized sustainably, while negative sound and vibration can be anticipated and mitigated, avoiding unwanted disturbance.

Sight

Architecture invites visual response. Buildings are judged as a success or failure on their aesthetic merits. Vision, the sense of sight, confirms the perception of the sense of touch. Vision perceives light, color, and spatial boundaries. While the eyes perceive and evaluate the visual qualities of a space, sight has a more expansive role, in that humans use sight to orient ourselves and move through space.

View

A view is closely tied to sight but also related to a sense of place. People become oriented within a building structure by what they can see in the building, the vista down a corridor, and their ability to navigate through architectural space. It is human nature to be drawn from the interior of a building by the views to and of the outdoors. View provides a strong a connection to nature and daylight.

Views from the interior to outside are essential for practical observations and information. What is the weather outside? What was that noise? The biophilic response prompted by views to nature improve our perception of emotional and physical well-being. The opportunity to change focus, resting eyes and mind, supports productivity.

Touch/Textures

Touch provides information; the skin can detect temperature, texture, weight, and density. Tactile evaluation, the way things feel, differs from visual evaluation in that it confirms the physical qualities that our visual perception implies. Touch creates interest and communicates thermal comfort, humidity, and temperature. The sense of touch communicates an understanding of physical qualities that connect humans and the world.

Texture is the look or feel of a surface. A tactile property, texture needs the sense of touch to be fully appreciated. Textures create a different experience; they allow more sensory input than just "seeing." Textures allow viewers to feel the building. Light enhances texture as it forms shadows, accentuating depth. The impression of texture can also be created with the play of light, creating shadows and patterns.

Smell

When compared to vision, the role of the human sense of smell is underappreciated as an influence of experience. Smell has more receptors than any of our other senses. Smell can trigger intellectual and emotional associations that enhance visual experience. The scent of freshly baked bread can elicit memories of another time and space. Smell is a meaningful way of experiencing the world. It helps establish the sense of place and is crucial to building a lasting memory.

Taste

The senses of taste and smell are deep, fundamental, and animal, tied to an earlier time in human evolution. Consider what it is like to have a stuffy nose and how it affects your sense of taste. Taste and smell are so closely tied that if the sense of smell is weakened, so is the sense of taste.

Taste may also be closely tied to place. As an example, consider the wines of Champagne, France. The physical properties of the wine are so intertwined with the physical properties of the environment that produces them that only wine using grapes from the Champagne region of France may be called Champagne.

Memories recalled by taste and smell are often connected by association to the built environment. Even so, taste is one of the more difficult senses to independently tie as a direct indicator of architectural place and space.

Biophilia

Biophilia is a hypothesis asserting that connection to nature can improve human health and well-being. Sustainable design has a synergistic relationship to biophilia. They share core qualitative values: occupant health and wellness, respect and connection to nature, and social equity. Passive design strategies that are crucial—the first strategies to be integrated into the design of sustainable buildings—support and enhance biophilic design strategies.

The three pillars of biophilia are nature in space, nature of space, and natural analogues.

Nature in space refers to direct access to actual natural elements in a space

- Daylighting strategies within interior spaces
- Dynamic and diffuse use of changing artificial light
- Potted plants
- Use of natural materials
- Ambient sounds: breezes, water flow
- Water features
- Direct access to wooded areas in city parks, urban forests, or restored wetlands

Nature of space refers to spatial characteristics of an interior that convey prospect, refuge, enticement, and peril.

- Prospect is provided through dramatic views out to open spaces.
- Refuge may be realized through a cozy enclosed interior space that provides an emotional sense of safety and protection.
- Enticement/mystery is often accomplished with a visual cue: a peek at a winding hallway that disappears out of sight.
- Peril may be achieved by direct visual connection to, or perception of, a potentially dangerous condition or a controlled risk coupled with knowledge of reliable safety. Some examples are a view from the top of a light well, a cantilevered platform, or a space that appears secluded but may be worth exploring.

Natural analogs refers to design elements that remind us of nature.

- Artwork and decorations that mimic nature's patterns such as leaves on trees, grasses
- molding decorative architectural elements that evoke nature without involving actual natural elements

Benefits of biophilia include contact with nature that generates emotional, physiological, and social benefits; and the innate emotional human response to nature that influences human perception and response to the physical environment.

Site Inventory

Thinking Across Scale

The site inventory documents specific conditions on a building site. Decisions made at the building-specific scale both mitigate the negative impact on broader concerns and contribute to the solutions of far-reaching concerns at the individual project scale and beyond the present moment in time. What happens locally ultimately and cumulatively impacts the environment globally.

TABLE 3.4 MACROSCALE SITE CONSIDERATIONS

Macro Scale Considerations Viewed through the Four Perspectives	

Experience
 	
Biophilia
Happiness
Apathy
	Performance
	
	Measurable climate change
	  -Sea level rise
	  -Temperature rise
	  -Frequency of natural disasters
	Regulation, zoning, and building code

Culture Historic context Vernacular architecture Education centers Human character Economic influences Social and political context Diversity, equity and inclusion	**Systems** Greenhouse gases increasing Sea level rise and loss of ice sheets Deforestation Loss of biodiversity Infrastructure Waterways Transit

Source: Sharon B. Jaffe

Macro context issues include global and regional concerns including cities, large suburban areas, and even larger rural areas. Table 3.4 identifies macroscale context issues organized by the four perspectives.

Micro context issues include community and site concerns. Consider what makes a community. The scale of community is interpreted as a neighborhood or a district. The site reflects the boundaries of the actual site. The site inventory includes nearby areas that have a direct influence on the project. Table 3.5 identifies microscale context issues organized by the four perspectives.

Site Inventory Documentation

The site is the base level of sustainable design. Each site has unique attributes: natural and humanmade, cultural, and financial, that create opportunities and challenges.The inventory is a listing that identifies all of the existing conditions. Analysis represents judgments made about the inventory and determining the opportunities and challenges so that appropriate actions and design responses may be considered. The understanding and analysis of the site inventory is critical to the next steps in the predesign and design processes. Site inventory is documented in the SDB site inventory matrix, illustrated by Table 3.6, and through site plans.

Site Inventory Matrix

The site inventory matrix (Table 3.6) organizes challenges and opportunities observed through research and exploration of the site. It is an easily accessible format to assess the information through the lenses of the four perspectives. Not every significance of each observation is relative to the project's guiding principles, the building program, and client preferences. The site inventory is a fundamental exercise. It requires a designer to identify conditions and concerns at the outset of the project before design ideas are formed or drawing begun. The process may seem complex and time-consuming but time invested in the early stages of a project provides

TABLE 3.5 MICROSCALE SITE CONSIDERATIONS

Micro Scale Considerations Viewed through the Four Perspectives

Experience	Performance

Biophilia
Adjacent development
Conditions that affect experience
    Iconic places and views
Sounds, smells, views
Textures, tastes and spatial sense
Sense of safety
    Emotions:
    Happiness, sadness, anger
	Information:
	Geo setting: urban, suburban, rural
	Environmental context
	Boundary of district
	Proximity to city center
	Community density/demographics
	Local economy
	
	Performance:
	Clear sky
	    Site prevailing wind and solar angles/path
	        regulation/zoning and building code
	Microclimate
	Solar exposure, sun angles
	Shade patterns: natural and built
	Topography – shape, slope & soil
	Total solar potential
	Water potential
	Wind potential
	Flood plain

Culture	**Systems**

Population diversity
Historic dontext
Vernacular architecture
Museums
Education/community centers
Local traditions and events
Equity:
    Social construct
    Economic diversity
    Social and political context
       and diversity
	Ecological:
	
	Site contamination
	Watershed
	Local wildlife and habitat
	Loss of biodiversity
	Waterways
	Technological:
	
	Infrastructure
	    Utilities
	    Communications
	    Stormwater
	Access/connectivity:
	    Roads, sidewalks
	    Public and private transit
	Alternate modes of transit:
	    Pedestrian and bike paths

Source: Sharon B. Jaffe

significant benefits. A deep and thorough understanding of site complexities prepares a designer to anticipate and incorporate appropriate and effective response to challenges and opportunities occurring throughout the design process. The process of observation, analysis, and organization of large quantities of information does get easier with practice as a designer develops a familiarity with the process and, through experience, an intuitive sense for prioritizing information. Not every cell in the matrix must have an entry. It is likely that, for most projects, the experience perspective is not relevant on the global scale.

Chapter 11, "Demonstration Project," provides examples of the site inventory and analysis process and a completed site inventory matrix. SDB site inventory matrix form may be found in appendix B.

TABLE 3.6 SITE INVENTORY AND ANALYSIS MATRIX FORM

Criteria Matrix: Interiors

The Four Perspectives Scale	Objective/Tangible Requirements				Subjective/Intangible Requirements			
	Performance		Systems		Culture		Experience	
	Issues	Design Decisions	Issues	Design Decisions	Issues	Design Decisions	Issues	Design Decisions
Macro Scale Including Global Regional District	Enter the most important 1 or 2 challenges or opportunities at this scale	Enter a specific design response	Enter the most important 1 or 2 challenges or opportunities at this scale	Enter a specific design response	Enter the most important 1 or 2 challenges or opportunities at this scale	Enter a specific design response	Enter the most important 1 or 2 challenges or opportunities at this scale	Enter a specific design response
	Enter the most important 1 or 2 challenges or opportunities at this scale	Enter a specific design response	Enter the most important 1 or 2 challenges or opportunities at this scale	Enter a specific design response	Enter the most important 1 or 2 challenges or opportunities at this scale	Enter a specific design response	Enter the most important 1 or 2 challenges or opportunities at this scale	Enter a specific design response
	Enter the most important 1 or 2 challenges or opportunities at this scale	Enter a specific design response	Enter the most important 1 or 2 challenges or opportunities at this scale	Enter a specific design response	Enter the most important 1 or 2 challenges or opportunities at this scale	Enter a specific design response	Enter the most important 1 or 2 challenges or opportunities at this scale	Enter a specific design response
Micro Scale Including Neighborhood, Site, Building	Enter the most important 1 or 2 challenges or opportunities at this scale	Enter a specific design response	Enter the most important 1 or 2 challenges or opportunities at this scale	Enter a specific design response	Enter the most important 1 or 2 challenges or opportunities at this scale	Enter a specific design response	Enter the most important 1 or 2 challenges or opportunities at this scale	Enter a specific design response
	Enter the most important 1 or 2 challenges or opportunities at this scale	Enter a specific design response	Enter the most important 1 or 2 challenges or opportunities at this scale	Enter a specific design response	Enter the most important 1 or 2 challenges or opportunities at this scale	Enter a specific design response	Enter the most important 1 or 2 challenges or opportunities at this scale	Enter a specific design response

Sustainable Design Basics: A methodology for the schematic design of sustainable buildings

Visually documenting the site through each of the four perspectives can identify several sets of priorities simultaneously. It is not uncommon for individuals to approach design projects with a bias that is an outgrowth of their personal or professional experiences. An engineer might be focused on the technical aspects of performance or systems, while an end user may primarily have an interest in the day-to-day experience working in the building. By focusing on each of the four perspectives separately, each is validated and carefully considered before an integrated assessment is assembled. Challenges and opportunities are organized and prioritized to inform the next two steps of the process: pre-planning and design. It is that analysis of challenges and opportunities that provides the answers to why a particular action or strategy might be applicable, and another judged not feasible.

4

Step 2 Pre-Planning

Step 4
**Design
Resolution**

4A Design Synthesis
4B Final Validation
4C Presenting the Project

~~ep 3~~
~~gn~~

3A
3B F
3C Bu   ninary Design
3D Gr   e Design
* Be   g Envelope
             Materials
          nd the Basics

Step 2
Pre-Planning

2A Research & Case Studies
2B Project Goals
2C Design Criteria
2D Spatial Relationships

Step
Conte

1A Project I
1B Guiding Prir
1C Macro / Micro
1D Site Inventory & Anal

Figure 4.0 *Sustainable Design Basics*, step 2
Source: Sharon B. Jaffe

RESEARCH AND ORGANIZATION

Pre-planning begins by researching and compiling building-related information, including:

- Case studies: carefully selected to supply precedent
- Project goals: from the four perspectives of performance, systems, culture, and experience

- Criteria matrix/expanded project program: Understanding the client functional and project energy, ecological, and conservation requirements
- Spatial relationships: Study the required spatial and functional requirements, opportunities to maximize beneficial adjacencies, and opportunities to leverage environmental interrelationships

The four perspectives—performance, systems, culture, and experience—continue to guide and organize the work in this pre-planning step, ensuring that the design of the sustainable project will respond to, and work holistically with, the natural environment. Completion of the tasks in step 2 will suggest sustainable design strategies to be tested and ultimately applied during step 3, design.

When working toward sustainability, everything is connected and the amount of information to be researched, organized, and applied to the design can be overwhelming. Be strategic. Work through complex issues by dividing the problem into smaller manageable parts. Approach each task with a high level of thoughtfulness and attention to detail. A good, integrative design considers a wide range of variables and relies upon the clarity of the pre-planning phase.

STEP 2A: CASE STUDY

Research is a critical aspect of the sustainable design process. For students or professionals new to the practice of sustainable design, the importance of research is magnified by inexperience. One particularly useful form of research is the case study, an in-depth exploration from multiple perspectives of a project with specific similarities to the design problem at hand. The case study provides valuable information related to building site, building typology, climate, building form, building systems, materials, and more. Analysis of the successes and failures of case studies identifies reasonable goals and benchmarks for design projects under development. Establishing clear benchmarks provides an unambiguous method to evaluate the relative success of the project.

Analysis of a case study requires extensive investigation and examination of the what, how, and why of a project. The best way to do this holistically and comprehensively is to use the four perspectives of sustainable design.

Selection

The usefulness of any particular case study lies in clearly identifying the issues relevant to the subject project. Once identified, the issues can be explored through carefully analysis of select case studies that address the issue or topic of inquiry. The designer's initial site inventory of the subject site will be beneficial because it documents many of the significant design issues early during the context step of the SDB methodology.

A case study can be general or specifically focused. Examples of focused case study topics include:

- Specific location/setting/climate
- Building typology

- User group
- Active and passive technologies
- Structural systems
- Elements that have some similarity to the subject design project

Analysis of a case study moves beyond theory to look at real-life approaches to problem solving. Case studies can vary widely and need not be limited to the type of project that is in question. A sustainable strategy applied to one building typology may have parallel application for another building typology. In considering appropriate case studies, the goal is to widen the search to increase the availability and diversity of information. Case study examples may come from distant locales, from ancient times, or even from unbuilt projects.

Case studies may relate to the subject of inquiry in varied ways. A case study provides the opportunity to benefit from the experience and knowledge of others, including the successes and the failures of their completed work. Analysis of case studies in the SDB methodology is to distill real-life data from a particular sustainable design project, understand how a specific strategy was applied, and evaluate the efficacy of the solution in order to extrapolate and apply the research to the subject project.

It is essential to understand the specific context of the case study to be able to evaluate the effectiveness, appropriateness, and applicability of a given sustainable design strategy to the subject design project. Case studies identify an individual situation or a limited collection of conditions, to research and collect relevant data. It is necessary to keep the case study focused and related to the specific inquiry for the resulting analysis to be applicable. While a case study cannot be generalized to apply to all situations, it is an excellent method to focus on specific examples of sustainable strategies employed relative to a particular building type, use, or climate.

It takes time to choose a case study, to research and compile relevant data, and complete the analysis required to document a project for a case study. Make a list of points or strategies to address and be sure all research ties back to those points. A case study uses multiple sources including research via websites, books, periodicals, architectural drawings, energy model results, and relevant data. Be sure to use multiple sources and different types of sources. Document all sources and credit intellectual and photographic work used. Analyze the case study at all scales. Investigate and consider the varied aspects of the case study and how different aspects interact and impact one another. When and where possible, interview building users and visit the case study subject in person. First-hand observations of context and existing conditions may provide information not otherwise available. Understanding the context and the challenges of the case study project is necessary to analyze and appreciate the effectiveness of the resulting design.

Precedents

A *precedent* is an established example, rule, strategy, principle, or characteristic that serves as a guide for consideration during the subject design project.

Case studies (original research or from research literature searches) are good sources for precedents to use as examples to guide current design efforts. Using clear applicable precedents to support a specific strategy adds authority to the particular design decision.

For instance, a case study project has a similar use, site condition or geo setting as the current design project site. This case study uses a particular sustainable technology effectively in a similar manner planned for the subject design, providing a precedent for sustainable technology to be used in the current design project.

An existing precedent creates a frame of reference and an example of a strategy applied to a similar situation with successful results. One caution: Clearly understand the example case study and the specific design challenge for which the case study will serve as an illustration, precedent or benchmark. The closer the parallel is from the case study to the prospective subject design project, the more persuasive the precedent.

Benchmarks

Benchmarks are numeric, measurable levels of performance that serve as a metric or an assessment tool. It is a method of determining the best practices, processes, and performance achieved in an area of focus. Benchmarking is a tool of comparison. Establishing a guideline, a standard or a point of reference to measure performance, through comparison, is extremely useful in determining the goals and objectives of a sustainable design project. Benchmarks serve as a measurement that may be used to quantify performance, and so that quantified performance may be more effectively compared to alternate technologies or applications, just as one might measure the length of two walls with a tape measure to compare the length of each wall relative to the other. Benchmarks often come from case study research. Terms that often describe a benchmark include performance metric and performance indicator.

Organize the Data

The *Sustainable Design Basics* methodology provides specific templates to streamline case study documentation. The case study matrix documents and organizes specific metrics and benchmarks identified for each aspect of the design project. Short text and numerical entries condensed to communicate benchmarks, metrics, systems, sustainable strategies, project goals, and other relevant information. The narrative power point slide template is used to explain the rationale, decisions, alternatives, support material, and images for the specific case study. See the appendix for a template.

Complete the Matrix

The case study matrix organizes research in columns under the four perspectives to assure that information collected is comprehensive and can be easily accessed and weighed as a holistic picture. Enter meaningful metrics, systems, and strategies from each case study into the matrix in the correlating cells to identify precedents that will guide the design proposal. Filling out the matrix may seem tedious and sometimes repetitive. Table 4.1 Case Study Matrix illustrates the matrix format and indicates the specific types of information to be recorded. The process of entering the information into the matrix requires thoughtful evaluation and analysis to create a familiarity with the data that will inform the sustainable design proposal and aids the designer's decision-making process. See Table 4.1 for a case study matrix form. Chapter 11, "Demonstration Project" contains a completed example of the case study matrix. Blank full-size matrices may be found in the appendix.

Performance

The "what" of a case study includes the performance of the building and building systems. Enter the overarching performance goals of the case study, and if applicable, the specific rating system and score.

Building performance achieved by the case study is critical to recognizing precedents and benchmarks.   Enter the actual quantitative numeric metric information. Where actual metrics are unavailable due to lack of history from recent projects, enter projected or energy modeled metrics.

- EUI: Energy use per square foot (kBtu/ft^2)
- Light: Percentage of occupied space with direct access to daylight window, spatial daylight autonomy (sDA), and daylight factor (DF)
- Air: Percentage of occupants within 30 feet of an operable window
- Water: Percentage of conservation or reduction, and rainwater harvested
- Stormwater: Percentage managed on site

Identifying systems and strategies employed to achieve the metric results is helpful when determining a sustainable strategy for similar building design challenges.

Performance information is critical to recognizing precedents and benchmarks for a sustainable design project.

Systems

The "how" of a case study includes technological and ecological strategies that are employed to accomplish the "what" of performance.

The matrix itemizes the stated ecological goals, objectives, strategies, and achievements of the case study as related to:

- Environmental integration of the building and the site
- Structural/construction systems used
- Energy efficiency systems to manage occupant behavior
- Cost savings strategies employed to meet green standards

TABLE 4.1 CASE STUDY MATRIX

Case Study Matrix

	Objective/Tangible Requirements						*Subjective/Tangible Requirements*		
The Four Perspectives	**Performance**					**Systems**	**Culture**		**Experience**
Projects and or **Rating Systems**	Stated Overarching Performance Goals or Guiding Principles or Rating System Selection/score					Stated Ecological Goals	Stated Equity Goals	Stated Cultural Goals	Stated Experiential Goals
Metrics (category)	Energy	Health and Wellbeing		Water			Stakeholder Engagement	Sense of Community	View
Metrics (sub)	**Energy** — Predicted consumed energy use intensity/ Predicted Net EUI	**Light** — % of floor area or percentage of occupant work stations achieving adequate light levels without artificial light	**Air** — % of floor area or percentage of occupant work stations within 30 feet of operable windows	**Water** — Predicted annual consumption of potable water for all uses, including process water	**Storm Water** — % of rainwater managed on site from max. anticipated 24-hour, 2-year storm event	**Ecological Integration** — % of landscaped areas covered by appropriate habitat supporting plants		Walk Score	Percentage of floor area or percentage of occupant work stations with direct views of the outdoors
Achievements (predicted or actual)	kBTU/ ft²/yr	xx% DF	xx%	Gallons	xx%	xx%	xx%	xx%	xx%
Systems + Strategies	What strategies used were the most impactful to reach the goals?	What strategies used were the most impactful to reach the goals?	What strategies used were the most impactful to reach the goals?	What strategies used were the most impactful to reach the goals?	What strategies used were the most impactful to reach the goals?	List 1 or 2 most impactful Passive strategies used	How the above goals are achieved	Strategies or policies used to meet cultural achievements	Strategies or policies used to meet experiential achievements

Sustainable Design Basics: A methodology for the schematic design of sustainable building

Source: Sharon B Jaffe

- Mechanical systems employed
- Renewable passive energy, light, air, and water strategies
- Technical infrastructure for active building systems

Culture and Equity

The "why" of a case study examines its social and cultural drivers. These include:

- Stated equity and inclusivity goals
- Initiatives: community or social motivations
- Policies: internal client or governmental
- How the culture and equity goals were achieved

Experience

This perspective examines the look and feel of the case study, the elements that impact emotion, and the aesthetics. These include:

- Sensory engagement: hearing, sight, smell, touch, and taste
- Spatial perception: whether the space is wide open, closed and tight, varied or static
- Biophilic conditions (the aspects of nature that contribute to human health): a connection to nature, the availability of daylight, natural breezes

Narrative

The case study narrative describes how qualitative support information generated during a case study project is related to the current subject project. It provides the context for the case study.

Information in the case study narrative, available on the companion website, includes project information on the macro- and microscale from all four perspectives: performance, systems, culture, and experience. A narrative structure is flexible enough to document the tangible and intangible aspects of the case study. Case studies may extend beyond technical performance of the subject project to include the values, experience, and involvement of the community. Each case study will have specific and unique elements.

The case study narrative template, available on the companion website, provides a flexible documentation system that will readily accept both text and images as required. It documents the key factual background related to the project, project team, and provides project context across scales.

Basic project information/facts
- Project data; name, location, project use type, year
- Client name and business type
- Project aspirations and motivation
- Principal project team: designers, engineers, special consultants, and contractors
- Stakeholders
- Construction type

- Applied standards, green standards, codes
- Construction cost per square foot
- Awards
- Significant identifying design approach and features
- Measures of success

Global, regional, and district scale
- Performance/Facts
  - Location
  - Climate
  - Local code
  - Local transit
  - Local infrastructure
- Systems
  - Ecological systems
  - Technological systems
  - Mechanical systems
- Culture and Equity
  - Global influences on the project
  - Physical characteristics of the surrounding community
  - Human, social, and cultural issues
- Experience
  - Inspiration
  - Aesthetics
  - Architectural vernacular and materials
  - Imagery perception

Site and building scale
- Performance/Facts
  - Construction costs
  - Program information
  - Special construction constraints and concerns
  - Special code concerns
  - Case study building plans
- Systems
  - Ecological system diagrams
  - For protected habitat, watershed, flood zone
  - Mechanical system restrictions
  - Technical system diagrams
- Culture
  - Description of project culture
  - Client/organization values
  - Underlying cultural drivers
  - Specific cultural expressions
  - Human equity policies, concerns, or expressions
  - Images
- Experience
  - Inspiration
  - Description of project experience

- Sensory
- Aesthetic

The demonstration project in Chapter 11 further explains the role of the case study for developing sustainable projects. Presentation of the case study is discussed in chapter 14.

Interpretation, Analysis, and Evaluation

Case studies help the designer by illustrating the application of sustainable design strategies, and what those strategies achieved in a real-world application. By understanding the application and results of sustainable strategies in a case study, a designer can construct a reasonable hypothesis for the subject project. Case study research allows the sustainable designer to take a shortcut through the iterative design process by building upon other designers' explorations and project results.

Before integrating case study findings into a current project, consider the key issues and the mitigating sustainable strategy applied. Analyze the strategy, alternatives, and assess the application of the strategy to the subject project based on desired outcomes and metrics. Evaluate each sustainable strategy and the outcome. Did the strategy perform as expected? If not, why not? How might the strategy apply to the subject sustainable design?

Case study research and analysis identify metrics achieved through identified sustainable strategies. In the early stages of a project, case study research that associates metrics with specific sustainable strategies provides the designer with a realistic understanding of probable outcomes. Understanding precedent and best practices informs and supports the process of setting goals and objectives.

STEP 2B: PROJECT GOALS

Goals, objectives, and rating systems all set targets for sustainable projects to achieve. Most tangible targets are performance oriented. Intangible drivers and achievements are often more difficult to measure and may be communicated through post-occupancy interviews, survey, and observations.

Case studies, building standards, research, and best practices are effective sources for metrics documenting what designers have achieved in previous projects. Metrics gleaned from research provide inspiration in the form of what is possible for a designer's current sustainable design.

Project goals are broad in scope. Goals are big-picture ambitions that align with the guiding principles established in step 1 of the SDB process. Project goals are developed from all four perspectives: performance, systems, culture, and experience. Goals can be measured and therefore they are tangible. Goals define clear sustainability targets for the design project. Chapter 11 provides examples as applied to the demonstration project.

Performance Objectives

In a society that is increasingly concerned about environmental impact, setting objective performance criteria for the overall building project is critical. It is easy for team members to inadvertently lose focus on overall building performance, during a sustainable design process while considering initial cost or to accommodate a specific aesthetically driven concept. Performance objectives are integral to overall project goals. They are informed by client requirements, code, and specific third-party sustainability standards, case studies, precedent, and program analysis. Objectives are *tangible* and *measurable*. Accomplishing objectives leads to realizing goals.

Establishing Goals and Objectives

While the goal of a project may be general, for example: to build a sustainable building that does not further degrade the local environment, specific objectives must be set to achieve the goal. The broadest objectives of a sustainable building are to reduce, reuse, recycle, and restore. Project objectives are established to accomplish the project goals using:

- Guiding principles established in step 1
- Project program requirements
- Successful strategies, precedents, and benchmarks documented during case study research discussed in step 2

Objectives are accomplished by following specific, concrete steps. Project goals and objectives might be organized as follows:

- **Goal:** Reduce the use of resources
    - **Objective:** Optimize passive heating, cooling and ventilation systems
        - **Metric:** reduced EUI
        - **Strategy:** building shape and massing, solar orientation, buffer space, space planning, thermal mass, WWR, thermal insulation, exterior shading, window and roof monitor locations, landscaping
    - **Objective:** Reduce and optimize energy consumption
        - **Metric:** EUI, percentage of daylight only lighting, energy generated
        - **Strategies:** careful building orientation, efficient planning, and intelligent use of material resources
    - **Objective:** Protect and conserve water
        - **Metric:** percentage of reduced potable water consumption, gallons of rainwater collection
        - **Strategy:** Use low-flow or waterless plumbing fixtures
        - **Strategy:** Harvest rainwater and graywater, reducing the potable water required
        - **Strategy:** Utilize xeriscape strategies saving on overall water and labor
    - **Objective:** Reduce life-cycle (inclusive of production, material, and transportation energy consumption) costs of processes, systems, and materials. Life cycle

effectively used as a point of comparison between similar buildings, materials, and products rather than an absolute measure.

- **Metric:** Energy consumed during the life cycle
- **Strategy:** Optimize systems and material use

- **Goal:** Reuse resources
  - o **Objective:** Use an existing building, effectively saving energy by applying embodied energy to the current project. Embodied energy is the energy expended in labor, material production, and construction, of an existing building.
    - **Metric:** percentage of reused building structure and materials
    - **Strategy:** adaptive reuse of existing and/or use of a heritage building
  - o **Objective:** Conserve the energy required to clear a green site and pull utilities to the site by using a site previously built on.
    - **Metric:** percentage of the site that requires clearing
    - **Strategy:** Select an existing building site
  - o **Objective:** Select materials with recycled content
    - **Metric:** percentage recycled content
    - **Strategy:** Select products with specific documented high percentage of recycled content
- **Goal:** Recycle
  - o **Objective:** Recycle water on site (i.e., capture graywater to be used for landscape irrigation)
    - **Metric:** percentage of water used that is recaptured as greywater
    - **Strategy:** install a branched drainage system from sinks and other light water use, measure graywater redirected/repurposed
  - o **Objective:** Reduce waste from daily operations—percentage composted, reused, or recycled
    - **Metric:** Percentage composted, reused, or recycled
    - **Strategy:** Locate recycling collection receptacles throughout a facility, create a culture of waste reduction, enact organization-wide policy rewarding employees directly for reaching waste reduction objectives
- **Goal:** Restore the local environment
  - o Objective: Reduce carbon emissions on a regional scale
    - **Metric:** Percentage of occupants using public transit or alternate transportation
    - **Strategies:** Select a site that has good transit connections, public access to bicycle trails, bicycle lanes, and sidewalks

The building owner's objectives are likely to be more nuances and specific to building rating systems or influenced by specific business requirements. They may include specific metrics and strategies:

- Objective: Meet or exceed LEED BD+C and LEED ID+C platinum criteria
- Objective: Harvest 90 percent of stormwater runoff
- Objective: Achieve effective interior light levels using daylighting
- Objective: Use effective building envelope construction techniques requiring only passive strategies to heat and cool the building

Building Standards as Benchmarks

The International Building Code recognizes and incorporates many standards established by independent and technology-based organizations such as ANSI (American National Standards Institute), ASTM (American Society for Testing and Materials), ASHRAE (American Society of Heating, Refrigeration, and Air Conditioning Engineers), and IES (Illuminating Engineering Society), among others. These organizations create standards through a consensus process documented and approved by a recognized reviewing bodies or organizations.

Green and Sustainable Building Rating Systems as Benchmarks

Green and sustainable building rating systems often serve as benchmarks because each system provides a specific standard and requires specific measured levels of performance from the building as a whole. Living Building Challenge, Well Building, LEED, Passive House, Green Globes, and BREEAM are but a few of the performance-based design standards. Performance-based codes and standards define the objective or the results without providing a specific method by which to achieve the level of performance. There are building standards that take a prescriptive approach, that list specific measures as requirements for compliance. An example of a prescriptive requirement is this statement: R values must meet or exceed R-value 25. Performance-based standards provide flexibility in how to achieve an objective. Prescriptive standards or codes eliminate the ambiguities that come with the interpretation sometimes required by more flexible performance standards.

Green building standards continually evolve to keep pace with new technology and developing societal demands. They are a voluntary rating system undertaken by the building owner and by extension, the project design team. Do not confuse rating systems with codes. Codes are mandatory. Some states, such as California, have mandatory green codes. Many local codes include the IECC (International Energy Conservation Code). Green or sustainable building systems and standards have common goals to promote environmentally responsible, cost-effective, healthier places to live and work. As such, there are many similarities between systems, yet specific requirements vary by system, building type or use, regulatory oversight, and global location. Green and sustainable building rating systems are adapted to national requirements and may address issues beyond building practices and materials.

A sustainable building does not require a green building rating system or achievement rating to be sustainable. It is the building performance and environmentally sensitive practices that determine the sustainability of a building. The specific metrics required to achieve a specific rating certification are what determines if a rating system is a credible benchmark, not the system ranking itself. Benchmarking energy management is a common practice and is often required by sustainability standards.

Using the Goals and Objectives Matrix

Goals and metrics extrapolated from case studies and other research are entered into the goals and objectives matrix to organize pertinent data where it is available for quick reference during the design process. (See Table 4.2.)

- Goals are outgrowths of the guiding principles. Goals are the means by which the guiding principles become tangible.
- Objectives are the multiple targets that must be achieved to realize the goals.
- Metrics serve as evidence that the objectives have been achieved. They are the measure to be achieved. In many cases the metrics are preset by a rating systems. SDB methodology focuses on a few key performance metrics: energy, daylight, air, and water.
- Benchmarks are the specific numerical targets that represent best practices or best performance that can be achieved for the category.
- List the proposed sustainable strategies that will be most influential in achieving the stated goals and objectives.

STEP 2C: CRITERIA MATRIX

Design Program

Each project is unique; each site, each client, and every opportunity require exploration to identify opportunities available and reveal the full potential inherent in each project. Sustainable design projects are innately individual and complex. Each project has a wide variety of needs and requirements to meet the functional building program, the building performance requirements, the cultural role the project plays in community development, and future use of the building. Satisfying these often-competing needs requires careful analysis, evaluation, and considered compromise. The pre-planning phase is the time to explore the nature of the project deeply, to prioritize needs, wants, and desires that drive the project according to the guiding principles.

The design program is a staple of the design processes. Typically, the functional programming or the spatial design program describing the proper sizing and relationship of spaces to support function is the basis of a design. Projects must accommodate spatial, organizational, and high-performance system requirements within the framework of financial budgets, scheduling, regulatory concerns, and construction delivery methods and interests. A genuinely sustainable design process requires more.

More than just the quantitative nature of building structure or performance, a sustainable project strives to express beauty, meaning, and humanity. Often considered intangibles, beauty, meaning, and humanity are perspectives equally as valid as performance. The expanded sustainable design program serves as a tool to transform the broad guiding principles into detailed planning requirements that become the source material for the criteria matrix.

TABLE 4.2 GOALS AND OBJECTIVES MATRIX

Goals and Objectives Matrix

The Four Perspectives	*Objective/Tangible Aspects* — **PERFORMANCE**					*Subjective/Intangible Aspects* — **SYSTEMS**	**CULTURE**	**CULTURE**	**EXPERIENCE**
	Energy	Health and Wellbeing — Light	Air	Water	Storm Water				
Guiding Principles	Insert Guiding Principle(s) from Step 1 in the SDB process					Insert Guiding Principle(s) from Step 1 in the SDB process	Insert Guiding Principle(s) from Step 1 in the SDB process	Insert Guiding Principle(s) from Step 1 in the SDB process	Insert Guiding Principle(s) from Step 1 in the SDB process
Stated Project Goals and/or Rating Systems	Stated Project Performance Goals					Stated Ecological Goals	Stated Equity Goals	Stated Culture Goals	Stated Experiential Goals
Objectives	Energy	Light	Air	Water	Storm Water				
Metrics	**Energy** Predicted consumed energy use intensity/ Predicted net EUI	**Light** % >300 lux (28 FC) at 3pm March 21 and/ or daylight factor (DF)	**Air** Percentage of floor area or percentage of occupant work stations within 30 feet of operable windows			**Ecological Integration** Percentage of landscaped areas covered by native or climate appropriate plants supporting native or migratory animals	**Stakeholder Engagement**	**Sense of Community** Walk Score	**View** Percentage of floor area or percentage of occupant work stations with direct views of the outdoors
Benchmarks	**xx/xx** kBtu/ft²/yr	**xx% DF = ?**	**xx%**	**xx**	**xx%**	**xx%**	**xx%**	**xx**	**xx%**
Strategies	List 1 or 2 proposed strategies to achieve the goals	List 1 or proposed strategies to achieve the goals	List 1 or 2 proposed strategies to achieve the goals	List 1 or 2 proposed strategies to achieve the goals	List 1 or 2 proposed strategies to achieve the goals	List 1 or 2 proposed Strategies to achieve the goals	List 1 or 2 proposed strategies to achieve the goals	List 1 or 2 proposed strategies to achieve the goals	List 1 or 2 proposed strategies to achieve the goals

Sustainable Design Basics A methodology for the schematic design of sustainable building

Source: Sharon Jaffe

Expanding for Sustainability

By utilizing the SDB methodology, the traditional design program can be expanded to include the goals and objectives of sustainability to:

- Minimize the negative environmental impact
- Minimize energy consumption, maximize energy efficiencies
- Enhance indoor environmental quality and occupant comfort
- Optimize building space and material appropriateness and quality
- Optimize lifecycle operational and maintenance practices
- Support and enhance the local community

The "expanded" sustainability program links discipline-specific requirements together into a comprehensive set of design criteria. Studying the adjacent and immediate microclimates, the engineering requirements for spaces of a building, along with the more traditional programming requirements, can yield increased comfort, better functionality, and even higher energy efficiencies. For example, the desire for increased daylight (without glare) and building efficiency can often drive a slimmer building profile, which allows light to penetrate deeper in the building, thereby increasing daylighting benefits.

In its final form, a sustainable design program will include:

1. Detailed function by function written statement describing all project needs and concerns, including sustainability benchmarks, and goals
2. Numeric summaries of spatial, furniture, and equipment requirements as the first indication of project budget requirements
3. Adjacency and spatial relationship information for interior spaces and interior/exterior spatial relationships

Understanding the Criteria Matrix

The program developed by the designer or presented by the client in a completed form is typically a multipage document in a format that is cumbersome for use in the design process. Classroom design projects often give lengthy narrative program statements that are difficult to translate immediately into space planning terms. The designer needs a concise and abbreviated format, with program elements organized in a practical sequence, so that information can be found without continually flipping through many pages of data, and where spaces, rooms, or functions are categorized and grouped with the project's adjacency requirements. See the appendix for the narrative of the demonstration project spatial design program and Chapter 11 for the demonstration project's criteria matrix.

The criteria matrix format, established in the textbook *Space Planning Basics* by Mark Karlen, is expanded in this textbook, *Sustainable Design Basics*. The matrix format visually organizes a great deal of spatial information and driving design factors into a condensed format. It applies to both small and large projects and is adaptable to both tight and open time frames or deadlines.

When time permits, the matrix can include all the project's design criteria; when production time is limited, the format can be condensed to identify only the most critical planning considerations.

As with previous matrices in the SDB methodology, the form of the criteria matrix is a rectangular grid of notation spaces with names of rooms or spaces (or functions) listed in the column to the left, and columns for text and numerical indications of program requirements in the columns to the right. Rooms, spaces, or functions with similar attributes may be grouped or clustered by department or division.

The complexity of the criteria matrix can be adjusted to meet the needs of a particular project, as well as the amount of time available. The criteria matrix approach is a quick and efficient organizer of necessary planning information that will return the time invested in organizing the information through streamlined, easy access throughout the design process.

Completing the Criteria Matrix

The criteria matrix, shown in Tables 4.3 and 4.4, organizes building design and sustainability criteria information using the four perspectives of sustainable design, similar to the other matrices used in this text. It includes essential information crucial to the space planning process. The process of filling out the matrix is in itself a good process because it forces the designer to think intently about the spaces in the building and site before starting drawings.

1. **Performance**
   Space required in square feet or metric, adjacency relationships, acoustic levels, and furniture requirements
2. **Systems**
   Passive design and active technology requirements such as thermal comfort, artificial lighting, ventilation, and daylighting
3. **Culture**
   Public/private nature of each space, and the sense of community needed in some spaces
4. **Experience**
   Sense of place and special design considerations

See the demonstration project in Chapter 11 for an example of a completed criteria matrix.

Criteria Matrix and New Buildings

Review the criteria matrix requirements and the total square footage required for the building. Be sure to add appropriate square footage for circulation. Circulation space for enclosed office plans is typically 28 to 33 percent of the usable floor area. Open offices require a higher circulation factor ranging from

TABLE 4.3 CRITERIA MATRIX INTERIORS FORM

Criteria Matrix Interiors

The Four Perspectives	Objective/Tangible Requirements						Subjective/Intangible Requirements			
	PERFORMANCE				**SYSTEMS**		**CULTURE**		**EXPERIENCE**
Design Criteria	Sq Ft.	Adjacencies	**Acoustics** Indicate required level of control: high, medium, or low	**Furniture Requirements**	**Active Systems** Specialized heating, cooling, ventilation, plumbing, lighting, equipment only	**Passive Systems** List specialized requirements below	**Privacy** Indicate the level of privacy required: high, medium, or low	**Special Cultural Considerations** Image, brand, sense of community	**Sense of place** Views, smells, textures, colors, sounds, special considerations, spatial sense, other intangibles
Rm #	Room Name								
1									
2									
3									
4									
5									
6									
7									
8									
9									
10									
11									
12									
13									
	Subtotal Sq. Ft.								
	Circulation @30%								
	Total Sq. Ft.								

Sustainable Design Basics: A methodology for schematic design of sustainable buildings

TABLE 4.4 CRITERIA MATRIX BUILDING AND SITE FORM

Criteria Matrix: Building and Site Form

The Four Perspectives	Objective/Tangible Requirements							Subjective/Intangible Requirements				
	PERFORMANCE				SYSTEMS		CULTURE			EXPERIENCE	
Design Criteria	Sq. Ft.	Adjacencies	Acoustics Levels *Indicate the anticipated sound level: high, medium, or low*	Outdoor Furniture Requirements	Infrastructure	Ecological Systems *Habitat, Storm-water, plant communities*	Safety Level *Public-private*	Special Cultural Considerations *Image, brand, sense of community, relationship to nature*		Sense of Place *Views, smells, textures, colors, taste, sounds*	Special Considerations *Spatial sense, other intangibles*
Area A #											
A1											
A2											
A3											
A4											
A5											
A6											
A7											
A8											
Subtotal Sq. Ft.					-	-	-	-		-	-
Total Sq. Ft.					-					-	-

Sustainable Design Basics: A methodology for the schematic design of sustainable buildings

Source: Sharon B. Jaffe

30 to 38 percent. (Gensler, 2012). Verify the total required square footage for identified spaces and circulation meet the square footage allocated in the project budget. If the difference is greater than 5 percent, adjustments must be made to the criteria matrix in the square footage requirement column. A significant difference between the required usable square footage and the square footage allocated in the project budget will require adjustment of either the program reflected in the criteria matrix or the project budget. Matching usable square footage to required square footage is part of the planning process that becomes easier with experience.

Criteria Matrix and Existing Buildings

If the sustainable building project is an existing building, it is necessary to review the criteria matrix requirements and reconcile the program requirements with the available square footage of the building shell. Calculate the required square footage by adding all of the square footage listed in the criteria matrix, including all required spaces and circulation in the total square footage. Determine the available square footage by either manually measuring the interior of the base building shell with a scale and calculating the usable interior square footage or using a software program measuring tools to calculate the building area. After determining the available square footage, check the total required square footage against the available square footage. As noted for new buildings, a tolerance of 5 percent either higher or lower is usually workable. A significant difference between available and required square footage will make the space planning process very difficult. If the difference is greater than 5 percent, adjustments must be made to the program requirements or the building.

STEP 2D: RELATIONSHIP DIAGRAMS

The relationship of spaces, as in adjacencies and proximity, is a central aspect of a sustainable building plan and must be completed with attention to detail. Relationship diagrams transition between written analysis of the spatial program and the graphic drawings of space planning. They are abstract interpretations of program information intended to represent adjacency and proximity relationships graphically. Relationship diagrams identify shared needs, functions, access, and circulation between spaces. See Figure 4.1 for a few examples. Relationship diagrams are not space plans. They continue the abstract interpretation of program information, and are part of the pre-planning process that precedes the planning solution.

Drawing Relationship Diagrams

Referencing the criteria matrix, individual functional spaces can be illustrated with circles so that their size and placement on paper represent the proper relationship to other spaces. Rooms and functions that should be close to one another are drawn close together on the paper, drawn at a distance from one another when they do not require proximity or may even suffer from proximity. Connecting lines between circles are used to indicate circulation patterns between spaces. Connecting

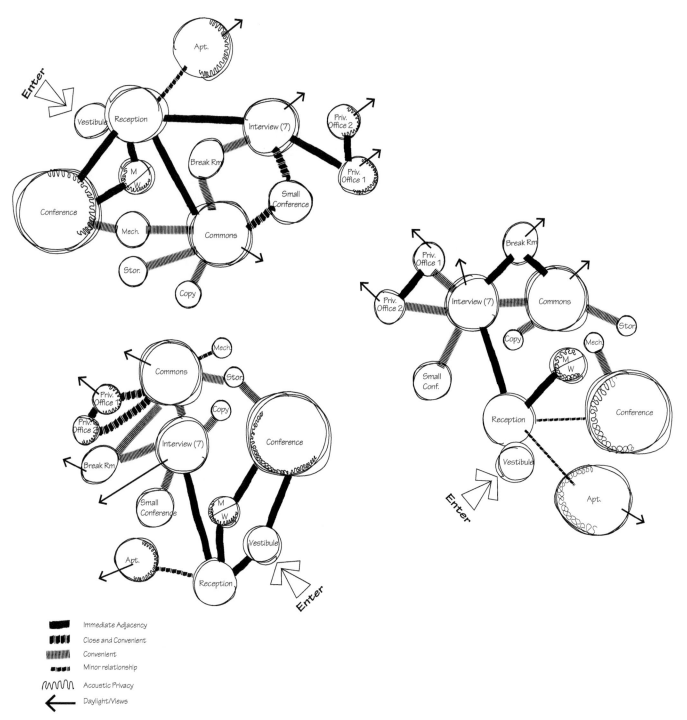

Figure 4.1 Relationship diagram examples
Source: Sharon B. Jaffe

lines can be coded by line weight or pattern to represent the varying degrees of connectivity or adjacency. Heavyweight lines indicate immediate adjacencies and necessary connections; lighter line weight is used for less critical adjacency. Additional lines and graphic codes are used to indicate additional program requirements (i.e., the point of entry, acoustic privacy, significant desirable views, access to windows or daylight). The relationship diagram is an abstract expression of relationships between spaces and does not relate to the building shell shape or configuration or an architectural scale.

Relationship diagraming is an iterative process. It is necessary to study multiple diagrams to explore a variety of relationship options. The intent is to work quickly and intuitively. Relationship diagrams are a design tool and not a finished product. A short roll of inexpensive tracing paper and a felt marker are helpful tools for the diagramming process. It is efficient to place a piece tracing paper over the original document and redraw rather than erasing and redrawing to make revisions.

FURTHER READING

Karlen, M., and R. Fleming. 2016. *Space Planning Basics* (4th ed.). Hoboken, NJ: John Wiley & Sons.

5

Step 3: Design

Step 4
**Design
Solution**
    ...ign Synthesis
    ...l Design Validation
    ...enting the Project

Step 3
Design

3A Preliminary Design
3B Passive Design
3C Building Envelope
3D Green Materials
    * Beyond the Basics

Ste...
Pre-...

2A Resear...
2B Project ...
2C Design Crit...
2D Spatial Relation...

Step 1
Context

1A Project Information
1B Guiding Principles
1C Macro / Micro Context
1D Site Inventory & Analysis

Figure 5.0 *Sustainable Design Basics,* **step 3**
Source: Sharon B. Jaffe

WHOLE BUILDING THINKING, SYSTEMS THINKING

> "A system is a set of entities and their relationships; whose functionality is greater than the sum of the individual entities."
>
> (Crawley et al. 2015)

A *system* is a set of individual elements organized as an interrelated, integrated network functioning collectively to perform a task or achieve a goal. A *building* is a whole system nested within a more extensive holistic system.

The building and site of a sustainable building can be designed together to respond to the more extensive systems in which they are nested. The building and site are within a neighborhood; the neighborhood is within the city. The city is a part of a region, and the nested systems continue to expand outward. Building structure and technology, along with the interconnected processes that interact and support one another, are a system. From initial project conception through an integrated design process, site selection, building design, construction, and occupancy, sustainability is accomplished by thinking of the entire building holistically as one system. Each decision and process affect the overall system. For instance, maximizing the use of daylighting impacts more than just the interior lighting system. It impacts the whole building and how occupants experience the space. Daylighting as a significant strategy will influence the building form, shape, orientation, exterior facade, and interior spatial relationships. It will impact the specification of appropriate HVAC systems, energy consumption and more. Consideration of multiple strategies, and the ability to leverage improved performance and experience from one strategy to impact another positively is all part of an integrated decision-making process.

The Sustainable Design Process is a Synthesis Process

Design is a process of analysis and synthesis. Research, inventory, and analysis are essential during the pre-planning phase. There is a transformation, a process of synthesis, required to negotiate the gap between analysis, which identifies and defines the problem, and the proposed responding solution.

Whether using a pencil or computer to draw shapes and forms, hundreds of different factors may be considered, often without conscious thought. The design process is often intuitive, which can make it challenging, but also stimulating and fun. Designing for sustainability adds a significant number of factors to any building project. The effects of climate change, habitat destruction, human health, and wellness, must all be considered during the design process. A building designed for sustainability will likely play many roles within its life cycle as owner, user, and community, needs evolve. The building will need to be flexible and evolve accordingly.

Resilience, meaning the ability to anticipate, adapt and endure future shocks and environmental stresses that may impact a project, is also a factor in the sustainable design process.

Fortunately, the pre-planning in step 2 of the SDB methodology helps to organize the research, understand the site, learn from precedents, understand the building program, and to set clear goals for the project. All of the background information, research, and analysis from steps 1 and 2 are synthesized into a coherent understanding of the design problem before step 3 is undertaken to achieve a genuinely responsive and resilient sustainable design.

Iterative Process

Sustainable design is an iterative process with many variables, factors, and drivers to be considered. Design solutions evolve. Multiple design ideas, concepts, and approaches are explored, developed, tested, and compared to one another. The integrated design process is interactive and nonlinear. It includes cycles of research, processing, analysis, and refinement before arriving at a final design. Rarely does a designer start with one idea and move forward to completion without referencing and reevaluating previously discarded ideas. This process can be challenging, sometimes discouraging, but ultimately rewarding. Patience is crucial to a successful process.

The first two steps of the SDB methodology generated a considerable quantity of information.

Step 1 identified relevant contextual information:

- Client and motivation
- Guiding principles that direct design efforts
- Macro and micro context
- Site inventory and analysis and intrinsic sustainable opportunities available at the site

Step 2 identifies pre-planning information:

- Research and case studies ascertain precedents and benchmarks.
- Project objectives and goals establish targeted metrics.
- Design criteria matrix summarizes the building program information.
- Spatial relationships that influence overall building shape and form.

All of these pre-planning activities are the groundwork required for step 3, design. Step 3 of the sustainable design methodology begins with the hand to paper, or computer, and the ideation process: design. Design is a complex process requiring many interdependent decisions. Dividing the many decisions of the design process into interim steps composed of closely interrelated decisions makes a complicated process more manageable. The interim steps for step 3 design include:

- Preliminary planning
- Passive design
- Building envelope
- Green materials

Some of the interim steps require mini steps to achieve.

Matrices

Throughout the *Sustainable Design Basics* process, matrices are used to organize, prioritize, and analyze critical tangible and intangible information, key design concerns, goals and objectives, and applicable design strategies. The design matrix (see Figure 5.1) is a comprehensive tool to help work through the nuances, complexities, contradictions, and benefits of different design ideas at each interim and mini step. The four perspectives—performance, systems, culture, and experience—form the structure of the design matrix. It provides a means to distill large amounts of information to essential factors, information, and reflections on the design response from each perspective. Information entered into the design matrix is readily available at crucial decision-making points.

At the conclusion of each interim step in the SDB methodology, design ideas developed from the four perspectives are analyzed in the context of the guiding principles and goals and objectives. The validation matrix supports and guides this analysis process. (See Figure 5.2.) The interim validation process identifies the strengths of each design idea to inform the synthesis of four ideas into one interim design scheme. Each interim step builds on those preceding it.

The design matrix and validation matrix are available in the appendix as blank forms and for download on the companion website. The demonstration project beginning in Chapter 11 illustrates how to complete all of the matrices used in the *Sustainable Design Basics* methodology.

3A PRELIMINARY DESIGN

Preliminary design in the SDB methodology is made up of a number of distinct smaller steps, including:

1. Building location and site integration
2. Building orientation
3. Building block plan
4. Building shape/space plan
5. Validation
6. Design synthesis

The order of these design decisions may vary to better suit a specific designer, client, or site. Even so, the last three tasks should remain at the end of the process.

Building Location and Site Integration

Locating a building on a site is a challenging task that requires the assessment and balancing of a variety of driving forces that shape design decisions. Often, there is more than one appropriate location choice. What is a designer to do? The overall goal is to integrate the building into a larger site plan, which may include parking, paths, outdoor elements, and more. In professional projects, the site plan may be designed by a landscape architect determining the building location as part of that process. Landscape architecture deals with the complexities of site design. In a collaborative project, the architects and designers work in concert with a wide array of stakeholders, led by the landscape architect, to determine the final building location. In an academic environment, students will often assume the various roles of professional design team members.

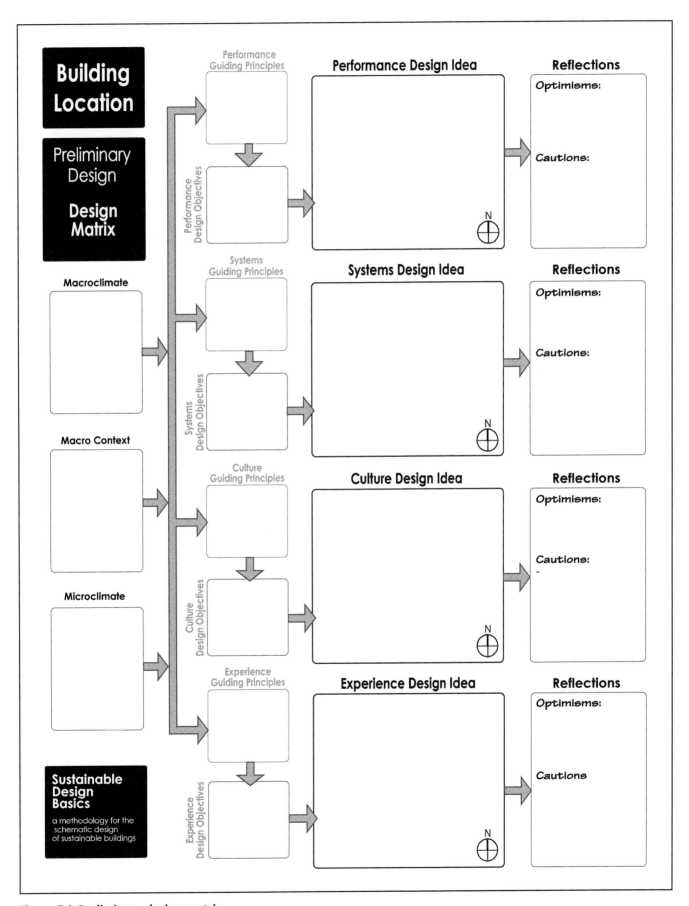

Figure 5.1 Preliminary design matrix

Source: Rob Fleming

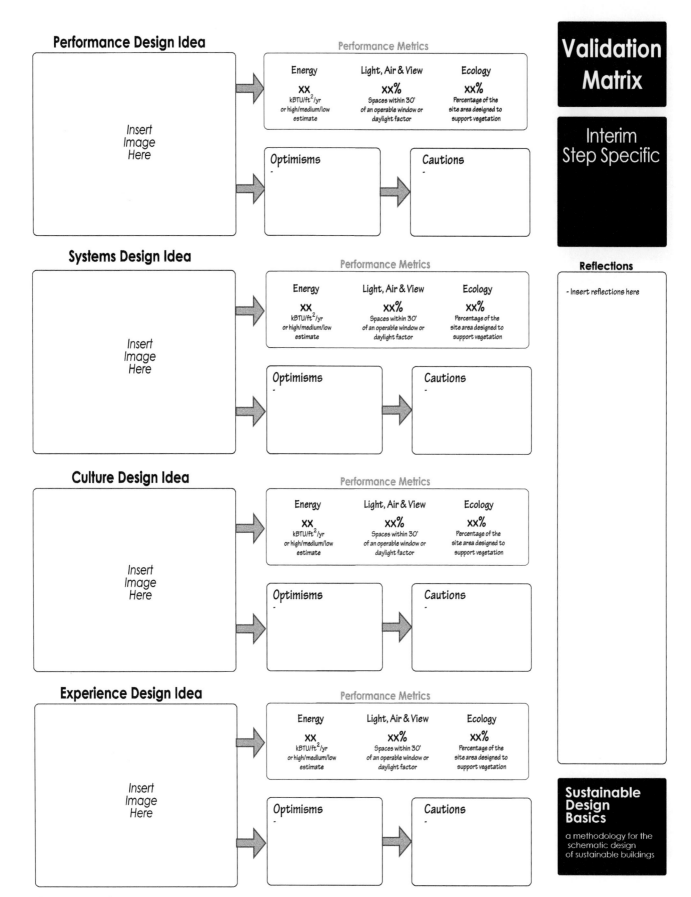

Figure 5.2 Validation matrix
Source: Rob Fleming

Site Inventory and Analysis

In the absence of an integrated team of design professionals, the research, inventory, and analysis, done and documented during step 1 (site inventory/site analysis matrix) provide guidance for locating the building. Site analysis drawings identify site conditions, natural resources, and solar orientation, the nexus of which recognizes the best building location. In the event of conflicts, the design matrix is a helpful tool to reassess priorities based on the established guiding principles, project goals, and objectives established earlier in the process.

Macroclimate

The macroclimate describes significant weather patterns established over time. Sites with high levels of snow encourage a building location closer to streets and sidewalks, minimizing the need for snow removal. Mountainous geography requires specific attention to topographic contours, to ensure the project is not susceptible to landslides, snow avalanches, or negatively impacted by water runoff from the mountain to the building.

Macro Context

Settlement patterns impact where to locate a building on a site. There are specific patterns that are characteristic for each settlement pattern. Urban settlement patterns respond to local zoning guidelines and the limited available space on a site that is appropriate for building. Urban patterns tend to favor locations that are close to, if not right up against, the sidewalk as a means to define the street edge and add life to the street. Suburban sites typically are larger than urban sites, with far fewer pedestrian sidewalks or amenities. Buildings are often set back behind large parking lots required by a car-centric culture and located farther from the road. Finally, rural settlement patterns can take advantage of the natural beauty of the rural landscape but can also isolate building sites requiring longer access roads.

The sketch in Figure 5.3 illustrates the basic settlement patterns discussed above. A sustainable designer is not required to follow these conventional patterns. Many times, conventional patterns need to be broken to establish a new model, to maximize solar power, or to protect a particular habitat.

Microclimate, Local Zoning, and Codes

Local townships reinforce, if not create, traditional settlement patterns to regulate planning and building practices. A building located on a particular site can optimize microclimates as well as create new ones. During the site inventory process, microclimates are discovered, mapped, and analyzed in order to optimize or mitigate conditions for a building location. For example, a site may have fierce northwestern winter winds. The building can be located to block those winds, creating a favorable

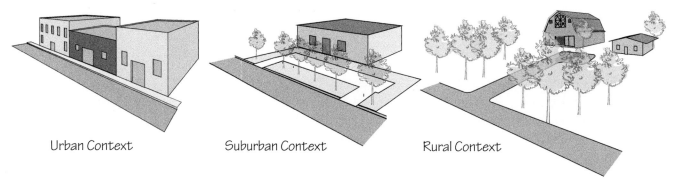

Urban Context   Suburban Context   Rural Context

Figure 5.3 Settlement patterns
Source: Sharon B. Jaffe

microclimate on the other side of the building. Local zoning and codes often require structures maintain setbacks. A setback is the minimum distance a building must be located from a road, floodplain, property line, or other feature requiring protection. Required setbacks reinforce urban patterns. Setback requirements vary by use, location, and local regulation.

Building Location Design Objectives and Design Ideas

Design objectives are broad statements of intent. It can be challenging to write design objectives. A designer may begin drawing with vague, even subconscious, design objectives. Locating a building on the site is more straightforward with clearly defined design objectives. Design objectives help prioritize and focus the approach to inherent site-specific conditions.

To define the design objectives, refer back to:

- The guiding principles established in step 1. These reflect the client and the project's "fundamental truth" and dictate essential project priorities.
- Goals and objectives (tangible and intangible) established in Step 2. Goals are the prioritized ambitions and objectives are the steps to be taken to achieve the goal.

It is very common to have multiple goals and objectives; competing interests may make it impossible to follow the objectives as if following a direct path to a destination. When objectives do not align, it is necessary to prioritize objectives in order to achieve the overarching project goals.

Design ideas are the actual creative work that moves a design project forward. Usually, at least one idea for the building location on the project site is drawn to fulfill the goals and objectives of each of the four perspectives established during steps 1 and 2 of the SDB methodology. Simple, quick drawings communicate intention.

In the SDB methodology, design ideas are explored through the four perspectives in response to design objectives. Table 5.1 illustrates building location design ideas

TABLE 5.1 BUILDING LOCATION: DESIGN OBJECTIVES AND DESIGN IDEAS.

Building Location

		Design Objective	Design Ideas	
Perspectives	**Performance**	• Locate the building(s) to maximize solar exposure for potential PV power and winter heat gain.	• Locate the building clear of shade from trees in SW corner of the site and clear of surrounding building shadows.	
	Systems	• Locate the building(s) respecting the local ecology.	• Locate the building away from the 100 year flood zone.	
	Culture	• Locate the building(s) near the main road for best visibility and access by the outside community.	• Locate the building near the street corner along the commercial corridor.	
	Experience	• Locate the building(s) to maximize views to and from the building.	• Locate the building with clear views of the park and interesting bridge structure.	

Source: Sharon B. Jaffe

that respond to specific design objectives. Typically, multiple design ideas will be explored for each design objective. The most effective design idea response will be entered into the appropriate design idea matrix for reflection and evaluation.

Design Objectives

- Consider how the building location may further the overall project goals.
- Review the site inventory matrix completed during step 1 to identify site-specific opportunities and challenges to be met and leveraged.
- Be sure the design objectives for this interim step, building location, reflect the guiding principles of the overall project.

Design Ideas

Exploring multiple design ideas for the building location based on the four perspectives reveal opportunities to accommodate varied concerns.

- Consider the relationship of the proposed building location to the site context.
  o Is the building a public destination or limited or private access?
  o What are desirable relationships between the building location and the street?
  o How will proposed building locations connect to public transit?
- How will the proposed building location integrate the building and the site? Parking? Walking paths? Outdoor amenities?
- How will the proposed building location interact with the macroclimate, macro context, and microclimate?

At this early stage of the design, a generic mark or form is used to define specific areas for the building location on the site rather than a specific building shape. Table 5.1 illustrates the exploration of design ideas for building location in response to design objectives.

Design Priorities

Much of the evaluation and prioritizing process is a subconscious, intuitive process that balances tangible and intangible factors as a designer processes information while drawing. Aligning design decisions with guiding principles is essential. There will be multiple project concerns that are of high priority. At this point in the design process, there may be more one good idea. Design ideas are not combined until later during design synthesis. All four perspectives have validity and all must be considered in the iterative design process.

Synergies and Tradeoffs

If the building locations based on each of the four perspectives suggest separate locations, which is the best? Often the best solution combines more than one good idea, fulfilling multiple objectives. Look for synergies, a combination of more than one idea for a more significant effect than the sum of the separate ideas. An example of synergy is when the proposed building location works for the culture of the community from the culture perspective and also has a great view that fulfills the experience perspective. Sometimes a designer must consider tradeoffs. An example of a tradeoff situation is a desirable location that protects local animal habitat but does not maximize solar radiation exposure vital for generating power. Tradeoffs made through the design process must balance the needs of the habitat with the need for solar radiation. Possible tradeoffs include locating the solar array in a more favorable position, remote from the building, perhaps over the parking lot. A remote location trades off the additional construction cost, energy degradation in transfer from generation site to use, and inconvenience of the remote location, in support of the guiding principle that preserves and enhances local habitat. Another tradeoff may be to reduce the building footprint and overall size to reduce the power requirement from solar. The project trades off interior space to reduce required energy consumption. Functional performance synergies and tradeoff possibilities are integral elements of the sustainable design process.

Building Orientation

Site Inventory and Analysis

A comprehensive site inventory and analysis identifies critical elements affecting building orientation such as views, sun angle, and direction of prevailing summer breezes.

Macroclimate

The macroclimate is a powerful driver of building orientation. Seasonal changes in sun angles are influenced and often altered by the geo setting of a site. The sun path and altitude discussed in detail in step 1 combined with different sun and wind orientations of the building can have a significant impact not just on energy savings but also on the user experience. Available view, natural ventilation, and daylight inside a building are significant factors in occupant comfort. Most people prefer glare-free, daylit spaces, which support occupant productivity and benefit the occupant health and well-being attributes required by all sustainable design rating systems. Figure 5.4 identifies the sun path and orients the building on the east-west axis favored for daylighting systems. Note that the solar path and building orientation shown in this figure is for the northern hemisphere. In the southern hemisphere, buildings would be oriented toward the northern sun.

Macro Context

Building orientation in large urban settings is significantly impacted by the prevalence of standard architectural approaches. While the benefits of orientation relative to sun and wind is almost self-evident, alignment with local settlement patterns is often an overriding driver of building orientation. As discussed, relative to building location, in both urban and suburban settings, buildings tend to be oriented parallel with streets. Orientation parallel to the street is also standard for commercial establishments motivated to maximize square footage available on standard rectilinear lots. There may be more flexibility in the rural countryside with large open areas, where land costs are lower and visibility from the road is less important for commerce.

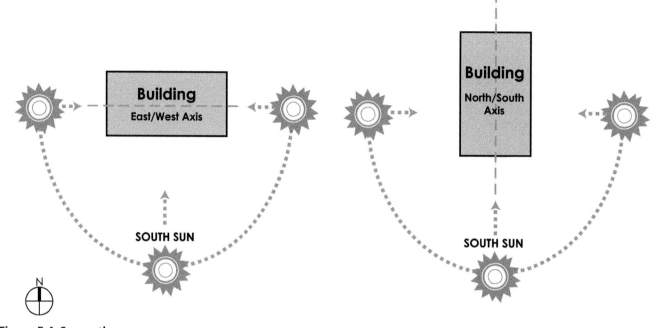

Figure 5.4 Sun path
Source: Sharon B. Jaffe

Microclimate, Local Zoning and Codes

As stated earlier, the shape of building lots and required setbacks from building lot lines often drive building orientation more than passive systems. The intent is to maximize building square footage and parking space. Many site plans are drawn by the civil engineer before the landscape architect gets involved. Often the result is a plan that does not optimize passive design opportunities. A sustainable designer may identify opportunities that another design professional may dismiss as atypical or too costly. Sustainable designers have the obligation to explore tangible and intangible opportunities, synergies and tradeoffs, initial investment balanced by operational and maintenance expenditures, before the true return on investment can be understood.

Design Objectives and Design Ideas

Guiding principles, overall project goals and objectives, and site context will suggest appropriate design objectives for building orientation. Objectives must reflect the conclusions of earlier research and be focused through the four perspectives. The preceding interim step, building location, serves as the basis for building orientation. As such some objectives may expand from, or relate to, building location objectives.

Design ideas for building orientation will be responsive to the specific design objectives. The site inventory and analysis from step 1, context, will inform and influence building orientation design ideas.

Consider the relationship of the proposed building orientation relative to macro context, macroclimate, micro context, and microclimate.

- How does the proposed building orientation relate to the macroclimate and available natural resources?
- How will the proposed building orientation optimize the macroclimate?
- What is the relationship of the proposed building orientation to the community and site context?
  - Is the orientation surrounding built structures, streets, and roads relevant to the proposed building orientation?
  - How will the proposed building orientation impact the natural habitat on site?
  - Will the proposed building orientation integrate the building with the broader community and with the site? Parking? Walking paths? Outdoor amenities?
- How does the proposed building orientation relate to the microclimate?
  - Optimize existing microclimates?
  - Create new microclimates?
  - Facilitate passive design strategies?

Multiple simple, quick drawings from each of the four perspectives carefully investigate and analyze building orientation possibilities. At this early stage of design, a simple rectilinear form represents the building. The true shape of the building will be determined later in the process. Resist the impulse to choose the best building orientation design idea. For now, allow each design ideas from the four perspectives to develop. Later in the process, guiding principles will help prioritize design ideas and determine which option, or combination of options, best fulfills the design objectives. (See Table 5.2.)

Design Priorities

Examining the site from the four perspectives expands design thinking and assures consideration of options that may not be obvious at first. This may also result in four different building solar orientations, one for each perspective. How does a designer choose the best option? Early in the design process, building location and solar orientation can be fluid. Ideation and careful evaluation of many options generated throughout the design phase are facilitated if commitment to a specific solar orientation is not made until the end of the preliminary design phase.

Synergies and Tradeoffs

The sketches in Table 5.2 illustrate solar orientations that differ based on the initiating perspective. The building orientation of the performance and culture perspectives both face south toward the sun, indicating design synergies. The systems perspective suggests that orienting the building to harvest breezes is very different than the view-oriented experience perspective. Experience and systems perspectives are tradeoffs. Choosing one orientation idea will force the designer to trade off the other to balance the driving forces.

TABLE 5.2 BUILDING ORIENTATION: DESIGN OBJECTIVES AND DESIGN IDEAS

Building Orientation

		Design Objective	Design Ideas	
Perspectives	**Performance**	• Building facilitates use of PV panels and use of solar energy as a primary power source.	• Orient the building to harvest the most sun possible.	
	Systems	• Building facilitates 100% natural daylighting for a greater part of the day.	• Orient, the building to maximize daylight, minimize glare, and to collect summer breezes.	
	Culture	• The building will act as an ambassador to the community and provide maximum visual integration into the surrounding community.	• Orient the building to define the road so that it fits into its surrounding built context.	
	Experience	• Provide landmark views for occupants of the building to the surrounding areas and from the surrounding areas to the building.	• Orient the building toward the views or to present an attractive and engaging form from the pedestrian and vehicle approach.	

Source: Sharon B. Jaffe

Preliminary Space Planning for Sustainability

Sustainable design is a holistic enterprise. It involves all aspects of the project site, building, and building interior, as related to the macro and micro environments it inhabits. Building orientation, shape, and form affect the space available for interior use.

What if the building's functions are considered before the building shape and form is finalized? Frank Lloyd Wright set a powerful architectural precedent: to begin a building design from the inside, allowing the exterior to be informed by the interior and to draw inspiration from the site.

Throughout academia, the building design process is routinely begun with shapes drawn on paper to express a building's design shape and form. Sometimes the shapes are drawn without consideration for the actual functional requirements or space plan inside the building. When a building shape is conceived without considering the function of interior spaces, it may be difficult to force the required rooms and spaces into the shapes with appropriate adjacencies.

The Block Plan

A block plan is the first rough explorations of a space plan: a method of exploration that uses trial and error to explore space planning options quickly. They are works in progress, not final floor plans. Developed early in the building design process, a block plan will explore the interdependent relationship of the building interior, building size, and mass relative to the building site. Understanding the nature of the interdependent relationship facilitates location of crucial building elements such as entrance and loading docks while positioning the building on the building site.

It is important to note that the preliminary block plan is not a design of a building and it should not include specific preconceived design ideas. If ideas about building design occur, they should be put aside for later use in the overall process. The preliminary space planning process only serves to indicate the optimal building shape to accommodate the performance, systems, culture, and experience preferences.

Space planning is an essential part of the building design process; it organizes and optimizes available interior space for effective and efficient function. A space plan can also be a sustainable strategy. Earlier, in step 2 of the SDB methodology, a building program developed by the designer (or presented by the client in a completed form) was integrated into an expanded criteria matrix. The criteria matrix organizes the program information to quickly identify all the required building spaces with sizes and functional requirements, including views, daylight, acoustics, and spatial adjacencies. A space plan must address all of the issues in the criteria matrix beyond simply accommodating various activities. Interior spaces should be planned to meet occupant needs while optimizing building energy performance. Space planned with an understanding of performance and systems preferences can facilitate and support passive design strategies that are critical to the success of a sustainable building project. Block plans developed with an understanding of passive design strategies produce a synergy for interior spaces. Efficient interior spaces facilitate passive building systems while increasing occupant comfort and enjoyment. The interior space layout developed through these block plans will be the basis for the building shape.

One of the critical strategies of sustainable design is to reduce consumption of the planet's resources. An efficient space plan is a sustainable strategy as a smaller building will use less material for construction, reduce systems size, reduce energy loads, and reduce operations costs. Well designed, a smaller physical footprint can improve organizational productivity and occupant satisfaction. Sustainable materials and products used in the construction, finish, furnishing, and maintenance of the building may also improve occupant health and wellness.

See *Space Planning Basics* (Karlen and Fleming, 2016) for more information on space planning, including block plans. This book is one of the most thorough and widely adopted textbooks, presenting a practical step-by-step approach to space planning.

Site Inventory and Analysis

Before beginning preliminary space planning with a block plan, consider the site opportunities. Each location or orientation design idea proposed during the previous mini steps have opportunities for daylight, breezes, sights, and sounds, which may prompt different preliminary planning responses, resulting in different block plan shapes. Block plans will help focus the preliminary space planning process to optimize integration of the building and site.

Building Codes

Building and zoning codes deal with almost every area of planning, design, and construction. The space planning process commonly addresses issues of code relative to use and occupancy classifications, types of construction, means of egress, ADA barrier-free accessibility, and fire-resistant construction. During the interim step, preliminary design, it is not necessary to get caught up in meeting specific codes but to keep code in mind while working quickly to develop block plan options.

As illustrated in Figure 5.5, preliminary planning diagrams are basic and straightforward. In the spirit of developing a holistic and integrated building, the preliminary design process makes use of the four perspectives as a helpful framework to generate first planning options that are different in meaningful ways. The goal of this step is *not* to design a final floor plan, but instead, through the block plan, to establish the spatial parameters required to develop the building plan, shape, and massing.

Macroclimate

Sun angles shift during different times of day and different seasons. In the early stage of space planning, consider the impact of sunlight on daylighting strategies and potential heat gain during all seasons. Building orientation will establish the

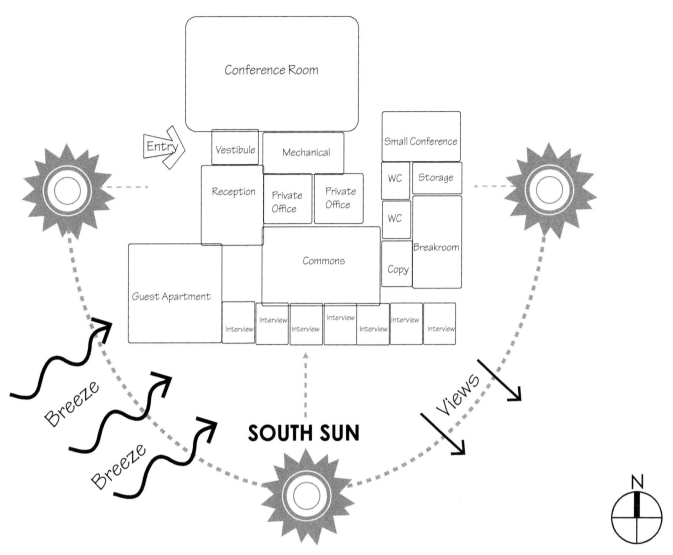

Figure 5.5 Building block plan example
Source: Sharon B. Jaffe

potential solar radiation contributions to daylight and heat gain. Consider how wind origination and seasonal changes in wind direction will impact natural ventilation. The space plan must maximize passive opportunities to effectively reduce building energy usage. Be sure to have the sun path and wind origination drawn on the site plan while working on bubble diagrams and block plans.

Macro Context

Settlement patterns impact the early stages of space planning. Consider community cultural patterns and quality of life concerns as bubble diagrams and block plans are developed. The variables of the building site, opportunities for views, ventilation, and daylight all have considerable influence on the interior space plan. The space plan, in turn, influences the building shape, form, and location on the building site. The building orientation, shape, massing, and position on a site are directly related to the urban, suburban, or rural contexts. (See Figure 5.6.)

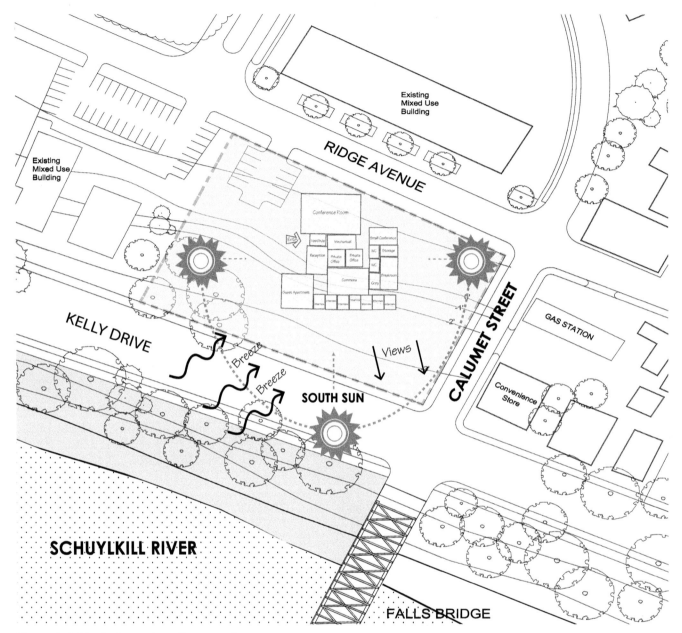

Figure 5.6 Block plan: microclimate and context
Source: Sharon B. Jaffe

Microclimate

Context and local conditions need to be included in the drawings when generating block plans and preliminary space planning diagrams. It is a good practice to draw block plans directly on the proposed site as a reminder of the site context. Consider all of the microclimate elements and factors while developing preliminary diagrams and plans, including solar path, solar angle, shadows, wind direction, vegetation, and views of the site and beyond.

The diagrams in Figure 5.7 indicate three microclimates and solar conditions that impact interior planning and daylight strategies. The first block plan illustrates a large open plan area on the southern side of the building with smaller private

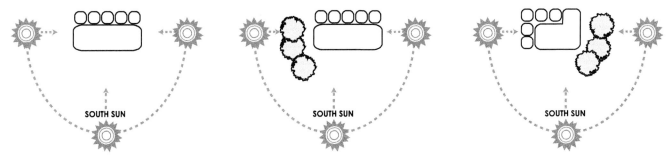

Figure 5.7 Block plan: sun path and glare
Source: Sharon B. Jaffe

spaces on the northern exposure. The site provides unobstructed south, north, east, and west solar exposures. Sunlight from the south and skylight from the north are relatively consistent throughout the day, providing advantageous conditions for passive daylight systems. However, the quality and quantity of sunlight from the east and the west change drastically with the arc of the sun's path throughout the day. Typically, western solar exposures are difficult to control. The low afternoon sun often generates excessive glare and heat gain due to the low afternoon sun, making interior spaces with west-facing windows uncomfortable. Passive solar responsive designs minimize east and west windows. Any necessary east and west windows are heavily shaded.

The second diagram is the same block plan as pictured in the first diagram with an addition to the surrounding landscape. The trees in the west help manage the potential afternoon heat gain and glare from west-facing windows, making the interior space much more comfortable. The direct sun exposure from the east is still challenging in early morning hours, requiring interior shades.

The third block plan has reorganized the interior spaces to provide a more comfortable daylight environment throughout the plan. Smaller private spaces that are less frequently used and frequented by fewer people have been moved to the west exposure to serve as a buffer for the main open plan area. Trees filter the low eastern light.

Design Objectives and Design Ideas

The mini steps preceding the block plan are informed by and reflect the conclusions of earlier research, the guiding principles, and project goals and objectives. The site inventory and analysis, compiled during step 1, context, and the research and criteria matrix completed in step 2, pre-planning, will be especially helpful in developing block plan objectives and design ideas that develop enriching interior building to exterior site relationships as well as beneficial interior spatial adjacencies. (See Table 5.3.)

Design objectives are shorthand statements that capture the essence and desired results of first the space planning diagrams, block plans. Design objectives are statements of conditions for the space plan to achieve.

TABLE 5.3 BLOCK PLAN: DESIGN OBJECTIVES AND DESIGN IDEAS

Block Plan

<table>
<tr>
<th></th>
<th></th>
<th>Design Objective</th>
<th>Design Ideas</th>
<th></th>
</tr>
<tr>
<td rowspan="4">Perspectives</td>
<td>Performance</td>
<td>• Arrange the spaces in the buildings to gain as much solar access as possible to the rooms that need it most.</td>
<td>• Plan the building to be compact to conserve heating energy Provide open plan space with south solar exposure for daylight and passive heat.</td>
<td></td>
</tr>
<tr>
<td>Systems</td>
<td>• Arrange the spaces in the building to harvest to maximize daylight, wind, and water.</td>
<td>• Locate the building to maximize breezes and away from the 100-year flood zone.</td>
<td></td>
</tr>
<tr>
<td>Culture</td>
<td>• Arrange the spaces in the building to best capture the mission and vision of the client and to connect spaces to the community.</td>
<td>• Locate the building entrance near the street corner along the commercial corridor providing opportunity for community engagement.</td>
<td></td>
</tr>
<tr>
<td>Experience</td>
<td>• Arrange the spaces of the building to maximize views, address acoustics, and engage the senses.</td>
<td>• Organize building space to have clear views of the park and interesting bridge structure.</td>
<td></td>
</tr>
</table>

Source: Sharon B. Jaffe

Design ideas respond to the stated design objectives from the each of the four perspectives. Use the building orientation design idea from each of the four perspectives as a starting point for the block plan from the corresponding perspective. Remember that the building orientation communicated location and orientation of the building with a simple shape of arbitrary size. The block plan developed for each perspective will establish the first suggestion of the building size and shape.

Draw multiple block diagrams from each of the four perspectives to carefully investigate and analyze interior planning possibilities. Rapidly drawn using simple shapes, these drawings communicate design intent. They are not intended to be fully developed floor plans.

While not a formal space plan, block plans will inform and influence building shape and size requiring clear and distinct edges. Refer to the criteria matrix and relationship diagram from step 2. Be sure program requirements are met and be sure to account for circulation and egress.

Design ideas will be responsive to the design objectives' four perspectives (performance, systems, culture, and experience), while considering the factors that influence overall productivity and occupant satisfaction.

Acoustics

Acoustic comfort – protecting occupants from unwanted noise – is directly related to productivity and therefore occupant performance. Acoustic distractions come from many sources, including noise from adjacent spaces, outdoor noise, mechanical building systems, and office equipment. In the preliminary space-planning stages of bubble diagrams and block plans, it is essential to consider the most fundamental aspects of acoustics.

- Group spaces with similar acoustic needs for privacy and sound control by separately grouping quiet and noisy spaces.
- Employ buffer zone spaces, usually storage areas, closets, and other nonoccupied spaces to reduce direct noise transmission from a noisy space to a quieter space.
- Be sensitive when planning spaces adjacent to mechanical areas inside the building and noise-producing elements outside the building.

Solar Access and Daylighting

Efficient, effective daylighting has more influence on the building's lifetime energy use than the artificial lighting system specified. Every sustainable design must maximize daylighting. These are a few strategies appropriate for the early development of a space plan:

- Locate activities according to light requirements.
- Put rooms with little need for daylight or view (infrequent use, service, washrooms) in nonperimeter areas or along walls with less desirable light.
- Locate tasks with higher lighting needs nearer the windows.

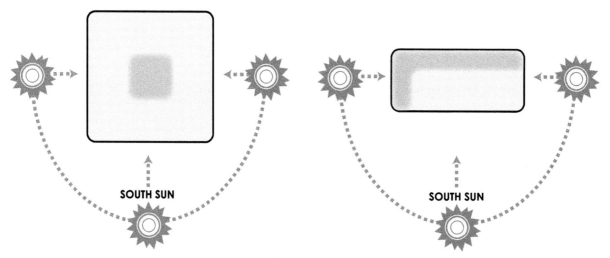

Figure 5.8 Block plan: daylight zones
Source: Sharon B. Jaffe

- Group tasks by similar lighting requirements for efficient use of electric lighting, and by similar schedules and comfort needs.
- Minimize use of west zones as occupied spaces. Western light is variable. It is difficult to optimize for daylighting or to avoid glare. Western exposure receives the highest solar heat gain, requiring higher cooling loads, and may be uncomfortable for occupants.

Daylight and natural ventilation are significant space planning influencers. Figure 5.8 illustrates how the geometry of a space impacts daylighting. Daylight from the perimeter of a deep plan will not reach the center of the plan. A long narrow plan, on an east-west axis, will provide good exposure for passive design strategies, including daylight, solar heat gain, and natural ventilation.

Natural Ventilation and Cooling

Natural ventilation is a low-cost, zero-energy-consumption opportunity for ventilation. Climate, microclimate, and prevailing outdoor conditions determine the effectiveness of natural ventilation. One key element in natural ventilation is operable windows, which introduce air movement to increase occupant comfort under a broader range of temperatures than still air. Control of one's environment through the opening and closing of windows can add to occupant comfort both physically and psychologically. Many people prefer "fresh" air because it connects occupants with the outside environment and typically has less CO_2, VOCs, and other contaminants that are the product of off-gassing and occupant load. The expanded criteria matrix indicates which rooms required natural ventilation. Ideally, 100 percent of all occupants will work within 30 feet of an operable window. Here are some basic strategies:

- Locate spaces near windows according to natural ventilation requirements. Open-plan space facilitates natural ventilation. Full-height partitions and private offices restrict airflow.
- Identify and utilize opportunities for both inlet and outlet natural ventilation windows.

- Locate spaces requiring limits on uncontrolled natural ventilation (e.g., labs) in space partitioned off from open natural ventilation to allow for independent ventilation controls.

Water

Identify plumbing fixture requirements and locations. Grouping plumbing fixtures will simplify supply and drainage system requirements. Code compliance, user needs, and existing service are critical location considerations for restrooms, janitor closet sinks, and other plumbing fixtures.

- Group restrooms and other rooms that require plumbing to minimize pipe runs.
- Locating restrooms along the edge of the building allows rainwater cisterns to be more easily integrated into the project as it evolves.

Privacy/Access

The cultural aspects of the plan determine the social interactions of the project among the end users. An interior space plan can create equity for the building users by making sure everyone has light and air.

- Provide shared spaces with access to daylight and natural ventilation.

Views

Occupant performance and satisfaction are closely tied to visual and thermal comfort. Visual comfort includes view as well as lighting. Access to natural views, daylight, and natural ventilation are incorporated into green building standards to provide occupant comfort and are considered significant components for occupant wellness.

- Provide natural views to the highest percentage of occupants possible.
- Provide access to operable windows for natural ventilation and control of individual environments to the highest percentage of occupants possible.

Design Priorities

As with the exploration of the earlier mini steps, building location and orientation, developing block plans as viewed via the four perspectives expands one's thinking and assures consideration of options that may not be obvious at first. It may also result in four or more different approaches to the block plan. At this stage in the design process, multiple options are a positive outcome. It is not necessary to choose a single block plan until the overall preliminary design interim step is complete.

Synergies and Tradeoffs

The block plan design ideas in Table 5.3 illustrate different approaches based on the four perspectives and stated design objectives. Notice that the diagrams targeting the performance, systems, and culture perspectives indicate building entry from an on-site parking lot, because it is the most efficient. The logical and consistent entry point in these perspectives provides synergistic or collaborative opportunities for perspectives to work together. The culture perspective also suggests a prominent entry from the corner of the site as a connection to the surrounding community. The experience perspective suggests entry from a path that could meander through a garden. The culture and experience diagrams/plans illustrate a tradeoff or compromise situation. Either idea will force the designer to compromise, reconcile, and balance competing diving forces.

Building Shape

Determining the shape of the building is the first real concrete step toward an actual building design. The building location, orientation, and block plans are critical steps in the process that determines the shape of the building.

From Block Plan to Space Plan

Developing the building shape requires refinement of the block plan to a preliminary space plan. Particular attention is focused on circulation within the building for productivity, through the building for egress, circulation through the site for amenity, and community access to the building. Lines and blocks allocating space for activities become walls and door swings that require spatial clearance. Verify that adequate area has been allocated to circulation and support areas such as (but not limited to) storage, mechanical space, janitor closets, equipment rooms, filing, and specialized work areas. Review the criteria matrix and relationship diagrams completed earlier in the SDB methodology.

- Are all required functions and spaces accommodated?
- Are all the spatial requirements met?
- Are there any code concerns?
- Are the spatial and amenity adjacencies correct?
- Is the circulation within the building intuitive for easy movement?
- Have visual and acoustic privacy needs been met?
- Does the plan facilitate natural ventilation, passive cooling, and daylight?

Revisions are made to the block plan as it evolves into the space plan before continuing on to the next steps. While it is important to be self-critical when evaluating and evolving the block plan to a space plan, remember this is still a work in progress, not a final plan. Using the SDB methodology, the space plan will continue to evolve through the next interim steps of step 3, design.

Site Inventory and Analysis

The site inventory and analysis provide context, specific drivers, and factors that influence the building shape. When the site inventory and analysis are investigated thoroughly, the primary options for building shape should become apparent quickly.

Building Orientation and Location

A simple building shape is usually the most energy and spatially efficient. A simple shape has less surface area, and subsequently less exposure to the outside elements of sun, rain, wind, and temperature. Less surface means an uncomplicated shape will gain less heat in the summer and lose less heat in the winter. Buildings with simple shapes and standard proportions generally require fewer materials and more easily accommodate standard mechanical and plumbing systems. As with many aspects of sustainable design, there are tradeoffs. A simpler design shape has a variety of performance benefits. More complex building shapes have a higher ratio of external wall area to floor area therefore may consume more energy materials resources. Although less energy and spatially efficient, a complex shape may have increased value from an experience perspective.

Macroclimate

Over the centuries traditional or vernacular architecture developed general rules for building shape and orientation based upon experience with local climate, materials, culture, and form that have over time been proven to be valid for specific functions. Those rules were based on context and attributes that are still applicable today.

Hot/dry climates
- North-south orientation may be preferable to reduce heat gain.
- Block the western sun with a permanent barrier to minimize late day heat gain.
- Minimize sun exposure; minimize the effects of wind.
- Use small windows.
- Optimize thermal mass to take advantage of the daily cycle of significant day to night temperature swings.
- Cluster buildings for the shade they offer one another.
- Courtyards are a cultural, architectural tradition, creating more comfortable micro-climates for surrounding structures.

Hot/humid climates
- Minimize sun exposure; maximize natural ventilation.
- Use lightweight construction to minimize radiation of heat.
- Space buildings far apart to maximize breezes.
- Courtyards are a cultural, architectural tradition, creating more comfortable micro-climates for surrounding structures.

Cold climates
- Orient buildings and openings for maximum protection from cold winds.
- Use south-facing windows (in the northern hemisphere) to maximize solar gains.
- Use compact shapes and small windows to minimize heat loss.

Temperate climates
- Maximize solar gain in winter; minimize solar gain in summer.
- Maximize breezes in summer; minimize breezes in winter.
- Take advantage of daylighting opportunities.
- With no extreme conditions, both heat and cooling are required.

Macro Context

At the macro scale, rating systems and standards encourage the integration of the building shape early in the design process as a means to make the building more energy efficient or to gain more daylight into the center of a building.

Settlement patterns impact the shape of a building. Climate and culture shape the patterns of urban development and culture. The four images in Table 5.03 are examples of this.

As discussed, relative to building solar orientation, street grids and shapes of adjacent and surrounding properties also drive building shape. A larger site in a suburban context allows greater freedom for building shape variation. Even so, due to the regular linear nature of building assemblies that lend themselves to straight walls and forms, buildings are often rectilinear in shape. Buildings in rural settings are frequently more complex, often composed of a collection of rectilinear shapes.

Microclimate, Local Zoning, and Codes

Just as the density of the urban landscape and streets drive building form, property lines and regulatory zoning also impact the shape of buildings.

Design Objectives and Design Ideas

The building shape design objectives build on the preceding interim steps.

Block plan design ideas, developed from each of the four perspectives, have evolved into preliminary space plans. These preliminary space plans serve as the starting point for building shape exploration. Building shape design ideas should accommodate the space plan from the same perspective with minimal adjustment. Later in the process, the space plan may be further adjusted as part of the preliminary design synthesis.

Design idea sketches for each of the four perspectives facilitate investigation and analysis of building shape possibilities. Simple, quick drawings communicate design intent. For each perspective, determine which shape, or combination of shapes, best fulfills the building objective.

Table 5.4 shows four possible building shapes, each meeting one of the four perspective's design objectives. All four shapes contain roughly the same square footage. There are many more possibilities. Each one of these is shown based on the four perspectives and would accommodate, with some modification, the bubble diagram or block plans developed earlier in the process.

Design Priorities

Each of the shapes in Table 5.4 reflects a successful interpretation of one of the four perspective's design objectives tying into the higher project goals and guiding principles of the project. Does one building shape, orientation, or location seem to be the consistent standout? That is not unexpected. Even so, the SDB methodology continues to explore options from all four perspectives during the early stages of design before too many advanced design decisions have been made. If changes to fundamental design decisions are required later in the design process, it will consume a much greater portion of the project budget.

TABLE 5.4 BUILDING SHAPE: DESIGN OBJECTIVES AND DESIGN IDEAS

Building Shape

		Design Objective	Design Ideas	
Perspectives	**Performance**	• Shape the building to maximize energy efficiency.	• Shape the building to be as compact as possible to conserve energy.	
	Systems	• Shape the building to harvest sun, wind, and light.	• Shape the building, to maximize daylight, minimize glare and to collect summer breezes.	
	Culture	• Shape the building to fit into the neighborhood architectural geometry.	• Orient the building to relate to and invite the community. Use rectilinear articulation similar to the variations in front facade depth experienced on small urban commercial corridors.	
	Experience	• Shape the building to be an element of delight for building occupants and community members alike.	• Create a sweeping curve to embrace the view and create a protected microclimate for sunny but cooler weather.	

Source: Sharon B. Jaffe

Synergies and Tradeoffs

The building shapes in Table 5.4 address the design objectives formulated via the four perspectives. Four different building shapes suggest opportunities for synergy where the combination of ideas and the shapes generated will produce a result preferable to an individual shape or idea. Look at the building orientation. While each shape will result in a different interior building plan, two of the four building shapes offer a similar solar exposure, and two of the shapes have a similar relationship to the building site. The experience idea has the start of a courtyard, which will provide interior to exterior visual and spatial connections and expanded daylighting and ventilation opportunities. The culture and systems ideas have similar rectilinear shapes, although the differences in solar orientation and building depth will impact the choice of appropriate strategies for passive heat gain, daylighting, and natural ventilation and cooling strategies. The performance design idea is not synergistic and would require tradeoffs during the synthesis process to effectively combine its strengths with any of the other four perspective ideas.

Building Massing

Building massing is the most basic elemental form of the building without windows, doors, and other details. As the purest form of a building, building mass is considered early in the design process because of its considerable impact on early sustainability decisions. Two of the most significant factors affecting the sustainability of a building are effective passive design strategies and minimizing a building's energy consumption; both hinge on appropriate building massing.

Building massing, location, shape, and orientation are interdependent; as individual aspects of a building, each effects the others. In this book, each aspect is discussed individually with the intent to dissect the design process. More experienced designers may choose to work with shape, orientation, and massing, simultaneously.

Floor to Floor Height and Daylighting

What height is best for the interior spaces? The distance between the floor and the roof or one floor and another significantly impacts the overall building height and the ability to bring daylight into the interiors. Access to fresh air, views, and daylight impacts the health and well-being of the building users. Increased window wall height provides opportunity for increased glazing area. The opportunity for window openings to be located higher on the perimeter wall allows daylight to penetrate deeper into the building. In cold climates, more heat will be required to heat the increased interior volume. In warmer weather, high ceilings allow the hot air to rise above the work level, providing greater occupant comfort. Figure 5.9 illustrates the increased daylight penetration depth that is a result of windows set higher on the perimeter wall. Increased glazing may result in unwanted glare and heat gain entering the space as sunlight in the summer. This topic is discussed in greater depth in Chapter 7, "Step 3B: Daylighting." However, a taller floor-to-floor dimension results in a taller building with more surface area exposed to the elements.

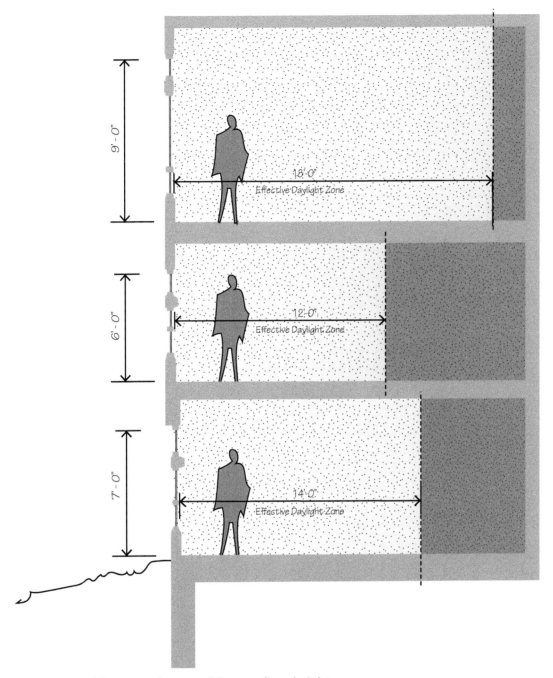

Figure 5.9 Building mass: increased floor-to-floor height
Source: Sharon B. Jaffe

Taller Buildings with Smaller Footprints

The building shape or footprint is two-dimensional. Mass is three-dimensional. A building may have a small footprint, either by design preference or necessity of a small building site. Building height is an early fundamental decision, along with building shape, location, and orientation. They all play a part in a building's ability to maximize sustainable strategies for natural ventilation, cooling, daylighting, and solar energy successfully while minimizing building energy loads.

Assuming the site has the space to accommodate either a tall building with a small footprint or a shorter building with a larger footprint, which is more efficient? As with many sustainable design decisions, it depends on many factors. The project guiding principles may express the desire to minimize site disturbance and maximize open space.

As illustrated in Figure 5.10, taller buildings with multiple floors reduce the total impact of the building footprint upon the site's open space. The taller building with the narrower plan allows daylight to penetrate deeper into the building floor-plate. The smaller and narrower floor plate increases opportunities for natural cross ventilation, and creates opportunities to use natural site features and green infrastructure in support of biodiversity. Increasing the daylight, views, and natural ventilation available to a higher percentage of building occupants achieves additional synergies by helping to meet the health and wellbeing metrics.

Zoning and Code

Multistory buildings in the United States are typically required by code to provide an elevator and two enclosed fire stairs. The reduced size of the multistory building footprint may be offset by the square footage required for additional stairways and elevators. Local zoning governs how much of the site the building footprint can use.

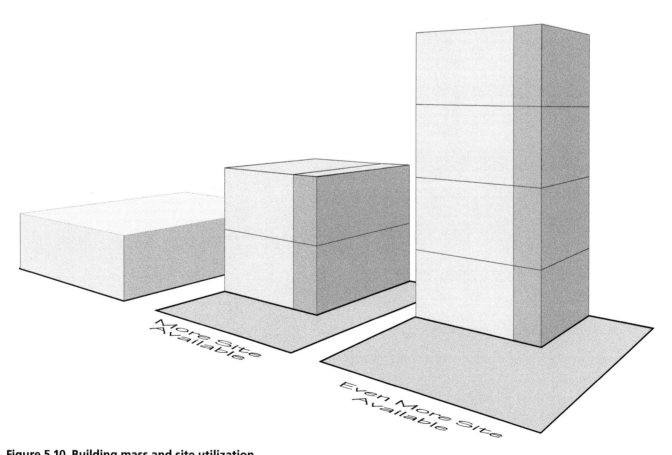

Figure 5.10 Building mass and site utilization
Source: Sharon B. Jaffe

A multistory building may be required on a given site in order to meet zoning code requirements for building setback greenspace while still providing adequate interior space for building functions. Similar to orientation, the shape of the site, required setbacks, and height limits all significantly influence building massing. Taller buildings with a smaller surface to volume ratio are potentially more environmentally sustainable due to decreased heat loss and greater efficiency in reducing energy consumption.

In Figures 5.11a and b, building massing has "maxed out" the extent of the setback and height limitations of the zoning code. Buildings that cover the maximum percentage of site allowable by code are not uncommon where clients' primary goal is to maximize return on investment. Increasing building height from a one-story building to a multistory midrise to limit site coverage may increase construction costs per square foot but result in higher potential rent per square foot on upper floors, thus increasing total revenues.

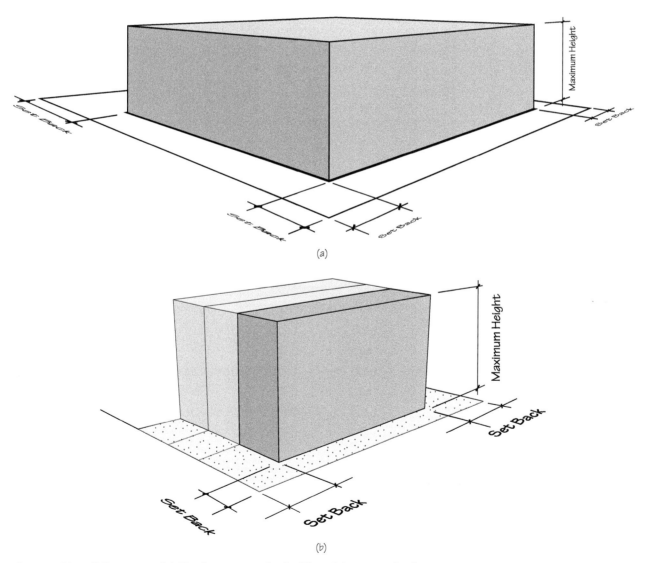

Figure 5.11 Building mass: (a) Single-story setback; (b) Multistory setback
Source: Sharon B. Jaffe

Surface Area to Volume Ratio

Surface area to volume ratio (also known as the aspect ratio) describes the total amount of exterior walls and roofs that are exposed to the elements. Winter winds, rain, and sun all hit the exterior of a building hard. As a rule, a building loses or gains heat through the exterior surfaces. One of the first steps in sustainable design is to reduce the amount of building surface exposed to the elements.

To determine the heat loss or heat gain of a specific massing concept, calculate the amount of exposed exterior surface area (area= length × height) relative to the interior volume (volume = length × width × height). That may sound complex, but it is pretty straightforward.

As illustrated in Table 5.5, option 1 has a far lower surface-to-air-ratio, making it more efficient for heating in the winter. Option 2 will have a 30 percent higher surface-to-air-ratio, thereby needing more heat, more energy, and ultimately leading to the emission of more CO_2 pollution. The tradeoffs in option 1 involve health and wellness. Although more efficient in energy consumption, reduced exterior surface area results in reduced access to daylight and operable windows.

Macroclimate

Macroclimate plays a significant role in determining the massing of the building. In cold, heating-dominated climates, the surface-to-air ratio is minimized to reduce heat loss. In hot, cooling-dominated climates, shading, natural ventilation, and the ability to dissipate heat become important. A tall, thin building reduces the heat collecting roof surface. Exterior shading devices prevent solar radiation from warming building walls or entering the building through direct sunlight while still allowing operable windows to provide natural ventilation. In many hot areas of the globe, air conditioning becomes very important for occupant comfort, so building massing options shift. Multiple buildings can be grouped to create shade for one another, reducing heat gain. Tall interior spaces allow warm air to rise above occupant level and, with appropriate planning, be vented out of the building.

TABLE 5.5 BUILDING MASS: ASPECT RATIO, BUILDING SHAPE TO BUILDING AREA

	Option 1 Simple Box	Option 2 Multiple Structures	Option 3 Elongated Box	Option 4 Courtyard
Total Roof Area	2500 S.F.	2500 S.F.	2500 S.F.	2500 S.F.
Total Wall Area	2,000 S.F.	4,000 S.F.	2,272 S.F.	3,600 S.F.
Total Surface Area	4,500 S.F.	6,500 S.F.	4,780	6,120 S.F.
Surface Variation from Option 1	—	+2,000 S.F.	+280 S.F.	+1,620 S.F.

Source: Sharon B. Jaffe

Macro Context

Macro context also influences the decisions that help determine building mass. While concerns for energy efficiency and habitat are crucial factors in sustainable design, the culture and experience perspectives are also sustainable design drivers. Massing of a building responds to urban, suburban, or rural conditions and their macro contexts. The characteristics of the different macro contexts are discussed in detail in step 1 of the SDB methodology. Urban, suburban, and rural macro context have different patterns that impact building massing. Urban form and pattern are dominated by street grids and buildings that define those street edges. Suburbia tends to be dominated by buildings floating as objects surrounded by open spaces and parking lots. Rural patterns are dominated by larger plots of land and building mass that is often lower and more spread out. However, design solutions are not required to repeat the patterns of existing development and can often introduce new patterns to the benefit of the sustainable building project and the surrounding community.

Microclimate and Local Project Requirements

The microclimate of the project site, the local context, and the project requirements are central elements determining building form (shape + mass). The site inventory is used to help locate the building(s), and now the inventory and analysis identify driving factors that influence the building mass. Surrounding buildings, natural elements, and zoning codes drive many of the building mass decisions. Good sun exposure available on site for daylight may influence the height of the building walls and windows locations. Openings located higher in a wall allow daylight to penetrate deeper into the building. A neighborhood community with zoning height restrictions may suggest breaking up the building mass into smaller connected buildings. Neighboring buildings can also influence massing. It may be a high project priority to match the height of adjacent buildings to maintain the urban pattern. Alternatively, the priority could be to make the building a sculptural landmark to be seen from many vantage points. The design matrix highlights important local conditions to which the building absolutely must respond.

Site Analysis

Local context and project requirements play decisive roles in determining building form (shape + mass). Surrounding buildings, natural elements, and zoning codes drive many of the decisions. Site inventory and analysis are valuable in locating building(s) on the site. Analysis will also help determine the massing. If there are prominent views to the building or from the building, it may be appropriate for the building to be taller, or stepped back in places to provide better visual opportunities. A varied building height line may help to avoid unwanted shadows from other buildings or trees.

Design Objectives and Design Ideas

It is typical to consider many conflicting project objectives while designing. Guiding principles of a sustainable design project may encourage a low building mass with optimizing area for solar panels. A tall, thin multistory building will "tread lightly on the site." There are many drivers and factors involved in sustainable design that apply to different aspects of the process. Primary drivers of the project, as objectives relative to each of the four perspectives, are organized in the matrix format.

Design Ideas

Design ideas for massing are preliminary designs that lead toward the resolved building design. Everything discussed previously in preliminary design influences the design of building mass. That means that each design idea contains hundreds of smaller ideas, objectives, and responses to factors. In that sense, this is a challenging but rewarding step. Table 5.6 organizes the building mass objectives with notations of the ways design ideas might approach the exploration of building mass.

The ideas from the performance perspective address the design objective to maximize solar energy by employing a large roof for the placement of PV on the roof and high walls to optimize opportunities for daylighting.

Design ideas from the systems perspective proposes multiple buildings to respond to the objective to limit the buildings impact on habitat.

TABLE 5.6 BUILDING MASS: DESIGN OBJECTIVES AND DESIGN IDEAS

Building Mass

		Design Objective	Design Ideas
Perspectives	Performance	• Design a building with a minimal exterior surface for the maximum square footage. • Optimize daylighting opportunities. • Optimize passive and active solar energy.	• Design a compact building to conserve embodied energy and energy for building operations. • Provide open plan space with south solar exposure for daylight and passive heat. • Design a building with higher than standard floor-to-floor heights to allow for windows placed high on the walls. • Design a building with a large roof to accommodate extensive PV array.
	Systems	• Minimize the building footprint on the site, providing areas for habitat restoration.	• Locate the building away from the 100-year flood zone. • Use multiple smaller structures to reduce the negative impact on existing habitat.
	Culture	• Building height, mass, and materials correspond to the local context. • Connect building with the community and invite foot traffic. • Integrate the building with community activities.	• Locate the building entrance near the street corner along the commercial corridor.
	Experience	• Create a distinctive structure of beautiful proportions. • Create a gateway experience for the community and visitors.	• Organize building space to have clear views of the park and interesting bridge structure.

Source: Sharon B. Jaffe

The idea from the culture perspective derives its form from the local context. The building mass "matches" other buildings in the area.

Finally, the building mass idea from the experience perspective explores a dynamic sculptural response to the site that maximizes views to and from the building.

Design ideas for building mass arise from those for building shape and incorporate all of the previous design decisions. Multiple massing design ideas should be drawn from each of the four perspectives. Focus on the overall massing. Specific details of roof shape, windows, and other building details are addressed in the subsequent chapters of this text. For each perspective, determine which option or combination of options best fulfills the design objective in building mass.

Synergies and Tradeoffs

Design ideas for massing have so many synergies and tradeoffs that it is often difficult to determine a clear path forward. Look for synergies and capitalize on those that are more pronounced. Some of the tradeoffs might challenge a designer to mitigate and balance drawbacks to maximize prioritized design opportunities. For example, the building mass design idea from the systems perspective of using smaller buildings could be combined with the design ideas from the performance perspective to create a composite design idea. The process of addressing tradeoffs and capitalizing on synergies occurs in the last step of the preliminary design process.

Validation

Synergies, and Synthesis of Preliminary Design

Preliminary design is an interim step of step 3, design, in the *Sustainable Design Basics* methodology. During preliminary design, the information observed, researched, and documented in step 1, context, and step 2, pre-planning, are invaluable. It is this background information, combined with the project guiding principles and goals, criteria matrix, and relationship diagrams that influence the preliminary design ideas for:

- Building location
- Building orientation
- Interior space bubble diagram or block plan
- Building shape
- Building mass

At this point in the SDB methodology, building design ideas have been developed by layering information and design decisions on the previous mini steps of preliminary design to create a composite design scheme for each of the four perspectives. There are now four solutions, one from each perspective: performance, systems, culture, and experience.

Validation Metrics

There are still many details left undetermined at this point of preliminary design. Broad generalizations have been made regarding windows, insulation, materials, and systems. Still to be explored is the building envelope, and specific determinations regarding windows, wall, and foundation. Building roof shape will make a significant impact on metrics. Yet, even at this early point in the sustainable building design, energy modeling software can provide an analysis of a simple 3D model that includes the most rudimentary information to make an impartial analysis in order to evaluate and compare designs. It is essential that each of the four perspectives consider the same metrics determined by the same process.

Validation metrics: Preliminary design includes
- **Energy**: EUI or estimated level: high, medium, or low
- **Light and air**: The percentage of space with direct access to operable windows or daylight autonomy
- **Water**: Not applicable at this early stage in the process
- **Ecology**: Site available for natural habitat

Software energy models will provide metrics for energy analysis EUI and daylight autonomy. Calculate the percentage of space with direct access to operable windows using a drawing program or manually. If the software is unavailable for an energy model, work with an instructor to make the best guess estimate of the energy consumption by the basic form design idea for each perspective. Still to be addressed are water conservation and rainwater harvesting strategies. Enter NA for "not applicable." Calculate the percentage of the site that supports natural habitat and ecology using a drawing program or manually. Information regarding specific software and software use will be available on the companion website.

The preliminary design validation matrix is a useful organizational tool for categorizing and recording required information from each of the four perspectives.

Validation Matrix: Preliminary Design

The preliminary design evaluation will compare the four different design ideas, one from each perspective, against the overall project goals. Early in the design process, the metrics provided are indicators of the design ideas' value. They do not prescribe a final result. Too many details requiring metric analysis are still missing. Figure 5.12 is an image of the validation matrix from the demonstration project in Chapter 11.

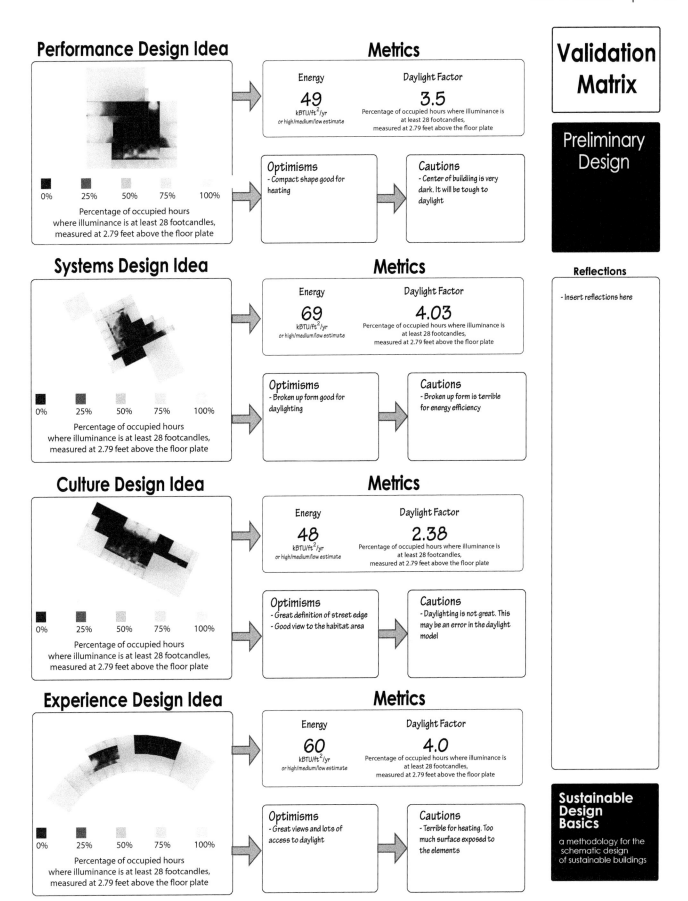

Performance Design Idea

Metrics

Energy
49
kBTU/ft²/yr
or high/medium/low estimate

Daylight Factor
3.5
Percentage of occupied hours where illuminance is
at least 28 footcandles,
measured at 2.79 feet above the floor plate

0% 25% 50% 75% 100%

Percentage of occupied hours
where illuminance is at least 28 footcandles,
measured at 2.79 feet above the floor plate

Optimisms
- Compact shape good for heating

Cautions
- Center of buildiing is very dark. It will be tough to daylight

Systems Design Idea

Metrics

Energy
69
kBTU/ft²/yr
or high/medium/low estimate

Daylight Factor
4.03
Percentage of occupied hours where illuminance is
at least 28 footcandles,
measured at 2.79 feet above the floor plate

0% 25% 50% 75% 100%

Percentage of occupied hours
where illuminance is at least 28 footcandles,
measured at 2.79 feet above the floor plate

Optimisms
- Broken up form good for daylighting

Cautions
- Broken up form is terrible for energy efficiency

Culture Design Idea

Metrics

Energy
48
kBTU/ft²/yr
or high/medium/low estimate

Daylight Factor
2.38
Percentage of occupied hours where illuminance is
at least 28 footcandles,
measured at 2.79 feet above the floor plate

0% 25% 50% 75% 100%

Percentage of occupied hours
where illuminance is at least 28 footcandles,
measured at 2.79 feet above the floor plate

Optimisms
- Great definition of street edge
- Good view to the habitat area

Cautions
- Daylighting is not great. This may be an error in the daylight model

Experience Design Idea

Metrics

Energy
60
kBTU/ft²/yr
or high/medium/low estimate

Daylight Factor
4.0
Percentage of occupied hours where illuminance is
at least 28 footcandles,
measured at 2.79 feet above the floor plate

0% 25% 50% 75% 100%

Percentage of occupied hours
where illuminance is at least 28 footcandles,
measured at 2.79 feet above the floor plate

Optimisms
- Great views and lots of access to daylight

Cautions
- Terrible for heating. Too much surface exposed to the elements

Validation Matrix

Preliminary Design

Reflections
- Insert reflections here

Sustainable Design Basics
a methodology for the schematic design of sustainable buildings

Figure 5.12 Preliminary design validation matrix

Source: Sharon B. Jaffe

Enter the following information for each perspective in the preliminary design validation matrix:

- Block plan
- Validation metrics for each of the four perspectives
- Evaluate the metrics of derived from each perspective.
  - Make a note of cautions and optimism for each perspective scheme
  - Cautions are observations of the design scheme that are cause for caution.
  - Optimisms are observations of the design scheme that are cause for optimism.
- Reflections
  - Think about the tradeoffs and synergies presented in the preliminary design scheme from each of the four perspectives. How does each perspective relate to each of the remaining three perspectives?

Synthesis

Once all the information is entered into the validation matrix, analyze and evaluate which aspects of which schemes yield the most significant benefit. The goal is to arrive at a design that incorporates the best aspects from each perspective.

Rarely is one perspective's approach a comprehensive solution. It is much more likely that good ideas incorporate aspects of each of the four perspectives approaches. Design ideas that coincide indicate substantial alignment of strategies, which should be synthesized into the final design.

Space Plan Revisited

The synthesized preliminary design now combines favorable features from all of the four perspectives to establish the base building size and shape. It is time to revise, resolve, and refine the preliminary space plan to a preliminary floor plan before moving on to the next interim step, the building envelope.

Rough Floor Plan

Specific relationships and adjacencies between spaces have been present throughout the iterative design process. It is possible that, during the multiple iterations of the preliminary design process, spatial requirements may have shifted. Refer to the criteria matrix as the rough floor plan is developed to assure that all requirements are met.

Preliminary block plans have evolved into space plans to establish the basis of the floor plan, organizing the building entry, circulation, egress, and interior rooms and spaces. Unlike a diagram, a floor plan is realistic. Dimensions are accurate; walls are drawn to the correct thickness; doors are drawn with the appropriate clearances; circulation space is drawn to meet ADA and building code requirements. Using the preliminary space plan as a guide, begin to draw the floor plan. Revise and refine the plan as spaces are drawn with walls and doors, and circulation.

Detail Demanding Spaces

Start with the more challenging spaces. Detailed spaces that are anchored by plumbing requirements such as kitchens and bathrooms are located in a floor plan, considering the organization of plumbing fixtures, location of plumbing chases, and minimizing the length of supply and drainage lines. Where permitted by code and regulation, consider locating toilets in relative proximity to rainwater or graywater collection for use flushing toilets. Whenever possible, locate restrooms in a manner that facilitates sharing a plumbing chase; back to back or side by side to reduce the quantity of piping required. Be sure that clearances at doors, in travel paths, and in individual toilet stalls allow clearance for wheelchairs and scooters. The 2010 ADA standards became mandatory in 2012. It is worth noting that, like many codes, the American with Disabilities Act (ADA) Guidelines state minimum requirements, not the ideal; the minimum requirement may not always be adequate. Individuals dependent on scooters – of which there are an increasing number – often struggle in spaces that meet ADA guidelines because scooters have a much larger footprint than wheelchairs. Restroom facilities must also consider issues of discrete access and visual privacy. Restrooms should not be too remote from the main traffic area in order to avoid long travel distance and provide easy access for those with urgency concerns. People in hallways or waiting areas should not be able to see into restrooms.

While codes are complex and beyond the focus of this text, design professionals must become familiar with the codes and regulations of the specific municipality and location of each project. Not all local codes adopt the most recent version of all other standards or codes. IBC, plumbing code, fire code, ADA guidelines, and barrier-free planning conventions are all codes that directly impact space planning.

Space Planning and Daylight, Ventilation, and Views

Space planning as a strategy for sustainable design integrates daylighting, natural ventilation, and views into the planning process early in the development of block plans. As diagrams become plans, sustainable strategies for daylight, ventilation, and views should be reinforced. Keep in mind all habitable spaces have requirements for daylight and air. Typically, the code requirements for residential buildings require windows to be at least 10 percent of the floor area with one half of that being operable windows. Beyond code requirements, daylight and access to windows have a clear and quantifiable impact on productivity and occupant satisfaction with their work environment.

Organizing open plan spaces along the equator side of a building provides the greatest flexibility for daylight penetration into a building. Studies indicate that the best arrangement using a traditional desk organization is with work surfaces perpendicular to the window wall. This arrangement avoids glare contrast between bright daylight and work surfaces and screens. Understand and plan the interior spaces to maximize the WWR, window locations, and shading to support optimizing building daylight and energy performance.

Space Planning and Daylight Obstructions

Avoid blocking daylight penetration with partitions. If partitions are required, consider using transparent or translucent materials for wall areas above 30 inches. Interior spaces on east and west sides of the building are impacted by low and shifting daylight angles, making effective daylighting a challenge. Often vertical circulation, restrooms, spaces that may not benefit from daylight, and other support spaces are grouped to buffer interior spaces from less than optimal solar exposure from the east and west facades. When it is necessary to use challenging west and east exposures, window treatments may mitigate some of the uncomfortable effects of glare. Automated and manual solar shades, blinds, and window louvers are among readily available, cost-efficient interior shading possibilities.

Passive cooling, natural ventilation, and views are closely tied to daylighting because all are dependent on the placement of building fenestration. Passive design strategies of this textbook include additional detailed information about window sizing, placement, and shading.

Acoustics

When transforming the block plan or space plan into a fully detailed floor plan, verify that the acoustic concerns are addressed as detailed in the criteria matrix. Examine the acoustic zoning of spaces. Grouping spaces with similar functional levels of sound and isolating them from spaces requiring relative quiet will go a long way to avoid conflict once the spaces are occupied. Buffer spaces, such as closets and storage areas, further insulate zones from unacceptable noise levels.

Space Plan Review

The space plan has refined the block plan locating partitions, doors, furniture, and perhaps suggested window locations. Take time to review that the space plan aligns with project guiding principles and goals and fulfills all of the requirements from the criteria matrix before moving on to the next interim step.

FURTHER READING

Allen, E., and J. Iano. 2017. *The Architect's Studio Companion* (6th ed.). Hoboken, NJ: John Wiley & Sons.

Ching, Francis D. K., and I. M. Shapiro. 2014. *Green Building Illustrated*. Hoboken, NJ: John Wiley & Sons.

Karlen, M., and R. Fleming. 2016. *Space Planning Basics* (4th ed.). Hoboken, NJ: John Wiley & Sons.

Step 3B: Passive Design

Figure 6.0 *Sustainable Design Basics*, **step 3**
Source: Sharon B. Jaffe

WHAT IS PASSIVE DESIGN?

Passive design is a sustainable design approach that utilizes freely available elements of the natural environment to maximize the comfort of building occupants. A well-designed sustainable building optimizes passive design strategies to minimize, if not eliminate, the need for fossil fuel-based energy sources. A building's energy efficiency and resilience are amplified by leveraging sustainable design strategies that use the free resources of the sun, wind, and water, to maintain comfortable temperatures, good air quality, and appropriate levels of natural light. Passive design strategies are relatively simple, require no moving parts or mechanical systems, and require minimal maintenance.

Passive design strategies work best when integrated into the early design process for new construction as a synergistic system since optimizing passive design strategies rely on the early design decisions determining building orientation and building envelope. Requirements for natural light must consider the implications for potential heat gain. The use of operable windows required for natural ventilation must examine the possibility of heat loss and gain through the windows. Critical design decisions can leverage each specific strategy benefit to realize synergies. A roof monitor may provide daylight and serve as a ventilation outlet. Both passive strategies serve their intended function, but are supportive and synergistic, improving both daylighting and passive ventilation. A holistic design approach optimizes the synergies of passive design strategies for superior overall building performance.

Passive design has been integral to vernacular architecture throughout the history of the world providing economic and environmental benefit through reduced energy consumption, reduced maintenance requirements, and increased occupant comfort and overall satisfaction.

Resilience

Resilient buildings function even when ordinary life is not ordinary. Climate change and increased frequency of extreme weather-related disruptions require designers to carefully evaluate the local context and plan for common disruptions and natural disasters. Each specific location has its particular conditions and vulnerabilities. Passive design strategies respond to these conditions to reduce a building's dependence on active or mechanical systems, which is extremely important when power is not available.

Globally, temperatures are increasing, and the weather is becoming more extreme. Designing with resilience as an objective is a smart approach in any environment. To design for resilience a building site is assessed for probable disruptions. Is the site vulnerable to severe wind, rainstorms, and associated flooding? Is the building site currently at risk, or likely to be at risk, in the future due to drought or fires? Will the site be threatened by rising sea, lake, or river bed levels, and the erosion caused by storm surges? Resilient design anticipates potential climatic challenges and integrates appropriate responses into the building design.

KEY ELEMENTS OF PASSIVE DESIGN

Passive design is a key consideration in the earliest design decisions for site integration, building location and orientation, building form, and the building envelope. Each one of these early design steps can significantly enhance or limit opportunities for passive design.

Climate refers to the variables of the local weather conditions in an area over a long period, impacting requirements for cooling, heating, and ventilation that support a comfortable interior building environment.

Site analysis may reveal inherent opportunities that support passive design strategies. Site contours, earth forms, and landscape plantings may be beneficial in directing or buffering winds, filtering out ambient noise, and providing shade. The site-specific changing solar path, angles, and the solar radiation available throughout the year suggest strategies to maximize solar energy.

Building location on a specific site reflects the connection of the site to the broader community and integration with the specific site. A building's relationship to the road requires zoning setbacks, parking access, and views, which may be employed to enhance community connections.

A *building orientation* that aligns with the sun will impact the building energy usage. In the northern hemisphere, an east-west building orientation provides an opportunity for passive solar heating and daylight from the south. In the southern hemisphere, a building's north face is oriented toward the sun and will have maximum exposure to solar radiation.

Building form or *mass* means that size, shape and material influence how solar heat gain is absorbed and stored within a building. Together, building orientation and building mass can maximize solar radiation.

The *building envelope* is an assembly of elements: roof, walls, windows, doors, and foundation. As the barrier that separates exterior and interior conditions, the design of the building envelope is critical to interface with, and leverage, surrounding site and climate conditions.

Insulation acts as a barrier limiting the unwanted transfer of heat or cooling, both into and out of the building. Insulation is a necessary component to support passive heating and cooling strategies. Different climates have varied insulation needs.

Thermal mass regulates and delays the effect of heat gain. High-density materials, like concrete, stone, and brick are all high-thermal-mass materials with the capacity to absorb and store heat when exposed to direct sunlight. As temperatures cool in the evening, thermal mass releases the heat collected during the day helping to maintain a comfortable and steady temperature inside a building. High thermal mass should be exposed to the sun and absorb heat in cold months but shaded so as not to absorb heat in the warm months. Thermal mass is most useful where there is a significant difference between daytime and nighttime ambient temperatures (approximately 50°F/10°C).

A *vestibule* or *airlock* at the entrance to a building will act as a buffer protecting interior spaces from outside temperatures, winds, and noise regardless of the specific solar orientation. Consider and utilize incidental passive heat gain and daylight. An airlock must be able to be closed off from both the outside and the inside, to buffer the interior space. Space must be allocated to allow people to enter and close the side of the airlock they entered before exiting through the other door.

The *building space plan* is a crucial element in realizing and maximizing passive design opportunities to increase occupant comfort and building efficiencies. The building facade facing the sun may have ample operable windows to provide opportunities for passive heat, passive cooling and ventilation, and views to outdoors. Generally, this will locate infrequently used building space and other support spaces, such as restrooms and mechanical rooms, to areas of the building farther away from windows and solar exposure. Spaces with functional requirements that limit daylight requirements should also be located to shield them from sun exposure.

Interior building spaces are planned with an understanding and consideration of the passive design attributes provided by a building's orientation.

Passive design attributes listed by building solar orientation as would be experienced in the northern hemisphere are:

South-facing spaces:

- Good daylight for most of the day
- Solar gain for most of the day throughout the year
- Horizontal shading required to prevent summertime overheating
- Good passive solar gain in winter

East-facing spaces:

- Morning sun and daylight
- Morning direct solar gain for thermal mass
- Cooler in the late afternoon

West-facing spaces:

- Afternoon sun and daylight
- Vulnerable to late afternoon overheating
- Vertical shading required to prevent afternoon glare
- Afternoon direct solar gain for thermal mass

North-facing spaces:

- Low daylight levels
- Limited or no heat gain
- Best suited for support and service spaces

Key Terms

Air temperature is the measurement of the kinetic energy, the motion of air gas molecules. Measured in degrees Fahrenheit or Celsius, the temperature is an indicator of the hot or cold level of an object or environment.

Air velocity represents the speed air travels described as the distance air travels in a given time frame (e.g., feet per minute). Air volume flow is air velocity multiplied by area represented by cubic feet per minute or CFM.

The *diurnal cycle* is a daily pattern or cycle as a result of the earth's rotation. The most familiar form is daily temperature change from day to night, a basic climate pattern.

Heat transfer is a measure of the thermal energy, heat that moves from one location to another location of lower temperature until a state of equilibrium is reached.

Humidity is the amount of water vapor in the air.

Relative humidity is the amount of water vapor or moisture in the air as a percentage of the maximum water vapor the air could hold in the same air temperature before full saturation. The warmer the temperature of the air, the more significant the amount of water vapor the air can hold. A significant factor in thermal comfort. In high relative humidity, the air is heavy with moisture limiting the effectiveness of the human body's natural cooling system, sweating. Occupants may feel sticky and uncomfortable in high relative humidity.

Radiant temperature or mean radiant temperature (MRT) averages the temperature of the surrounding surfaces and area of radiant energy (heat). It is the weighted mean temperature of all the surrounding objects. As a measure, MRT is used to express the influence of surrounding surface temperatures on occupant comfort. In practice, occupant thermal comfort is higher when there is no difference or a relatively small difference between surrounding surfaces and an occupant.

Resultant temperature. Also known as operative temperature measures the human thermal comfort based on air temperature and air speed. Average air temperature and surrounding surfaces temperatures are a significant factor in thermal comfort. Occupants will feel comfortable if the resultant temperature remains within the targeted comfort range.

Thermal comfort or *human thermal comfort* is a measure of occupant comfort in the thermal environment. Human thermal comfort is highly subjective and dependent on an individual's perception of comfort. Primary environmental factors in thermal comfort are air temperature, relative humidity, air movement, surface temperatures, and direct solar heat gain. Primary personal factors that impact thermal comfort include an occupant's activity level, type, and quantity of clothing, an individual's perception of temperature and body acclimation to the surroundings.

A *psychometric chart* is a graphic presentation of air properties, temperature, and relative humidity that may be used to define zones of occupant comfort. Highly subjective and dependent on an individual's perception of comfort. It is an oddly shaped graph that may be used to analyze and design for environmental conditions.

Predicted mean vote index (PMV) is a thermal comfort model that predicts the response of a larger group of people to the thermal environment.

Predicted percentage dissatisfied index (PPD) is a prediction of the percentage of occupants of a particular thermal environment that will be dissatisfied. Thermal comfort is highly individualized. Approximately 5 percent of the people in a group will be dissatisfied with the thermal environment even at its most optimized.

PASSIVE DESIGN STRATEGIES

Key passive design strategies are addressed individually in this section in response to separate fundamental principles. In reality, different passive strategies are used in combination and studied together as synergistic strategies provide benefits greater than the simple addition of each individual strategy. Passive design strategies may also maximize specific contradictory opportunities requiring design tradeoffs. Tradeoffs and synergies are essential to effective passive design. Data gathered during the initial site survey, research, and case studies, provide an enormous amount of information. It may seem overwhelming. Using the SDB methodology design matrix helps sort through, prioritize, and determine, which passive design strategies can be implemented most effectively to achieve project objectives and goals.

Passive Design in Macroclimates

Passive strategies are most effective when designed for specific climates. In some climates, passive heating is a benefit and helps to reduce total operational energy cost. In hot climates passive heating is an undesirable natural climate condition. The inherent heat gain typical in hot climates requires higher levels of cooling to create comfortable conditions inside the building. The opposite occurs in cool climates that require higher levels of heating to realize thermal comfort.

Passive Strategies Organized by Macroclimate

All climates
- Building orientation: orient the building to maximize or minimize solar radiation as appropriate to the macroclimate and specific microclimate.
- Vernacular architecture: consider integrating indigenous building practices into passive design strategies such as structures raised off the ground on piles to facilitate air flow in hot, humid climates.
- Building form must suit the macroclimate. For example, in year-round cold climates, the ratio between perimeter exterior surface area to the interior area is optimized for a compact building footprint, reducing the opportunity for heat transfer through the building envelope.
- Insulation: Maximize building envelope insulation to reduce unwanted heat transfer.
- Interior space plans should facilitate passive strategies. Open plans provide opportunities for shared daylighting, passive heat distribution, and cross ventilation for passive cooling. Buffer spaces may be utilized to insulate spaces from extreme temperature swings.
- Daylight is desirable in all climate zones. Careful control methods are required to either block or allow solar heat gain to enter the building with daylight based upon specific climate requirements.

Hot/dry climates

In hot dry climates, the temperature swings may be extreme. With little vegetation or humidity to hold the ambient warm air, hot daytime temperatures drop at night. Cold nighttime temperatures can make for chilly mornings. Heat is often required until the sun rises high enough in the sky.

- Orient and locate buildings to minimize sun exposure.
- Design a compact building form to reduce heat gain through exterior surface areas.
- Include buffer spaces in the building plan.
- Courtyard or patio with vegetation and a small body of water will cool ambient air supply for natural ventilation.
- Tall floor-to-ceiling dimensions allow space for hot air to rise above living areas and facilitates stack ventilation.
- Roof design with a high pitch provides high insulated air space to maintain cooler temperatures on lower levels.
- Roof design should reflect solar radiation and have high levels of insulation. Consider light-colored roof, double roof or fly roof with integral ventilation, and a single roof with high insulation levels and air cavity.
- Use thermal mass to store heat during the day, release heat in cooler night temperatures.
- Insulate the building envelope to reduce unwanted heat gain in the heat of the day and retain heat in cold nights.
- Design natural ventilation to provide cross ventilation at body level.
- Consider smaller window openings with horizontal shading in thick light-colored walls that may serve as thermal mass.
- Operable windows that reduce heat transmission through window glazing to reduce cooling loads but support natural ventilation.
- Locate windows on building facades facing away from the equator and direct sunlight. Locate windows to distribute air through the building interior spaces.
- Roof and impervious surfaces used as catchment areas for rainwater harvesting. Locate cisterns to be shielded from the sun or locate underground.

Hot/humid climates

In hot humid climates the temperature and moisture level are consistently high. Warm air holds more moisture than cold air. As temperature increases, so does the potential for high humidity levels. Ventilation and protection from solar radiation are the two passive strategies effective for improved thermal comfort in this climate. The evaporation of a body's perspiration from the skin to the air is a cooling process. Ambient air saturated with water vapor is less effective than dry air for evaporative cooling.

- Utilize the building surrounds and plantings to cool the area around the building.
- Structures raised above the ground provide ventilation below the structure and reduce moisture from entering the structure from the ground.
- Employ moisture barriers between the building envelope and the ground.
- Buildings designed as detached units with space around the exterior of the building allows the building envelope to radiate excess heat instead of retaining it.
- Design buildings configured as a long thin floor plan to facilitate cross ventilation.
- Tall floor to ceiling dimensions provides space for hot air to rise above living areas and facilitates stack effect ventilation.

- Courtyards, breezeways, deep verandas, and other outdoor shaded areas may provide cooler air supply for natural ventilation.
- Recessed courtyards allow cold air to sink
- Design roof structures that shade all building elevations.
- Utilize light colors for roof finishes to reflect solar radiation.
- Design roof structures that insulate and ventilate. Consider a double roof/fly roof structure
- Shield all opening in the building envelope from the sun. Locate shielding shade based on the seasonal sun path.
- Highly insulate the building envelope for all conditioned spaces.
- Design building spaces that are not conditioned with highly permeable material to encourage natural ventilation and airflow when the interior dew point is lower than the exterior dew point.
- Employ thermal buffer spaces when planning the interior of the building.
- Locate functions that produce unwanted heat in remote or external locations.
- Relatively high WWR (window to wall ratio)
- Shade windows to minimize exposure to solar radiation. Western exposure glazing must be shaded from direct sun.
- Specify window glazing with low light transmission and high insulation properties to avoid ambient or conducted heat gain or cooling loss.
- Design exterior window shading that also protects from precipitation allowing windows to remain open during rain showers.
- Locate smaller low windows on the windward side of the building and larger windows on the leeward side of the building and roof openings to facilitate ventilation.
- Design ventilation paths to direct air currents across occupant skin.

Continental/cold climates

Cold climates have seasons with extreme seasonal changes. Summers are short with mild to warm temperatures. Winters are cold with harsh weather conditions. Effective passive design strategies in continental cold climates that both resist heat loss and promote heat gain based on the season.

- Optimize building orientation to protect against harsh winds and maximize solar gain. East-west orientation provides opportunities for heat gain and daylighting.
- Use topography, vegetation, and landscape, to shelter the building exterior from harsh winds.
- Buildings organized in clusters minimize exposure to cold winds.
- Open spaces between buildings should be positioned and finished to reflect solar rays on to the building during cold months.
- Minimize building envelope surface to limit heat loss.
- Maximize building envelope insulation to keep warm air inside the building.
- Consider a multilevel compact form with solar access to most if not all spaces.
- Use building materials that have quick heat gain and release heat slowly.
- Color building exterior exposed to the sun in cold months dark colors to absorb solar radiation.
- Tightly seal all aspects of the building envelope.
- Slope roof structure to shed snowfall and accommodate added load and drainage requirements for snow and ice.
- Lower ceilings minimize heating requirements.
- Size and locate operable windows to maximize solar heat gain opportunities and minimize heat loss through glazing.

- Utilize window glazing with low levels of temperature transfer and windows with high insulation values. Consider multilayer glazing.
- Provide solar shading on equator-facing elevation and multilayer glazed windows.
- Adjustable shading is required on west-facing windows to control afternoon heat gain.
- Space plan the building interior to maximize distribution of solar heat gain where required and minimize drafts from convective air movement.
- Integrate buffer and sunspaces into the space plan.
- Use convective air movement to maintain a consistent temperature and distribute warm air through and around the interior spaces.
- Employ night cooling or night purge of excess heat.
- Use cross ventilation for warm season passive cooling.
- Reduce the velocity of interior air currents during cold months to retain heat.

Temperate climates

This climate has the most diverse climate conditions. A temperate climate has four distinct seasons. Summer and winter conditions are often beyond building occupant thermal comfort levels. It is likely that multiple passive design strategies will be required to meet building occupant thermal comfort levels during different seasons. Careful site analysis and research will identify specific conditions that provide opportunities or require intervention. Evaluate the tradeoffs and synergies of passive design strategies for each season.

- Maximize building envelope insulation to keep conditioned air inside the building.
- Optimize building orientation to maximize solar gain. East-west orientation provides opportunities for heat gain and daylighting.
- Use topography, vegetation, and landscape, to shelter the building exterior from harsh winds.
- Roof spaces may serve as thermal buffer zones when ventilated in the summer and sealed in the winter.
- Buildings organized in clusters minimize exposure to cold winds.
- Open spaces between buildings should be positioned and finished to reflect solar rays on to the building during cold months.
- Passive solar heating is key to achieving thermal comfort in cold seasons.
- The sun altitude can vary significantly requiring tradeoffs between daylighting strategies and passive heating and cooling strategies.
- Carefully size and position windows for ventilation and solar heat gain.
- Multiple passive cooling and natural ventilation strategies are required, depending on the local wind consistency and pattern.
- Use cross ventilation and convective ventilation to move air through and around the interior spaces for passive cooling in warm seasons and natural ventilation.
- Shaded courtyards, gardens areas, and landscape with water features cool the low-level air on the windward elevation before drawing it into the house.

Passive Design Strategies in Macro Context

At the global scale, rating systems play a huge role in determining the need for energy-efficient strategies. Passive design strategies are extremely energy efficient in that they require no fossil fuel energy expenditure. When passive strategies cannot fulfill the entire need, they can still serve as a support for mechanical systems. Mechanical systems can be smaller when used in tandem with passive systems, thereby lowering the volume of fossil fuels consumed and CO_2 emissions produced.

Building orientation optimized for passive design strategies may not align with the typical regional or neighborhood configuration of buildings. Rural and suburban buildings are often in a more open context, positioned on large sites surrounded by parking lots, which may allow the building to rotate to face the sun. In urban conditions, the orientation, shape, and massing of a building are more constrained. It is not uncommon in an urban context for passive strategies to require an original and clever application to mitigate and adapt to conflicting conditions of the prescribed building orientation and site. See Chapter 12, "Beyond the Basics," to learn more about how to address this challenge.

PASSIVE SOLAR HEATING

Passive solar heating (Figure 6.1) captures free and natural energy from the sun for heat. The goals of passive heating are simple: Meet the needs of human comfort while reducing the fossil-fuel required to generate heat through a mechanical heating system.

Passive heating necessitates the weighing both potential synergies and tradeoffs before determining the appropriate strategy. Strategies that allow solar radiation to enter the building are synergistic with many daylighting strategies. In temperate and cold climates strategies used to gain heat in cold seasons may generate excess heat in the warmer seasons creating a need for air conditioning, potentially creating a tradeoff. Overheating can be mitigated by using appropriate shade and ventilation strategies. The most effective passive heating strategies utilize the previously

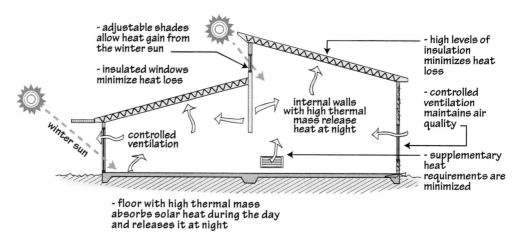

Figure 6.1 Introduction to passive solar heating. Passive heating is a vehicle to reduce carbon emissions. Passive heating supports the fight against global warming while reducing building operations and maintenance costs. However, passive heating is a challenging strategy to understand and master.

Source: Sharon B. Jaffe

addressed building design approaches: building massing, building shape, building orientation, window to wall ratio (WWR), and building envelope.

- Maximize windows facing the equator using an east-west building orientation, consider WWR (window area to wall area ratio). Too high a WWR can result in too much light entering the building, creating uncomfortable daylighting glare.
- Maximize controlled solar access.
- Direct heat gain to thermal mass.
- Minimize windows facing away from the equator to reduce unwanted heat loss.
- Minimize east- and west-facing windows to prevent glare and unwanted heat gain from the varied angles of the sun that may create unwanted summer heat gain and glare.
- Select windows that are appropriately rated for each exposure.
- Increase levels of insulation in building envelope to retain heat.
- Minimize air infiltration.

Key Terms

Heat transfer is the flow of heat flows from hot to cold materials or objects until reaching parity.

Radiation is heat transfer between objects that are not in contact with one another. Energy, in the form of heat, is emitted from a heat source.

Convection is the transfer of heat energy through the air. As air is warmed it becomes less dense, hence lighter; as the air rises away from the warming source it cools, becoming denser, and sinks. This process sets up a cycle of air movement. Hot air rises, cold air drops. This process is the basis of the stack effect discussed later in this book.

Conduction transfers heat through direct contact with an object. An example of conduction heat is a pot heated by placing it on an electric stove coil burner. Two objects at different temperatures in physical contact will transfer heat from the warmer object to the colder object until reaching a uniform temperature.

Sensible heat is heat from sun, lights, equipment, and people.

Latent transfer. Moisture from ventilation air, perspiration and respiration, and cooking vapors

Diurnal variation of temperature is the variation from high to low temperature during the same day.

Passive heating strategies may complement the previously well thought out building design decisions that provide heat gain in desired places and block heat in others (see "Passive solar heating strategies: options and considerations").

Passive solar heating strategies: Options and considerations

Passive heating uses the available solar energy from the sun and natural occuring air movement to maintain comfortable temperatures without mechanical assistance. Passive heating requires good solar exposure that is dependent on building location and orientation. Effective passive heating works with the microclimate, site elements such as shade trees and windbreaks, and is interwoven with effctive building envelope design. Simple systems collect, store, and release, solar energy in response to amibient conditions without elaborate, technology based, controls.

Direct solar heat gain is supplied by the radiant energy of the sun. Spaces that are warmed act as the solar collection, storage, and distribution systems. Determine the amount of direct solar gain available at a specific location. Solar energy enters the space through glazing, falling directly and indirectly on thermal mass. (See Figure 6.2, Direct solar heat gain)

Place and size windows to optimize direct solar gain in cold weather seasons. Window glazing area for direct heat gain should range between 7%-12% of the floor area. Shade is required to block heat gain in hot weather seasons.

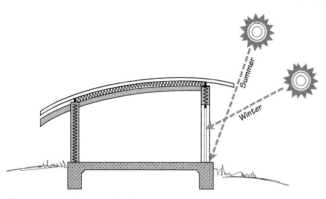

Advantages
- Energy saving
- Cooling

Disadvantages
- Potential overheating
- Overlighting/glare

Synergies
- Thermal mass
- Daylight

Tradeoffs
- Cooling
- Finish constraints

Figure 6.2 Direct solar heat gain
Source: Sharon B. Jaffe

Sunspaces are glazed spaces, outside of the programmed occupied space of the building envelope. Sunspaces directly face the sun to serve as heat buffers and/or heat collection spaces that may provide warm air to the rest of the building. Sunspaces generally are not conditioned space; sunspaces are intermediary space that serve as an additional layer of separation from exterior conditions. An atrium, conservatory or vestibule may serve as a sunspace. Sunspace glazing should be vertical. Sloped glazing may result in overheating. Pair each square foot of direct sun-facing glass with 3 square feet of 4-inch-thick masonry thermal mass for effective solar heat gain storage.

Sunspaces may support passive heating strategies by naturally warming air through direct heat gain. That pre-warmed air can flow into adjoining spaces via operable vents at the top of the common wall, often a trombe wall. Cool air is returned from main building spaces through vents in the lower portion of the common wall to be heated in the sunspace. This arrangement creates a conductive loop. In very cold climates consider glazing that reduces conductive heat loss during the day and nighttime insulation. (See Figure 6.3, Sunspaces and solar heat gain)

In warm weather seasons, sunspaces may need additional integral shading designed to prevent overheating.

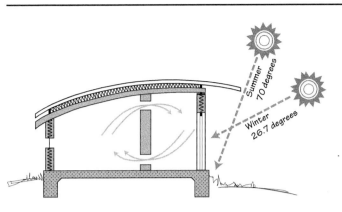

Advantages
- Energy conservation

Disadvantages
- Potential overheating
- Potential inefficiencies
- Over lighting/glare
- May be drafty

Synergies
- Thermal mass
- Daylight

Tradeoffs
- Cooling
- Additional enclosed space
- Direct view

Figure 6.3 Sunspaces and solar heat gain
Source: Sharon B. Jaffe

Thermal mass refers to high-density materials, such as masonry and water, that act as the solar collection, storage, and distribution systems. Ideal materials for thermal mass are dense and heavy to absorb and hold heat, are good heat conductors and will release stored heat slowly as the ambient temperature drops. Thermal mass distributes the solar heat from where it is collected and stored to the building by convection, conduction, and radiation. (See Figure 6.4, Thermal mass and solar heat gain)

Slabs that serve as thermal mass floors must be insulated under and around the edge of the slab to prevent unwanted heat transfer to adjacent materials, surfaces or spaces. Do not cover thermal mass floors with carpet or rugs. Covering the thermal mass will reduce the ability of the floor to absorb heat. External or Internal walls can be used as thermal mass walls (brick, concrete block) when they are in direct sunlight or near a radiant heat source. External walls used for thermal mass must be insulated on the exterior and exposed on the interior building. Rules of thumb suggests the thickness of a floor slab or wall equal four to eight inches and the area of thermal mass be equal to six times the glazing that receives direct sunlight. Dark colored surfaces collect the greatest amount of solar radiation. Look for a low SRI for greater solar radiation absorptance. Thermal mass is most effective in climates with temperature swings of 50°F from day to night. Thermal mass prevents rapid temperature fluctuations.

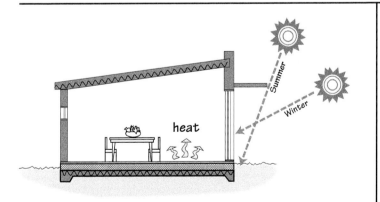

Advantages
- Energy saving
- Supports cooling with high diurnal temperature fluctuation
- Reduces interior temperature fluctuations
- Delayed heat transfer

Disadvantages
- Heat is absorbed until mass and air reach parity
- Slower heat distribution

Synergy
- Daylight

Tradeoffs
- Cooling
- Finish constraints

Figure 6.4 Thermal mass and solar heat gain
Source: Sharon B. Jaffe

Buffer spaces create an insulation layer of spaces between the building envelope and interior conditioned space. Spaces with low energy requirements such as storage, utility, restrooms, etc. and rooms that produce an internal heat load like kitchens, may be grouped on the side of the building farthest from the equator. In the northern hemisphere, this is the north side of the building. These service spaces buffer the overall building thermal loads reducing the heat loss without interrupting solar access. Evergreen trees and landscape planted on the north and west sides of the building will buffer the interior from the cold north and potential overheating from the western sun. (See Figure 6.5, Buffer spaces and solar heat gain)

cold winds

Figure 6.5 Buffer spaces and solar heat gain
Source: Sharon B. Jaffe

Advantages
- Reduces energy requirements
- Reduces temperature transfer through building envelope
- Reduces interior temperature fluctuations
- Solar shading
- Reduces exterior noise infiltration

Disadvantages
- May increase total building area
- Slower heat distribution

Synergies
- Trombe wall
- Double ventilated facade

Tradeoffs
- Direct view
- Natural ventilation

A **Trombe wall** facilitates indirect solar gain and thermal mass heat storage. Trombe walls are positioned directly in the path of solar radiation/sunlight. A Trombe wall is a glass-faced 8 to 12-inch-thick thermal mass wall that is a dark heat absorbing color and generally a foot or thicker. The glazing is set off the Trombe wall 1"– 6" creating an air space that traps the radiant heat holding it close to, and further warming, the thermal mass. Water is a very effective heat sink and can retain approximately 5x the heat than concrete. Solar energy/heat that is absorbed and stored in the trombe wall will be slowly released over time to the occupied space(s) reducing day to night temperature fluctuations. A Trombe wall is most effective in climates with temperature swings of 50°F from day to night. A passive heating strategy, Trombe Wall depends on the synergy between indirect heat gain, thermal mass, radiant heat, and appropriate glazing properties to maximize efficiency. In very cold climates glazing that reduces conductive heat loss during the day and night time insulation may be appropriate. (See Figure 6.6, Trombe wall and solar heat gain)

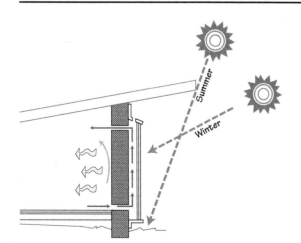

Summer

Winter

Figure 6.6 Tombe wall and solar heat gain
Source: Sharon B. Jaffe

Advantages
- Energy saving
- Supports cooling with high diurnal temperature fluctuation
- Reduces interior temperature fluctuations
- Delayed heat transfer

Disadvantages
- Heat is absorbed until mass and air reach parity
- Slower heat distribution

Synergy
- Cooling

Tradeoffs
- Daylighting
- Finish constraints

A **double skin façade** (Figure 6.7) is a two layers façade system spaced to create an air space between the two layers. The outer layer of glazing provides an opportunity for solar radiation to heat air in the cavity between the interior building envelope and the outer face glazing layer. The heated air rises and is either released to the outside from vents at the top of the façade or is released into the interior of the building through vents in the interior layer depending upon the seasonal need.

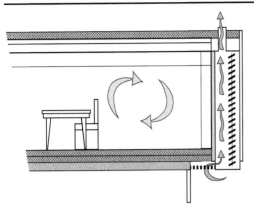

Advantages
- Energy saving
- High insulation value
- Optimized shading reduces cooling load

Disadvantages
- Higher initial capital cost
- Higher WWR

Synergies
- Insulation
- Thermal mass
- External shading

Figure 6.7 Double skin facade and solar heat gain
Source: Sharon B. Jaffe

Microclimate

At the microclimate scale, it is essential to orient the building toward the equator; in the northern hemisphere, orient the building to have direct access to the southern sun. Shading from trees and other buildings will block attempts to gain heat. The building location step should have addressed this, but sometimes the realities of a project do not permit for the solar orientation or access desired.

Passive heating can also occur outdoors. Outdoor spaces that are sheltered by the landscape, building, or vegetation, are often utilized as a warmer microclimate. When the sun falls directly on pavers, natural stone, or another hardscape, the thick, solid surface functions as thermal mass, absorbing and storing the heat from the sun, then releasing the stored heat to warm cooler ambient air. The heat released from the thermal mass of the hardscape warms the microclimate, making it a comfortable place to sit and enjoy on all but the coldest days.

Figure 6.8 illustrates a building with a central exterior courtyard buffered from cold north winds by the building structure. The courtyard is open to the south sun. Ground pavers functioning as thermal mass absorb direct heat gain from the sun. This warm microclimate will add to the buildings general thermal comfort, create a protected, welcoming, and warm outdoor area while adding a nominal amount of heat to the south side of the building.

Design Objectives and Design Ideas

The four perspectives will drive significant exploration of passive heating opportunities. Table 6.1 illustrates possible cold climate design objectives from the four perspectives and design ideas that respond to those objectives. Many variations of design ideas may require exploration to thoroughly address the design objectives. Enter the final design idea from each of the four perspectives into the design

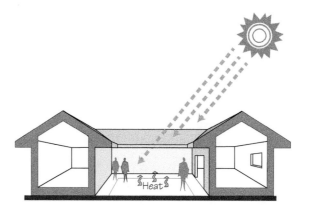

Figure 6.8 Passive solar heating/microclimate
Source: Sharon B. Jaffe

decision matrix. After fully exploring all of the four perspectives, evaluate and prioritize the design ideas and determine which takes precedence based on project guiding principles and client priorities.

Design Priorities

All of the design ideas in Table 6.1 have merit. The guiding principles, goals, benchmarks and other precedent research state which design ideas are most important to the project at hand.

A client interested in providing building occupants with outdoor access may prioritize the experience perspective that creates a south-facing wind-sheltered outdoor area that provides a comfortable outdoor temperature extending use beyond traditional seasons. Local conditions and features specific to the building along with the design decision matrix will help prioritize the most appropriate design approach.

TABLE 6.1 PASSIVE SOLAR HEATING, DESIGN OBJECTIVES AND DESIGN IDEAS

Perspective	Design Objective	Design Idea
Performance	Collect as much passive heat as possible to reduce the need for active mechanical heating	Use glazing angled to catch winter sun angles combined with thermal mass floor and trombe wall.

TABLE 6.1 (CONTINUED)

Perspective	Design Objective	Design Idea
Systems	Create a winter garden micro climate that collects heat in the winter.	Use a central atrium with thermal mass floor to gather heat in the winter.
Culture	Encourage connections to surrounding community using local architecture roof form and materials. Connect indoor and outdoor spaces that facilitates heat gain on the south façade for building users to enjoy.	Pergola with deciduous flowering vines over a stone veranda create an outdoor space for summer. Connecting corridor that runs along south facade acts as a buffer space from exterior veranda to interior spaces.
Experience	Provide outdoor space for four-season use, even on cold yet mild days.	Central open courtyard with thermal mass floor. Glazing positioned to maximize solar gain in winter with horizontal shade to block heat gain in summer.

Source: Sharon B. Jaffe

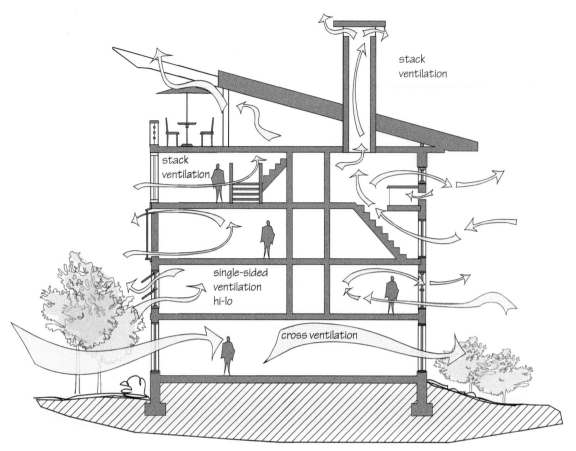

Figure 6.9 Passive cooling and natural ventilation
Source: Sharon B. Jaffe

Synergies and Tradeoffs

Passive heating strategies frequently will have conflicts with daylighting, passive cooling, and natural ventilation design objectives and ideas (Figure 6.9). Ultimately the guiding principles and project priorities drive required compromise.

PASSIVE COOLING AND NATURAL VENTILATION

"The most effective method to lessen energy use for mechanical cooling is to eliminate the need for it through climate-adapted design" (Kwok and Grondzik, 2011, p. 137). Passive cooling limits heat gain and uses free and natural wind for ventilation to dissipate heat through convection and increase occupant perception of thermal comfort through evaporation. The goals of passive cooling are similar to passive heating: meet the needs of human comfort while reducing the fossil-fuel required to cool the space through the use of a mechanical system.

Passive cooling and natural ventilation reduce the need for fossil-fuel-based mechanical HVAC systems to provide cooling and air circulation. Carbon emissions are reduced, supporting the fight against global warming while reducing building operations and maintenance costs.

Passive cooling and natural ventilation strategies present both potential synergies and tradeoffs with daylighting and heating. Strategies that allow solar radiation to enter the building are synergistic with many daylighting strategies. In temperate and cold climates, passive heat gain strategies used in cold seasons may generate excess heat in the warmer seasons creating a need for air conditioning, potentially creating a tradeoff. Ventilation and shade may be necessary during warm seasons to prevent overheating. The most effective passive cooling and ventilation strategies involve design strategies previously addressed: building massing, building shape, building orientation, window to wall ratio (WWR), and the building envelope. For instance:

- Orient the building to maximize openings for natural ventilation.
- Position openings on opposite sides of the building to facilitate cross ventilation.
- Consider window to wall ratios (WWR). High WWR may result in unwanted heat gain, increasing cooling loads.
- Window size, placement, and rating are selected to correspond with building exposure.
- Integrate exterior horizontal shade into the design for windows facing the equator; this blocks direct sunlight and unwanted heat gain, yet allows indirect sunlight to enter for daylighting.
- Minimize east- and west-facing windows to prevent glare and unwanted heat gain from the varied angles of the sun. If required, use vertical fins to block solar heat gain.
- Utilize an open space plan to facilitate cross ventilation.
- Incorporate high levels of insulation into the building envelope to retain cold air and reduce heat transfer.
- Minimize air infiltration with a tightly sealed building envelope.

Key Terms

Ventilation is the movement of fresh air into and through an area. Ventilation significantly impacts indoor air quality, temperature, and humidity levels. Air movement in a building greatly influences an occupant's perception of thermal comfort.

Convective air flow is the movement of air as a result of air pressure differences between one part of the building to another. Warm air is less dense than cool or cold air due to the tendency of warm air to expand. Warm air will rise. Cold air contracts, becoming denser and dropping to lower areas of the building. This effect is also known as the stack effect. The cold air sinking and hot air rising create air currents of circulation.

Bernoulli's principle of differential pressure relates to passive ventilation. Differences in wind speed and air pressure generate air movement. As air moves faster, the air pressure drops. Outdoor breezes, high above the various ground elements, have fewer obstructions, allowing it to move faster, and so has lower air pressure. Lower air pressure passively draws fresh air into and circulating through the building. This principle requires a significant difference in height between air inlets and outlets. There can be no obstructions between the two.

The *Venturi effect* is created by a natural tendency for air to equalize pressure across two zones. The creation of a positive (high) pressure air zone and a negative (low) pressure air zone can increase airflow through a building creating a cooling effect.

Evaporative cooling is when liquids change to gas when heated through the process of evaporation. When water evaporates, it absorbs heat and produces a cooling effect. Water features such as fountains or ponds in a courtyard provide passive cooling, acting as heat sinks absorbing some of the heat from the air as it passes over the surface of the water, thereby lowering the temperature and increasing the humidity of the air.

People experience both evaporative and convection cooling through perspiration. As an individual perspires, the perspiration absorbs heat from the body as it changes from fluid to gas through evaporation. As perspiration and air move across the skin, heat is transferred through convection from the body to the air cooling the body surface.

Convection cooling transfers heat through the air. As air is warmed it becomes less dense, hence lighter, as the air rises away from the warming source it cools, becoming denser, and sinking. Hot air rises cold air drops. This process sets up a cycle of air movement and is the basis of the stack effect.

Radiant cooling is the transfer of heat via interior building surfaces (floor, ceiling, or wall). A pipe system is circulating cooled water, or a water mix is embedded into the surface of a mass. The cooled building surface absorbs the heat from the rest of the room, cooling by radiation and convection. Ceiling-based radiant cooling systems have the advantage of gravity and physics. Hot air rises while cold air sinks.

Thermal emittance is the measure of a material's ability to release heat it has absorbed.

Solar reflectance measures the solar energy that is reflected away from a surface. It is expressed as a fraction of the total solar energy.

Key Metrics

The effectiveness of passive cooling and ventilation strategies is influenced by a variety of factors and can be evaluated by a number of criteria.

Distance of building occupants from an operable window

PPD: Percentage of people in discomfort

ACH: Air changes per hour. Air change rate is a crucial aspect of ventilation and indoor air quality. Air changes with the supply of clean, fresh air, and the removal of stale humid air. Air change rate also impacts building interior temperature control. Code and best practice standards regulate specific air change rates in buildings.

EUI: Energy use intensity. Often expressed per square foot per year, EUI divides one year of building energy consumption by the total building square footage. Sustainable buildings often use EUI as an essential benchmark to establish targets for a design project and a metric for comparison with other similar buildings to determine relative efficiency. Natural ventilation and passive cooling can replace the need for active ventilation and air conditioning, thereby saving energy and reducing the total energy consumption of the building.

SRI: Solar reflectance index measures the ability of a surface to radiate solar heat by reflection. The index range is 0–100. The higher an index number, the lower the surface temperature. Material with a high SRI can reduce solar gain into the building.

These passive cooling and natural ventilation strategies may support the previously well-considered building design decisions that reduce heat gain and facilitate ventilation. Some may pose conflicts with previous building design decisions, thereby requiring careful evaluation.

Passive cooling and natural ventilation strategies: Options and considerations

OPERABLE WINDOWS

It might seem odd that something as simple as operable windows is a "strategy." However, today, many buildings are designed only with fixed windows, denying occupants natural ventilation, and the sounds and smell of outdoors. Different types of windows (Figure 6.10) have varied characteristics relative to ventilation, acoustics, and weather protection. Long horizontal strip windows ventilate a space more evenly.

- Tall windows that open at top and bottom can use convection and outside breezes. They vent hot air out from the top of the room and draw fresh, cooler air in the bottom.
- Windows provide building occupants control of their environment, increasing the occupant satisfaction.
- Clerestory windows are located at or near the roof line and can help vent hot air from the top of the room or building facilitating convection ventilation.
- A transom is a window over a door opening allowing air and light to circulate even when visual privacy is desirable.
- Rule of thumb: Operable windows/louvers should be 20 percent of the floor area, with the inlet size roughly matching the outlet.
- A smaller inlet paired with a larger outlet can increase air movement velocity.

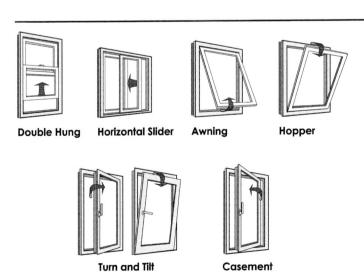

Double Hung   Horizontal Slider   Awning   Hopper

Turn and Tilt   Casement

Figure 6.10 Passive cooling: windows

Source: Sharon B. Jaffe

Advantages
- Source for natural ventilation
- Fresh air = increased productivity
- Occupant self-determination

Disadvantages
- Occupant control of thermal envelope
- Leak conditioned air

Synergies
- Ventilation and cooling are interdependent
- Support daylighting strategies
- Interior planning

Tradeoff
- Passive heat gain

BUILDING VOIDS

Courtyards, atriums, and light wells are all vertical spaces that are exposed to the sky even while located within the building's footprint. Creating a void in the overall building mass (Figure 6.11) provides additional perimeter wall surface facilitating passive cooling and ventilation.

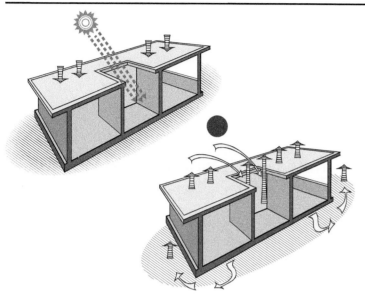

Advantages
- Increases cross ventilation opportunities
- Increases cross daylight opportunities
- Can cool warm air and warm cold air
- Shelters building from heat and cold
- Shelters building from high winds

Disadvantage
- Additional square footage required but not maximized

Synergies
- Evaporative cooling
- Daylighting
- Night flushing

Tradeoffs
- Building skin to volume ratio
- Passive heating

Figure 6.11 Passive cooling: building void
Source: Sharon B. Jaffe

CROSS VENTILATION

Cross ventilation (Figure 6.12) uses naturally occurring cool wind or breeze and changing air temperatures to move air through the building. Wind from the windward facade creates positive pressure entering the building through an inlet window (or other intakes) as it moves through the space absorbing the warm interior air, lowering air pressure and exiting through an outlet window (or other outlets) on the leeward side.

- Locate large openings on both windward and leeward faces with inlets at higher pressure zones.
- Offset windward inlets and leeward outlets, rather than locating them directly across from one another, to better distribute air flow.
- Placing inlets low in the space and larger outlets high in the space creates air currents through active occupant zones to support evaporative cooling effects.

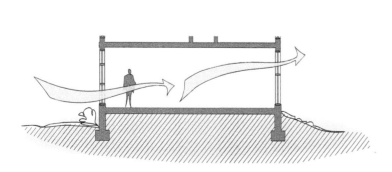

Advantages
- Passive cooling and natural ventilation reduces the need for mechanical systems, reducing energy consumption

Disadvantages
- Precipitation
- Intake of fresh air can introduce noise, dust, allergens, or pollutants

Synergies
- Daylight
- Views

Tradeoff
- Heating

Figure 6.12 Passive cooling: cross ventilation
Source: Sharon B. Jaffe

STACK EFFECT

The stack effect (Figure 6.13) uses a combination of convection techniques: Bernoulli's principle and the Venturi effect to ventilate a building. Air moves as a result of the difference in air pressure. Air pressure varies due to temperature and moisture differences through the building. Warm air rises through the building to escape through a high window or roof vent. To reduce the pressure at the base of the building, more cool air is drawn through low inlets creating air circulation.

SOLAR (THERMAL) CHIMNEY

A solar or thermal chimney uses basic convection principles. A chimney, or an air shaft, is built with solar orientation and a finish that maximize solar radiation/heat gain on the equator side of the building. As the chimney absorbs solar radiation, it warms the air inside the chimney. This process begins a convection cycle. When the air cools, it is once again pulled back into the chimney. During cold seasons when heat is required, vents at the top of the chimney are closed, forcing the warm air into the building. During warm seasons the top vent is opened, allowing the warmed air to exit the top of the chimney, pulling new air from outside into the building's lower inlets and circulating it through the building.

Architects and builders have used these strategies to provide cooling without mechanical means for centuries. The strategies are manifestations of simple physics. Warm air rises, cold air sinks. Both strategies – the stack effect and the solar chimney – work together to move air through the building, providing valuable cooling, ventilation, and energy savings.

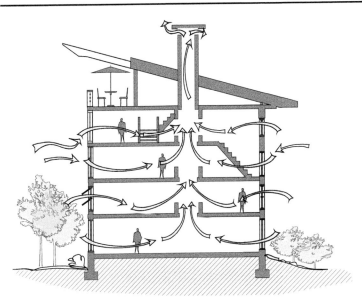

Figure 6.13 Passive cooling: stack effect

Source: Sharon B. Jaffe

Advantages
- Does not require natural wind to ventilate; utilizes the air pressure differential
- Uses gravity and temperature; no mechanical system required

Disadvantages
- Rarely controls temperature completely; usually utilized as an assisting system
- Intake of fresh air can introduce dust, allergens, or pollutants.

Synergies
- Massing and orientation
- Window size and location
- Roof monitor

Tradeoff
- Potential heat loss in cold season

DOUBLE SKIN FACADE (DSF)

This is an external layer of glazing that creates a second skin over a building envelope (Figure 6.14). The second layer of glass provides the opportunity for solar radiation to heat air in the cavity or corridor between the building envelope and the glazing. The heated air rises and is either released to the outside from vents at the top of the facade convection to warm the interior of the building by releasing heated air through vents in the interior layer, similar to a solar chimney. The air cavity between the double facade can also function as a corridor buffer space, with fresh air intake and exhaust that facilitates natural ventilation. Shading methods, either exterior or the interior between the two facade layers, can control solar heat gain that, uncontrolled, would require mechanical ventilation and cooling systems. Most commonly used in temperate climates.

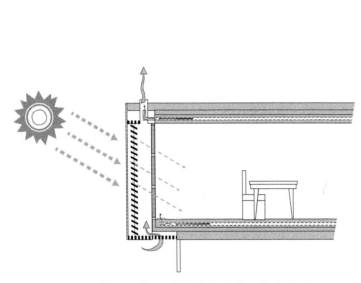

Advantages
- Maximizes daylight opportunities
- Secondary glass skin lowers wind load and allows fresh air supply to be regulated
- Second glazed skin and airspace provide acoustic insulation from exterior noise.
- Preheats supply air for natural ventilation

Disadvantages
- The potential for overheating air between layers of glazing inhibiting natural ventilation
- Potential for condensation
- Noise travel between adjacent spaces reflected by second glazing layer
- Significant additional cost

Synergies
- Daylight
- Ventilation
- Passive heating

Tradeoff
- Cooling

Figure 6.14 Passive cooling: double skin facade (DSF)
Source: Sharon B. Jaffe

ROOF VENTING

Ridge vents (Figure 6.15), cupolas, and roof monitors, facilitate passive ventilation and cooling utilizing the stack effect. Venting located high in the roof allows air movement to escape through the top of the building, accelerating the rate of air movement in the building. This increased convective flow facilitates cooling of the building, improving occupant thermal comfort and satisfaction.

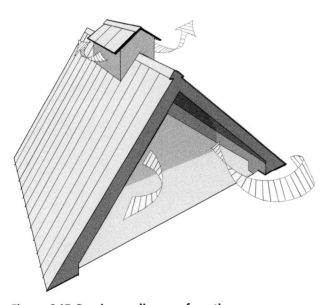

Advantages
- Stack effect venting
- Roof monitors with operable windows facilitate natural ventilation and daylighting

Disadvantages
- A roof may be compromised for solar photovoltaic arrays by shade from larger venting structure, limiting the available area to generate energy.

Synergies
- Daylight
- Stack effect
- Cool roof

Tradeoff
- Potential heat loss in cold season

Figure 6.15 Passive cooling: roof venting
Source: Sharon B. Jaffe

COOL ROOF/ROOF MATERIAL/COLOR

A cool roof (Figure 6.16) minimizes solar absorption and maximizes thermal emittance. The material and color of a roof can impact the ability of a building to reflect heat and thereby cool itself without the use of mechanical air conditioning, thereby saving energy, building operation costs and reducing greenhouse gas emissions. "Albedo" indicates the total reflectance of a specific roof system; emittance is the ability to radiate heat; and solar reflectance is the ability to reflect sunlight. Together, these three characteristics are good indicators of a roof's ability to stay cool, which, in turn, helps keep the interior of the building cool. Most impactful for buildings in climates where the cooling load is greater than the heating load. A cool roof helps reduce the citywide summer temperatures, which rise due to a preponderance of hard heat absorbing materials, also known as the urban heat island effect.

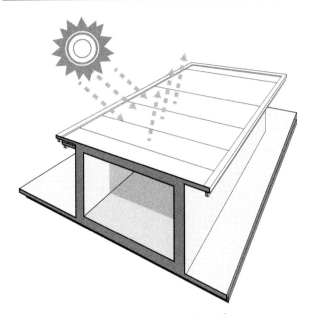

Advantages
- Reduce interior cooling requirement saving energy and money
- Increased interior thermal comfort
- Cooler outside air, reducing urban heat island effect

Disadvantage
- Increased cold weather heating requirement. A cool roof will absorb less solar radiation in the winter as well as the summer. Typically, in warm climates, the reduced heat from a cool roof is less of a burden than the increased need for cooling due to traditional dark roofing.

Synergies
- Natural ventilation and passive cooling
- High thermal insulation
- Daylighting top light strategies

Tradeoff
- Desirable heat gain in cold seasons

Figure 6.16 Passive cooling: cool roof
Source: Sharon B. Jaffe

VEGETATIVE ROOF

Also called an *extensive green roof*, a vegetative roof (Figure 6.17) absorbs solar radiation (heat). The vegetation and soil, or growth medium, release moisture as temperatures rise. The water is then released back into the atmosphere as water vapor latent heat transfer, also known as evapotranspiration. Evapotranspiration is as effective than high albedo roofing, if not more so.

EARTH TUBES

Also called earth-air heat exchangers, earth tubes (Figure 6.18) gather fresh air from a remote location away from the buildings and brings that air through a tube buried in the earth below the frost line, where a consistent 55°F degree temperature cools the air. Cooling/heating capacity is due to a temperature difference between air and soil. Most effective in dry climates with extreme heat or cold temperatures.

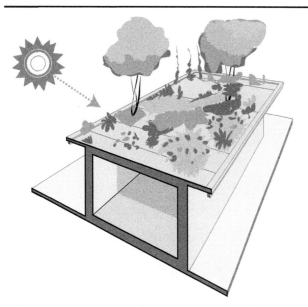

Figure 6.17 Passive cooling: vegetative roof
Source: Sharon B. Jaffe

Advantages
- Supportive of other passive and active cooling technologies
- Increased Insulation
- Synergistic with other passive strategies
- Reduces rainwater run off
- Reduces urban heat island effect

Disadvantages
- Building structure must be designed to support the potential additional load
- Expense
- Ongoing maintenance

Synergy
- High levels of insulation

Tradeoff
- Limits rainwater harvest quantity and quality

Figure 6.18 Passive cooling: earth tubes
Source: Sharon B. Jaffe

Advantages
- Constant earth temperature
- Minimal low-tech equipment
- Low operational cost

Disadvantages
- Initial installation cost
- Access to tubes for maintenance
- Pest/vermin/allergens/dirt
- Climate-dependent

Synergies
- Convection cooling
- Solar chimneys

Tradeoff
- Soil excavation may impact habitat

CHILLED BEAM

A chilled beam (Figure 6.19) uses water pumped through metal cooling coils surrounded by fins that cool air by convection. Naturally rising warm air is cooled by the chilled beams. A chilled ceiling slab is synergistic with convective air flow. Most effective in hot, dry climates.

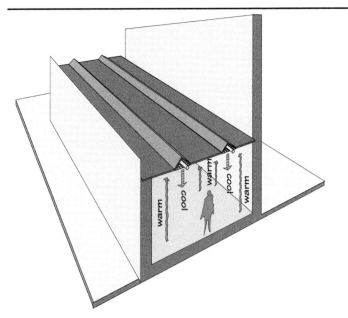

Advantages
- Quiet; no moving parts
- No large mechanical room required
- Can be evenly placed for proper distribution
- Lower energy consumption than traditional cooling systems
- Slab floor moderate diurnal temperature swings
- Structurally integrated
- Radiant cooling removes sensible heat

Disadvantages
- More expensive than traditional systems
- Potential for condensation and increased humidity

Synergies
- Natural ventilation
- High ceilings
- Convection airflow
- Roof monitors

Figure 6.19 Passive cooling: chilled beam
Source: Sharon B. Jaffe

EVAPORATIVE COOLING

Evaporative cooling (Figure 6.20) can be used to cool buildings in relatively dry hot climates. When water evaporates, it absorbs heat, producing a cooling effect. Water features, such as fountains in courtyards, or a pond near a building or on a building roof, will produce a cooling effect on surrounding air as the water evaporates. *Misters* create a fine water mist that almost instantly evaporates into the air, producing a cooling effect. Evaporative cooling is most successful in hot, dry climates, where adding humidity to the air is beneficial, and the ambient dry air facilitates efficient evaporation.

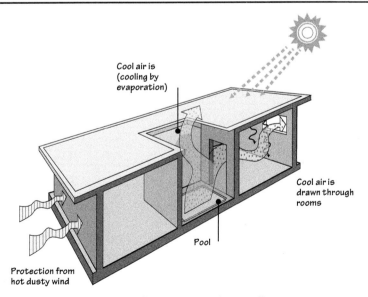

Advantages
- Simple and inexpensive
- Supplies needed humidity in dry climates
- Water feature aesthetics

Disadvantages
- Ineffective in humid climates
- Ineffective in rain
- The potential for bacteria and insects
- Requires water supply
- Require ventilation, no breeze = no cooling

Synergy
- Natural ventilation

Tradeoff
- Water required to function

Figure 6.20 Passive cooling: evaporative cooling
Source: Sharon B. Jaffe

THERMAL MASS WITH NIGHT-TIME PURGING OR FLUSHING

This is effective when daytime outside air temperatures are too warm to cool building occupants, but night time ambient air temperatures are much cooler (Figure 6.21).

Thermal mass combined with ventilation is a passive cooling strategy. During the day, a thermal mass of substantial size and density is needed to act as a heat sink to absorbs and store heat ambient air temperature. Thermal mass is located so cool evening breezes will cross the surface removing stored heat from the day, releasing it into the cooler night air. This strategy is most effective in climates with significant diurnal temperature variation for buildings that are occupied during the day but not at night. Thermal mass with nighttime purging evens out the peaks and dips of ambient temperatures.

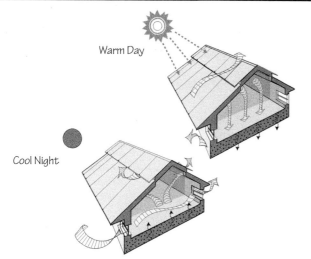

Warm Day

Cool Night

Advantages
- Even out diurnal temperature fluctuation
- Minimal resources required

Disadvantages
- Material and finish constraints
- Climate limitations

Synergies
- Nighttime cooling
- High levels of insulation

Tradeoffs
- High levels of insulation increase initial costs
- Acoustic reverberation

Figure 6.21 Passive cooling: night purge
Source: Sharon B. Jaffe

WINDOW SHADING

Window shading (Figure 6.22) is a time tested, inexpensive yet effective way to keep direct solar heat gain out of a building. Horizontal shading refers to overhangs and shading elements that protrude from the building. Exterior window shading prevents direct heat from solar radiation from entering the space and adding to the heat load. Horizontal shading works best

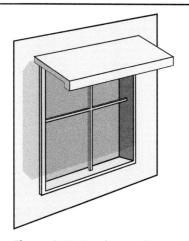

Advantages
- Limit direct heat gain
- Limit glare

Disadvantage
- Too much shading limits daylight

Synergy
- Daylight exterior light shelf

Tradeoffs
- Direct solar heat gain
- Daylight

Figure 6.22 Passive cooling: window shade
Source: Sharon B. Jaffe

when the sun is high in the sky to minimize the required depth of shading. West and east exposures to solar radiation are typically too low for effective horizontal shading; instead, vertical shading or "fins" are used to block the low sun as it moves around the building. Coordinate all window shading strategies with daylighting strategies.

Windows and Window Shading

Windows connect building occupants to the world outside a building. Windows and window shading also play a significant role in passive heating, passive cooling, natural ventilation, and daylighting. Some of the most effective tools in optimizing natural ventilation and passive cooling are the operation, size, position, and shading of a window (Table 6.2).

- Orient the building to present the longest facade to the prevailing winds. Design window and door openings in that facade to provide natural ventilation access points and optimize cooling breezes.
- Prevent unwanted heat gain through windows with effective exterior shading and appropriately specified glazing.
  - Low SHGC is better for blocking heat gain.
  - Low U factor is indicative of better insulating properties.
  - Higher VT allows more daylight and solar radiation to travel through window glazing.
- Locate operable windows on both windward and leeward sides of the building to increase cross ventilation air flow. Air moves from high pressure, windward, to low pressure, leeward.
- Size windows and other air inlets to direct air circulation and control airspeed.
  - Outlets larger than inlets increase air velocity.
  - Locate inlets low and outlets high to direct airflow through occupied spaces air across occupants' body to facilitate convection and evaporative cooling.
  - Avoid locating inlets high in interior spaces. High inlets will direct air currents across the ceiling and not in the work zone.
  - Large window openings on opposing facades reduces air velocity but will maximize air volume.
- Low horizontal windows are more effective as fresh inlets than vertical windows.
- Windows positioned high on the leeward wall or above the roof line encourage stack effect ventilation, enhancing air flow and ventilation.
- Specify glazing that optimizes VT and SHGC to the climate, functional requirements, and specific conditions.
- Design the interior space with an open floor plan eliminate obstructions and maximize cross ventilation.

Microclimate

Natural ventilation requires an understanding of the microclimates of the site. Airflow is influenced and modified by a variety of factors and various scales, including prevailing winds, temperature, climate, and topography. The topography of a site

TABLE 6.2 WINDOW SHADING STRATEGIES

Condition	Shading System
Southern exposure in Northern Hemisphere	Landscape features such as mature trees or hedges; consider deciduous trees if seasonal solar heat gain is desirable.
Southern exposure in Northern Hemisphere	Exterior fixed solid horizontal overhang
Southern exposure in Northern Hemisphere	Exterior, fixed solid horizontal overhang with a downward lip, or downward angle reduces required projection for adequate shading
Southern exposure in Northern Hemisphere	Exterior, multiple fixed, solid, horizontal overhang breaking up window height and reducing required projection for adequate shading.
Southern exposure in Northern Hemisphere	Exterior, solid, horizontal overhang with adjustable angle and depth adapts to seasonal solar requirements.

TABLE 6.2 (CONTINUED)

Southern exposure in Northern Hemisphere	Exterior fixed horizontal louvered overhang	
Southern exposure in Northern Hemisphere	Exterior, multiple adjustable horizontal louvered overhang breaks up window area to be shaded, reducing required projection. An adjustable angle provides seasonal adaptability. Will restrict view.	
Eastern exposure has morning sun and heat gain. Western exposure sun has heat gain in the afternoon.	Exterior vertical and angled fins. When using static, set angled fins, evaluate spacing and fin length for each exposure. Adjustability mitigates changing solar angles. Fins will restrict view.	
Eastern exposure has morning sun and heat gain. Western exposure sun has heat gain in the afternoon.	Exterior vertical fin & horizontal overhang, create an eggcrate formation. Will severely restrict the view.	

Source: Sharon B. Jaffe

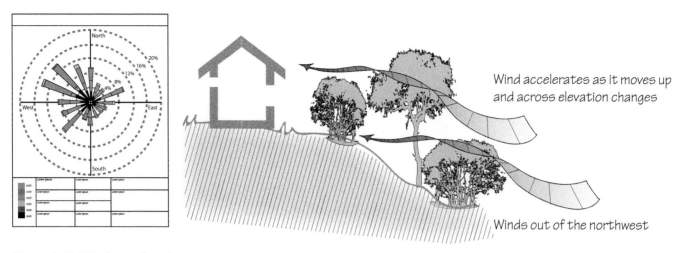

Figure 6.23 Wind speed and topography
Source: Sharon B. Jaffe

will impact wind speed and direction (Figure 6.23). Ridges, hills, and mountains create barriers that direct winds up and over slopes. Generally, airflow increases with the compression of the winds as it moves up the slope on the windward side of a hill, expanding and cooling as air reaches the ridge. The highest speed is at the crest of the hill. Leeward winds descending a slope are compressed under gravity's influence, becoming warmer, denser, and drier.

The built urban environment modifies prevailing winds. The height and spacing of buildings, prevailing wind speed, ambient temperature, and the resulting thermal effects of the building themselves impact air flow. Airflow is a complicated interaction between a variety of elements. In general, cities are less windy than rural areas due to buildings' wind blockage and friction slowing the wind. However, the urban setting often aligns buildings in the same direction, causing buildings to act as a funnel for wind, increasing its speed. When wind flows through constricted spaces along the streets and sidewalks between tall buildings, the pressure difference causes increased wind velocity. The Venturi effect, previously described in this chapter, is exemplified by the severe winds felt by pedestrians walking between tall buildings in dense urban environments.

A wind rose diagram communicates general measures of wind direction and speed taken at a specific location. The spokes of the wind rose diagram indicate the direction and frequency of the wind from a specific direction, while the color on the spoke indicates the strength of the wind or wind speed. Often, at the building site scale, wind patterns will differ from the wind rose diagram. External landscape elements influencing wind direction and ambient temperatures will significantly impact natural ventilation and passive cooling opportunities.

Trees and vegetation moderate air temperature, humidity, and air movement in the microclimate. In addition to the cooling effects of shade provided by the tree canopy and ground cover, moisture from vegetation increases humidity, an effect known as evapotranspiration. Evapotranspiration is a combination of evaporation and transpiration processes. Evaporation is the movement of water from the surface soil, plants, and bodies of water into the air. Transpiration is the physiological process of water movement taken from the soil and released as water vapor through the leaves of the plant. The office of U.S. Geological Services estimates that 90 percent of moisture in the air is from evaporation, 10 percent of moisture in the air is from transpiration (U.S. Department of the Interior | U.S. Geological Survey, 2018). Transpiration rates will vary based upon the ambient temperature and humidity. Plant life helps to reduce ground temperatures as trees and vegetation shield the ground from solar radiation. Transpiration releases excess water to the air, helping to cool the surrounding environment. Typically, cities have fewer trees and plants, resulting in less evapotranspiration and less of its cooling effect on the ambient air. The urban heat island is a result of increased heat-absorbing surfaces such as pavement, asphalt, and concrete building forms, waste heat from daily activity, and reduced vegetation.

The urban environment has complexities that impact natural cooling and ventilation. Buildings tend to follow the street grid, playing a critical role in activating the street. Urban site areas are limited, restricting opportunities for different shapes and orientations that facilitate natural breezes. Municipal codes often set limitations on minimum window opening size and minimum distance from the adjacent buildings. The code restrictions' intent is to address both ventilation requirements and fire prevention concerns.

As previously explained, the interior space plan can facilitate or obstruct cross ventilation, playing a significant role in achieving adequate ventilation.

Design Objectives and Design Ideas

Distinct project objectives for passive cooling and natural ventilation are organized via the four perspectives: performance, systems, culture, and experience (Table 6.3). Significant exploration of passive cooling and ventilation opportunities occurs in the design ideas generated to address the design objectives and shaped by local context and microclimate. The design decision matrix will help evaluate, prioritize, and determine which perspective takes precedence based on project guiding principles and client priorities.

Design Priorities

Access to passive cooling and natural ventilation are priorities for all four perspectives. Locating building occupants near the perimeter of the building facilitates their access to natural ventilation and passive cooling. A narrow floor plan is typically required to meet these criteria.

A deep building plan reduces the effectiveness of natural ventilation. Cross ventilation is effectual in narrow footprint buildings with open interior spaces. Floor plan depth should not exceed two and a half times the ceiling height. For example, a building with ten-foot-high ceilings, an open office plan, and windows located for cross ventilation should be no deeper than twenty-five feet. Single-sided ventilation

TABLE 6.3 PASSIVE COOLING DESIGN OBJECTIVES AND DESIGN IDEAS

	Design Objective	Design Idea
Performance	Reduce energy consumption	Limit heat gain to limit the need for air-conditioning. High levels of roof insulation Shade south-facing glass. Natural ventilation. Automated clerestory windows vent excess heat. Open floor plan facilitates cross ventilation.
Systems	Use natural ventilation and passive cooling to limit or eliminate the need for mechanical ventilation	Use the building roof form to accelerate breezes through the building to acheive passive cooling and ventilation.
Culture	Accelerate breezes through the building using local vernacular acrhitectural forms.	Limit heat gain to limit the need for air-conditioning. High levels of roof insulation. Shade south facing glass. Building roof monitor facilitates stack effect. Smaller low air inlet, higher larger outlets, accelerate breezes through the building.
Experience	Provide cross ventilation in all areas for breezes through out the building and shade the south side of the facade.	Central courtyard reduces depth of floor plan, provides cross ventilation throughout building. Smaller fresh air inlet and larger air outlet on opposing walls increases air velocity. Shade and water feature in courtyard cools ambient air.

Source: Sharon B. Jaffe

may be functional in thinner buildings with open interior spaces, although considerably less successful than cross ventilation.

Natural ventilation in a building with a deep plan may use central, high ventilation outlets to break up the deep plan and enhance air circulation.

Examples of central ventilation outlets include:

- Cupolas
- Operable roof monitors
- Ridge vents
- Sawtooth roof with operable vents or windows
- Clerestory windows
- Wind tower, wind catcher
- Courtyard or atrium, as a central building void

Centrally located roof venting strategies use the stack effect, the difference in air pressure created between the inlets and outlets of the building envelope. As heat escapes through high outlets, cold air is sucked in through the lower-level inlet windows. In summer, the opposite happens. Courtyards and atriums support natural ventilation and passive cooling strategies by breaking up a deep building plan and providing enhanced ventilation opportunities. The addition of void space in the form of an atrium or courtyard provides opportunities to boost cross ventilation.

Natural ventilation (Figure 6.24) and passive cooling are essential systems to combat high humidity and essential for thermal comfort and to maintain healthy indoor air quality. A high level of relative humidity is unpleasant. People feel sticky and in hot temperatures with a high level of relative humidity. In a cold surrounding, high relative humidity makes people feel even colder than the actual temperature. High relative humidity also raises air quality concerns. Mold thrives in high-humidity, high-temperature environments. High levels of condensation occur in high-humidity environments, potentially damaging building components.

Low relative humidity feels dry and often results in conditions that are uncomfortable to occupants, causing static electric shocks and dry throats. In hot, dry climates with low humidity, a fountain or other small body of water in an atrium, courtyard,

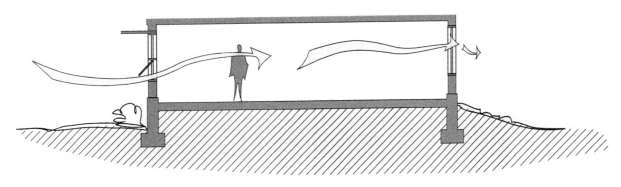

Figure 6.24 Natural ventilation through cross circulation
Source: Sharon B. Jaffe

or other shared space can help cool and humidify the dry, hot air, providing intermediary remediation.

Synergies and Tradeoffs

Passive cooling and natural ventilation are combined in this section to associate the synergies between the two passive strategies. Natural ventilation and day-lighting are both highly dependent on the geometry of the spaces to be served. They have similar proportional and reach limitations. Both influence occupant perception of thermal comfort. The design idea sketches in Table 6.3 demonstrate closely aligned and often overlapping passive design strategies. Strategies that overlap indicate synergies that should be used to drive future building design decisions.

WATER CONSERVATION AND RAINWATER HARVESTING

Water is a precious resource. The human body is 60 percent water. Without water, life as we know it would cease to exist. In some parts of the world, the scarcity of clean, potable water is a serious concern and water is highly prized. In other parts of the world, clean water is available on demand without recognition of its importance.

Green building standards include water efficiency and conservation as vital aspects of a sustainable building. Worksheets and formal calculations of water conservation and efficiencies are often integral to building certification submittals. For water, as in other passive design strategies, the first step toward conserving water is to reduce the demand by reducing usage. Low-flow plumbing fixtures for sinks, bathtub, showers, and toilets can reduce indoor water use up to 40 percent. The Department of Energy's Lawrence Berkeley National Laboratory (Berkeley Lab), in a 2017 study, found a link between water usage and heat mitigation strategies in urban areas. Cool roofs reduce the demand for water by reducing ambient air temperatures, thereby reducing the demand for urban irrigation.

Water used for drinking, cooking, and bathing must be clean, potable quality, but water used for landscape irrigation or to flush toilets does not need to meet that same standard. The U.S. Geological Survey estimates that 12 percent of water used in the United States for building operations does not require clean drinkable water. Graywater is the water that has been used by laundry machines, dishwashers, bathtubs, and sinks. Graywater may contain traces of dirt, food, grease and even look dirty, but it must not have had contact with feces either from plumbing fixtures or washing diapers. Graywater is suitable for irrigation and other nonpotable water use. In some areas, graywater supports indoor plumbing functions such as flushing toilets. Regulations and codes that stipulate the reuse of any graywater vary widely, so a careful investigation of local regulations is vital before integrating graywater reuse strategies into a sustainable design project. Rainwater collection and graywater reuse for landscaping needs will reduce the usage of clean drinkable water.

Key Terms

Potable water is water that meets quality standards suitable for human consumption.

Graywater is untreated wastewater from bathtubs, showers, and bathroom wash basins that has not come into contact with water closet waste.

Blackwater is wastewater from water closets and urinals. Blackwater is not suitable for any human contact (either direct or indirect).

The *catchment area* is the surface used to collect rainwater. A roof or other impermeable surface may serve this function.

The *delivery system* transports rainwater from a collection surface to a storage reservoir or cistern. On a traditional home, gutters may serve this purpose.

A *reservoir* is a tank that stores collected rainwater until it is needed.

An *extraction device* can be a simple as a scoop or bucket or a pump or infiltration device.

Key Strategies

Water conservation and efficiency strategies can be implemented to reduce water use, waste, and loss. Strategies to save water include:

- Reduction in potable water consumption
- Minimization of wastewater
- Low-flow plumbing fixtures and fixture fittings
- Water efficient appliances (clothes washers, dishwashers)
- Water treatment equipment (softeners, filtering systems)
- Locally adapted landscape
- Rain barrels and cisterns
- Water reuse and alternate sources of water (graywater, rainwater, stormwater, cooling condensate, cooling tower blowdown, and foundation drain water)
- Vegetated green roofs
- Proper maintenance for prevention/repair of leaks

Key Metrics

Vital benchmark metrics for water conservation are:

- Predicted annual consumption of potable water for all uses, including process water
- Eliminating or minimizing use of potable water for irrigation.

Encouraged metrics to monitor a project's water conservation efforts include:

- Actual annual consumption of potable water for all uses
- Percentage of water consumed on site from rainwater capture
- Amount of graywater or blackwater captured for reuse
- The capacity percentage for on-site management of 24-hour rainwater from a 2-year storm event

Rainwater Harvesting

Rainwater can be a ready source of water. Cisterns store rainwater collected from rooftops and other impervious surfaces. One inch of rain on 2,000 square feet of roofing can mean a harvest of approximately 1,200 gallons of water. Cisterns may be located either above or below ground to supply water as needed for irrigation. Rainwater harvesting is a cost-effective technique that provides a ready supply of nonpotable water available for irrigation. Local and other building codes regulate the amount of permissible rainwater runoff and permeable surface and can be quite restrictive in efforts to safeguard overall water quality and infrastructure. Collecting rainwater also slows runoff and eases the pressure on the stormwater sewer system.

Rainwater harvesting systems have four essential components:

1. Catchment area constructed from nontoxic material. Avoid painted surfaces and overhanging vegetation.
2. Conveyance system such as downspouts, gutters or other devices that direct runoff flow.
3. A storage tank or cistern must have a secure lid/cover, inlet filter, overflow pipe, and the ability for cleaning.
4. Extraction tap or pump that does not contaminate collected water must be used.

Methods of Rainwater Harvesting

All impervious surfaces will have rainwater runoff. Rainwater runoff can be redirected and collected in ponds, reservoirs, and cisterns.

Rooftop rainwater harvesting is prevalent in urban areas which often use the roofs of buildings to collect rainwater. The direction and slope of a roof will determine the rate or speed the water will leave the catchment area. All impervious surface roofs can be used to harvest rainwater. A steep slope roof will shed water more quickly than a flat roof. Design all roof and drain systems to allow uncomplicated collection and storage of rainwater for later use.

Rainwater harvesting benefits
- Protects local waterways from debris and contaminants in stormwater runoff
- Conserves potable water
- Reduces the strain on the infrastructure (and saves municipal sewer fees)

- Reduces erosion and flooding around a building
- Provides irrigation water
- Serves as a backup water source

Rainwater harvesting key strategies
- Shape the roof to collect rainwater
- Funnel water toward the cisterns
- Do not use green roofs, which allow some water to trans-evaporate into the air.
- Strategically locate and use retention ponds.
- Direct all stormwater on site toward ponds to support natural habitats.

Stormwater Management

Stormwater is rainwater and snowmelt that does not soak into the soil but instead becomes surface runoff. Surface runoff, if not managed and collected, either flows directly to waterways, into storm sewers, or floods roadways and surrounding grounds. A substantial amount of dirt and debris is collected by stormwater runoff, the rainwater that flows over the ground, roads, and other impervious surfaces. The dirty stormwater flows into rivers and streams, polluting these sources of drinking water.

Negative impacts of unmanaged stormwater runoff
- Overburdening sewer systems.
- Polluting rivers and waterways with fertilizers, oils, and other pollutants.
- Damage to aquatic life and habitat.
- Extreme stormwater runoff contributes to flooding and the resulting flood damage.

Methods to manage stormwater runoff
- Permeable paving allows rainwater to percolate through the ground, filter naturally, and return to the aquifer.
- Gutter and downspouts can redirect rain and stormwater shed by the roof to cisterns or other collection areas.
- Green roof surfaces utilize stormwater in place.

Rainwater harvesting strategies: Options and considerations

SLOPED ROOFS
Sloped roofs (Figure 6.25) serve as effective catchment areas. The angle of the roof uses gravity to direct rainwater toward collection devices, usually roof gutters connected to a downspout or piping system, that drain collected rainwater through enclosed piping to a rain barrel, cistern, or other collection containers. High sloped roof structures such as a shed roof or a butterfly roof are especially effective in directing rainwater.

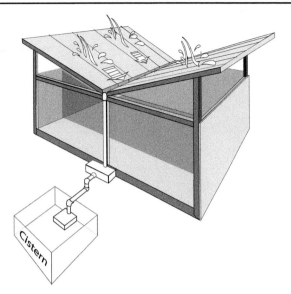

Advantages
- Aesthetic
- Rainwater collection
- Wind resistance
- Accommodate larger or high windows

Disadvantages
- Complex construction
- Increased maintenance requirements
- Heavy rain, snow, and ice dams may threaten the structure

Synergies
- Daylighting
- Natural ventilation
- Passive heating

Tradeoff
- No overhang for shade

Figure 6.25 Rainwater, sloped roof
Source: Sharon B. Jaffe

CISTERNS

Cisterns (Figure 6.26) are large storage tanks that capture rainwater. Locate any cistern as close as reasonably possible to the water use point. Do not locate cisterns downhill from any form of sewage disposal facilities, septic tanks, sewer, or drain lines. Do not place cisterns in low-lying areas prone to flooding. Cisterns support stormwater management and collect water for reuse from roofs or other impervious surfaces. Stored water is either drained by gravity or pumped to its end-use location.

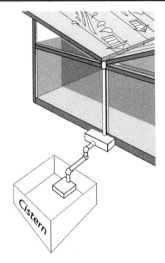

Advantages
- Water storage for later use
- Facilitates stormwater management

Disadvantages
- Above ground/appearance
- Above ground/freeze
- Above ground/algae
- Below ground/cost
- Pipe maintenance

Figure 6.26 Rainwater, cistern
Source: Sharon B. Jaffe

PASSIVE DESIGN VALIDATION

Validating the passive design strategies employed requires determining if the passive design strategies meet the stated tangible and intangible design objectives.

Passive design objectives will vary widely by the client, project guiding principles, and project requirements; the ability to achieve passive design objectives is significantly influenced by early building design decisions that respond to macroclimate, microclimate, and site conditions: building location, building orientation, building shape, and building mass.

Factors critical to the success of passive design strategies include:

- Solar path relative to site and building to optimize solar radiation for passive heating
- Wind direction and velocity to harness for natural ventilation and passive cooling
- Annual quantity, pattern, utilization, and management of precipitation, reducing potable water requirements
- User/occupant participation and support

Passive design strategies are most effective when the building design responds to the surrounding natural and built environment, maximizing the opportunities presented. A building adapted to the local context and climate has reduced energy needs and provides increased if indirect, opportunities for occupants to intersect and benefit from the local environment.

A sustainable design project will have design objectives from all four perspectives.

The performance perspective demands increased energy efficiency. Passive design strategies reduce the need for powered heating, cooling, ventilation, and lighting. Reduced requirements equate to reduced energy consumption. Energy consumption is measured as EUI or energy use intensity.

The systems perspective engages the passive design systems and the buildings interface with the technological, mechanical, and surrounding ecological systems.

The culture perspective objectives reflect the expectations and opportunities of the surrounding community. The significance and prioritization of each passive design strategy will change with macroclimate, culture, and community. Vernacular architecture will often provide indications of effective passive strategies.

The experience perspective objectives aim to inspire. Passive design strategies address experience objectives by optimizing thermal comfort. The implementation of passive strategies may further respond to the experience perspective, utilizing all of the senses in the detailing of passive strategies in ways that are engaging, aesthetically pleasing, and provide opportunities for building occupant interaction and control.

SDB methodology step 1, context, set general expectations when guiding principles are determined. Step 2, pre-planning, set more specific goals and objectives. The first step in the validation process is to confirm that the passive design strategies address the intentions expressed in these earlier steps.

The design validation matrix is a tool used throughout the design process for organizing the observations, evidence, metrics, and reflections that support the design decisions made. The design validation matrix role the SDB methodology is addressed in Chapter 10, "Design Resolution."

Multiple responses are possible to implement passive design strategies addressing each of the four perspectives objectives. Passive heating, natural ventilation, and daylighting are interrelated, providing synergies and requiring tradeoffs to achieve a balanced that reflects the overall project guidelines.

Methods of passive design strategy evaluation include:

Quantitative metrics
- Energy modeling and computer simulations
  - EUI
  - Daylight simulation
- Water usage and conservation calculations
- Percentage of building and occupants with access to fresh air and views

Qualitative metrics
- Reflections
  - Physiological
  - Psychological
  - Sociological
  - Aesthetic expression

Quantitative metrics provide computational evidence. Quantitative metrics indicate the level benchmarks and metrics are projected to achieve. Qualitative metrics are more subjective. Qualitative assessments provide key measures of success—such as community engagement, stakeholder satisfaction, and occupant happiness—that data-driven metrics cannot provide. Guiding principles and various intangible objectives developed during the pre-planning stages are the focus of qualitative evaluations and validations. After a project is completed, validation of building performance may continue measuring and comparing actual performance and systems metrics to energy and daylight modeling. Qualitative evaluation and validation may take the form of survey and interviews measuring occupant and community satisfaction.

FURTHER READING

Allen, Edward. 2005. *How Buildings Work: The Natural Order of Architecture* (3rd ed.). New York and Oxford: Oxford University Press.

Allen, Edward, and Joseph Iano. 2017. *The Architect's Studio Companion: Rules of Thumb for Preliminary Design* (6th ed.). Hoboken, NJ: John Wiley & Sons.

Grondzik, Walter T., and Alison G. Kwok. 2019. *Mechanical and Electrical Equipment for Buildings* (13th ed.) Hoboken, NJ: John Wiley & Sons.

Kwok, Alison G., and Walter T. Grondzik. 2011. *The Green Studio Handbook: Environmental Strategies for Schematic Design* (2nd ed.). Boston: Architectural Press.

Lechner, Norbert. 2009. *Heating, Cooling, Lighting: Sustainable Design Methods for Architects* (3rd ed.). Hoboken, NJ: John Wiley & Sons.

7

Step 3B: Passive Design, Daylighting

Step 3
Design

3A Preliminary Design
3B Passive Design
3C Building Envelope
3D Green Materials
 * Beyond the Basics

Step 4
Design
solution

ign Synthesis
I Design Validation
enting the Project

Step
Pre-

2A Resear
2B Project
2C Design Crite
2D Spatial Relation

Step 1
Context

1A Project Information
1B Guiding Principles
1C Macro / Micro Context
1D Site Inventory & Analysis

Figure 7.0 *Sustainable Design Basics*, **step 3**

Source: Sharon B. Jaffe

DAYLIGHTING

Daylight is a passive design strategy. It is free light! Zero fossil fuel energy is consumed to produce the daylight to illuminate a building interior. Strategic use of daylighting can eliminate the need for artificial light during much of the day. Using daylight instead of artificial lighting reduces energy consumption, thereby reducing operational costs and carbon emissions required for artificial lighting. Daylighting has the potential to save energy and associated costs required to reduce the heat generated by artificial lights. If artificial lights are not on, the cooling system need not work as hard, saving the direct cost of energy required to power the artificial lights and the cost of the energy required for cooling and the first costs required for a larger cooling system. But daylight is much more than an energy- and cost-saving strategy. Daylight can dramatically reveal building architecture while benefiting occupants' health, and increasing their comfort and productivity.

Daylight for the interior of a building comes from:

- Intense direct sunlight during clear skies, which also introduces heat
- Reflected sunlight from the ground and nearby objects
- Diffuse, ambient light from the sky
- Diffuse sunlight during cloudy skies
- Interior reflected light from interior surfaces

Daylight is not the same as sunlight. Direct sunlight introduces heat to interior spaces. Not all daylit spaces want or need direct sunlight. The desirability of heat gain from sunlight will vary by climate and may vary in the same climate by season. Daylight strategies use diffuse or indirect light.

Design for passive daylighting requires a holistic approach. Consistent daylight without glare can be challenging to achieve. Fundamental determinants for effective daylighting include the building site microclimate, the orientation of a building on the site, the massing of the building, building fenestration, the interior floor plan, and interior finishes. These elements control solar radiation exposure and are all critical to achieving appropriate and comfortable levels of daylight. As noted throughout this text, each building system is part of the larger overall building. The macro and micro context of the building and the multitude of design strategies required for the whole building influence daylighting. However, the openings in the building—the fenestration—are what lets light into the building and determines the success of daylighting design.

One of the primary challenges of daylighting is getting the daylight into the building in the places and in the quantity that it is needed. The ideal building mass for daylighting optimizes opportunities for natural light penetration into the building with a high floor-to-floor dimension. A high floor-to-floor dimension allows windows to be located higher above the finished floor, facilitating daylight penetration deep into the building. A narrow building footprint reduces the depth of the spaces where daylight is required and increases the perimeter of the building, thereby increasing the total potential daylight area. An east-west axis maximizes the elevations with the most uniform solar exposure.

Window placement and selection have a significant influence on daylighting as well as passive cooling, natural ventilation, passive heating, and active building systems. Best daylighting practices carefully implemented may also capture savings by reduced cooling loads and downsizing cooling equipment.

Skylights, roof monitors, and clerestories influence roof form by shaping and facilitating daylight from above, directing it deeper into building plans as required. However, top lighting has limitations in multistory buildings.

The amount of light available varies from season to season, time of day, and local weather. Even the local air quality can affect available daylight. An effective and efficient daylight system must include controls not just for the daylight but also for the artificial lighting system. If there is sufficient daylighting to provide for the necessary illuminance of required tasks, artificial light should not be on. Using daylight instead of artificial light saves the energy required by an artificial lighting system and improves the interior environment.

Conversely, if there is not enough daylight, the artificial lighting system should be switched on. Artificial lighting systems can be controled manually or automatically. Automated systems use daylight sensors and dimming to make the artificial lighting system responsive to the daylight system. The artificial electric lighting systems can be programmed to supplement available daylight as needed.

An effective daylighting system uses direct, diffuse, and reflected daylight to provide a reasonable amount of light in the building where needed; it will provide enough light for good visual performance, as well as lighting contrast for visual comfort. Building fenestration, specific glazing material, sun control and shading, and daylight controls interconnected with artificial lighting controls are all part of a daylighting system. The integrated design approach evaluates and maximizes each system as part of the whole building system, utilizing the expertise of each discipline during the design process, enhancing the probability of overall success of long-term comfort, energy, and cost savings.

Key Terms

Sunlight is light that results from a direct beam of energy/radiation from the sun. Sunlight includes both light and heat.

Daylight is light from the ambient and diffuse light of the sky.

Ultraviolet (UV) radiation is an element of sunlight/solar radiation. Invisible to most people, UV is the component of sunlight that causes the body to increase levels of melanin in the skin, produce vitamin D, and promote the creation of serotonin. However, UV exposure can damage the human eyes and skin; it can also degrade building finishes.

Visible light is the wavelengths of light visible to most people. Color is a property of visible light.

Visual comfort in its most basic sense is the absence of discomfort. Although specific green building standards may have distinct visual comfort metrics, visual comfort and quality of daylight require glare control, views out of the building, adequate and uniform illuminance, quality color rendition, and some occupant control of light levels.

Glare is the result of too much light. Glare is extreme brightness contrasting with the general visual field creating excessive contrast. The perception of glare is highly dependent on the position of an individual. A window or a poorly directed light fixture can be direct sources of glare. Direct glare can be eliminated by changing the amount of light or the direction of the light. Indirect or reflected glare is too much light reflected off a surface or object. Modify indirect glare by removing glossy surfaces from view to reconfigure how the light hits the reflective surface.

Light reflectance value (LRV) measures the percentage of visible and usable light reflected by a surface color or material. Light reflectance values range from zero value for the color black (all light and heat is absorbed) to 100 percent for pure white light (all light is reflected).

Window wall ratio (WWR) is calculated only from vision glass. Net glazing divided by gross interior wall area equals the window wall ratio. WWR calculations exclude insulated spandrel glazing. The 2015 IECC allows 30 percent WWR and increases to 40 percent for climate zones 1–6 with other factors. Daylighting design must balance daylight penetration against solar heat gain.

Effective aperture is a measure of window glazing's ability to transmit light. EA is equal to WWR multiplied by visible light transmittance (VT). A starting point EA for north- and south-facing facades is 0.30, with minimal glazing on east and west elevations. In high-performance buildings, glazing is selected to optimize each elevation. Typically, larger windows use darker glass, while clear glass is used in smaller windows.

Daylight glass and *vision glass*. Daylight glazing is located above occupant eye level (7'-6" above the finished floor). Daylight glazing allows light to enter the space but does not provide a view for occupants to see out of the building. Vision glazing, located between 2'-6" and 7'-6" above the finished floor, lets daylight into a building while also allowing occupants to see out. High-performance buildings may specify high transmission glazing for daylighting and moderate transmission glazing to provide views.

Apparent brightness is an important psychological aspect of daylighting. It is the impression of brightness in a space; it may or may not correlate with the actual levels of illumination. Rooms with nonuniform lighting appear brighter than uniformly illuminated areas. The elements of variation and contrast within design tolerances create more exciting spaces that appear brighter. Spaces that are illuminated solely from side lighting, such as light from a side window, typically result in a dark ceiling, dark walls below the window openings, dark floor, and dark side walls. The general darkness resulting from side lighting a room or space presents a cave-like appearance with a low level of apparent brightness.

A *clear sky* has less than 30 percent clouds. It is brighter at the horizon.

A *cloudy sky* has 30–80 percent clouds, with conditions varying from clear to overcast throughout the day.

An *overcast sky* is more than 80 percent clouds and provides the most uniform sky illuminance. An overcast sky can be three times brighter at a high point than at the horizon.

Side lighting refers to light entering the building from openings perpendicular to the ground and lighting the space from the side. Windows, French doors, and bay windows all provide side lighting.

Top lighting refers to light entering the space from above, parallel to the floor. Skylights, roof monitors, and sawtooth roofs all provide top lighting.

North light, in the northern hemisphere, is the general natural light in the sky. North light provides excellent daylighting. Artists have valued northern light for centuries. North light offers an even ambient light without the extremes of shifting light and shadows that are caused by the sun's movement throughout the day. North light is a consistent color temperature throughout the day. Ambient north light is less damaging to fabric and other interior finishes than direct light.

East and west light is very uneven and difficult to integrate into a daylighting system. The sun angle continually shifts as the sun moves from east to west throughout the day, making it difficult to control direct sunlight and glare. As a result, daylight designs minimize daylight openings in east and west facades or use shading to prevent glare and redirect sunlight.

South light, in the northern hemisphere, provides direct sunlight all day. Southern light has the maximum potential for sun and daylight, although it changes tone and warmth and casts sharp shadows throughout the day. Shading must be used to prevent glare.

The *daylight zone* or daylight area, is the portion of a building that consistently receives a substantial amount of daylight throughout the day. Codes and standards require daylight zones to be controlled separately from other lighting systems.

Key Metrics

Daylighting metrics analyze both the quantity and quality of daylight. Daylighting metrics are essential to a designer's evaluation of various daylighting strategies and glazing specifications necessary to balance lighting and cooling load requirements.

Daylight factor (DF) is the ratio between indoor and outdoor illumination at a given time under overcast skies. DF is a design criterion indicating the minimum target for adequate daylight that allows for quick comparisons of daylight penetration for different building configurations. Established as a criterion for spaces throughout the building, DF is usually related to the light levels required for functions and tasks. An average DF of 5 percent and a minimum DF of 2 percent supply adequate lighting. Using the DF is an imprecise methodology. At certain times of the year, for portions of the day, additional lighting may be required. Over 5 percent DF provides plenty of light, rarely requiring artificial light, but has a high probability for overlighting, uncomfortable glare, and solar heat gain, all of which may be problematic. Note that the daylight factor does not take direct sunlight, local climate, facade orientation, or movable shading into account. That said, the daylight factor is relatively accurate for dense urban areas in temperate climates and is still preferable to no analysis.

Climate-based daylight modeling (CBDM) enables daylight assessment to be integrated with thermal modeling. CBDM can accurately assess solar gains and glare based on building location and facade orientation.

Target illuminance is the minimum light level, measured in lux or foot-candles, based on function, task, and occupants age.

Illuminance on the horizontal plane is a measurement of the lighting levels on a horizontal surface, usually desk height. Recommended lighting levels for detailed office work are 300–500 lux or 27–46 FC.

Foot-candles (FC) is a unit of illumination that measures the quantity of light on a surface or object. Consider a single candle burning. A candle without shielding of any kind emits light in all directions. A single ray of light from that candle hits a perpendicular surface one foot away. The intensity of that ray is one candlepower. The illumination or light from that ray on the perpendicular surface is equal to one foot-candle. If any of the candlelight rays are hitting a one-square-foot surface one foot away, then the entire surface is illuminated to one foot-candle. One foot-candle is equal to one lumen per square foot (IES ED50).

IES RECOMMENDED LIGHT LEVELS

Space Type	IESNA
Open offices	30–40FC
Private offices	30–50FC
Conference rooms	30–50FC
Corridors	10 FC
Dining areas/pantry	10–30FC
Fitness areas	30 FC
Restrooms/ locker rooms	10 FC
Utility spaces	30 FC

A *lumen* is a unit of light quantity. One lumen per square foot is one foot-candle.

Lux (lx) is a unit of illumination that measures the amount of light on the surface. One lumen per square meter is equal to one lux.

Visible transmittance (VT or VLT), or visible light transmittance, is the percentage of visible light that reaches and passes through the glazing to the building interior. High VT appears clear, and low VT reduces the amount of light available for visual tasks.

Annual sun exposure (ASE) is the percentage of the floor space that gets too much direct sunlight. Too much direct sunlight causes visual discomfort or glare and increases cooling loads. ASE indicates the percentage of the floor area that gets more than 1000 lux for at least 250 or more occupied hours per day.

Infiltration and Distribution

Getting daylight where it is required takes careful planning. Sidelight-oriented daylight on the south- and north-facing elevations will generally reach into the building one and a half times the height of the window header; assisted by a light shelf, the daylight may reach as far as two times the height of the window header. East and west facades present more of a challenge because of the variable low angles of the sun path that creates glare. Glare is uncomfortable, causing building occupants to pull down shades and otherwise block the light, thereby negating daylighting benefits. Achieving daylighting objectives requires awareness and accommodation of the limitations of daylighting penetration as part of early design decisions for building location, orientation, shape, and mass.

The geometry of the subject space, color, and reflectivity of the surfaces, and most importantly the placement of the windows, dictates the depth of sidelight daylight zones. A general rule for determining the depth daylighting will reach into the building is one and a half times the height of the top of the window (the window header) from the floor. Figure 7.1 illustrates this rule. Windows positioned with the top of the window high on the wall will allow daylight to enter farther into the building than similar-size windows placed lower on the wall. Increasing glazing area will increase daylight intensity, but will not increase the depth of the daylight zone.

Another significant metric of daylighting is the percentage of the floor plan that is in the daylight zone. Green building standards often have specific daylight requirements expressed as a minimum percentage of the floor plan to be daylit. Just as building orientation, shape, and overall building mass are carefully evaluated to maximize daylight infiltration, building proportions are also considered to assure daylight reaches the highest percentage of the building footprint.

The diagrams in Figure 7.2 describe three different building footprints. All of the building diagrams represent 4050 square feet. All three buildings plan to utilize perimeter windows with a head height of 10 feet above the finished floor. Building A has a very narrow and long building shape, providing 100 percent daylighting of the building footprint without interior partitions. It is a rare building that does not have some core and support space that does not require daylight. Building B responds to the need for a central core area. Although it is also rectilinear, it has a slightly deeper floor plan than building A. The deeper floor plan may provide some construction economies and reduces exterior surface area, which supports passive

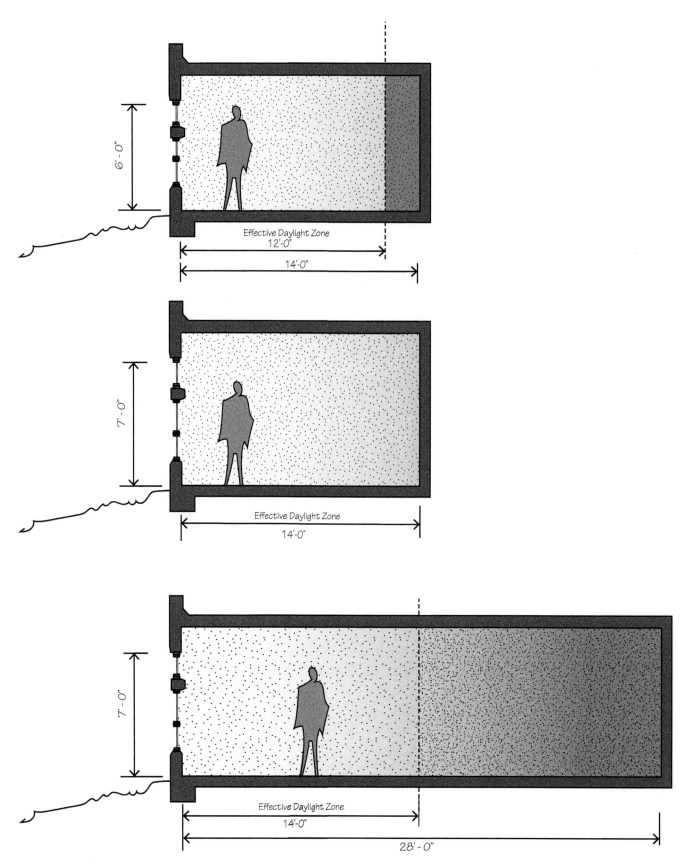

Figure 7.1 Effective daylight zones in section

Source: Sharon B. Jaffe

heating strategies while providing daylight for 78 percent of the building footprint. Building C is the same overall square footage as Buildings A and B. The square proportions reduce the perimeter surface area, which limits opportunities for temperature transmission through the building's perimeter. The tradeoff is that the increased depth of the floorplate reduces the available daylight zone to 72 percent. While the difference illustrated by the diagrams may seem minimal, it is significant. LEED V4 ID+C Commercial Interiors Indoor Environmental Quality (EQ8) requires 75 percent daylighting coverage. The variation in massing changes the building geometry enough to make it a challenge to meet the daylighting requirement.

"Use a combination of side lighting and top lighting to achieve a total daylighting zone (the floor area meeting the following requirements) that is at least 75 percent of all the regularly occupied spaces" (U.S. Green Building Council).

Daylighting requires adequate solar exposure, window area at appropriate locations, shading systems, accommodations in the building facade, and interior space plan to be effective. Understand that a daylighting system does not eliminate the need for an artificial lighting system. Justification of the initial construction cost of a daylight system can be found in the increased building performance and increased occupant comfort, health, and productivity. Electric lighting in buildings consumes over 15 percent of the energy produced in the United States, according to the U.S. Department of Energy. A properly designed daylighting system can reduce the demand for artificial

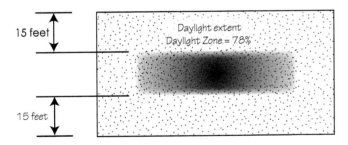

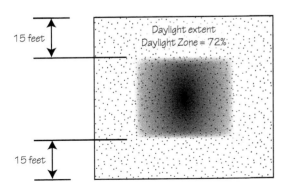

All buildings 4050 sq. ft. per floor.

All buildings have perimeter windows on all sides of the buildings.

Window head height of 10 feet above the finished floor.

Figure 7.2 Effective daylight zone extents in plan

Source: Sharon B. Jaffe

lighting, eliminating or reducing the heat generated, lowering costs for electricity, and possibly reducing the size of the HVAC system required. Daylighting also contributes to an improved interior experience. People are attracted to natural light and appreciate the visual connection to the natural environment. Multiple studies document the increased comfort, satisfaction, and productivity of building occupants in daylit buildings.

Daylighting strategies: Options and considerations

NARROW FLOOR PLAN, BUILDING ORIENTATION, AND BUILDING MASSING

Buildings that are longer on their east-west axis with a narrow footprint are efficient for daylighting. The amount of useful daylight and unwanted glare varies by facade orientation. A single-story building with a deep plan can achieve adequate daylighting using top lighting. However, single-story buildings are often not the best practice for efficient land use. Multistory buildings with a thinner profile, or narrow footprint, provide opportunities to maximize daylighting potential and views from side windows. (see Figure 7.3) Central void space such as a courtyard or atrium also provides access to daylight. Taller than typical floor-to-floor heights allow for higher window placement that will introduce daylighting deeper into the building.

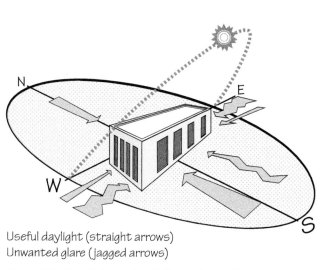

Useful daylight (straight arrows)
Unwanted glare (jagged arrows)

Figure 7.3 Daylight and building orientation
Source: Sharon B. Jaffe

Advantages
- North elevation
  - No direct sunlight
  - Ambient daylight only
- South elevation
  - Direct sunlight all day
  - Maximum potential for sun and daylight
  - Shading required to prevent glare

Disadvantages
- Higher skin to volume ratio
- Synergies
- Occupant proximity to windows
- Direct heat gain opportunity
- Passive cooling and ventilation

Tradeoffs
- Higher skin to volume ration
- Heating and cooling costs

BUILDING VOIDS

Courtyards, atriums, or light wells, are all vertical spaces exposed to the sky within the building's footprint. (See Figure 7.4) As with cooling and ventilation, void spaces facilitate getting more of the floor area close to the perimeter.

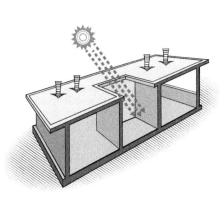

Figure 7.4 Daylight and building void
Source: Sharon B. Jaffe

Advantages
- Increases cross ventilation opportunities
- Increases daylight opportunities
- Can cool warm air and warm cool air
- Shelters building from heat and cold
- Shelters building from high winds

Disadvantages
- Addition square footage required but not maximized

Synergies
- Evaporative cooling
- Daylighting
- Night flushing

Tradeoffs
- Building skin to volume ratio
- Passive heating

HIGH CEILINGS

High ceilings allow for window heads to be set higher in a wall, resulting in greater penetration of daylighting into the building. A high ceiling presents opportunities for an interior and exterior light shelf without impacting vision glass. (See Figure 7.5) Daylight efficiency is increased using ceiling heights of 11 feet or higher.

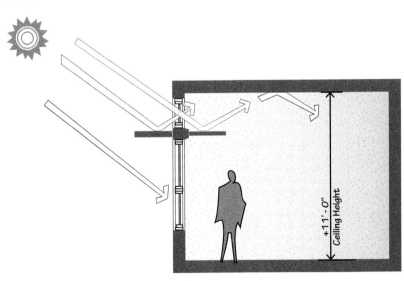

Figure 7.5 Daylight and high ceilings
Source: Sharon B. Jaffe

Advantages
- Increased opportunity for daylight glass height and quantity
- Passive cooling: supports convection airflow and related passive cooling strategies

Disadvantage
- Heating: high ceilings create increased volume for heating and allow hot air to rise above occupant level

Synergy
- Cooling and ventilation

Tradeoff
- Increased heating load

SLOPED CEILINGS

A sloped ceiling directs more daylight into the building. A sloping ceiling at the perimeter window increases the brightness of the ceiling and allows raising the window head without increasing floor to floor height. (See Figure 7.6) The higher window head height increases the depth daylight will reach inside the building.

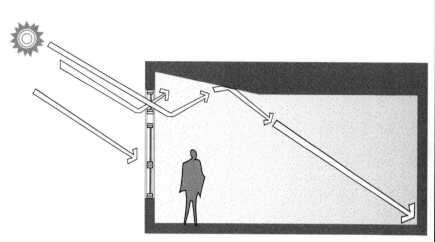

Figure 7.6 Daylight and sloped ceilings
Source: Sharon B. Jaffe

Advantages

- Increased opportunity for daylight glass height and quantity
- Reduces overall volume and increased heating demand resulting from the increased volume.
- Lower overall ceiling keeps heat closer to occupant level

Disadvantage

- Heating: high ceilings create increased volume for heating and allow hot air to rise above occupant level

Synergy

- Cooling and ventilation

WINDOWS

Windows are the primary source for daylight side lighting into a building. Window configuration and placement impact daylight distribution. Windows facing north or south provide more consistent daylighting throughout the day. The variable angle of eastern and western sun resulting from the daily sun path creates challenges to shading east and west elevations from glare and heat gain, suggesting that east- and west-facing windows should be avoided or minimized. The most effective daylighting systems coordinate the daylighting window layout with the interior space plan.

Tall window head heights facilitate daylight penetration into the building. High continuous horizontal windows are more useful for daylighting than individual vertical windows. Locating the top of windows close to the ceiling line increases distribution depth. Glazing below desk height does not add appreciably to useable daylight. Unless a full wall view is essential to the application, minimize glazing below 30 inches.

The general rule is *usable* daylight will penetrate a space one and a half times the distance from the window head to the floor, two times the distance when using a light shelf. (See Figure 7.7)

A high visible transmittance (VT) used for daylight glazing allows more daylight through the glazing than the moderate VT used for vision glazing to reduce glare that exceeds comfort levels.

U value or U factor is indicative of thermal conduction through the window. Like many window traits, macroclimate, and functional requirements determine the preferred U value. A lower U factor is better at retaining heat inside the building. High-performance windows may combine technologies, including thermal breaks, low-E coating, films, and multiple glazing layers, to reduce the U factor of the window assembly.

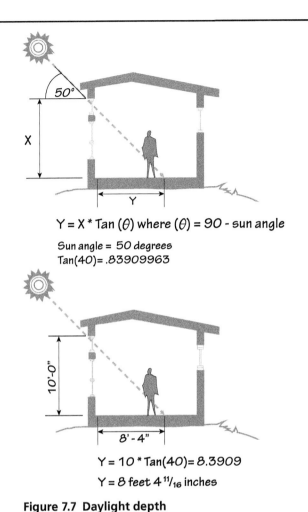

$Y = X * Tan\ (\theta)$ where $(\theta) = 90$ - sun angle

Sun angle = 50 degrees
Tan(40)= .83909963

$Y = 10 * Tan(40) = 8.3909$

$Y = 8$ feet $4\,^{11}/_{16}$ inches

Figure 7.7 Daylight depth
Source: Sharon B. Jaffe

Advantages
- Free source of light
- Views

Disadvantages
- Potential heat loss
- Potential heat gain
- Occupant interference w/natural ventilation strategy

Synergy
- Cooling and ventilation

Tradeoff
- Heating

Vision Glass and Daylight Glass

These optimize views while minimizing the heat load and reducing the solar radiation that enters a space. Separate window openings for daylighting and views allows for different glazing specification and facilitates appropriate horizontal shading and light shelf positioning. Daylighting glass is positioned over 7 feet above the finished floor using high transmission glass to maximize daylight distribution. Vision glass is positioned below 7 feet and uses lower transmission glass to control glare. (See Figure 7.8)

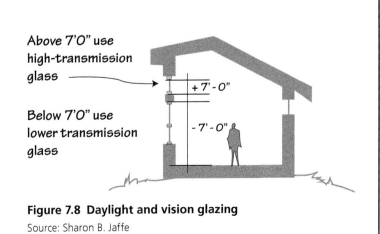

Above 7'0" use high-transmission glass

Below 7'0" use lower transmission glass

+ 7' - 0"

- 7' - 0"

Figure 7.8 Daylight and vision glazing
Source: Sharon B. Jaffe

Advantages
- Opportunity to vary VT and U factor per functional requirement.
- Opportunity to use varied interior shade controls on different windows

Disadvantage
- Maintenance may be awkward

Synergy
- Exterior/Interior light shelf

Tradeoff
- Potential seasonal heat loss for high quality year-round daylighting

EXTERNAL SHADING

External shading is an inexpensive but effective way to keep sun glare and direct solar heat gain out of a building throughout history. Solar radiation—the heat gain that accompanies sunlight—is blocked by external shading before it enters the space, reducing the cooling load of the building. Interior blinds and shades may be very helpful in controlling the light component and potential glare of sunlight but do not manage the accompanying heat. Solar radiation may be welcome in cool seasons when heating requirements dominate energy consumption, yet undesirable during hot times of the year when increased cooling is required. A strong understanding of sun angles for specific building orientation, massing in the specific climate, latitudes, and the particular building site, is required to plan external shading to effectively block or permit solar radiation to enter spaces as required.

Horizontal Shading

Refers to overhangs and shading elements that protrude from the building. Horizontal shading (Figure 7.9) works best when the sun is high in the sky, minimizing the required depth of horizontal shading. Exterior horizontal shading can be designed to block high angle sunlight in summer and allow lower angle sunlight in winter. An external horizontal solar shade that is also reflective may also function as an exterior light shelf to reflect light into the building when positioned between vision glass and daylight glass. Reflected daylight avoids the heat gain of direct sunlight. A building envelope with deep facade configuration, exterior overhangs, or applied light shelves or louvers creates integral horizontal shading. Fixed and adjustable horizontal shading devices are available in a variety of configurations and materials, ranging from fabric awnings to stainless-steel fins.

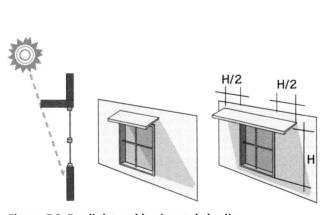

Advantages

- Block direct sunlight, allowing ambient sunlight to enter building, reducing heat gain
- Reduce the impact of sun movement on interior daylighting
- Limit glare
- Reduce cooling load

Disadvantages

- May inhibit access for cleaning and maintenance
- May collect snow and ice
- Too much shading limits daylight

Synergies

- Exterior light shelf
- Passive cooling

Tradeoff

- Potential seasonal heat loss for high-quality year-round daylighting

Figure 7.9 Daylight and horizontal shading
Source: Sharon B. Jaffe

Vertical Shading

Similar to horizontal shading, vertical shading (Figure 7.10) addresses the need for shading from the solar radiation on the east and west ends of the sun's path. On the west and east elevations, the sun is typically too low for horizontal shading to be effective; instead, vertical shading or "fins" are used to block the low sun as it moves around the building. Fins can be stationary or adjustable.

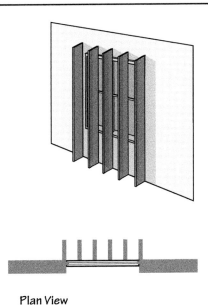

Plan View

Figure 7.10 Daylight and vertical shading
Source: Sharon B. Jaffe

Advantages
- Daylighting: If the fins are light colored, they block direct light and heat from entering the building but bounce desirable diffuse light into an interior area or room.
- Limit glare from low sun angles

Disadvantage
- Interferes with a clear view

Synergy
- Passive cooling

Tradeoff
- Natural ventilation

Landscape Shading

In warm and hot climates, trees, shrubs, and other vegetation can provide solar-radiation-blocking shade for the building. See Figure 7.11. Deciduous landscape shade is particularly useful in temperate climates where shade is desirable in the warm seasons, but direct heat gain is beneficial in the cold season.

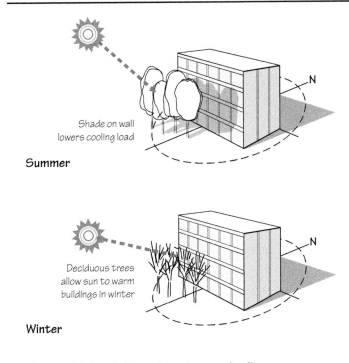

Shade on wall lowers cooling load

Summer

Deciduous trees allow sun to warm buildings in winter

Winter

Figure 7.11 Daylight and landscape shading
Source: Sharon B. Jaffe

Advantages
- External shading with deciduous vegetation during summer allows solar heat gain in cold seasons.
- Connection to nature

Disadvantages
- Vulnerable to natural disease and pests
- Only available during growing seasons, not on the occasional unseasonably warm day or week in an offseason

Synergy
- Passive cooling

Tradeoff
- May block distant views

LIGHT SHELVES

These are solid light-colored horizontal surfaces that reflect daylight deep into a building. Light shelves are most effectively used on equator-facing elevations above vision glass and below daylight glass to increase daylight distribution. Daylight is bounced, or reflected, off the light shelves toward the ceiling, increasing ceiling brightness. Daylight may then reflect off a light-colored ceiling, increasing daylight penetration into a room or interior space up to two times the window head height. (See Figure 7.12) A light shelf's reflective surface finish must be cleaned and regularly maintained to avoid a sharp loss in efficiency. Interior and exterior light shelves will have different lengths. The optimal size of a light shelf is calculated based on the sun angle, height, and window dimension. The width of the light shelf should be the same as the height of the vertical glass above it.

An *exterior light shelf* is a reflective horizontal surface installed on the exterior of a building, designed to redirect a portion of the incident light through the daylight glass above the sunshade to the building interior. Horizontal window shading may serve multiple functions for shade and reflecting light.

An *interior light shelf* is a reflective horizontal surface installed on the interior of a building located at the exterior window wall to reflect daylight from exterior windows further into the interior space of the building.

A *baffle* is a light shelf oriented vertically. Often used with top lighting strategies, baffles reduce glare and distribute daylight.

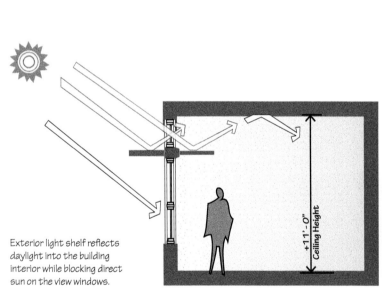

Exterior light shelf reflects daylight into the building interior while blocking direct sun on the view windows.

Figure 7.12 Daylight and light shelf
Source: Sharon B. Jaffe

Advantages
- Increased level of brightness compared to window side light
- Increase depth of daylight penetration
- Increase ceiling brightness
- Block direct sunlight, allowing ambient sunlight to enter building, reducing heat gain
- Reduced impact of sun movement on interior daylighting
- Limit glare
- Reduce cooling load

Disadvantages
- May inhibit access for cleaning and maintenance
- Exterior light shelves may collect snow and ice
- Too much shading limits daylight

Synergy
- Passive cooling

Tradeoff
- Potential seasonal heat loss for high-quality year-round daylighting

TOP LIGHTING/DAYLIGHT FROM ABOVE

Top lighting introduces daylighting into buildings through openings in the roof. Buildings with a deep footprint utilize top lighting to introduce light beyond the reach of side daylighting from windows. Top lighting is an effective strategy for a single-story building, the top floor of a multistory building, or above an atrium/void space in a multistory building. There is the potential for both heat gain and heat loss as a result of removing portions of the insulated roof and replacing it with glazing. The overall building design must mitigate or avoid the negative impact of top lighting strategies on thermal comfort. Mitigation strategies may include the configuration of the roof to prevent direct sunlight from entering the building through top lighting, internal baffles to diffuse direct sunlight, and a variety of top lighting fenestration options.

A *clerestory* is a window located high above eye level near or above the roof. (See Figure 7.13) Clerestory windows can introduce light deep in a building plan where perimeter window light would not reach. Operable clerestory windows support passive ventilation and cooling. North- and south-facing clerestories maximize daylighting opportunities.

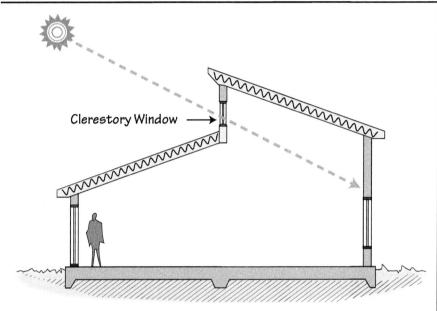

Clerestory Window

Advantages
- Introduce light deep into a building
- Operable clerestory facilitates convection air flow

Disadvantages
- Roof form may be compromised, resulting in a roof angle that does not accommodate optimum angle for solar photovoltaic arrays

Synergies
- Convection air flow
- Passive cooling

Tradeoff
- Potential heat gain and loss through additional glazing

Figure 7.13 Daylight and clerestory
Source: Sharon B. Jaffe

Sawtooth Roof

Often seen in warehouse and industrial buildings, this roof structure is particularly well suited to provide daylighting for buildings with deep open floor plans (See Figure 7.14). Operable windows support passive ventilation and cooling.

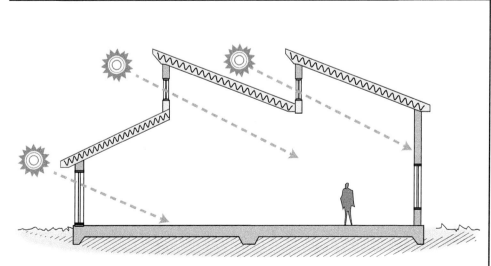

Advantages
- Introduce light deep into a building
- Operable clerestory facilitates convection air flow

Disadvantages
- Roof area available for PV reduced
- Roof angles compromised for PV arrays

Synergies
- Convection air flow
- Passive cooling

Tradeoff
- Potential heat gain and loss through additional glazing

Figure 7.14 Daylight and sawtooth roof
Source: Sharon B. Jaffe

ROOF MONITOR

This is a raised area of the roof, usually straddling a ridge, with openings, louvers, or vertical windows to admit daylight and facilitate ventilation. (See Figure 7.15) Roof monitors that have a sloped back wall help diffuse the light and reduce direct sunlight glare. Roof monitors can be spaced throughout the roof to maximize daylighting.

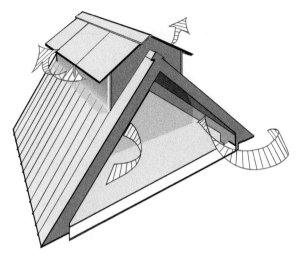

Figure 7.15 Daylight and roof monitor
Source: Sharon B. Jaffe

Advantages
- Introduce light deep into a building
- Operable window facilitates convection air flow

Disadvantages
- May allow direct sunlight/heat gain into a building; consider overhangs or shading similar to sidelight windows
- May introduce glare; consider baffles, angled back wall or deep wells cut off and limit glare

Synergy
- Passive ventilation and cooling

Tradeoffs
- View
- Occupant control

Skylights

Skylights are primarily a daylighting component and have a variety of options. They may be a transparent or translucent glass or plastic, domed or flat, stationary or operable. Some skylights open, also providing ventilation opportunities. A challenge of daylighting with skylights is that skylights may also allow excessive solar heat gain with daylight and heat loss at night.

Standard flat or domed skylights create horizontal windows on a flat or sloped roof and allow high levels of direct sunlight and heat gain into the building. (See Figure 7.16) Skylights may be spaced throughout the roof to maximize daylight for a single-story building or on the top floor of a multistory building.

Deep well skylights use a well to block direct sunlight. A deep well can drop down into interior space or be built up above the roof. While skylights provide more uniform lighting for more hours of the year than roof monitors, skylights add to direct heat gain.

General rules of thumb for even daylight from skylights are:

Skylight = 2–4% of floor area
Space skylights on center 1.5 × the floor to ceiling dimension

Solar tubes, or solar pipes, are similar to skylights in that they can introduce daylighting to sections of a building side daylighting does not reach. There are a few basic variations of solar tubes. Fixed or flexible tubes extend from the roof through the ceiling to distribute, with or without mirrors, a large quantity of diffuse light from a relatively small surface opening on the roof. The small surface area of the roof penetration minimizes heat loss.

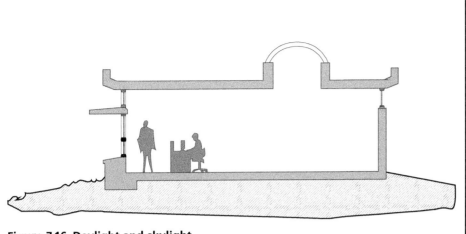

Figure 7.16 Daylight and skylight
Source: Sharon B. Jaffe

Advantages
- Introduce light deep into a building
- Operable skylight facilitates convection air flow

Disadvantages
- Heat gain
- Energy loss
- Potential glare

Synergy
- Vented skylight supports passive cooling

Tradeoff
- Potential heat gain and loss through additional glazing

Double Skin Façade

A double skin façade (DSF) is an external layer of glazing that creates a second skin as a light source over a building envelope. The second layer of glass allows air warmed by solar radiation to be contained outside the interior spaces of the building, where it can be vented to outdoors before entering conditioned space. (See Figure 7.17)

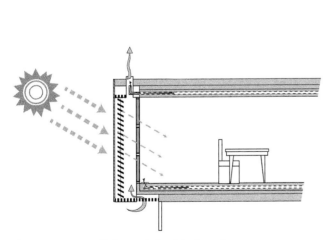

Figure 7.17 Daylight and double facade
Source: Sharon B. Jaffe

Advantages
- Maximizes daylight opportunities
- Secondary glass skin lowers wind load and allows fresh air supply to be regulated.
- Second glazed skin and air space provide acoustic insulation from exterior noise.
- Preheats supply air for natural ventilation

Disadvantages
- Potential for overheating air between layers of glazing inhibiting natural ventilation
- Potential for condensation
- Noise travel between adjacent spaces reflected by second glazing layer
- Significant additional cost

Synergies
- Daylight
- Ventilation
- Passive heating

Tradeoff
- Cooling

BUILDING FORM

A building's mass, form, and architectural characteristics can provide shading and mitigate thermal heat gain through exterior features such as balconies, deep facades, deeply recessed windows, and facade projections. (See Figure 7.18) Interior details such as splayed window apertures, adjacent walls, and sloped roofs facilitate daylight distribution.

Advantages
- Block direct sunlight allowing ambient sunlight to enter building reducing heat gain.
- Reduce the impact of sun movement on interior daylighting
- Limit glare
- Reduce cooling load

Disadvantages
- May collect snow and ice
- Too much shading limits daylight

Synergies
- Exterior horizontal shading
- Passive cooling

Tradeoff
- Potential seasonal heat loss for high-quality year-round daylighting

Figure 7.18 Daylight and integral shading
Source: Sharon B. Jaffe

Controls that integrate daylighting with the building, mechanical, and electric powered lighting systems, are required to optimize daylighting systems fully and realize potential energy savings. Both ASHRAE 90.1 standard and IECC include daylighting control requirements. When there is enough daylight, artificial light must be turned off to realize energy savings. If there is not enough daylighting, electric or artificial lighting must be turned on by manual or automated controls. Automated daylight controls may include daylight sensors that regulate the electrical lighting system responses to interior daylight levels.

Daylight controls require a clear strategy for managing the integration of electric lighting systems and daylight systems. Daylight harvesting systems adjust the level of electric lighting to utilize available daylight to maintain desired light levels. An effective integrated daylighting and electric-powered lighting system recognizes and appreciates the programming requirements of the building occupants and understands the significance of lighting on visual experience beyond the quantity of light required. Controls for powered lighting may include:

- Separate switching in daylight zones; lights are turned off when daylighting meets set light level
- Stepped dimming to set specific light levels, supplementing variable daylight; for example, 100 percent, 50 percent, and off

- Multilevel stepped lighting controls with multiple interim levels, minimum of 2 levels between off and 100 percent on
- Continuous dimming, a gradual dimming of electric lighting to supplement available daylighting to target light levels

Daylight systems and artificial or electric lighting systems may struggle to find a balance between the four perspectives. Lighting control systems should strive to bridge the divide through integration, producing buildings that are more energy efficient and less maintenance intensive than traditionally designed buildings, while enhancing the productivity and the quality of life for building occupants.

Microclimate, Local Zoning, and Codes

Building codes have minimum requirements for light and air in buildings. Sustainable designers work to design buildings that require no artificial lighting when the sun is shining, and the sky is cloud free. To evaluate daylighting potential, a designer evaluates daylight feasibility.

Feasibility Factor

$$\text{WWR (window to wall ratio)} \times \text{VT (visual transmittance)} \times \text{OF (obstruction factor)} = \text{daylight feasibility factor}$$

A feasibility factor of more than .25 is an indication that daylighting has the potential for significant energy savings. Less than .25 feasibility factor requires a reevaluation of the site to explore the possible removal of obstructions. If obstructions cannot be removed or relocated, investigate increasing the WWR or the VT. Daylighting principles may be applied for occupant comfort and views even if daylighting is not a viable energy cost-saving strategy. The reflectivity of exterior and landscape materials is also an important factor to be evaluated.

Interiors Scale

At the interiors scale, the space plan, interior finishes, and material selections can aid or hinder the ability to reflect daylight deep into the building.

Building interiors designed to utilize and integrate daylight zones while minimizing glare can use daylighting most effectively. Space plans that prioritize maximum occupant access to daylight locate open office areas at perimeter window walls of a building. Partitions of private perimeter offices or other enclosed spaces may block light from reaching spaces deeper inside the building. When private spaces must be located at the perimeter of a building, share daylight by using demising glass walls or high clear windows above sight lines. Areas that do not require daylight, or those that require controlled artificial light, should be located in non-perimeter spaces. Low sun angles in the early day and late afternoon on east and west facing glazing present challenges for daylight systems. West facing glazing has an increased probability of uncomfortable glare and heat gain from direct sunlight. Functions that are time-limited or task-specific, service spaces, and infrequently occupied spaces are better located away from the building perimeter or in western perimeter zones.

Position computer monitors, video screens, and other equipment screens carefully in daylit spaces. High contrasting bright light behind an internally illuminated screen can cause eye strain. A bright light behind the screen user may cause veiled reflections on the screen, making the screen more difficult to see clearly. Screens positioned parallel to the direction daylight enters a building, generally perpendicular to the window, reduce the incidence of veiled reflections and high contrast glare.

Open office areas, especially open areas that use furniture systems with workstation panels, must be planned to support daylighting distribution and access to ventilation and views. Low workstation panels, 43 inches or less, will maintain views and daylight distribution patterns. Work surfaces, with or without video or computer screens, are best positioned perpendicular to windows to avoid casting shadows on the work surface. Open-plan offices with low partitions are inherently louder spaces in which to work, and limit privacy. Acoustics are likely to be a significant tradeoff to allow greater daylight penetration. This design approach has a significant functional impact. As such, end-user involvement should be solicited in decisions to pursue this approach.

Interior materials and finishes significantly influence the success of a daylighting system design. Effective, even distribution of daylight deep into the interior space requires light-colored ceilings to reflect and bounce light. Interiors with high-LRV colors, smooth, modestly reflective surfaces, and finished ceilings produce the best daylighting results. Avoid dark colors. Dark colors, rough exposed surfaces, unfinished wood, and exposed ductwork and mechanicals in ceilings all absorb some daylight.

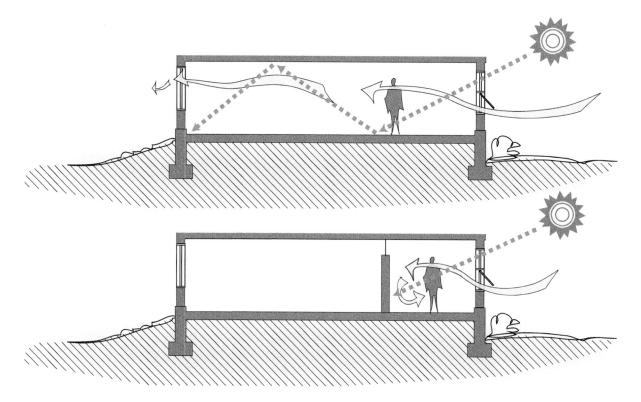

Figure 7.19 Daylight and interior scale
Source: Sharon B. Jaffe

Light-colored materials (>80% LRV) and matte finishes in all daylighted spaces increase efficiency through interreflections, also significantly increasing visual comfort. Highly reflective surfaces may cause uncomfortable glare. Desirable light reflectance values (LRV) as recommended by the Illuminating Engineering Society are ceilings greater than 80 percent; walls 50 to 70 percent (higher if wall contains window); floors 20 to 40 percent; furniture 25 to 45 percent. High-LRV material finish on the wall opposite the daylight wall will help balance the brightness of daylight windows.

As important as quantity of light on the horizontal plane or work surface is for visual requirements, the light quality, brightness or lightness, of interior space is primarily observed by the light levels on vertical surfaces. As a generalization, building occupants prefer light, bright spaces. Windows and daylight are highly prized, and well-lit spaces increase both building occupant productivity and mood. High contrast between the relatively high light levels on horizontal planes and lower light levels on the walls and ceilings give the impression of dark and uncomfortable spaces. A broad distribution of daylight on all surfaces in interior space is essential for the perception of brightness and occupant visual comfort.

Objectives and Design Ideas

The pre-design phase of a project sets specific daylighting design objectives. Informed by industry standards, code requirements, and case study research, design objectives indicate the target and intention for daylighting quality and quantity. Design ideas are the various methods implemented to achieve targets and intentions. Usually, there are multiple ways to achieve an objective; therefore, there may be several design ideas for each objective. *Sustainable Design Basics* methodology views a project through the four perspectives of performance, systems, culture, and experience, to explore varied design solutions. Developing separate objectives for each perspective in the early design exploration stage assures a considered and holistic design response. Ultimately, the design ideas explored through the four perspectives are evaluated and synthesized into a focused response that supports the overall project objectives and goals. This design integration process is explained and demonstrated in the demonstration project in chapter 11.

Design Priorities

The design ideas illustrated Table 7.1 indicate a shared priority, to locate people near the perimeter of a building to take advantage of daylight. Typically, an effective daylight strategy requires a narrow building to allow daylight to reach all parts of the building floor plate. In a "deep" building, it is more challenging to meet illumination requirements with daylighting. Single-story buildings, or the top floor of a multistory building, may address the "deep" plan challenge with the use of top lighting in the form of roof monitors, skylights, or other roof shape configurations that provide daylight access. Unfortunately, top lighting does not mitigate the absence of views. An open space in the building's mass, or void, such as an atrium or courtyard, is another approach used to address the challenge of daylight distribution in a deep building. A courtyard or atrium reduces the enclosed depth of the building while introducing additional perimeter side lighting that delivers daylight to more building users.

Table 7.1 DAYLIGHT: DESIGN OBJECTIVES AND DESIGN IDEAS
Source: Sharon Jaffe

	Daylighting	Design Objective	Design Idea
Perspectives	**Performance**	Meet required light levels with daylighting 75% of operational hours. Meet or exceed objectives set during Step 2 Goals and Objectives. Meet or exceed prescribed levels of daylighting for targeted green rating without adding to cooling load.	Simple structure that is easy to build, with overhanging roof lines and exterior horizontal sun shade to shade windows from direct sunlight and glare. Interior light shelf to reflect light deep into the building. Locate storage and no light functions on the north side of the building.
	Systems	Maximize use of skylight and daylight while blocking potential heat gain. Create a comfortable exterior room/area that supports daylight and shading strategies. Provide comfortable daylight with out glare or unwanted heat.	Use north lighting to maximize ambient daylight without heat gain. Use light shelves to reflect daylight deep into the building to limit or eliminate the need for artificial lighting. Use exterior pergola for shading outside the south windows creating a comfortable outside area.
	Culture	Connect occupants of the building with daylight and views at all times to support overall health and wellness. Provide spots of daylight inside the building bring the outside in. Utilize the building orientation to organize interior spaces.	Limit heat gain to limit the need for air-conditioning. Use high levels of roof insulation. Shade south facing glass. Building roof monitor facilitates daylighting in the central interior of the building creating a natural gathering spot.
	Experience	Use daylight as an organizing element of the building. Use daylight to create a welcoming and dynamic central gathering space available to all building occupants.	Central courtyard reduces depth of floor plan while providing ample and focused daylight. Daylight, plantings, and water feature in the central courtyard create an indoor environment with an outdoor sensibility.

Daylighting has the potential to improve overall lighting, building performance, and energy savings. Daylight also enhances the interior environment aesthetically and physically. Building occupants prefer daylit spaces. Daylight adds to a general sense of well-being, reduces eye strain, boosts mental focus, and increases productivity and occupant satisfaction.

Validation

Daylight design objectives will vary widely based on specific program requirements, visual tasks, and aesthetic aspirations. Accomplishing daylight objectives will require consideration of factors from the macroscale to the microscale. Critical factors to achieve effective daylighting include the relationship between the solar path to site and building, the availability of daylight influenced by building orientation, massing and fenestration, the placement of work surfaces, interior materials, and surface finish reflectance, and the needs of an individual to accomplish visual tasks.

Daylighting for a sustainable design project will have objectives from all four perspectives. The performance perspective asks for increased energy efficiency by reducing the required electric lighting requirements to provide appropriate light levels. The systems perspective requires the daylighting system to support the objectives of other passive systems for natural ventilation, passive cooling, and passive heating while reducing the need for the electric lighting system to meet targeted lighting levels. Daylight levels, as well as methods to introduce daylight to the interior of a building, are influenced by the culture perspective. The configuration of the building, building fenestration, and massing are influenced by the desire to meet or contrast the architectural expression of the surrounding community. The experience perspective asks the designer to consider the ability of daylight to reveal architectural form, and to provide connection to nature and the surrounding environment to nurture the sensory perception and appreciation of the beauty that strengthens the psychological connection to "place."

There are multiple daylight design responses to each of the design objectives from each of the four perspectives. Often, it is not possible to achieve the objectives of all four perspectives 100 percent. It is much more common to require a balance between the four perspectives through tradeoffs and synergies that reflects the overall project guiding principles. A client with an aesthetic-driven mission may be willing to sacrifice some degree of energy performance for a building that provides a daylight experience that reflects the organization's aesthetic aspirations or facilitates specific daylight-driven functions. An organization deeply rooted in the architectural culture of the community may be willing to trade off some degree of daylighting to preserve the overall appearance of a classic window fenestration thereby increasing the need for insulation of the thermal envelope.

Effective daylighting solutions are not as simple as achieving a set lighting level. Daylighting solutions are nuanced. A synthesis of the tradeoffs, contradictions, and distillation of hundreds of individual pieces of information that inform design decisions is required to resolve the four perspectives into a single focused daylight design. An interim analysis and validation of the daylight schemes provide the necessary metrics that a designer uses to evaluate and meld four perspective design ideas into one.

Methods of daylight performance analysis include:

- Mathematical models
  - Lumen input
  - Daylight factor
- Daylight computer simulations and models
  - Computer software with 3D modeling and daylight simulation
  - Most 3D architectural modeling software includes the capacity for some daylight simulation and analysis either as part of the native program, extensions or through program plug-ins. SketchUp, Revit, Autodesk Ecotect, and Vector-works have varying degrees of capability for daylight analysis and simulation with a variety of companion plugins.
  - Sefaria is a program plugin used in the SDB demonstration chapter.
  - Building performance software
  - Specific lighting simulation programs (i.e., RADIANCE)
- Physical architectural scale models and measurements
  - A scale model with daylight apertures can be used to evaluate daylighting schemes. May be used under real or artificial sky or light.
  - Advantages of physical models are they require no mathematical knowledge. Visual results are very close to reality. Photographs and measurements taken with light measurement instruments can document results. Cautions: Accuracy requires an accurate model, including dimensions and material reflectance, and appropriate measurement instruments. A physical scale model may be time con-suming and expensive.
- Full-scale mockup models and measurements
  - A full-scale (1:1) mockup model including daylight apertures of the subject space can be used to test and validate daylighting strategies under the real or artificial sky. Advantages include the experience of the illuminated space, very accurate results, option to include specific artificial lighting as to be specified, effects of different glass areas and locations can be studied, real measurements can be taken to establish illumination levels. Disadvantages are that the process is space, time, and expense intensive.
  - Lawrence Berkeley National Laboratory's FLEXLAB can simulate whole-building environments.

Daylight systems and artificial or electric lighting systems may struggle to find a balance between the four perspectives. Lighting control systems strive to bridge the divide through integration, producing buildings that are more energy efficient and less maintenance intensive than traditionally designed buildings while enhancing the productivity and the quality of life for building occupants.

FURTHER READING

Ander, Gregg D. "Daylighting." Whole Building Design Guide (WBDG), a program of the National Institute of Building Sciences, www.wbdg.org/resources/daylighting.php.

DeKay, M., and G. Z. Brown. 2014. *Sun, Wind, and Light* (3rd ed.). Hoboken, NJ: John Wiley & Sons.

Karlen, M., J. R. Benya, and C. Spangler. 2012. *Lighting Design Basics*. Hoboken, NJ: John Wiley & Sons.

Kwok, A., and W. Grondzik. 2011. *Green Studio Handbook* (2nd ed.). Hoboken, NJ: John Wiley & Sons.

Lechner, N. 2014. *Heating, Cooling, Lighting: Sustainable Methods for Architects* (4th ed.). Hoboken, NJ: John Wiley & Sons.

National Oceanic and Atmospheric Administration. (n.d.). NOAA Solar Calculator. Retrieved from Earth System Research Laboratory, www.esrl.noaa.gov/gmd/grad/solcalc/.

8

Step 3C: Building Envelope

Step 4
Design
Solution

4. ...ign Synthesis
...l Design Validation
...enting the Project

Step 3
Design

3A Preliminary Design
3B Passive Design
3C Building Envelope
3D Green Materials
* Beyond the Basics

Step...
Pre-...

2A Resear... ...dies
2B Project ...
2C Design Crite...
2D Spatial Relation...

Step 1
Context

1A Project Information
1B Guiding Principles
1C Macro / Micro Context
1D Site Inventory & Analysis

Figure 8.0 *Sustainable Design Basics*, **step 3C**

Source: Sharon B. Jaffe

WHAT IS THE BUILDING ENVELOPE?

The building envelope (Figure 8.1) is an assembly of systems that includes the foundation, exterior walls, roof, floor, windows, doors, and any other openings in the building exterior (e.g., clerestories, roof monitors, and skylights). Together these interrelated elements make up the physical separation between the unconditioned outdoors and the conditioned interior spaces. The building envelope prevents unwanted heat, cold, water, light, and noise from negatively impacting the space inside the building.

The building envelope is the interface between indoor and outdoor space; its design is complex, serving many functions and directly impacting passive strategies for solar heating, passive cooling, natural ventilation and daylighting. Together with other building systems, the building envelope ideally responds to the local climate and optimizes the energy efficiency and interior comfort of a building.

FUNCTIONS

The building envelope physically separates conditioned and unconditioned environments. The various building envelope components function as a system to provide structural support, regulate temperature and air flow and serve as a barrier to protect the building interior and building occupants from the elements of nature.

- Structure: The building envelope may be a part of the structural system, as with some masonry block, stone, and brick buildings. Independent of the building structure system, the building must still support its weight and transfer lateral forces, such as winds and earthquakes.
- Control or barrier: The building envelope serves as a barrier protecting the interior from water infiltration and condensation, air infiltration, and noise. The building

Figure 8.1 Introduction to the building envelope
Source: Sharon B. Jaffe

envelope is required by code to serve as a barrier to fire, heat, and smoke, to protect occupants within a building, and to prevent a fire from spreading to other structures.

- Daylight infiltration: The decisions regarding building fenestration and the location, size, glazing properties, of windows, doors, and other openings are expressions of the building envelope that are vital to the success of a daylighting system.
- Thermal insulation: The building envelope directly interacts with the macroclimate and microclimate. It is required to moderate extremes in heat and cold, and by doing so, reduces the consumption of energy required to mechanically heat, cool, and ventilate a building.
- Aesthetic appearance: The building envelope is the architectural expression seen from outside the building. Its aesthetic appearance has the potential to communicate information about the building quality and its occupants while contributing to the character of the surrounding community. The interior appearance and operations of the building envelope influence the productivity and satisfaction of occupants.

THE BUILDING ENVELOPE IN THE SDB METHODOLOGY

Step 3 of the *Sustainable Design Basics* methodology explores the interim steps of preliminary design and passive design in the previous chapters. The process of establishing specific perspective-focused design objectives based upon the project goals and objects established in step 2 is now familiar. The evaluation of the strengths of each design idea and the synthesis of the most responsive design ideas from each of the four perspectives form a single interim design scheme built on preceding interim steps. This methodology provides a holistic and ordered exploration through the four perspectives while limiting design variables for the beginning sustainable designer. The synthesized design scheme from passive design daylight is a starting point for building envelope explorations and design.

Resilience

Buildings designed to be resilient are meant to continue to function in the face of natural and human-made disasters. Resilient buildings anticipate and protect against possible destructive scenarios. In hurricane-prone areas, they are built to withstand high wind loads and heavy rain, and to resist, accommodate, and quickly drain flood waters. Resilient buildings will locate mechanical systems on the upper floors above flood levels to avoid destruction. In earthquake-prone areas, they are built to withstand the shaking and lateral movement of seismic loads. Resilient buildings are designed to accommodate internal change, large and small modifications, that are made to a building over time as successive generations adapt a building to its current needs.

How quickly or slowly buildings evolve is based on a variety of factors. A building can take a "high-road" or "low-road" approach to structure. High-road buildings are built to be very strong to resist the forces of nature and to last a long time. Low-road buildings are built with some redundancy, and are flexible, lightweight structures without grand architectural intent.. When they cease to fulfill the need of the day, the low road building can be easily modified, disassembled and reassembled with the materials available for reuse. Both of these approaches avoid obsolescence that requires demolition of the building and the waste of a considerable quantity of building materials and associated embodied energy. Resilient buildings are the ones that can adapt to evolving needs.

BUILDING ENVELOPE AND MACROCLIMATE

Ideally, the building envelope is designed to respond to macroclimate of climate and weather; and microclimate, which is influenced by the terrain, landscaping, and the building itself. The building envelope must accommodate seasonal changes that trigger expansion and contraction. Explorations of daily and seasonal environmental changes are integrated into the building envelope design to leverage opportunities and mitigate challenges for the benefit of the interior environment and enhanced building performance.

The perception of comfort is circumstantial and adaptive, changing with the surrounding environmental conditions and the activities performed. A building envelope that is designed to be responsive to the macroclimate and microclimate with the intention of maximizing passive strategies reduces the amount of energy required to mitigate uncomfortable interior conditions. Over the centuries of architecture, especially before mechanical systems became common, rules of thumb were used in thinking about building shape, building envelope, and building structure. Table 8.1 presents some of those rules of thumb.

TABLE 8.1 BUILDING ENVELOPE DESIGN STRATEGIES BY MACROCLIMATE

	Implication	Design Strategy	Material Notes
Macroclimate: Hot/Dry	High temperatures, low humidity	Minimize sun exposure and maximize shade. Shade the building and breezeways to limit heat gain.	Exterior shade materials including: landscape vegetation, thatch, built shade structures including awnings, screens, pergolas, and arbors
	High temperatures, low humidity	Reduce building surface-to-area ratio. Compact building shape and floor plan minimizes external wall area limits surface for heat gain. Minimize size of east and west façades that otherwise receive extended sun exposure.	Light-colored exterior materials: concrete, brick, or whitewashed. Local material: mud, brick
	Minimize sun exposure and maximize shade	Cluster buildings with compact footprints positioned to shade one another	Local material: mud, brick, not a lot of lumber
	High temperatures, low humidity	Shaded courtyards with pools of water facilitate evaporative cooling, cooling the ambient air supply for natural ventilation intake.	Exterior shade materials including: building roof, landscape, thatch, awnings, screens, pergolas, and arbors. Light-colored exterior materials: concrete, brick, or whitewashed.

	Implication	Design Strategy	Material Notes
Macroclimate: Hot/Dry	Large temperature swings from day to night	Locate fenestration to facilitate natural ventilation, cross breeze, stack effect, high level windows or vents for night time flushing of hot air. Intake cool air through lower windows. Deep roof or other built overhangs shade smaller windows. Limit if not eliminate windows on east/west exposures.	Thermal mass for building and walls of concrete, mud, adobe, white-washed to reflect solar heat. Exterior shade materials including: building roof, landscape, thatch, awnings, screens, pergolas, and arbors. Window glazing with low U factor, low SHGC
	Large temperature swings from day to night	Large thermal mass has the ability to absorb heat gain keeping interiors cooler in the day, releasing the heat during cooler evenings to mitigate temperature swings	Local material for exterior building structure. Whitewash to reflect solar heat gain. Interior flooring for thermal mass heat storage
	High temperatures, low humidity	Interior space uses high ceilings; hot air rises above occupant living space	Light-colored interior materials.
	High temperatures, low humidity	Light-colored surfaces reflect solar radiation and radiant heat gain	Light-colored exterior materials: concrete, brick, or whitewashed. Light-colored interior materials.
Macroclimate: Hot/Humid	Temperature range remains steady heat	Avoid thermal mass, use lightweight porous material. Insulated eastern and western walls	Timber of steel stud frame construction; avoid storing heat that would be released in the evening maintaining high temperatures
	Temperature range remains steady heat	Shade building keeping sun off roof and wall surfaces to avoid heat gain	Exterior shade materials including building roof, landscape vegetation, thatch, awnings, screens, pergolas, and arbors.
	Temperature range remains steady heat high humidity	Raise first living level above the ground to capture cooling breezes. Maximize ventilation at night.	Wood, bamboo, and other lightweight materials assembled to allow facilitate ventilation.
	Condensation resulting mold concerns	Insulate surfaces prone to condensation. Windows that may be left open for ventilation in all weather. Materials that do not support bio growth.	Thatch roof, wood is available; insect, rodents, pests are a concern. Concrete is used to avoid pests but not as porous for ventilation.
	Temperature range remains steady heat	Covered external living areas positioned to catch prevailing breezes, shield walls from sun exposure and act as buffer zones	Shade with solid materials to block sun that minimize heat retention and tolerate exposure to solar radiation.
	Temperature range remains steady, heat, high humidity	Windows that can be left open in wet conditions to maintain natural ventilation during precipitation	Shelter windows with awning, overhang or shutters, or use casement or louver windows.
	Temperature range remains steady, heat, high humidity	Air movement is required. High ceilings: hot air rises above occupant living space. Large windows on at least two walls maximize cross ventilation.	Building materials porous to air but not rain.
	High steady heat, high humidity, concern for mold	High ventilation Limit materials that support mold,	Interior mold-resistant materials; tile, stone, laminate flooring Moisture-resistant drywall, paint that contains mold inhibitors.
	Temperature range remains steady heat	Light color surfaces reflect solar radiation and radiant heat gain	Whitewash, sun-bleached materials

High humidity can rarely be fully controlled by passive measures. Advanced active technology such as air conditioners, dehumidifiers, desiccants, and other equipment specifically designed to control humidity and driven by renewable energy may be required to control high humidity levels. Humidity levels above 70% for extended periods is an attractive condition for mold growth.

(continued)

TABLE 8.1 (CONTINUED)

	Implication	Design Strategy	Material Notes
Macroclimate: Cold	Low temperatures, require more heat than cooling	Maximize insulation, thick walls for thermal mass. Seal building to eliminate air infiltration, airtight envelope. Small compact floor plan to reduce exterior building skin to limit heat transfer surface.	Indigenous materials Darker colored material. High R-value building envelope materials including prefab wall panels, straw bale walls. Fiberglass window and door frames do not expand and contract and do not conduct heat or off-gas.
	Maximize solar gain, minimize opportunities for heat loss	Equator facing larger windows for solar heat gain. Limit windows and window size on other exposures. Direct sun for solar heat gain by thermal mass inside the building.	Glazing low U-factor, high SHGC. Interior flooring including stone, tile or concrete flooring for thermal mass heat storage.
	Heavy snows increase load on roof, reflect sun reducing potential heat gain, increases exterior brightness and glare.	Sloped roof that easily sheds snow and rain. Roof materials that absorb heat.	Green roof insulates for hot and cold. Design simple roof form, use durable insulating roof materials. Darker colors. Slate, metal standing-seam, cement tile, wood shake, shingle.
	Cold temperatures, great differences in external and interior temperatures	Low interior ceilings to reduce volume of air to be heated.	Closed plenum ceiling.
Macroclimate: Temperate	Seasonal extremes for hot and cold	Insulation keeps heat in during cold seasons and heat out in warm seasons.	Wood, stone, clay soil is typically available for construction. Advanced materials for wall insulation.
	Seasonal extremes for hot and cold	Multipaned operable windows keep heat in during winter; operable windows aid natural ventilation in warm seasons.	High U factor window glazing, wood, stone clay soil is typically available for construction. Advanced materials for wall insulation.
	Building shape—rectangular on east-west axis.	Deep overhangs allow winter sun to enter building and heat thermal mass in the winter while blocking sun in the summer	Utilize dense material for thermal mass, such as concrete and stone.
	Seasonally hot	Cross ventilation, limit depth of floor plan. Smaller inlet opening offset from larger outlet facilitates air movement while mixing fresh air through the interior space.	Inlets and outlets can be louvered openings, windows that are screened or shaded from solar radiation to limit heat gain.

BUILDING STRUCTURE AND THE BUILDING ENVELOPE

The building envelope and the building's structure are closely tied both physically and functionally. The structural system impacts a building's energy footprint. A number of material factors influence the choice of a structural system: embodied energy, thermal mass, moisture control, and the ability to control infiltration.

The role of building structure is to support and transfer building weight, or gravity load, and lateral loads produced by the natural environment, through elements of the building structure system to the ground, allowing the building to stand. In short, the structural system is what holds the building up. The structure of a building may be integral to the building envelope, as in a masonry wall, or may be an independent framing system, like wood or metal framing, which supports the upper floors, walls, and roof. The type of structural system employed, frame or planar support, influences decisions for building envelope.

Different structural systems can accommodate different maximum distances between support elements, affecting the flexibility of the building interior. Previous design decisions regarding building shape and form will suggest the suitability of one structural system over others. The structure of the building envelope is determined in the early design stages, based on the priorities established through project guiding principles, and goals and objectives.

Types

Types of basic building structure systems (Table 8.2) include the following.

Bearing wall: A wall carries its weight as well as the weight of the floors and roof transferring the combined weight to the ground and transfers the combined weight to the ground.

Column and beam: Columns (the vertical structure elements) and beams (the horizontal structure elements) support the weight of the building itself, the building contents, and occupants, transferring the load through the horizontal beams to the vertical columns down through the foundation and ultimately to the ground. Subcategories of column and beam include the common skeleton frame structure and truss system. Walls are not load bearing, allowing for design flexibility.

- A skeleton frame system uses a network of columns and connecting beams to transfer building load, leaving the exterior envelope and interior spaces independent from the structure.

- A truss system uses a triangulated structural frame assemblage that distributes force among the assemblage members, allowing it to span long distances efficiently.

Free-span structure: Engineered wall frames, engineered horizontal beams, and trusses transfer building load to provide an interior space free of vertical structural elements.

Each building structure system and each material has specific basic structural and aesthetic properties and qualities that determine the most appropriate choice for a specific application or given project. The specifics of structural systems are an essential aspect of building technology studies and beyond the scope of this textbook. However, a rudimentary understanding of structural systems will allow evaluation of the sustainability concerns during the schematic design of a sustainable building.

TABLE 8.2 COMPARATIVE BUILDING STRUCTURE SYSTEMS

	Clear Span	Column	Bearing
	Column-free interior space	Framework carries the load, w/ stabilizing infill for rigidity	Wall carries the load of structure above
Heavy timber		X	
Concrete		X	
Steel frame		X	
Steel stud			X
Wood stud			X
Engineered wood	X		
Truss	X		

Materials

Building structure systems have individual material properties that are more, or less, environmentally sound. Each project weighs the tradeoffs of specific structural materials for a sustainable building, including the inherent embodied energy of a material, structural suitability, resource consumption, and future resilience.

Building Structure and Macroclimate

Over the centuries, especially before mechanical systems became common, architectural rules of thumb were used in thinking about building shape and structure. Following are observations and cautions for material usage based on climate regions:

Hot/dry climates
- Mud, brick, and limited lumber are available in this climate zone.
- Wildfire zones require fire resistant and self-extinguishing material.

Hot/humid climates
- Wood building materials are available but require high maintenance because wood will warp and rot.
- Concrete is stable despite high humidity.
- Concrete masonry unit (CMU) structures manage high humidity and limit the risk of termite and pest infestation.
- Steel framing must be treated against corrosion when used in humid climates.

Cold climates
- Cold climates often are located in mountainous, forested regions where lumber and stone are available.
- In extremely cold climates with permafrost, elevate buildings with ventilated air-space between the building and the ground. Breaking the contact between the building and the ground helps control heat loss through heat transferred from the building to the ground.

Temperate climates
- Wood, stone, and clay soil are typically available.

Macro Context

Rating systems and standards are used to help design teams make decisions that will benefit the project from a sustainability perspective. For example, a steel structure may have a 95% recycled content level, making it conform to some rating systems' benchmark for the use of recycled materials. Other rating systems, like the Living Building Challenge, are more concerned with the toxicity of materials and will, therefore, encourage the use of renewable, nontoxic, low-energy materials. Urban, suburban, or rural macro contexts' may suggest a more appropriate or recognizable structural system that often falls within the skill sets of local builders.

TABLE 8.3 BUILDING STRUCTURE DESIGN OBJECTIVES/DESIGN IDEAS

		Design Objective	Design Idea
Perspective	Performance	• Use the least amount of structure to support the maximum amount of square footage in the building.	• Use steel frame structure to minimize material required and maximize space.
	Systems	• Use an ecological renewable structure system. • Use a low pollution solution.	• Use heavy timber wood structure.
	Culture	• Use a structural system that provides open spans to support the large spaces needed to meet client requirements. • Use a structural system that can be disassembled at the end of the buildings service life.	• Use steel structure to maximize space between columns. • Use laminated wood to maximize space between columns with a lower carbon foot print system.
	Experience	• Use structural systems that are expressive.	• Use exposed natural finish heavy timber for a biophilic experience. • Sculpt the heavy timber columns to create an interesting sculptural experience.

Design Objectives and Design Ideas

The four perspectives will drive significant project specific exploration and opportunities related to building structure (Table 8.3). The design decision matrix will help evaluate and prioritize which perspective and design idea takes precedence, based on project guiding principles and client priorities.

Design Priorities

Throughout the design process, and particularly at this stage in schematic design, it is necessary to review the client's guiding principles to determine the priority for each possible structural system choice. The design matrix will help evaluate the design approach to the building structure.

Synergies and Tradeoffs

The design ideas generated through the four perspectives (see Table 8.3) present a synergy between the systems idea and the experience idea. Both call for the use of heavy timber. The performance and culture ideas are synergistic as they both call for the use of steel structure. If steel is desirable, it is necessary to evaluate the tradeoffs and benefits comparing heavy timber relative to the advantages of the steel frame structure. In design, there is not one perfect solution. A building design project requires hundreds of compromises.

Building Structure Systems: Options and Considerations

Traditionally, a building design must balance conflicting demands of structural requirements, code requirements, material costs, and aesthetics. When designing a sustainable project, the choice of structure requires the evaluation of embodied energy, thermal properties, function, local availability of materials, and labor as they all have a significant impact on a building's overall environmental impact and building resilience. In the Pacific Northwest of the United States, for example, a high proportion of building construction uses local wood and engineered wood products. It is a practice that reduces overall life-cycle CO_2 emissions while supporting a local economy with close ties to the timber industry. In Florida and other hot, humid climates, structures made of concrete masonry units (CMU) reinforced with steel rebar are a response to damaging local insects and provide a structure that benefits a building through the inherent insulating properties of thermal mass that keep building interiors cooler.

Advantages and Disadvantages of Structural Systems

Steel frame: Steel columns and horizontal beams create a "skeleton" frame with a three-dimensional rectangular grid to support attached floors, roof, and walls. They are assembled with bolts, welded joints, or rivets.

Advantages
- Lighter-weight quick construction
- Wind and earthquake resistant
- Flexible interior space

Disadvantages
- Loses strength at high temperature
- Prone to corrosion in humid environments

Common building applications
- High-rise buildings
- Industrial buildings
- Warehouse buildings
- Multifamily residential buildings

Light-gauge steel construction uses galvanized steel studs, sized similarly to lumber, similar to wood frame construction. A frame of steel members is built and sheathed with surface material, stabilizing the frame; connections are made with self-tapping screws.

Advantages
- Lighter weight, quick construction
- Wind and earthquake resistant
- Noncombustible material
- High weight-to-strength ratio

Disadvantages
- Loses strength at very high temperature
- Additional blocking required for axial loads

Common building applications
- Low-rise residential
- Small-scale commercial
- Small-scale industrial

Concrete frames use reinforced concrete beams and columns in a skeleton arrangement.

Advantages
- Durability, compression strength
- Inexpensive
- Can use any perimeter exterior cladding
- Noncombustible; eliminates fireproofing
- Fly ash, recycled content
- No VOCs
- Reduced vibration and sound conduction

Disadvantages
- Cement production produce GHG
- Uses substantial resources to produce

Common building applications
- Commercial
- Industrial

Concrete slab construction uses horizontal slabs of reinforced concrete to construct floors and ceilings, typically used with steel or concrete columns and beams.

Advantages
- Durable and low maintenance
- Flexible form
- Thermal mass
- Noncombustible eliminates fireproofing
- Inhospitable to pest and mold

Disadvantages
- Heavy
- GHG emissions from cement
- Uses many resources to produce

Common building applications
- Commercial
- High-rise multifamily residential

Light wood frames use wood lumber for construction. A frame of wood members is built and sheathed with surface material, stabilizing the frame; connections are made with nails or screws.

Advantages
- Lightweight material
- Quick construction
- Flexible configuration
- Wall frames can be built flat and then raised into place

Disadvantages

- Combustible
- Low levels of wind resistance

Common building applications

- Low-rise residential
- Small-scale commercial
- Small-scale industrial

Timber frame construction is a traditional building system using heavy timber joined with lap, mortise, tenon, and other wood joints to create a frame structure. **Post-and-beam** construction is a similar construction system using manufactured steel connections and may span large building areas.

Advantages

- Renewable material (FSC)
- Wood stores CO_2, reducing CO_2 emissions
- Low embodied energy
- Lightweight
- Insulating properties

Disadvantages

- Natural wood material must be handled appropriately and is subject to rot, pests, structural frame movement.
- Frame movement may result in finish material cracking.
- Exterior exposed for aesthetic results in thermal bridging.

Common building applications

- Traditional barn structures
- Residential single-family homes
- Old industrial buildings

BUILDING FOUNDATIONS

A building foundation (Figure 8.2) transfers the overall building load to the ground; keeps out wind, groundwater, soil gases, and water vapor; and resists temperature transfer between the conditioned space and the surrounding ground. The type of building foundation – shallow or deep – is determined by building load, building type, soil type, and other site conditions and constraints. The choice of a foundation influences the installation and ongoing access to utility lines.

Shallow foundations are common in residential and smaller commercial buildings. Sometimes called footings, they transfer building load to the ground near the surface of the soil and include concrete slab on grade, spread footing, and rubble trench.

Deep foundations transfer building load into the ground using piles or pilings drilled deep into the ground. Tall commercial buildings use deep foundations. A pile can be reinforced concrete, steel, timber, or a composite.

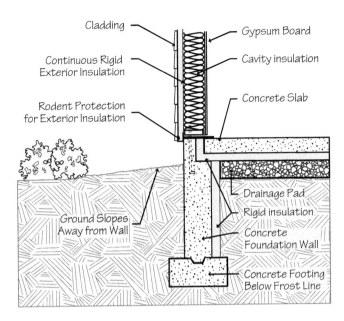

Figure 8.2 Building foundation
Source: Sharon B. Jaffe

Building Foundations and the Macroclimate

The following are observations for usage based on climate regions:

Hot/dry climates
- Foundations are shallow because the frost line is very high.
- Current recommendations call for insulation in all climate zones.

Hot/humid climates
- Foundations are shallow because the frost line is very high.
- Foundations may be open and support building ventilation.
- Current recommendations call for insulation in all climate zones.

Cold climates
- Foundations are deep (below the regionally designated frost line) and insulated.

Temperate climates
- Foundations are deep (below the regionally designated frost line) and insulated.

Microclimate, Local Zoning and Codes

Soil types and site typography are drivers for foundation choices. The local code determines the minimum soil and drainage requirements and testing. Code requires a foundation capable of accommodating specific building requirements and generally prescribes the minimum dimensions and depth the foundation must extend below the frost line. On a site with soil not capable of supporting a typical concrete foundation, pilings may be required. The pilings are required to sit on a solid rock to support the foundation of the building.

Site Inventory and Analysis

The site inventory and analysis from step 1 is critical. Refer to the inventory analysis about the site topography, soil conditions, and water table levels that will impact the selection of appropriate foundation and structure.

Basements

A basement contributes to larger overall building size. A larger building consumes more energy than a smaller building. Traditionally, a basement allows for storage space and locating mechanical equipment below grade, thereby freeing up more space for active work areas and support functions of the building. A basement is an additional level of the building below ground, requiring more extensive excavation, site modifications, additional insulation, vertical circulation and moisture barriers. After construction, a basement must be conditioned to avoid high humidity and potential mold growth. Constructed with concrete walls, a material with an extremely high embodied energy level, a basement is also resource intensive. Foundations are expensive and permanent which makes the building location step in the design process is critical. Once built, it is difficult and costly to make a change to the foundation design of a building. Many clients opt for a "slab-on-grade" building where a basement is eliminated to save money and make construction easier.

Resilient buildings adapt and continue to function despite changing natural or temporary disaster conditions. Resilience is present at various scales. At the building scale, specific macroclimates and microclimates have specific vulnerabilities. In an area vulnerable to flooding, Mechanical equipment in the basement is vulnerable in floods. Mechanical spaces located above grade on upper levels contribute to a building's operational resilience, allowing the building's utilities to continue to function in a disaster.

Foundation Systems

Slab on grade is a single poured concrete slab several inches thick that serves as a building foundation. Usually, wire mesh is incorporated into the concrete to reduce cracking. The edges of the slab may be poured to be thicker with reinforcing rods to create integral footing or supported by a footing and foundation wall (creating a T shape in section) below the frost line. A slab-on-grade foundation is usually set on gravel or other aggregates to facilitate drainage. Following are observation for usage based on climate regions:

Advantages
• Low cost and ease of construction
• Durable
• No elevators or stairs to the basement
• Less site disturbance than basement foundation

Disadvantages
• Less insulation buffer with the ground than crawl spaces and basements
• No access to plumbing buried in or below a slab
• No below-grade occupied spaces, storage, or mechanical room

Common applications
- Warm climates with minimal earth movement
- Commercial or retail with rooftop mechanical equipment

Crawl spaces are spaces with just enough room for a person access the space while crawling, usually 24 to30 inches in height. Crawl spaces are usually created using pier and beam construction with concrete footings and cast concrete or masonry wall construction.

Advantages
- Better insulation for heating and cooling
- Space to install utility lines and ductwork
- Less expensive than a basement

Disadvantages
- Vulnerable moisture and resulting mold/fungi
- Vulnerable to erosion
- Vulnerable to weather-related damage

Common applications
- Smaller buildings
- Moist climates prone to water accumulation

A *basement* is an area of usable space below grade. In cold climates, foundations and walls must be below the frost line to avoid soil movement that accompanies the freeze and thaw cycle. Economics balance the incremental costs required to extend the depth of a foundation to accommodate a full basement with additional space. Basement foundations require excavation, perimeter drainage, insulation, and venting. Basements may be on site-built footings of poured concrete. Walls are usually precast or poured in place reinforced concrete, or concrete block; the floor is most often a poured concrete slab. The slab floor is poured after the walls and should incorporate drainage and insulation below the floor.

Advantages
- Storage and mechanical space for building
- Good thermal buffer for occupied spaces above
- Space to install utilities
- Wind-related weather event shelter
- Additional space for mechanical, storage, occupiable spaces

Disadvantages
- Elevator and egress requirements
- Moisture can be a problem leading to mold
- More expensive than some other solutions
- Flooding potential

Common applications
- Residential where space is premium
- Cold and temperate climates

- Areas with a low water table, stable soil
- Sloped sites
- Commercial

An *open foundation* supports a building on piers, piles, or columns with the bottom of the first level framing several feet above grade. Piles and piers may be constructed of timber, poured concrete, steel, or masonry.

Advantages
- Low cost of construction
- Good for cooling as air moves freely
- Lightly touches the site
- Resilient to flooding and wind

Disadvantages
- Elevator and egress requirements
- Expensive
- Requires deep embedment, coastal erosion
- Dark space underneath building only suitable for parking
- Insulation required underside of the floor above
- Potential to collect debris, which can fuel a potential fire below the building

Common applications
- Coastal areas, which must resist wave loads, erosion, and wind gusts
- Areas prone to flooding
- Smaller buildings
- Hot humid regions; aids ventilation

EXTERIOR WALL ASSEMBLY

Combined with the windows, roofs, and ground floor, exterior walls are the critical barrier between the raw elements of nature and the spaces providing comfort inside the building (Figure 8.3). Exterior walls are directly related to building structure and foundation. There are two types of exterior wall:

- Load-bearing wall supports its weight as well as that of the floors and roof above.
- Non-load-bearing wall supports only its own weight. An alternate load-bearing structure such as columns and beams carry the weight of the overall building.

All exterior walls must withstand and manage the weather, including the sun, wind, and precipitation, in ways that provide protection as well as leverage natural resources. Exterior wall design varies in different regions and macroclimates of the world.

Exterior walls are one of the more permanent building elements. Bearing walls that carry the overall building load are problematic. Making changes after construction requires extreme care. In a resilient building, to the degree possible, exterior walls are designed to allow for internal space modifications without requiring a significant

Exterior Wall Example:

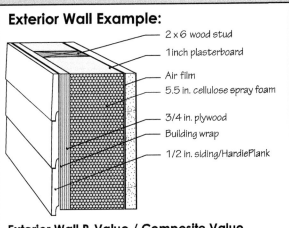

- 2 x 6 wood stud
- 1 inch plasterboard
- Air film
- 5.5 in. cellulose spray foam
- 3/4 in. plywood
- Building wrap
- 1/2 in. siding/HardiePlank

Exterior Wall R-Value / Composite Value

	Material	R-Value
Through Stud	1" plasterboard	1.2
	Air film inside	.68
	2 x 6 wood stud	6.87
	¾" plywood	0.94
	Building wrap 0.1"	0.17
	½" siding/HardiePlank	3
	Total R-value of composite	12.86
Through Cavity	1" plasterboard	1.2
	Air film inside	.68
	5.5" cellulose spray insulation	37.4
	¾" plywood	.95
	Building wrap 0.1"	.17
	½" siding/HardiePlank	3
	Total R-value of composite	**43.4**
	Percentage stud area	18.75

$$12.86 \times .1875 + 43.4 \times .8425 = \textbf{38R}$$
Total composite value of wall assembly

Figure 8.3 Wall assembly composite R-value
Source: Sharon Jaffe

response from the exterior wall system. Resilience provides for changing conditions over time and is hugely location driven. Ongoing climate change would, in some locations, suggest increased insulation in exterior walls beyond current condition requirements. Earthquake zones might require redundant framing and connections. Hurricane-prone areas may need walls that can withstand higher than maximum wind loads for short periods. Designs would provide exterior wall connections to roof and foundation that can account for the increased load and redundant load paths. In a flood-prone area, a resilient building may be raised above flood level and use flood barrier walls or ground-level materials that will not support mold growth despite prolonged exposure to floodwaters.

Key Terms

Insulation is a material that reduces unwanted heat loss or gains by increasing thermal resistance. Insulation materials reduce heat transfer by trapping air in the material to slow conductivity. Considerations include effectiveness, durability, material cost, the energy required to manufacture the insulation material (embodied energy), impact on air quality (toxicity), and installation method. Effective thermal insulation is available in a variety of materials.

R-value is a measure of an insulating material's capacity to resist heat flow. The higher the R-value, the greater the insulating power. A higher R-value indicates a higher thermal resistance. *The International Building Code* (IBC), *International Energy Conservation Code* (IECC), and sustainable building standards mandate specific R-values. All building materials have thermal transfer properties. R-values are additive. A building's thermal envelope can be an assembly of layers of materials. A composite R-value is calculated by adding the effective R-values of each of the assembly's components.

An *air barrier* is an element that controls the movement of air across the exterior wall system.

Infiltration is the introduction of outside air into a building, typically through cracks in the building envelope and through use of doors for passage. Infiltration is sometimes called air leakage. The leakage of room air out of a building, intentionally or not, is called exfiltration.

Wall assembly: The exterior wall is much more than materials on the outside of a building. An exterior wall is an assembly of several layers of construction. An exterior wall assembly typically will include the exterior finish material, airspace, sheathing, structure, insulation, drywall, and other finish material on the interior. The R-value of a wall assembly is calculated by simply adding up the R-values of the different layers of construction. International Building Code (IBC) Code, International Energy Conservation Code (IECC), and sustainable building standards mandate specific R-values. All building materials have thermal transfer properties that can be found in reference material, integral to many building design software programs, and a variety of state and federal department of energy listings.

Air infiltration: Remember that R-value does not account for holes in the walls, which allow air infiltration; it also has a significant impact on whether a wall is keeping a building warm. Proper design of the wall details, sound constriction practices, and appropriate use of insulation materials all contribute to an air-tight building.

Macroclimate

The macroclimate and anticipated weather conditions profoundly influence building materials used for exterior walls. Exterior wall systems, both assembly and materials, must be well suited to the climate for adequate protection from temperature, moisture, and air infiltration through the building envelope skin. Following are observation sfor usage based on climate regions:

Hot/dry climates
• Thermal mass

Hot/humid climates
• Wood material possible; rot and pests are a concern
• Concrete often used to limit pests
• Thermal mass opportunities

Cold climates
• Thermal mass
• Highly insulated, resulting in thick walls

Temperate climates
• Walls incorporate insulation

Macro Context

At the global scale, rating systems and standards are used to improve the performance of walls and helps guide the selection of eco-friendly wall materials. Different rating systems have different requirements, and the selected rating system plays a role in shaping the wall selection.

Settlement patterns impact exterior building walls, as customs in a region provide specific context. Urban, suburban, and rural contexts each have a traditional vocabulary of construction. Urban structures may be of a larger scale, relating to a commercial application or serving as multifamily residences, and will use material and modules appropriate to the locale. Urban exterior walls are often composed of masonry, metal cladding, and glazed curtain walls. Residential urban structures integrate similar materials scaled to residential proportions. Large and mid-rise commercial and suburban retail structures are likely to use structures and exterior walls similar to urban structures. However, small-scale commercial suburban structures may utilize construction methodologies similar to traditional residential construction using on-site construction using wood or steel frame or masonry techniques.

Urban Context

Exterior wall design considers the local context and what might fit in aesthetically and culturally. The city of Philadelphia is vibrant with red brick buildings occupied by businesses and residences. Insulation, air, and vapor barriers integrated into the wall assembly on the interior of the building may be invisible to the casual observer, but they mitigate seasonal temperature shifts, maintaining comfortable conditions. The urban context also provides opportunities for experimentation and innovation. In Philadelphia, "green" buildings boasting impressive energy efficiency are using SIPs (structural insulated panel). Torre de Especialades in Mexico uses a smog-eating material that is activated by sunlight, converting smog into less harmful substances (calcium nitrate and water), along with some undesirable carbon dioxide.

Suburban and Rural Context

The macroclimate and available materials dominate the design of exterior wall design in suburban and rural contexts. For example, in suburban Phoenix, Arizona, stucco walls with high thermal mass are ubiquitous and constitute the primary suburban context. In the Pacific Northwest, building structures reflect local culture and history through the use of FSC wood from regional sources.

Microclimate, Local Zoning and Codes

Local microclimate and building codes will also influence the exterior wall assembly. In colder climates, many codes require a minimum R-value, which will influence wall thickness. The immediate context, including the structures and landscaping immediately surrounding a building site, often influence the choice of a building's exterior finish materials.

Design Objectives and Design Ideas

The four perspectives will drive a significant part of the exploration and ideation around building walls (Table 8.4). The design matrix will help evaluate and prioritize which perspective takes precedence based on project guiding principles.

Synergies and Tradeoffs

The design ideas outlined in Table 8.4 clearly highlight the conflict between performance perspective and the experiences perspective. A designer may trade off the advantages of the thick, highly insulated wall that provides increased thermal mass for an extensive glazed wall if the guiding principle and project goals and objectives prioritize the experience of the view through the glazed wall.

Materials

Wood stud framing is a conventional wood frame construction that easily accommodates a variety of architectural styles and is simple to construct and modify. FSC wood materials are manufactured and readily available in a variety of standardized sizes and grades. Wood is a growing natural resource that can

TABLE 8.4 EXTERIOR WALL ASSEMBLY: DESIGN OBJECTIVES AND DESIGN IDEAS

		Design Objective	Design Idea
Perspective	Performance	• Save energy • Minimize framing	• Double the level of insulation required by code in cold climates. • Increase thermal mass • Use a buffer zone or double skin façade to mitigate temperature extremes
	Systems	• Utilize locally available ecologically friendly materials	• Utilize locally manufactured SIP system
	Culture	• Respond to the local context	• Use brick as the predominate building material to integrate with the surrounding community
	Experience	• Beauty for beauty's sake • Allow materiality to be express in pattern and texture	• Use zinc metal walls to reflect the colors of the sky. • Use extensive glazing with minimal framing to connect the building interior and the site.

be managed sustainably as a renewable resource. Exterior wall framing with wood studs must support the floor, roof, and wind loads. Traditional wood stud framing spaces 2×4 studs 16 inches on center with multiple studs at corners and the intersections of stud framing. Optimized, resource-efficient, advanced framing combines 2×6 studs spaced 24 inches on center with wood structural panel sheathing to meet structural requirements while saving materials, labor cost, and reducing thermal bridging. The 2×6 stud increases the wall cavity insulation depth for higher R-values, providing space for an R20 minimum. Use of engineered wood I-joists for floor framing and glulam for floor and roof structure increases the permissible span distance and consequently the overall resource efficiency.

Advantages
• Material savings
• Reduced thermal bridging
• Reduced labor costs
• Maximize cavity space for insulation
• Stronger than metal stud for load bearing, hanging cabinets, doorways, and window installation
• Easier to cut in the field than metal

Disadvantages
• Requires informed builder
• Requires informed building inspector
• Coordination 24-inch building module with other building materials
• Less framing for interior drywall and exterior siding attachment
• Vulnerable to warping and rot

Common applications
• Residential and small commercial building

Steel stud framing is similar to wood framing construction using light-gauge steel studs and tracks to create the wall frames. Unlike wood framing, steel stud framing has no structural strength and is not intended for load bearing. Steel stud framing becomes rigid once drywall or sheathing is attached.

Advantages
- Lightweight
- Will not warp or rot
- Not vulnerable to fire or termites
- Less expensive than wood
- Recyclable

Disadvantages
- Cutting metal
- Mounting cabinets or equipment on metal stud wall requires additional blocking
- Requires greater embodied energy to produce

Common applications
- Below-grade walls
- Commercial non-load-bearing walls

Masonry construction has a high compressive strength, is fireproof and durable, and the thermal mass provides insulation from summer and winter temperature variations. Masonry materials include brick, stone, concrete, and concrete block. Contemporary masonry structures are more likely to use concrete masonry units (CMU) or reinforced concrete, for smaller, low-rise buildings.

Advantages
- Thermal mass
- Fire resistant
- Strong, load bearing
- Durable, termite resistant
- Resistant to extreme winds
- Integral construction finish for brick, stone, and some concrete block
- Very low maintenance
- Acoustic separation

Disadvantages
- Weight on foundation
- Less resilient to lateral loads and shifting soil
- Resource intense material
- Slow on-site construction
- A higher level of construction coordination
- Higher construction material and labor costs

Common applications
- Commercial
- Residential
- Institutional

Structural insulated panels (SIPs) usually consists of an insulating material sandwiched between two structural faces. Sips are manufactured in a factory and arrive ready to use at the building site. SIP insulation material is commonly available as EPS foam and is also available with straw-bale or hempcrete. Given that the structural material and the insulation are integrated, SIP constructions that can be correctly handled and installed contribute to a highly insulated and airtight building. SIP materials are suitable for ceilings, floors, and walls.

Advantages
- Strong and stable structure
- Resistance to wind and seismic events
- Airtight construction
- Fast on-site construction
- Reduced workforce labor
- High R-value, energy saving

Disadvantages
- May limit building form; simple boxy forms easier to construct
- Requires more coordination to integrate infrastructure utilities
- Vulnerable to pests and moisture
- Requires specialized knowledge for construction
- Possibly too airtight; careful attention to HVAC required
- Difficult to modify design during construction

Common applications
- Residential urban single and multifamily

Nonstructural facing (infill panel/cladding/curtain wall). When the building structure is a frame system, and the exterior walls are not load bearing, an exterior curtain wall transfers its load or weight to the building structure through the floor planes from which the curtain hangs. A curtain wall is a thin (2-inch-thick or less) framed wall containing modular in-fill panels that span several floor levels. Often in-fill panels are metal, glass, or thin stone.

Advantages
- Reduced construction cost
- Lightweight modular construction
- Provides flexible daylight opportunities
- Provides flexible opportunities for views
- Limits moisture infiltration
- Design and aesthetic flexibility
- May provide additional structural stability

Disadvantages
- Less durable than other options
- Requires more maintenance than some other exterior facade materials
- Lower R-value; inefficient as insulation
- Access for cleaning
- Greater opportunity for glazing leakage

- Wide swings in temperature and humidity
- Controls required for solar heat gain, condensation
- Fire safety requires a perimeter system and knock out panels

Common applications
- High-rise commercial building
- Advanced building envelope applications with double-skin systems
- Advanced building envelope applications with "smart" curtain wall that controls visible light transmittance

Which is the Most Sustainable?

The client's guiding principles, the macroclimate, context, and microclimate—all will drive the approach to and selection of exterior wall design. At this early stage in the design process, a variety of options are investigated and studied, testing each option's feasibility for the project. Design criteria vary based on project priorities.

Performance perspective
- Maximize insulation value and air tightness
- Low embodied energy of wall materials
- Durability
- Optimize cost and R-value
- LCA value

Systems perspective
- Proven, a reliable construction system
- Product disclosures available, providing environmental impact information
- No VOC or off-gassing material
- Simple maintenance

Culture perspective
- Local contractors proficient in required construction
- Exterior materials match local context
- Materials available locally

Experience perspective
- Material, texture, and color of the exterior wall material is aesthetically pleasing
- Provides a unique, distinctive identity to the building

WINDOWS

Windows are the visual connection between inside and outside. Windows frame views, provide real-time weather information, and allow the sun to brighten a room. Windows are located and sized based on functional passive ventilation requirements, daylight requirements, and aesthetic requirements. Overall occupant productivity increases with operable windows that provide natural light and ventilation. Windows can also be a source of glare, unwanted heat gain, or loss.

Key Terms

Window to wall ratio (WWR) measures the percentage of glazing, or glass, relative to the total exterior wall area. Total exterior wall area includes all exterior walls even if there is a section of the wall without a window. Include any enclosing wall exposed to the exterior environment in the wall area calculation of this formula. Window glazing conducts heat at a different rate than walls. The size and orientation of the glazing area impacts building heating, cooling, and lighting loads. Calculate WWR by dividing the glazing area by the total wall area.

Window energy performance ratings. The National Fenestration Rating Council (NFRC) establishes independent window, door, and skylight energy performance ratings. Certified products are independently tested, and labeled to facilitate comparison of product performance. The performance information is typically listed on a label (Figure 8.4) that is affixed to each window.

Solar heat gain coefficient (SHGC) quantifies how much solar energy from outside passes through the window as heat. SHGC is a ratio between 0 and 1. A lower SHGC is better at blocking solar heat gain. Low SHGC is desirable in climates that require cooling for thermal comfort. Appropriate SHGC varies based on climate, solar orientation, and complementary sustainable strategies employed.

U-value measures the rate of heat loss, moving from inside to outside through a window assembly. A lower U-factor indicates window's superior insulating properties.

Additional Window Performance Ratings

Visible transmittance or visible light transmittance (VT or VLT) quantifies visible light that passes through window glazing as a number from 0 to 1. A higher VT allows more daylight to pass through the glazing (glass). A building with a higher WWR, meaning a more significant percentage of window area, requires less visible transmittance.

Air leakage (AL) measures air infiltration through a window. A lower number implies a higher comfort level with fewer drafts.

Condensation resistance (CR) is an optional evaluation rating. Window manufacturers are not required to include this on the performance label. Windows are rated based on resistance to condensation. CR is between 1 and 100. Higher numbers indicate increased resistance to condensation.

Types of Window Configurations

Windows come in many shapes and sizes; both operable and fixed. Windows affect the essential aesthetics of a building and have an impact on energy consumption, and maintenance requirements. The type and rating appropriate for a specific window are heavily dependent on climate, orientation, natural ventilation, and operational requirements. It is common for a sustainable building to have windows with different ratings based on relative solar orientation.

Philly Doors & Windows
Series 1776
Vinyl Clad Wood Frame
Double Glazed · Argon Fill · Low E
Product Type: **Vertical Slider**

National Fenestration Rating Council®

ENERGY PERFORMANCE RATINGS	
U-Factor (U.S./1-P)	Solar Heat Gain Coefficient
0.35	*0.32*

ADDITIONAL PERFORMANCE RATINGS	
Visible Transmittance	Air Leakage (U.S. / 1-P)
0.51	*≤0.3*
Condensation Resistance	
51	—

Manufacturer stipulates that these ratings conform to applicable NFRC. ratings are determined for a fixed set of enviornmental conditions and a specific products size. NFRC does not recomend any product and does not warrant the suitabitly of andy product for any specific use. consult manufactur's literature for other product performance information.

www.nfrc.org

Energy and building codes require exterior windows, skylights, and doors to be tested and labeled.

Prescriptive values for **U-factor** and **SHGC** have been established for fenestration based on orientation, climate, and function: operable, fixed, or entrance door.

Figure 8.4 Window performance label
Source: Sharon B. Jaffe

Macroclimate

Windows and doors are the primary interface between humans and the outdoors. They also serve as the barrier between the elements and the comfort of the protected building interiors. Following are observations for usage based on climate regions:

Hot/dry climates
- Shade all openings in the building envelope.

Hot/humid climates
- Equip all windows facing all directions with overhangs.
- Locate windows to facilitate natural ventilation.
- Window design or shading structure serves as a barrier to precipitation so windows can remain open regardless of weather.
- Window frames other than wood are best. (Wood is vulnerable to pest infestation and rot.)
- Shade all openings in the building envelope.

Cold climates
- Locate windows facing the equator. for maximum heat gain

Temperate climates
- Locate windows facing the equator, provide seasonal shading.
- Minimize windows facing west and east, shade with deep overhangs or external shading that is adjustable.

Macro Context

At the global scale, rating systems and code requirements play a critical role in determining the window selection. The U-value as discussed earlier contributes to the overall energy efficiency of a building and windows also help to daylight spaces leading to higher scores or compliance in a rating system. The view is also considered essential in a sustainable building. Window placement is key to the success of a project

Settlement patterns have a significant impact on building envelope aesthetic. The urban, suburban, and rural contexts can influence the design aesthetic of the building envelope, fenestration arrangement, and window selection.

Urban Context

Design of the building envelope windows may differ in urban contexts. In a high-density urban environment with tall buildings, glass curtain walls are common. In a less dense urban area, "punched" or individual windows may be more common. Windows and doors are critical drivers of the quality of the urban context where security and vitality are crucial to a high quality of life. Urban environments lacking windows and doors result in limited views, fewer eyes on the street, and more limited building occupant interaction with the surrounding community.

Suburban Context

Traditionally windows in suburban commercial developments are more likely to be separate and distinct individual windows. More recently, sizable suburban developments, such as office parks, are seeing the application of urban pattern window designs using more curtain wall glazing and continuous bands of windows on upper levels with ground-level windows and doors addressing end-user needs. Large suburban retail spaces are also adopting urban window standards and more commonly using large expansive store windows.

Microclimate, Local Zoning and Codes

At the micro-scale, window selection and placement are essential. Specific views of the landscape need to be accommodated by appropriate window size and location. In the urban environment, proximity to other buildings can be problematic and may facilitate the spread of fire. Local codes determine the required distance of a window from adjacent structures.

Design Objectives and Design Ideas

The four perspectives will drive a significant portion of the exploration, ideation, and evaluation of exterior building windows (Table 8.5). Each perspective drives a different option. The design decision matrix will help evaluate and prioritize the design relative to the project guiding principles, project design goals and objectives, microclimate, and context.

Synergies and Tradeoffs

The ideas generated by the performance perspective, limiting operable windows will be appreciated by the mechanical engineer attempting to design an efficient mechanical system that is not compromised by operable windows. Studies have shown that people value autonomy, so building occupants appreciate the ability to open and close windows. The design idea to use operable windows for human comfort generated by the systems perspective conflicts with fixed windows generated by the performance perspective. Which is more important: human well-being or energy efficiency? These are the types of challenges sustainable designers face daily.

Design Priorities

The client's guiding principles, the macroclimate, the context, and the microclimate will guide selection and approach to window size, location, performance, and design. At this stage, a variety of options are investigated and studied, testing each option's feasibility for the project.

Window Shading

Windows make significant contributions to the overall building performance and occupant well-being in any given space. Each window has opportunities and challenges generated by the specific climate and solar orientation. Appropriate window selection, position, and size are vital to managing the amount of sunlight entering a building. Changing solar position may create dynamic sunlight conditions that require careful management.

TABLE 8.5 WINDOW DESIGN OBJECTIVES AND DESIGN IDEAS

		Design Objective	Design Idea
Perspective	**Performance**	• Minimize energy consumption by using small windows. • Use windows with the lowest U-value and best solar heat gain coefficient (SHGC).	• Minimize the size and quantity of windows to reduce heat and cooling transfer • Use small punched openings on the south side of the building • Use nonoperable windows to avoid occupant interference with HVAC system balance.
	Systems	• Prioritize windows for access to daylight and fresh air for optimal occupant well-being.	• Use large operable windows on all sides of the building for access to fresh air.
	Culture	• Use window shape, type, and forms consistent with local context. • Use windows to connect the building to the streetscape.	• Use windows on the street side facade. • Use windows with the shape, proportion, size, and detailing traditionally used in the surrounding community.
	Experience	• Use windows as a biophilic connection to outdoors. • Use windows as design elements to create delight	• Use large windows and window walls on all facades (except facing parking) to connect building occupants with natural surroundings. • Use windows with minimal frames to maximize connection with surroundings.

Interior Shading

Interior shading options may address unwanted or excessive interior sunlight. Interior controls such as vertical blinds, venetian shades, and other window treatments, may be used to control excess light and glare. However, interior shading will impact daylighting systems and must be planned for and coordinated early in the passive design process. Use of shading after occupancy will certainly impact overall building performance. Perforated solar shades available in a variety of light transmittance levels may help mitigate uncontrolled glare. Solar shades can be automated or manual. Automated interior shading can be more easily integrated, and accounted for when coordinating automated daylight and building systems. Private spaces may find greater occupant satisfaction with manual controls. It is important to remember that direct sunlight is as much heat as it is light. Interior shading may mitigate excessive glare from sunlight, but it cannot reduce the solar heat gain that has already entered the building.

Exterior Solar Shading

Exterior solar shading (Figure 8.5) is a building element that is highly dependent on building location, orientation, massing, and construction. Integration of exterior solar shading techniques with the building envelope and building fenestration support the management of daylight penetration, reflection, and potential heat gain through windows. It is important to remember that exterior solar shading will affect the quality and quantity of daylight and must be closely coordinated with daylighting and building systems.

Exterior horizontal shading has historically been an inexpensive but effective way to keep direct solar heat gain out of a building. Horizontal shading refers to overhangs and shading elements that protrude from the building. Horizontal shading works best when the sun is high in the sky to minimize the depth required for effective shading.

Advantages
- Limit direct heat gain
- Limit glare

Disadvantage
- Too much shading limits daylight.

Synergy
- Daylight exterior light shelf

Tradeoffs
- Direct solar heat gain
- Daylight

Vertical shading. On the west and east walls the sun is typically too low for effective horizontal shading; instead, *vertical shading* or "fins" are used to block the low sun as it moves around the building.

Advantages
- Daylighting: If the fins are light colored, they block direct light and heat from entering the building but bounce diffuse light into the interior space.
- Limits glare from low sun angles

Disadvantages
- Interferes with a clear view
- Difficult to control heat gain from low angles

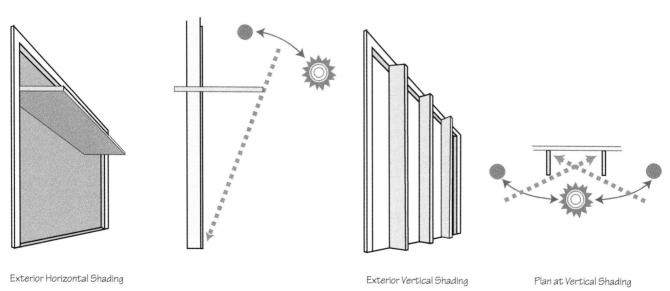

Exterior Horizontal Shading

Exterior Vertical Shading

Plan at Vertical Shading

Figure 8.5 Windows: exterior shading
Source: Sharon B. Jaffe

Synergy
• View

Tradeoff
• Natural ventilation

Which Is the Most Sustainable?

The client's guiding principles, macroclimate, context, and microclimate will guide window selection and shading approach. At this early stage in the design process, a variety of options are investigated and studied, testing each option's feasibility for the project. Design criteria may be viewed through the lens of the four perspectives and will vary based on project priorities.

Performance perspective
• Best U-value/performance
• Best SHGC
• Best visible light transmittance
• Operable

Systems perspective
• Maintenance minimal
• Environmental impact of vinyl, wood, or metal

Culture perspective
• Relate window style to the local context
• Exterior materials match existing context

Experience perspective
• Beautifully detailed windows
• Thicker window frames on operable windows function as a pattern to punctuate the design

ROOF SYSTEMS

Traditionally, the roof has one primary role: to protect the interior space of a building from the elements of sun, temperature, wind, and water (rain and snow). Commercial buildings often expand the role of the roof to include housing the building's mechanical equipment; heating, ventilation, and cooling (HVAC) system compressors; and vents, exhaust, intake, and other equipment associated with building systems. Commercial and residential buildings use roof surfaces for supplemental amenity spaces such as sun decks, lookouts, and roof gardens. Flat or modestly sloped roofs accommodate and ease access to amenity space and for maintenance of the roof and any roof mounted equipment.

Roofs play a large part in the look of a building. Sustainable design can leverage sustainable strategies with aesthetics and building appearance. A shed roof with clerestories facilitates top lighting with natural daylight. A flat or low slope roof allows for easy integration of vegetation, supplying the insulation and stormwater management of a vegetative roof. A roof angled to optimize solar radiation supports solar hot water and photovoltaic panels.

At this early design stage, it helps to establish the broad construction characteristics of the project. Do not try to determine so much detailed information that it slows the design progress.

Resilience

A roof must be resilient to function in the face of shifting conditions. Choosing a durable, weathertight roofing material that retains strength and requires minimal maintenance adds to the resilience of a roof. The design and functionality of the roof support the overall building structure's ability to withstand the impact of changing climate conditions, weather, and potential disasters. In cold climates, roofs carry substantial weight in snow loads. Therefore, increasing the structure of the roof improves the capacity to carry higher snow loads provides an additional margin of safety. High insulation levels at the roof and careful detailing to prevent thermal bridging and deep roof overhangs to protect the house and windows from direct sun will help moderate the impact of temperature changes.

Key Terms

A *cool roof* reflects more sunlight and absorbs less heat from the sun than conventional roofs.

Solar reflectance index (SRI) is a measure of the surface ability to reflect solar radiation (visible, infrared and ultraviolet rays from the sun) and thermal emittance (the ability to release absorbed energy/heat) and thereby stay cooler in the sun. Higher SRI values indicate greater ability to reflect and release heat from the sun, reducing heat transfer to the building. SRI values are available for roofing material through the Cool Roof Rating Council Standard (CRRC-1).

Macroclimate

Roofs provide shelter and have done so throughout history. Roofs serve as protection and a barrier between the elements of sun, wind, and rain, providing comfort for the interior. Climate influences the form, structure, and material of the building's roof. Following are observations for usage based on climate regions:

Hot/dry climates
- Flat roofs with parapets
- Low slope roof structure vented at peak
- Self-venting roof structure, radiant barrier, i.e., double or fly roof structure

- High SRI material allows air circulation (i.e., light-colored S-shaped clay tile)
- Insulation, green roof

Hot/humid climates
- Sloped roofs are opportunities for rain harvesting
- Thatch allows ventilation
- White metal roofing

Cold climates
- High sloped roofs to shed rain and snow have rain-collecting potential
- Consider snow load and falling snow/ice
- Darker color materials
- Green roof

Temperate climates
- High sloped roof to shed rain and snow: potential for collecting rain

Macro Context

At the global scale, rating systems play a significant role in determining the roof construction, slope, form, and material. Insulation R-values apply to the roof as well as the walls. Selection of roof structure and building materials should accommodate insulation for appropriately high R-values. A high SRI is also desirable for most green building rating systems. Both high insulation R-values and a high SRI rating for the contributes to the ability of a roof to support a cooler interior building temperature and overall building energy efficiency.

Settlement Patterns

Settlement patterns influence building structures and subsequently influence roof structure based on aesthetic architectural context and expectations.

Urban Context

While the roof forms can vary in urban environments, commercial buildings most often address the cost-benefit aspects of roof function and form. Flat or low sloped roofs that maximize useable interior space while providing opportunities to locate mechanical equipment or additional amenity space are most common in urban settings.

Suburban Context

Function and aesthetic standards influence roof structure. In a suburban setting, this can mean peaked roofs for specific fast-food chain restaurants, flat roofs on strip malls to provide access to roof mounted mechanical equipment, and a variety of residential roof configurations that relate to the specific variation of local house style.

Microclimate

Roofs serve as protection and a barrier between the elements of sun, wind, and rain the comfort of the interior. The weather and specific shading patterns influence structure, form and material selection of a building roof enabling it to leverage site opportunities. A site with unobstructed access to the sun's radiation should incorporate solar energy and daylighting strategies into the roof form and structure. Sites with consistent winds can maximize natural passive ventilation using roof monitors and wind scoops.

Micro Context

Codes, local regulations, and other planning ordinances generally include maximum roof heights and often govern the shape or material of a roof. Adjacent buildings and mature trees will impact roof configuration and appropriate applicable sustainable strategies. A roof with a high SRI will support reduced urban heat island effect. A roof configured to maximize rainwater harvesting supports water conservation by reducing demand for potable water.

Form

The four perspectives present significant and varied questions to consider as the design of the roof is developed. The design decision matrix will help evaluate and prioritize which perspective takes precedence based on project guiding principles.

Performance perspective
- Use, size, and mounting of PV array
- Roof color and material impact on performance
- Facilitate synergies: natural ventilation and daylighting

Systems perspective
- How will the roof system manage drainage and accommodate vents, stacks, and other building system roof penetrations?
- Is regular roof access required? What equipment will be roof mounted?
- Green roof offers an opportunity to support local biodiversity

Culture perspective
- Influence of regional climate, adjacent buildings, local aesthetic norms
- Local building materials and resources

Experience perspective
- How will the roof express the building aesthetic and communicate the client brand?
- The roof shape is a dominant proportion of the building structure and form from the exterior on low- or mid-rise buildings. The roof form influences the interior building experience.

Roof Form: Options and Considerations

The form or shape of the building roof must meet both functional and aesthetic criteria that vary greatly by location. Regional climate, building structure, available building materials, and local tradition influence roof form and character. As one of the most visible elements of the building envelope, a roof is an opportunity for a strong aesthetic expression of building form.

The roof is an opportunity for a strong aesthetic expression. This is especially true for a low or midrise building where the roof is a substantial proportion of the building structure. The roof form projects an aesthetic sensibility seen from the exterior and influences the interior experience by shaping and controlling space and light. Table 8.6 reviews sustainable strategies that affect roof form.

High Slope Roofs

High slope roofs efficiently reflect solar heat, shed storm water, snow, and avoid ice dams. A highly sloped roof can be set to an optimal angle for active solar panels. High sloped roofs with evident solar photo voltaic panels also communicate a strong sustainability statement that reinforces the need for and the economic viability of environmental responsible buildings.

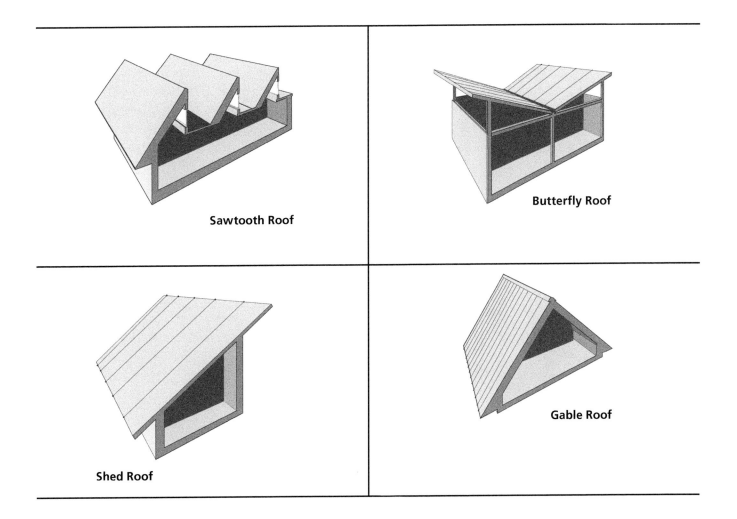

Sawtooth Roof

Butterfly Roof

Shed Roof

Gable Roof

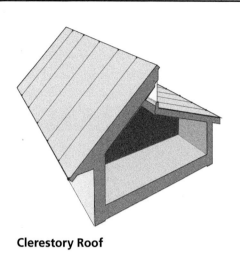

Clerestory Roof

Advantages
- Visibility and aesthetics
- Durable, longer lifespan
- Storage in larger attic or loft
- Limits pooling water and snow load
- Facilitates air flow through ridge and eaves

Disadvantages
- Expense for larger, more complex roof
- Additional weight on foundation
- Decreased rooftop space for systems

Common Applications
- Cold climate
- Residence
- Hospitality

Flat or Low Sloped Roofs

Flat—or more accurately, low slope roofs—are roofs that slope 4 inches or less per 12-inch length. They provide for easy roof access for roof maintenance, incidental exterior roof functions, such as decks, observation platform, roof garden, as well as to mechanical equipment, vents and stacks. Low sloped roofs do not shed rain water and snow as efficiently as roofs with a steeper slope making it more vulnerable to standing water and leaks. A low slope roof can extend beyond the exterior walls of the building providing a roof overhang to shade windows and doors from unwanted heat gain and protect a greater portion of the building exterior envelop from the elements. PV panels can be mounted to low sloped roofs mounted flat or set to the optimal angle for a specific location. Low sloped roofs can be further optimized when functioning as a vegetative roof.

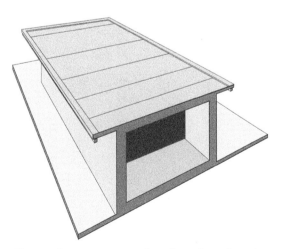

Flat roof; more accurately, a low sloped roof

Advantages
- Simple function, simple construction
- Requires less material than high sloped roof
- Less expensive that more complicated roof structures
- Roof top area for utilities, roof deck, or roof garden
- Aesthetic clean line
- Ability to cantilever for shading, solar control
- Easy mounting of PV panels
- Without extreme ceiling peaks heating and cooling circulation is easier to design

Disadvantages
- Vulnerable to water pooling and snow load
- Higher maintenance requirements
- Fewer appropriate materials
- May limit attic space.

Common Applications
- Commercial buildings
- Buildings with roof deck
- Green roof
- Warm, dry, and temperate climates

TABLE 8.6 SUSTAINABLE STRATEGIES THAT AFFECT ROOF FORM

Photovoltaic panels may be effectively used on a flat or pitched/sloped roof. Roofs sloped to the appropriate angle can facilitate efficient solar collection without extensive mounting hardware, simplifying installation, maintenance, and reducing structural load to the roof.	
A **vegetative roof**, sometimes called a **living roof**, or a **green** roof, is a roof that has been covered with plant material. The benefits of a vegetative roof include improved building/roof insulation, passive cooling, reduced stormwater runoff, mitigation of the urban heat island effect, and reduced carbon dioxide and pollutants in the environment.	
Rainwater harvesting influences the roof form relative to the direction and slope of the roof and drainage systems allowing the collection and storage of rainwater to be used at a later time. Collecting rainwater reduces rain and stormwater runoff, easing the pressure of storm water sewer systems.	
Roof monitor facilitates natural ventilation and daylight. Outdoor natural breezes, wind currents, and air pressure differences move air through and ventilate the building without mechanical means. Operable windows in roof monitors can support natural ventilation and daylighting.	
A **solar chimney** or thermal chimney is both a cooling and heating strategy. A tall stack structure may be used to help regulate temperature and ventilation as part of a natural ventilation system. Direct solar energy warms the air, causing it to rise by convection and vent out the top of the chimney drawing cooler air in from the bottom. The chimney must be higher than the overall roof. Output vents should face away from prevailing winds. The effective use of a solar chimney can may be leveraged combined with a Trombe wall.	airflow
Daylighting A deep building footprint may struggle to provide adequate daylight to interior spaces. The roof can b e configured to provide daylighting from above for spaces that do not receive adequate daylighting from vertical windows. Top lighting configurations include roof monitors, clerestory, sawtooth roof, horizontal skylights and solar tubes. 3-5% of the roof area should provide adequate daylighting for the building interior space.	

(continued)

TABLE 8.6 (CONTINUED)

Shading Roof overhangs, wide eaves, deep porches, and verandas reduce unwanted glare and heat gain from direct sunlight.	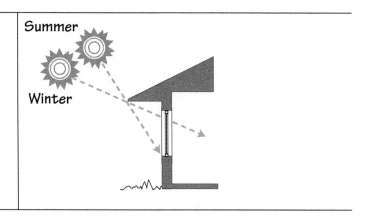

Source: Sharon B. Jaffe

Design Objectives and Design Ideas

The four perspectives will drive a significant portion of the approach, discussion, and evaluation of the design of a building's roof. The design decision matrix will help evaluate and prioritize the approaches. (See Table 8.7) Each perspective drives a different option. The design decision matrix will help evaluate and prioritize the design relative the project guiding principles, context, and microclimate.

Selecting the Most Sustainable Roof for a Project

Guiding principles, goals, and objectives set the parameters for specific criteria. How to meet specific criteria is highly influenced by the research and design decisions preceding the building envelope design. Climate and the site opportunities for sustainable strategies are key drivers.

Roof form design criteria can be categorized and explored using the four perspectives.

Performance perspective
- Best R-value
- Best air tightness
- Lowest first cost
- Best long-term cost
- Depth of roof
- Durability

Systems perspective
- Maintenance requirements
- Global environmental impact
- Building scale health risks
- Support local ecology

Culture perspective
- Alternative insulation materials: Does the builder have the willingness to try a new material?

Experience perspective
- Interesting shape experienced by the community
- Interior spaces created by roof form
- Use for garden or roof deck

TABLE 8.7 ROOF FORM: DESIGN OBJECTIVES AND DESIGN IDEAS

Roof Form

		Design Objective	Design Ideas	
Perspectives	**Performance**	Optimize roof angle for solar exposure facilitating passive or active systems. Maximize energy efficiency.	Shed roof with optimal angle for PV panel solar gain. Use roof materials with high R and SRI values to maximize energy efficiency.	
	Systems	Roof must support daylighting and passive ventilation.	Roof monitor positioned to provide daylight at the center core of the building and support passive ventilation.	
	Culture	Roof form to reflect surrounding context so the building fits into the community.	Roof structure will be flat with a gabled roof monitor to relate to gabled roofs of surrounding residential buildings.	

(continued)

TABLE 8.7 (CONTINUED)

Roof Form

Experience	Roof must make a clear positive statement for sustainable strategies. Provide opportunities for high interior ceilings.	High pitched shed roof at optimal angle for solar radiation will accommodate PV in clear sight of community while providing vaulted interior spaces.	

Source: Sharon B. Jaffe

VALIDATION, SYNERGIES, AND SYNTHESIS OF DESIGN

The building envelope is an interim phase of step 3, design, in the *Sustainable Design Basics* methodology. All of the explorations and design decisions from the preceding steps influence the exploration and design of the building envelope. Guiding principles, goals and objectives, criteria matrix, and relationship diagrams created earlier in the process ensure that the building envelope design synthesizes ideas from all four perspectives: performance, systems, culture, and experience.

Validation

The building envelope investigation has made decisions for windows, wall composition, foundation, and building roof shape by considering design ideas from each of the four perspectives. The variables make a significant impact on validation metrics. When using energy modeling software, adding the building envelope information will provide a more precise set of metrics for analysis and evaluation. Evaluate the building schemes with the updated building envelope information for the performance perspective, the systems perspective, the cultures perspective, and the experience perspective.

Understanding how the design solutions from each of the four perspectives compare to the project goals and each other is the purpose of the validation process. It is not necessary to select the one design idea that has the highest energy performance but to look at all the options holistically in light of the project guiding principles and project goals to discover the best solution. Sometimes a lesser performing option is selected.

Validation metrics for preliminary design include:

- **Energy:** EUI or estimated level: high, medium, or low
- **Light and air:** The percentage of space with direct access to operable windows or daylight autonomy
- **Water:** Water efficiency/% reduction, rainwater management/quantity collected
- **Ecology:** Protect/restore habitat, percentage of open space

Design Synthesis

Exploring preliminary design, passive design systems, and the building envelope through the four perspectives result in the rapid development and evaluation of many different design ideas. It is remarkable and inspiring to see how many options are possible. Given the number of design ideas quickly generated as part of the SDB methodology, it is not surprising that not every idea makes it into the final design resolution. However, each ideation explored along the way moved the design a bit closer to the final design resolution, even if only by supplying the opportunity to investigate, evaluate, and validate various sustainable strategies and combinations of strategies.

The structure, foundation, roof, walls, and windows determine the building form and profoundly influencing the overall character and expression of the building. Use the validation matrix metrics, optimism, cautions, and reflections, to analyze and evaluate the design ideas. Design schemes from the four perspectives will present synergies and tradeoffs that will inform the initial decisions for the synthesized building form. It is not unusual to attempt to include some of the best parts of each of the earlier ideas into an integrated design solution. Synthesize the four perspectives design ideas into one design scheme that incorporates the best aspects from each perspective.

Space Plan Refinement

The synthesized building envelope combines favorable features from all four perspectives to refine the basic building form. Depending upon the opportunities created by the synthesized building form, it may be appropriate to revise, resolve, and refine the rough floor plan as an interim step before the final design resolution in step 4 of the *Sustainable Design Basics* methodology.

Look for and capitalize on design opportunities presented by the synthesized building form in the space plan. Has the expression of the roof form created a volume better suited to open office planning than enclosed conference space? Revisions to the rough space plan may be required to adjust it to conditions presented in the synthesized building form.

At this point, the space plan remains in a loose form to facilitate the expected revisions required by step 4, design resolution, as the building design continues to evolve.

FURTHER READING

Ching, Francis, D. K., and I. M. Shapiro. 2014. *Green Building Illustrated.* Hoboken, NJ: John Wiley & Sons.

Kibert, C. J. 2007. *Sustainable Construction; Green Building Design and Delivery* (2nd ed.). Hoboken, NJ: John Wiley & Sons.

Kwok, A., and W. Grondzik, W. 2011. *Green Studio Handbook* (2nd ed.). Hoboken, NJ: John Wiley & Sons.

Step 3D: Green Materials

Figure 9.0 *Sustainable Design Basics*, step 3
Source: Sharon B. Jaffe

BASICS

A building's design is closely associated with its materiality. Selecting appropriate materials for a building project involves understanding structural and functional requirements, budget parameters, and individual material or product properties and characteristics. Traditional building projects commonly evaluate materials relative to structure, function, and aesthetics. In an energy-conscious world, both embodied and operational energy consumption require careful consideration relative to the building orientation and configuration, the systems specified, construction processes, and the specified materials. Sustainability demands the evaluation of a materials environmental impact from its extraction or production and processing, through all phases of its use, end of useful life, and beyond: to recycling, upcycling, or downcycling, into a useful product or, as a last resort, disposal.

Green and sustainable building projects integrate principles of sustainability at all scales, into the design process, construction, operations, and the deconstruction or demolition of the built environment. Materials used in the built environment directly impact ecology and humanity both globally and locally, and an individual's health and wellness. Unfortunately, building material production, use, and disposal have negatively impacted the environment and human health. To limit and mitigate adverse consequences it is necessary to investigate, research, and evaluate the materials used to build, finish, furnish, and maintain the built environment.

The broad goal for sustainable projects is to limit resource consumption, manage material use for efficiency, and eliminate toxicity. Beyond using materials that do not harm the ecosystems of the world, it is possible to use materials that support the environment and an equitable society, and contribute to human health and wellness without depleting the world's limited natural resources. Each sustainable building design project will establish criteria to align with the project guiding principles, the client requirements, client preferences, and the project budget.

Key Terms

Environmentally preferred products (EPP) have a lower environmental impact and reduce the adverse effect of a product on the environment or people as compared to competing products.

Embodied energy is the total amount of energy used to produce a finished product. Embodied energy includes the energy used to grow, extract, manufacture, and transport a product to the point of use.

Circular economy is ideally a regenerative economy. The intention is to keep resources in use as long as possible, minimizing the loss of energy and materials through innovative design and efficient manufacture of durable goods that can be repaired, maintained, and ultimately recycled, repurposed and reused for new goods. A circular economy is an alternative to the traditional linear economy of manufacture, acquisition, consumption, and disposal that feeds landfills.

Life-cycle analysis (LCA) calculates the present and future, cradle-to-grave environmental impact over the life cycle of a material or product. LCA provides information for designers to make sound, responsible decisions regarding a product or material, facilitating an understanding of the impact and environmental footprint beyond product performance. There is no single standard for LCA methodology.

LCA accounts for the environmental and social impact of all that goes into a product or material: labor, energy, materials, and emissions at all stages of a product or materials life.

- Design of the material
- Raw material: procurement and processing
- Manufacturing, including energy consumption, and use of recycled or virgin material
- Packaging and distribution
- Product use and consumption
- Post-consumer disposal or reuse

Environmental performance and sustainability goals are *not* an element of LCA, although most green standards require an accounting of embodied energy supporting a life-cycle approach to promote resource efficiency.

- LEED v4 applies life-cycle assessment thinking to the whole project and product level. Material and resources credit category focuses on minimizing the embodied energy of products and materials.
- Living building challenge (LBC) under the materials petal, requires embodied carbon footprint information.
- BREEAM International has opportunities for credits resulting from life-cycle assessment in three categories: materials, management, and energy.

Closed-loop recycling is a process that recycles manufactured product and uses it in the production of the same (or similar) product without negatively impacting the quality of the product. Steel, glass, and some types of plastics (e.g., nylon carpet fiber) are examples of materials that may utilize closed-loop recycling.

Indoor environmental quality (IEQ) includes a range of concerns affecting occupant health including lighting quality, noise, temperature, humidity, odors, vibration, and air quality. Many building processes, features, and elements, directly and indirectly, impact IEQ including:

- Outdoor environment: climate and outside air quality; landscape, natural pollen, soil/dust particles, pesticides; gases and emissions from adjacent sites
- Building structure and materials: air infiltration; water intrusion, material emissions
- Building operation and maintenance: ventilation system performance and operational schedules; housekeeping and cleaning schedules, routines and products; equipment maintenance
- Building interior contents: equipment and appliances; furniture and material emissions and maintenance
- Building occupants: activities; metabolism; personal hygiene; personal health

Indoor air quality (IAQ) U.S. EPA and the National Institute for Occupational Safety and Health define good indoor air quality as adequate ventilation and distribution of fresh air, control of airborne contaminants, and maintaining acceptable temperature and humidity levels.

According to ASHRAE Standard 62.1, the definition of acceptable indoor air quality is "air in which there are no known contaminants at harmful concentrations as determined by cognizant authorities and with which a substantial majority (80 percent or more) of the people exposed do not express dissatisfaction."

Better indoor air quality (low concentrations of CO_2 and pollutants and high ventilation rates) can lead to productivity improvements of 8 to11 percent. (Alker 2014)

Cradle to grave is a phrase that describes material production from material extraction through disposal.

Cradle to cradle is a phrase that describes the cyclical process of material production from material extraction through manufacturing, use, end use, demolition, removal and collection to its remanufacture for use again.

Key Metrics

Third-party material certification substantiates the environmental attributes of specific products. The certification of a specific product or process that is performed by an organization independent of the manufacturer or producer of the product.

Material safety data sheet (MSDS) provides information regarding potentially significant levels of airborne contaminants, handling and storage precautions and requirements, health effects, odor descriptions, combustibility, and procedures for cleanup.

Safety data sheet (SDS) serves the same function as MSDS. SDSs inform contractors and others of immediate risks a material may pose. SDSs provide information regarding materials, including (but not limited to) ingredients, hazards, handling and storage, exposure and personal protection, toxicology information, disposal, and regulations.

Environmental product declaration (EPD) is a document that quantifies the life-cycle environmental impact of a product. A product's EPD is independently verified and registered. EPDs are standardized voluntary disclosures that facilitate product comparison. EDP is *not* an environmental performance or green certification but may be used to qualify products for some green building rating system credits. However, some green building rating systems reward the use of EPD as a means to encourage transparency and full disclosure regarding the environmental impact of materials.

Green building rating systems have similar goals, each with specific requirements for material and resource use. The following list identifies some elements incorporated into rating systems metrics:

Health Product Declaration (HPD) is a standardized voluntary disclosure that facilitates comparison of products for the built environment relative to health and wellness. Designed to provide transparency and easily integrated with major green building standards, an HPD provides disclosure of 100 percent of all known ingredients. A product's HPD is independently verified and registered.

Volatile organic compounds (VOCs) are chemicals that can vaporize from material surfaces into indoor air at average room temperatures (a process known as off-gassing). VOCs are measured in grams per liter or pounds per gallon. Most are relatively inert at average indoor concentrations but may react and create a variety of irritants. VOCs include various acids and aldehydes with the potential to cause eye and upper respiratory irritation, nasal congestion, headache, and dizziness. Solvents, paints, adhesives, carpeting, and particleboard are all examples of materials that can produce VOCs.

Toxicity/off-gassing is the process whereby a synthetic material gives off a chemical (VOC) in the form of a gas. Commonly associated with the "new" smell of products, off-gassing is also present in cleaning products. Avoid products that emit VOCs to prevent off-gassing. Off-gassing may have a smell, but it can also be odorless.

CFC (chlorofluorocarbon) is a class of chemical compound used in the production of some aerosol sprays, refrigerants, and solvents. Although inert and nontoxic in the lower atmosphere, as CFCs deteriorate as they rise into the stratosphere, actively destroying the ozone layer and contributing to global warming.[1]

HCFC (hydrochlorofluorocarbon) is a class of chemical compound developed as a temporary substitute for CFC. HCFCs are not as damaging, but are still damaging. The gradual but complete cessation of new production and import of HCFCs is anticipated by 2020.[2]

Carbon footprint is the amount of carbon dioxide and other carbon compounds produced as the result of fossil fuel consumption. A manufacturing process used to produce goods, transportation to move goods, or any process that uses fossil fuel contributes to the product's carbon footprint. Methods to reduce carbon footprint include avoiding the use or reducing the use of material that produces carbon dioxide, using renewable energy resources, extending the useful life of a product, and consuming or using less for longer.

Salvaged material has been recovered from an existing building or construction site and reused in another building. Examples include structural beams, doors, brick, wood trim, and stone.

Reused materials are salvaged to be used again in the current form. reused materials avoid expending additional energy to remanufacture the product.

Recycled materials or materials with significant recycled content include those such as steel, where a good percentage of the product is put back into the manufacture of goods at the "end of life." Some green building rating systems reward reuse of materials and require documentation of the percentage of recycled material used in the qualifying product or material.

Post-consumer recycled material describes a product that has already served its original purpose, but the used material is an element of a new product instead of

---

[1] S. A. Montzka, *What are hydrochlorofluorocarbons (HCFCs)?* Retrieved August 16, 2018, from Earth System Research Laboratory: www.esrl.noaa.gov/gmd/hats/about/hcfc.html.

[2] Ibid.

being thrown away in a landfill. For example, some cellulose building insulation incorporates old newspapers into new product. Green building rating systems reward reuse of materials and require documentation of the percentage of post-consumer recycled material used in the qualifying product or material.

Pre-consumer recycled material is a material that is a byproduct of the production process, including scraps and breakage, reused in the manufacture of an alternate product before reaching the consumer. An example is mineral (slag) wool, a by-product of the steel blast furnace process. Acoustical ceiling panels use the mineral wool fiber. Green building rating systems reward reuse of materials and require documentation of the percentage of pre-consumer recycled material used in the qualifying product or material.

Rapidly renewable materials are plant based materials capable of quickly replacing the harvested material. Examples include sustainably harvested wood, straw, and bamboo. Avoid slow-growth and endangered species of wood.

Nonrenewable materials are materials harvested from natural resources that are not capable of self-regeneration, replacement, or restoration. Examples include metals and stones and items that "do not grow."

Local source. Sustainability includes a thriving economy. Local material sources are preferred. Locally sourced materials support the local economy and reduce the need to expend energy to transport materials long distances to the building site. Two separate but related distance measurements are considered to determine local sourcing: the distance measured between the point of a material's extraction or harvest to the project location, and the distance measured between the processing or manufacturing location and the project location. Different green building rating systems have different definitions and criteria for local materials. LEED has a 500-mile radius limit for local sourcing. LBC identifies both distances traveled and the percentage of total project materials budget that must meet specific distance criteria.

Material Consumption

In 1900, 41 percent of the materials used in the United States were renewable, for example, agricultural, fishery, and forestry products; by 1995, only 6 percent of materials consumed were renewable. The majority of materials now consumed in the United States are nonrenewable, including metals, minerals, and fossil-fuel derived products. (2020 Vision Workgroup 2009). That statistic means many products come to the end of their useful life and end up in a landfill. To use less is the original green strategy.

Construction of the built environment dominates overall material consumption (36 percent of materials consumption in weight), fossil fuel energy carriers (28 percent), and biomass for food and feed (20 percent) (OECD 2015). Sustainable designers evaluate materials and production processes using products that do not pollute the environment or deplete natural resources. Optimized construction techniques and construction processes that reduce waste also conserve natural resources.

Sustainable or green building rating systems have focused on energy efficiency and environmental stewardship. More recently, human health and wellness, which have been part of some green building rating systems, are becoming core considerations. The increased interest in occupant health and wellness, and more broadly the human experience, is more than altruistic. A competitive commercial market economy advances the interests of occupant wellness. Typically, staff salaries and benefits account for the highest portion of business operational costs (Alker 2014). Studies document increased employee productivity closely tied to the quality of a building's interior environment. The real estate rental market has also noted a demand for healthier environments that address human health and wellness and associated amenities in the workspace (Alker 2014).

Contemporary life has transformed the human experience. People now spend the majority of life inside the built environment. U.S. Environmental Protection Agency has determined that average Americans spend 93 percent of their life indoors: 87 percent indoors and an additional 6 percent of their life inside their cars. (Klepeis et al. 2001) Many contemporary chronic health issues trace their origin to the failings of the built environment. Increased attention and focus on a healthy interior environment are seen in the expanding role that human health and wellness play in green rating systems.

The materials and products used to build, furnish, and maintain the built environment in concert with building systems are critical elements in achieving a healthy indoor environment quality (IEQ). As material science has advanced so has the understanding of the negative impact of toxicants even in small amounts present in materials. Toxicants may be carcinogenic or otherwise impact the endocrine system, neurological system, or other aspects of human health. Some typical building finishes can emit harmful toxicants negatively impacting occupant health. Painted walls may emit volatile organic compounds (VOCs). Exposure to VOCs may cause headaches, nose and throat irritation, even nausea, dizziness, and vomiting. Adhesives, particleboard, and plywood may contain formaldehyde, a well-known VOC. Toxic fabric treatments are commonplace, including toxic flame retardants. Toxins can migrate out of the products and into people. Increased awareness of the impact of interior environment and interior air quality on human health and wellness has prompted changes in codes, standards, and regulations, as well as increasing efforts to remove toxic chemicals from the built environment.

Sustainable design is a holistic, integrated process. Materials are significant both as an element of a sustainable building design project and as part of the building system. To facilitate and support healthy, sustainable building strategies it is crucial to understand the attributes, content, production, and life cycle of materials and how materials may interact.

Research

Advancing technology is continually creating opportunities for material use, producing new advanced products, and uncovering information impacting established materials. Research, while time-consuming, is necessary to identify and evaluate sustainable products. Case study research may help identify sustainable materials. Information gathered from a manufacturers' sell sheet is not always complete and transparent. Environmental Product Declarations (EPD) and Manufacturer Safety Data Sheets (MSDS) are useful resources to understand life cycle environmental impact and safety concerns. Third-party certification organizations are also helpful. Third-party testing and certifications are specific to an established criterion, testing for specific attributes. Designers must understand the criteria used for each certification and verify the validity of results for ingredients, contents, and components for materials and products that are assemblies. Local regulations, codes, industry standards, and local environmental concerns may also have regulatory controls that influence the selection of project materials.

EVALUATION

It can be challenging to determine if a material or product is appropriate for a project that strives towards sustainability. Architects and designers working on sustainable and resilient projects are required to investigate and evaluate material and products suitability. Understanding the full specification and complete content of a product or material can be an involved process. Considerable research is often required. It requires asking a lot of questions, sometimes directly from the technical teams of manufactures, before there is enough specific and applicable data to interpret and evaluate.

Compare similar products against the specific project criteria for materials. Verify that reputable sources generate the data used for comparison. Product comparisons should be between similar products for the same function compared against the same criteria.

Material and Product Sustainability Standards

Standards are specific guidelines and criteria that, used consistently, ensure that evaluation of products is fair. Standards may be prescriptive (dictating the specific methods by which to achieve the result), or performance-based (dictating the desired result but not how to achieve the result).

Standards and certifications have been established to assist in the evaluation and selection of sustainable or green materials. Standards are established to provide a basis of comparison for assessment. Sustainability or green product standards may address a variety of concerns that impact the triple bottom line, including environmental, human health, social, and ethical issues. While most sustainability standards are voluntary, many green standards are integral to government regulations and codes.

A wide variety of stakeholders are involved in the development of green standards, including sustainability professionals, engineers, specific sector experts, and industry and manufacturing organizations. Standards (the criteria by which to measure the product) and certifications (the verification of compliance to the standard) are intended to validate a product's green claims. It is essential to understand the specifics of each standard and certification to understand the relevance to the evaluation of each specific product and application.

Product and Material Standards Development Organizations

A few of the organizations that establish standards are:

International Organization for Standardization (ISO) publishes the ISO 14000 environmental management family of standards. It is a collection of standards that companies and organizations may use to manage their environmental responsibility. Initially established as voluntary standards, ISO 14000 standards, like many voluntary standards, have found their way into codes and legislation.

ASTM International, formerly American Society for Testing and Materials, is a global organization that has developed technical, highly scientific standards for testing and classification applicable to certifications in a diverse range of industries.

American National Standards Institute (ANSI) oversees the creation, dissemination, and use of U.S. standards for a broad range of products and business sectors. ANSI is the official U.S. representative to ISO.

Material and Product Standards

Building codes address the issue of sustainability for materials and products from the broadest standard.

- International Building Code (IBC) and its ancillary codes include many provisions related to sustainability
- International Energy Conservation Code (IECC) for energy conservation
- International Mechanical Code (IMC)
- International Green Construction Code

Green building rating systems contain specific requirements and restrictions for products and materials applied to both new construction and renovation. All green building rating systems encourage the use of materials and products that are environmentally preferable. Some green building standards have criteria for materials that are more stringent than others.

- **LEED** (Leadership in Energy and Environmental Design), third-party certification for sustainable buildings. The material and resources (MR) credit support an LCA approach to materials and focuses on minimizing embodied energy while maximizing resource efficiency.
- **BREEAM** (Building Research Establishment Environmental Assessment Method), is an international third-party certification for sustainable buildings. BREEAM's material assessment category utilizes a whole building approach to reduce negative environmental and social impact of materials used in the built environment.
- **Green Globes** is a third-party certification for sustainable buildings available for buildings located in the United States and Canada. The rating system's resources, building materials, and solid waste assessment area emphasizes the use of bio-based materials, minimizing consumption, low environmental impact, and reuse and recycling of waste.

- **Passive House Institute US (PHIUS)** is a strictly performance-based building standard for sustainable buildings. PHIUS focuses on energy conservation achieved through airtight building envelopes and high-performance building components. Building envelope, insulation, building components, systems, and airtight construction are key to this standard. As the standard is energy-performance-based, it does not address specific materials beyond code requirements in a consequential manner.
- **International Living Future Institute Standards: Living Building Challenge (LBC)** defines a rigorous materials criterion, including vetting of all materials, systems, and products, to avoid over 15 chemicals on the LBC "red list" known to be harmful to human health and the environment, which are commonplace in the building industry. LBC also calls for sourcing materials within distances as established by material weight, categorized by Masterspec section.
- **WELL Building Standard** is a performance-based interdisciplinary system for measuring, certifying, and monitoring features of the built environment that impact human health and wellbeing. Monitored features include air, water, nourishment, light, fitness, temperature, sound, materials, mind, community, and innovation. Evidence-based scientific research that explores the connection between buildings and occupant health and wellness is the foundation of the WELL Building Standard.

Standards for Building Material and Products

Life-cycle assessment is prominent in the evaluation and qualification of a sustainable project.

The following standards are among various standards that apply to sustainable building projects.

ASTM Standard E-2129 Standard Practice for Data Collection for Sustainability Assessment of Building Products is the standard that provides instruction on how to collect the data required to evaluate the sustainability of specific building materials and products. The standard does not interpret the data; it provides the questions that require answers to properly evaluate the impact of a material or product on the environment.

LCA is a prominent factor while addressing five main categories.

- Materials: Environmental impact, recycled content, recyclability, toxicity, renewable resource use, and VOCs of materials
- Manufacturing process: Clean energy use, waste reclamation, water use, waste production, GHG emissions, and toxic chemical use
- Operational performance of installed product
- Indoor air quality
- Corporate environmental policy

ASTM E2432-17 Standard Guide for General Principles of Sustainability Relative to Buildings sets out basic sustainability principles and identifies methodologies for assessment. It is used by manufacturers to evaluate sustainable products.

ANSI/ASHRAE/USGBC/IES Standard 189.1 Standard for the Design of High-Performance Green Buildings is an integrated, comprehensive standard focused on energy conservation, directs appropriate product selection by performance options.

Standards for Interior Architecture, Interior Design, Materials, and Products

The list below is not exhaustive but represents the principle standards that guide the sustainable finishing of the interior built environment.

ANSI A138.1 is a multi-attribute sustainability standard of green squared specifications for sustainable ceramic tiles, glass tiles and tile installation materials.

ANSI/BIFMA e3 is a furniture sustainability standard that provides measurable market-based definitions and establishes performance criteria for increasingly sustainable furniture.

ANSI/NALFA LF 02 is a multi-attribute sustainability standard for laminate flooring.

NSF/ANSI 140 is a sustainability assessment for carpet.

NSF/ANSI 332 is a sustainability assessment for resilient floor coverings.

NSF/ANSI 336 is a sustainability assessment for commercial furnishings fabric, based on life-cycle assessment principles.

NSF/ANSI 342 is a sustainability assessment for wallcovering products.

NSF/ANSI 347 is a sustainability assessment for single-ply roofing membranes.

UL 100 is a sustainability assessment for gypsum board and panel products.

South Coast Air Quality Management (SCAQMD) is **[[an organization]]** concerned with regulating air pollution in southern California

Product Certification

A product certification may cover only one or a limited set of environmental, health, or social attributes. Identify the standards and certifications that match the specific need and project values.

Single-attribute certification validates product attributes relevant to a specific environmental concern. Single attribute certifications address focused issues as diverse as forestry management to chemical emissions.

An example of a single-attribute certification is the Energy Star program. Administered by the Environmental Protection Agency (EPA) in the United States, Energy Star is a voluntary program that provides independent certification of energy efficiency as measured against similar products. Energy Star certification results in the right to use the Energy Star label, which identifies products that meet energy conservation standards. It does not address other issues that may signify a product is environmentally or socially responsible.

Examples of single-attribute, issue-specific certifications and the specific issue addressed are listed below.

Energy Star: energy efficiency
Water Sense: water efficiency

Greenguard: chemical emissions (off-gassing)

Fair Trade International: fair trade standards including equitable employment, production, and trade practices

Leaping Bunny: animal testing

Salmon-Safe: water quality protection

USDA Organic: organic food, agricultural products

Multi-attribute certification validates product claims of multiple environmental, social, and economic attributes. Examples of multi-attribute certifications are listed below.

Cradle 2 Cradle (C2C) is a third-party certification, a biomimetic approach advocating regenerative design for products. C2C evaluates five quality categories: material health, material reutilization, renewable energy and carbon management, water stewardship, and social fairness. A product receives an achievement level in each category—Basic, Bronze, Silver, Gold, or Platinum—with the lowest achievement level representing the product's overall mark. The criteria for C2C is consistent across industries for all products.

Declare is the Living Future Institute product database that identifies product origin of raw materials and assembly location(s), ingredients and composition, and end-of-life disposition options. The Declare database lists the most harmful materials used in building and construction in its Red List. The Declare program provides transparent public disclosure in a consistent format, enabling a simplified evaluation of products and materials.

ECOLOGO is a third-party certification program run by UL Environment for products that meet multi-attribute, life-cycle-based sustainability standards. Certified products may include building materials, flooring, cleaning products, office products, and electronics. Product certification criteria vary across categories. Products certification is a pass/fail basis.

GreenSeal is a third-party certification for low chemical emissions that supports healthier indoor environments for a wide variety of products, services, and companies such as cleaning supplies, fluorescent lamps, and windows that meet GreenSeal standards. GreenSeal criteria uses a life-cycle approach to the evaluation of performance, energy and water efficiency, toxicity limits, indoor air quality, waste reduction, and manufacturing processes. GreenSeal is an ANSI-accredited standards developer whose products are certified on a pass/fail basis.

Green Squared certification verifies products in the tile industry and tile installation that are in conformance with ANSI A138.1.

Sustainable Materials Rating Technology (SMaRT) is a standard and certification system for products that incorporate life-cycle assessment, environmental performance, social performance, and business benefits into its evaluation and certification process (http://mts.sustainableproducts.com/SMaRT_product_standard.html).

There are different types of certifications and environmental labels. Not all labels are equal. First-, second-, and third-party levels of certification define the degree of separation between the certifier and the company whose product is being certified. When evaluating a certification or claim consider the party and standards behind the certification. A certifier or certifying agency can be ANSI approved, further attesting to the objectivity of the certification process.

First-party material eco-friendly labels are "self-declared" labels. A company establishes its standards and states the product's environmental performance. The manufacturer supplies information for certification. First-party material eco-friendly labels require no external testing or verification. These labels must be carefully evaluated for veracity. Often they are corporate strategies or part of marketing strategies. Examples of first-party material eco-friendly labels are listed below.

Eco-friendly, green, sustainable, pure, and **natural** are general terms that are often self-declared by a company. There may or may not be a standard or metrics applied to determine the claim. The terms are not clearly defined and are open to interpretation. Without applied criteria and independently verified metrics, these terms may be used as a fair representation of product attributes or merely a catchy marketing term.

Second-party material certification uses an industry-based standard or criteria to which the product strives. Independent third-party organizations may conduct the testing. Test data is measured against industry-established standard. Examples of second-party certification programs are:

BIFMA Level is a sustainability certification program for furniture, BIFMA (Business Institutional Furniture Manufacturers Association) is a second-party material certification.

CRI Green Label Plus is a sustainability certification program for carpet established by the carpet industry and targeted toward specifiers addressing indoor air quality (IAQ). The certification identifies low-emitting products by measuring the total VOC (volatile organic compounds) emissions and individual chemical concentrations.

SFI Sustainable Forestry Initiative, developed by the forestry and paper industry, is a standard and certification that encourages sustainability through the perpetual growing and harvesting of trees and the protection of wildlife, plants, and air and water quality. LEED does not accept this for LEED credit.

Third-Party Material Certification

Third-party certification is considered the leadership standard for product certification. Independent third-party certification substantiates that materials or products meet defined national or international (ISO, ANSI, ASTM) standard criteria or other manufacturers' claims such as energy consumption, air and water emissions, content, processing, and other attributes that impact the environment. The specifics of the standards vary by certification program, and not all certifications are equal. It is vital to look for established, well-respected, and recognized third-party certifications. Third-party certification can be specific to a product or industry relative to a specific concern, a single attribute certification, or based on life-cycle factors for multi-attribute certification. It is necessary to understand the standard(s) and claims the certification supports and how it applies to the specific application. Examples of third-party certification programs are:

Cradle 2 Cradle (C2C) is a third-party certification, a biomimetic approach advocating regenerative design for products.

Declare is a Living Future Institute product database that identifies product origin of raw materials and assembly location(s), ingredients and composition, and end-of-life disposition options.

Design for the Environment (DfE) is a certification that assesses the chemical safety of products relative to the environment and human health as well as performance. Administered by the EPA (Environmental Protection Agency), this certification assesses a wide variety of products ranging from cleaning supplies, paints, and films.

ECOLOGO is a third-party UL Environment certification for products that meet multi-attribute, life-cycle-based sustainability standards.

Forest Stewardship Council (FSC) is a global forest certification that applies to forest management and chain of custody of lumber and wood and products derived from wood. FSC signifies product comes from a source practicing forest management that meets FSC standards.

Greenguard is a third-party UL Environment certification program relating to standards for low emissions of VOCs into indoor air.

Green Seal is a third-party certification for a wide variety of products, services, and companies ranging from cleaning supplies, fluorescent lamps, to windows that meet Green Seal Standards.

Indoor advantage relates to indoor air quality certification for office furniture.

SMaRT Certified is a standard and certification system for products that incorporate life cycle assessment, environmental performance, social performance, and business benefits into its evaluation and certification process (http://mts. sustainableproducts.com/SMaRT_product_standard.html).

Beyond specific sustainability or green standards, manufacturers may have individual products evaluated by a third party to substantiate specific "green" claims. Certification of a specific level of recycled content, bio-based and rapidly renewable resources, material ingredient content, waste diversion, energy conservation, water conservation, biodegradable materials, and sustainable manufacturing processes are all among common green attributes. Manufacturers may seek independent certification outside of a specific certification label program for these sustainable attributes.

Material and Product Evaluation

In addition to determining that materials and products meet specific standards, consider the environmental impact of the material or product throughout all of its life stages by referencing the EDP (Environmental Product Declaration). In addition to certifications, additional clarifying information may be required to make an accurate evaluation. Request the information from the manufacturer. Which products best meet the project-specific criteria? Consider the strengths and weakness of each product. Often, there are tradeoffs between options. There may be a product that has less desirable aspects that are balanced by other very favorable characteristics or performance metrics. Conversely, a product with favorable characteristics may have just one unacceptable characteristic that cannot be mitigated or balanced, thereby removing the product from consideration.

Evaluate green materials as individual elements using a variety of criteria. When evaluating materials, consider the following:

Environmental impact
- Life-cycle analysis
- Location of material extraction, manufacture, and assembly

- Embodied energy
- Energy efficiency
- Carbon footprint
- Water efficiency
- Rapidly renewable material

Building codes requirements

- IBC: International Building Code
- Local building and fire codes
- IgCC: International Green Construction Code
- IECC: International Energy Conservation Code

Durability/performance history

- Useful life
- Track record
- Warranty
- Maintenance and repair requirements

Impact on human health

- Toxicity
- IEQ: Indoor Environmental Quality
- IAQ: Indoor Air Quality

Selection

Material and product selection will occur throughout the design process. Selecting appropriate materials and products for a sustainable building project involves understanding structural and functional requirements, budget parameters, individual material, and product properties and characteristics. Sustainable building projects have many common objectives, yet each project will have project-specific criteria and may prioritize one criterion over another in the evaluation process. Priorities set by the client, the project guiding principles, and project objectives filtered by human health and wellness concerns will influence the relative desirability of one specific product over another. Weigh materials evaluations from the perspective of structure, function, aesthetics, environmental impact, and impact on human health to select the materials that best meet project criteria.

Material and product choices impact the future of our world literally and figuratively. The materials used to construct the built environment have an ecological and environmental impact on the planet and human health. Regulations cannot keep up with the information and innovation regarding the myriad of materials available. Green building standards such as LEED, Living Building Challenge (LBC), Green Globes, and BREEAM all include criteria for green building materials. Designers must review objective material assessments to understand ingredients and content of materials and products relative to health and wellness in addition to energy efficiency, durability, thermal properties, reflectance, aesthetic, and cost.

Key Strategies

Usage. Use less. Reduce the materials required by sizing the building correctly. Select materials for building structure and building envelope that do not require applied finish materials. Consider exposed or polished concrete finish surfaces and prefab elements such as SIPs.

Reuse. Salvaged building materials save natural resources and reduce landfill contributions. Lumber, millwork, hardware, and certain plumbing fixtures are appropriate for reuse. Do not sacrifice energy or water efficiencies.

Recycle. Specify and use materials and products that incorporate pre-consumer and post-consumer recycled materials rather than producing new materials and products. Using materials that incorporate a significant percentage of recycled content reduces the demand for virgin raw materials, strengthens the market for recycled material, and diverts material that would otherwise go to landfills.

Durability. Long-term durability refers to the material's ability to withstand the conditions of use and wear without deterioration of function over time, eliminating or reducing the need for replacement. Durable products conserve embodied energy and may offset higher initial purchase cost with lower maintenance and operational costs.

Life cycle. Consider the entire life cycle of the building, from extraction and manufacturing to transport, operations, and maintenance and eventually the end of life. Design with resilience, adaptability and eventual deconstruction as part of the original plan.

Renewability. Rapidly renewable materials are made from fast-growing plants and bio-based materials harvested within a ten-year cycle. Bamboo, cork, wheatboard, and hemp are a few examples. Sunlight is the primary energy input required to produce these materials. Rapidly renewable materials typically have a more limited life cycle impact environmentally, economically, and socially.

Health and wellness. Use materials and products that support both the local environment and human health and wellness. Do not use products or materials that contain toxic materials or emit chemicals into the air through off-gassing.

Transparency. Environmental product declarations (EPDs) and material ingredient reporting tools, like Health Product Declarations, provide information on the contents of products and the manufacturing process. EPDs address the materials, ingredients, and processes used to make products. Other tools provide information about who makes them. Together, these three declarations address the triple bottom line and provide a complete set of information by which to select products.

Local, indigenous materials. Transportation consumes energy and produces pollution. The use of local indigenous material eliminates the negative impact of transport and often supplies materials and products better suited for local climatic conditions. Specifying and using local materials supports the social equity aspects of a sustainable project by supporting the local economy and creating local jobs.

Nontoxic and low-emitting materials. Avoid materials that use compounds that adversely impact indoor air quality (IAQ). Nontoxic implies products that will not cause adverse health effects. Low-emitting materials release only small amounts of compounds that negatively impact IAQ. These compounds may be present in adhesives, sealants, flooring, carpets, paints, composite wood products, and ceiling and wall systems.

Design for deconstruction. Buildings designed and built with an understanding of the value of deconstructed and salvaged material and material reuse may avoid sending materials to landfills. Buildings that are constructed simply are generally deconstructed simply. Simplified connections, prefabricated building systems, and modular assemblies facilitate building deconstruction while maintaining the value of salvaged materials.

Green material maintenance. Durability and longevity of green materials require proper maintenance. Maintenance of a green building must be effectual, efficient, and environmentally sound. Products and processes with low to no environmental impact are compulsory. Green Guard Certification Standards list emissions for a range of building products.

OVERARCHING OBJECTIVES

- Support for human health and wellness
  - Do not use materials that pollute or are toxic during their manufacture, use, or reuse.
    - No or low VOC levels
    - No or low CO_2 levels
    - No flame retardants
    - Reference Living Building Challenge (LBC) Red List
    Indoor environment quality (IEQ) and indoor air quality (IAQ) are fundamental aspects of building performance requiring toxin-free green material selection and maintenance practices.
  - Avoid materials that support mold.
- Reduce consumption.
  - Design spaces efficiently to reduce the number of materials required. Evaluate anticipated space utilization and the total size of the building required. Determine if, and which, functional requirements can share useable square footage reducing the overall size of the building.
  - Reuse building elements. Consider salvage from deconstructed buildings, items no longer in use in other associated buildings, reconditioned office furniture, and antiques. Examples of commonly available salvage building materials include brick, stone, lumber, interior wood and tile flooring, doors, glazing, and used and reconditioned furniture.
  - Recycled material. After right-sizing a building and exhausting opportunities for material reuse, select materials with high post-consumer recycled material content and, secondarily, pre-consumer recycled that can be recycled at the end of the material useful life.
  - Optimize all materials and products for efficient resource use. Whenever possible, use less. Optimized materials minimize environmental impact.
  - Optimize all materials and products for efficient energy use.
- Minimize environmental impact.
  - Select materials that are low in embodied energy. Sustainable materials support energy efficiency throughout the material life cycle from extraction/harvest through the end of useful life.
  - Select materials that prioritize water conservation in processing.

- Select materials that are durable.
- Select materials that are renewable and reusable and recyclable at the end of useful life.
- Select materials that are locally extracted or locally harvested.
- Select locally manufactured materials.

A sustainable building project requires materials that are sustainable, environmentally friendly, and green. Evaluate and select green materials to align with the project guiding principles, goals, and objectives. Set project specific sustainable material goals for the assessment process of prospective sustainable materials. Assessment of materials begins with research followed by evaluation and a final selection.

Design Objectives and Design Ideas

The four perspectives will drive significant project specific exploration and opportunities to select materials for exterior and interior building construction and finish materials (Table 9.1). The design matrix will help evaluate and prioritize which perspective and design idea takes precedence based on project guiding principles and client priorities.

New Materials and Long-Term Sustainability

The introduction of new and innovative construction materials and technologies requires architects and designers to research to evaluate the efficiency and capability of the innovation. Case study evaluation may be helpful for short-term results. However, durability, reliability, and longevity results require time for reliable data. Frequently, first project applications are the first real-world testing and evaluation. Do not rely solely on manufacture product data sheets and sales literature. New materials with little real-world application pose an inherent risk that must be recognized and thoroughly discussed with clients before making decisions.

Environmental Impact Evaluation Tools

Evaluation of environmental impact plays a significant role throughout a sustainable design project. The ability to estimate anticipated embodied and operational energy performance, to identify and quantify potential emissions to land, water, and air based on the materials and products of a specific design strategy is a powerful tool. Understanding the impact of design decisions on building performance, human and ecological health, and economic viability during the early stages of design allows designers to use the data to make better decisions, maximizing opportunities and avoiding potential adverse effects. During the design development phase, cost-benefit analysis can compare design scenarios under consideration and identify viable alternatives. LCA provides a way to evaluate multiple human health and ecological impacts simultaneously. LCA outputs of energy use, global warming potential, habitat destruction, resource depletion, and toxic emissions can inform comparisons of materials and support the material and product specification process with technical data.

There are a variety of environmental impact tools ranging from wide-ranging LCA tools to more specific tools that identify chemical toxins. Environmental impact

TABLE 9.1 THE RELATIONSHIP BETWEEN A DESIGN OBJECTIVE (GOAL) AND THE DESIGN IDEA (STRATEGY) USED TO ACHIEVE THE OBJECTIVE

		Green Materials	
		Design Objective	**Design Idea**
Perspective	**Performance**	• High-performing, durable materials • Healthy environment	• Evaluate materials using LCA, EPD, and MSDS. • Select materials that will support embodied and building operation energy conservation. • Specify materials that optimize raw resources.
	Systems	• Finishes should support a bright, open, and airy space. • Support building systems.	• Select materials that absorb and reflect heat. • Select materials that support daylighting strategies.
	Culture	• Create a healthy Indoor environment for building occupants. • Reflect the local environment in the building materials. • Reflect the no-nonsense, pragmatic local culture.	• Select no-VOC materials. • Choose locally produced products and other products with a low embodied energy content. • Maximize post-consumer recycled content.
	Experience	• Create a building with exterior and interior spaces that inspire. • Create a comfortable environment inside and outside. • Reflect the exterior environment and community.	• Select materials that provide a distinct appearance. • Select natural green materials that have a human-friendly feel.

tools are available through a web-based interface, plug-in applications to building information modeling (BIM) software, and stand-alone programs.

Following is a listing of environmental impact evaluation tools commonly used in the United States.

BEES (Building for Environmental and Economic Sustainability) is a North America–based life-cycle assessment and life-cycle costing software tool providing side-by-side comparison of environmental impact and cost of building material and products. The web-based program is best suited for the specification or procurement stage of a project. The BEES program uses the ASTM standard for multi-attribute decision analysis to combine the environmental and economic performance into an overall performance score. It was created by the National Institute of Standards and Technology and supported by the EPA Environmentally Friendly Purchasing Program (http://www.bfrl.nist.gov/oae/software/bees.html).

TALLY is an LCA plugin application for Autodesk Revit that helps quantify the environmental impact of building materials with LCA. Based on building information modeling (BIM), it uses the United States government standard method of measuring embodied carbon. Developed by Kieran Timberlake's affiliate company, KT Innovations, partnered with Autodesk and thinkstep, Tally details BIM models to recognize materials that are not modeled explicitly, like the concrete in steel assemblies, specificity, and detail to LCA modeling.

Athena Impact Estimator is a free LCA tool that is well suited for the conceptual phase of a project. It can simulate and evaluate cradle-to-grave impact of whole buildings, as well as building assemblies such as walls, roof, and floors. It is North America-centric and focused on material options for building core and shell. Output information includes the regionally adjusted environmental impact including embodied energy use, global warming potential, solid waste emissions, and air and water pollutants (Athenasmi.org).

Pharos Project, a product of Healthy Building Network (HBN), is an independent database that profiles chemicals and materials for a variety of health and environmental hazards, identifying and documenting the environmental safety and social performance of building products in the marketplace. While it is not a traditional LCA tool, it addresses the impact of the product on human health and the chemicals used in manufacturing (Pharosproject.net).

TRACI is a tool of the U.S. EPA for the reduction and assessment of chemical and other environmental impacts.

MATERIAL AND PRODUCT RESOURCES

- EPD Registry: Online central database of EPDs
  - Free, searchable
  - U.S. and international
  - www.environdec.com/EPD-Search/
- Cradle to Cradle: Certified products registry
  - More than building products
  - www.c2ccertified.org
- ECO-Specifier: product, case studies, resources
  - Global
  - www.ecospecifier.com
- ANSI BIFMA Sustainability Certification Program for Furniture
  - Levelcertified.org
- Declare: Living Future Institute
- UL Spot: Searchable database of materials and ingredients; previously Greenwizard.com
  - https://spot.ul.com

Transparency by Perkins+Will is a database of industrial chemicals and toxic substances, the "Precautionary List," which raises the awareness and understanding of chemicals of concern providing the framework from which to make an alternate selection. Product HPD, MSDS, and EPD, sheets may be reviewed against the listing. (https://transparency.perkinswill.com/)

GreenSpec directory is a listing of environmentally preferred building products published by Building Green Inc. that includes descriptions, manufacturer information, and links to additional resources. It is important to note that GreenSpec compiles the lists but does not test or verify manufacturer claims. (Greenspec.com)

A WARNING ABOUT GREENWASHING

Greenwashing is a general term used to describe the presentation of information that implies an environmentally responsible action or product that is vague, not verifiable, irrelevant, or inaccurate.

Deception by presenting partial information—whether purposeful or incidental—occurs with some frequency. Building professionals cannot accept information presented without verification and further investigation. It is critical to know the whole story behind a material or product.

These are just two examples of partial information greenwashing:

- A company advertises that it is using renewable energy sources. This claim sounds very progressive and environmentally friendly, except the company is only using renewable energy for 10 percent of its energy requirements. Indeed, 10 percent is better than not using any renewable sources, but the statement is deceptively crafted. This deception is a form of greenwashing.
- A fruit tree orchard advertises the ecological benefits of trees as carbon sinks. The company does not advertise its use of harmful pesticides to keep the fruit on the trees damage free. This is greenwashing through omission.

So, Is It Green?

Note that much of sustainability depends on the context. Some sustainable designers and educators have adopted an open approach to evaluating a sustainable design. "Cautions" and "optimisms" are terms that invite open discussion of context and variables. As an example, consider the "cautions" and "optimisms" of two materials:

Bamboo flooring
Caution
- A product of Hunan province of China
- Long-distance transport
- Manufacturing process: Poor manufacturing processing and installation practices can compromise the durability of bamboo flooring.
- Substrate and adhesives composition: Toxic preservatives and binders that contain formaldehyde may be used.

Optimism
- Durable
- Short regeneration time of three years
- Processing without preservatives or with benign boric acid justifies using bamboo instead of conventionally harvested wood flooring.

Recycled composite plastic lumber
Caution
- Expensive
- High energy use required for manufacture
- Small percentage of virgin plastic required to manufacture
- Susceptible to warping, discoloration, and melting
- Not recyclable: A growing plastic lumber market could increase plastics production and waste volume.

Optimism
- Made from recycled waste: Although it comes from nonrenewable petroleum, it diverts much plastic from landfills.

- Highly durable
- Maintenance free
- Pesticide treatments unnecessary

Currently, there are no easy, clear-cut answers for sustainable materials. Maintain a healthy skepticism when evaluating manufacturers' claims. The answer to the question "Is it sustainable?" often is: It depends. It depends on what are the project-specific environmental criteria.

Like all things relating to sustainability, evaluation of materials is better considered holistically rather than in isolation. Life-cycle assessment addresses the impact of a material or product through all life stages but is not always available or practical for every selection. Consider synergies with other materials and design strategies, along with the metrics and fundamental strategies listed earlier in this section. A full life-cycle approach balances the penalties from one stage of the life cycle with overriding benefits in another. Recognize that most material selection requires some tradeoffs relative to environmental effects at different points of the building and material lifetime. Overarching project guiding principles, specific goals, and strategies for a project will present priorities and criteria to advance the material selection process.

Be sure to see additional standards and evaluation information in the appendixes.

FURTHER READING

Alker, J. 2014. *Health, Wellbeing and Productivity in Offices*. Retrieved from World Green Building Council website: www.ukgbc.org/sites/default/files/Health%2520Wellbeing%2520and%2520Productivity.

Binggeli, C. 2014. *Materials for Interior Environments*. Hoboken, NJ: John Wiley & Sons.

Bonda, P., K. Sosnowchik, and S. Minchew. 2014. *Sustainable Commercial Interiors* (2nd ed.). Hoboken, NJ: John Wiley & Sons.

Kibert, C. J. 2008. *Sustainable Construction: Green Building Design and Delivery* (2nd ed.). Hoboken, NJ: John Wiley & Sons.

Klepeis, N. E., W. C. Nelson, W. R. Ott, J. P. Robinson, A. M. Tsang, P. Switzer, J. V. Behar, S. C. Hern, and W. H. Engelmann. 2001. "The National Human Activity Pattern Survey (NHAPS): A Resource for Assessing Exposure to Environmental Pollutants." *Journal of Exposure Analysis and Environmental Epidemiology* (May–June) 11(3): 231–252.

OECD. 2015. *Material Resources, Productivity and the Environment*. OECD Green Growth Studies. Paris: OECD Publishing.

Thompson, R., and M. Thompson. 2013. *Sustainable Materials, Processes, and Production*. London: Thames & Hudson.

2020 Vision Workgroup. 2009. *Sustainable Material Management: The Road Ahead*. Report No. EPA530R09009 (June). Retrieved from Environmental Protection Agency website: www.epa.gov/sites/production/files/2015-09/documents/vision2.pdf.

10

Step 4: Design Resolution

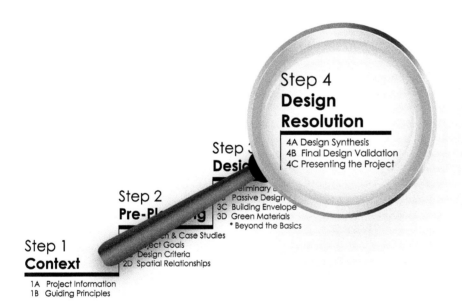

Step 4
**Design
Resolution**

4A Design Synthesis
4B Final Design Validation
4C Presenting the Project

Step 3
Desi

Step 2
Pre-Pl   g

eliminary
Passive Design
3C Building Envelope
3D Green Materials
* Beyond the Basics

n & Case Studies
ject Goals
Design Criteria
2D Spatial Relationships

Step 1
Context

1A Project Information
1B Guiding Principles

Figure 10.0 *Sustainable Design Basics*, **step 4**

Source: Sharon B. Jaffe

The final step in the SDB methodology, design resolution, features the last concrete actions in the sustainable design methodology. This step includes design synthesis, final validation, and presentation.

The section of design synthesis explores how design projects continue to evolve. The section of validation includes an overall description of the validation process, followed by a summary of the final validation process. The last section focuses on the strategies for effectively presenting a sustainable design project.

STEP 4A: FINAL DESIGN SYNTHESIS

At the end of the active or passive systems step in the SDB methodology, the designer should take one last opportunity to review and fine-tune the design. This process typically focuses on what may be called design resolution. It is a process that often includes a review of a few traditional design principles. First, the height, shape, and form of the building may change to provide a more unified and spatially pleasing composition. There is an art to creating beauty through architectural design. Established design principles and approaches that are the foundation of design practice are employed to bring about a satisfying building form and spatial resolution. This book does not address the aesthetic evaluation of building design. Some of the traditional design principles and methodologies design that refine the design of a building project include:

- Proportion
- Rhythm
- Hierarchy
- Spatial variety
- Spatial transitions
- Site integration
- Materials and finishes

The fundamental design skills required to utilize these design approaches are developed through education, design training, and design experience. Three-dimensional modeling (computer or physical) is often utilized during the design synthesis step to allow the design team to manipulate and study the design, as completed thus far, at eye-level from many viewpoints. Sometimes changes are needed to create a higher or lower spatial definition of space in both the building interior or on the exterior of the building. In the absence of a 3-D model, hand-drawn perspectives, sections, and elevations can be used to develop the three-dimensional aspects of the project.

Furthermore, during this process, landscape elements begin to be better defined and integrated with the architectural concept. While the design of the site is not a focus of this book, the demonstration project does illustrate some fundamental site design solutions that support the overall sustainable design goals and add significant design elements to the project. The demonstration project presents the evolution of a design from simple 3-D models to a more sophisticated final design as an example of the impact of the design resolution process.

The Design Synthesis Matrix

The design synthesis matrix (Figure 10.1) supports the evaluation and integration of the four perspective ideas at the end of each step in the design process. It is not a presentation tool. It is an organizational device and opportunity for the designer to share and reflect on what they have created. Chapter 14, "Demonstration Project: Final Presentation," covers specific examples of how to present the synthesis.

Macroclimate, macro context, and microclimate: The example matrix emphasizes the significance of climate and context. Climate and context information are shown in the matrix to maintain the focus on bioclimatic design aspects of the project. Often, climate and context tend to fall away as an emphasis further into the design process. Its good practice to represent them graphically as a reminder of their continued importance. The most influential microclimate design driver is recorded in the appropriate box.

Main image: The top space in the design synthesis matrix contains the most relevant and informative image as an expression of this step in the process. The example in Figure 10.1 uses a 3-D representation of the building. A floor plan or section may be used at the top in other cases. The image is meant to reflect the design synthesis to that point in the process. Final design synthesis requires additional pages and a different format for presentation. Chapter 14 discusses a variety of options for presentation and presentation format.

Section: A section drawing appears in the matrix. This is not intended to be a diagram like the ones drawn to explain how air moves through or light enters a building. Instead, it is a drawing that records the latest iteration of the design.

Daylight analysis and metrics: The next section of the matrix presents a daylight analysis and metrics. Daylight metrics are the most current performance-based projections from the energy modeling process. If the interim validation process has not generated a daylight diagram, place an available image that helps to visualize the light in the space. An interior perspective or section illustrating the extent and intensity of daylight in the building is acceptable.

Reflections: A series of "optimisms" and "cautions" are included to allow the designer or design team to reflect upon how the project is progressing. In many cases, the cautions lead to "next steps" to be resolved in the next iteration. The optimisms will remain and will be accentuated in subsequent steps.

The design synthesis matrix does not have a specific layout because each design project and each step often generate various types of drawings with multiple orientations. It is not required to complete a matrix precisely as it is in Figure 10.1. A second matrix may add other influential issues, such as site design or specialized interior design information. Think of the matrix as a framework that expresses a holistic approach to design. Depending on the resources available, some areas in the matrix may not have appropriate inputs, and they may be left blank, or filled with other types of information.

STEP 4B: FINAL DESIGN VALIDATION

A sustainable design project is evaluated according to a variety of standards, to varying degrees of detail, using a variety of methods. Determining the sustainability of a project is dependent on the definition of sustainability. The answer is usually: 'Well,

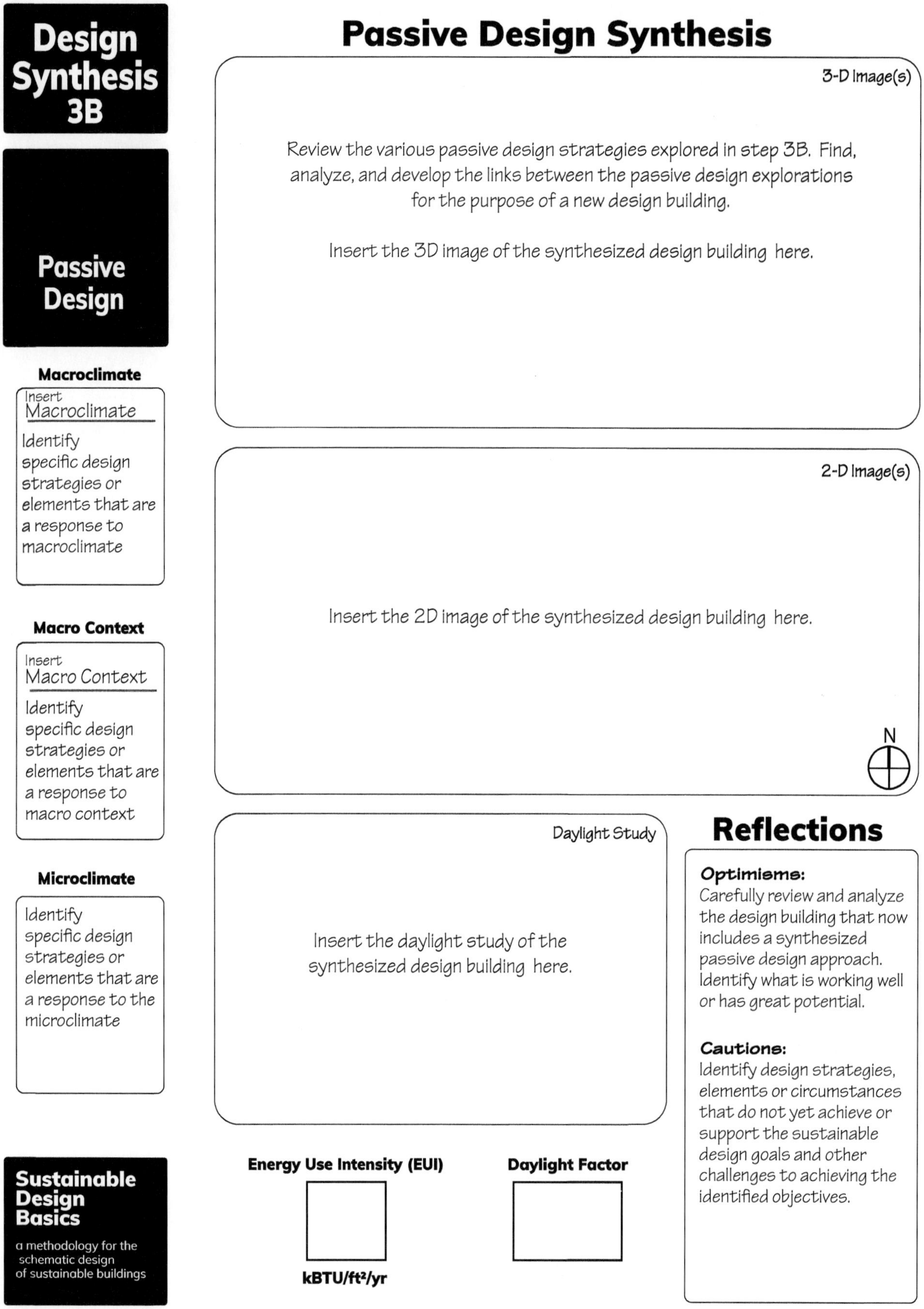

Design Synthesis 3B

Passive Design

Passive Design Synthesis

Passive Design Synthesis

3-D Image(s)

Review the various passive design strategies explored in step 3B. Find, analyze, and develop the links between the passive design explorations for the purpose of a new design building.

Insert the 3D image of the synthesized design building here.

Macroclimate

Insert Macroclimate

Identify specific design strategies or elements that are a response to macroclimate

Macro Context

Insert Macro Context

Identify specific design strategies or elements that are a response to macro context

Microclimate

Identify specific design strategies or elements that are a response to the microclimate

2-D Image(s)

Insert the 2D image of the synthesized design building here.

N

Daylight Study

Insert the daylight study of the synthesized design building here.

Reflections

Optimisms:
Carefully review and analyze the design building that now includes a synthesized passive design approach. Identify what is working well or has great potential.

Cautions:
Identify design strategies, elements or circumstances that do not yet achieve or support the sustainable design goals and other challenges to achieving the identified objectives.

Sustainable Design Basics

a methodology for the schematic design of sustainable buildings

Energy Use Intensity (EUI)

kBTU/ft²/yr

Daylight Factor

Figure 10.1 Passive Design Synthesis Matrix with completion instruction
Source: Rob Fleming

it depends." What are the sustainability goals? What does the site analysis reveal? What does the client want? Project context and pre-planning processes contain the supporting information and evidence required to answer all of these questions. More specifically, the basis for project evaluation is the criteria set in, and by, the project guiding principles and project goals. Validation is the process of determining whether the project met principles and goals. Validation also provides ongoing evidence upon which to base design corrections or advances during the design process. For example, a daylighting simulation will communicate to the design team whether spaces are getting enough light. Then the design team can change the design to better meet daylighting goals for the project. This chapter will explain in greater detail why validations are a critical part of the sustainable design process and how validation is utilized at different points in the SDB methodology.

The validation process substantiates the performance of the integrated sustainable design strategies relative to the projected energy demands. Early validations are performed throughout the *Sustainable Design Basics* methodology, at interim steps, to facilitate the design decision-making process. Validations are both quantitative and qualitative, often referred to as tangible and intangible.

Completed validation information is communicated to the client. The SDB methodology requires the collection, generation, and processing of a staggering amount of information throughout the design process. Validation provides essential information to demonstrate successfully reaching benchmarks, achieving objectives, and meeting the stated project goals in support of the overarching guiding principles. Chapter 14, the demonstration project, contains more guidance on how this is achieved.

Relationship between Project Goals and Validation

Most would agree that sustainable buildings should use less energy, have better daylight, be more comfortable for occupants, and therefore have healthier employees. However, sustainability is a sliding scale. How much better is enough? For example, the LEED Green Building Rating System offers four levels of certification, which represent increasingly higher performance levels of a project. Validating a sustainable design project without defined goals is not a very useful process. For example, a designer might add solar panels and say, "the project saved energy." However, how much energy was saved, and is enough energy saved? Did the amount of energy saved through sustainable strategies help the project achieve its overall energy goals? Without the context and framework of the goals, the different sustainable strategy may not be worth the investment.

Evidence-Based Design

The validation process is unique and powerful because it allows the design team to make critical decisions based on *actual evidence*. Designers are already very good at making decisions based on intangible goals to strengthen culture or increase beauty. Now, through the use of evidence-based design as made possible by the validation process, designers can begin to address and pursue the goals of saving energy and water. Designers can also pursue the goal of increasing physical comfort through better daylight, more fresh air, or more views to nature.

Validation occurs throughout the design process, not just at the end. It is important to note that early, and critical, design decisions require validation to provide qualitative and quantitative information to evaluate each step of the SDB methodology.

Multiple Versions and Iterations

A useful validation compares and contrasts multiple, distinct design ideas. Validating diverse ideas allows the design team to make comparisons based on evidence. For example, two different design ideas have dramatically different energy performance levels. The design team must confront the reality that the design idea they are most excited about may be a very low-performing project when it comes to energy or daylight. The discrepancies between design ideas will push the team to take action to move on to the next step. One possibility is to rework the preferred design idea to realize better performance. Another option is for the team to revise the design of the high-performing design to include some of the qualities most appreciated in the preferred previously poor-performing design idea. Yet a third alternative is for the team to apply the lessons learned from the high-performing and low-performing designs to develop an entirely new design idea. In Figure 10.2, four different design ideas are compared using daylight factors and EUI values.

Expanded Validation

Government regulations, industry standards, building codes, and rating systems define additional goals and objectives. Intangible and subjective aspects like experience or culture also need validation. Validation for intangible objectives includes an evaluation of *experience,* which measures the ability of the spaces designed to stimulate, soothe, and engage the senses. *Systems* are evaluated and validated by the ability to meet ambitious ecological goals. The approach to validation through *culture* begins with understanding room adjacencies, individual spatial requirements, and the varied needs for connectivity and separation related to behavior, communication, and social interaction. Validation evaluations for culture extend beyond the creation of positive environments in the building and building site to contributions to the community, and perhaps less directly, the city and region. The design process itself is also evaluated for its level of inclusiveness, a vital aspect of the cultural foundations of any design project.

Sometimes a design team will forgo the highest energy performing project in exchange for a desired cultural or experiential benefit. The most common example

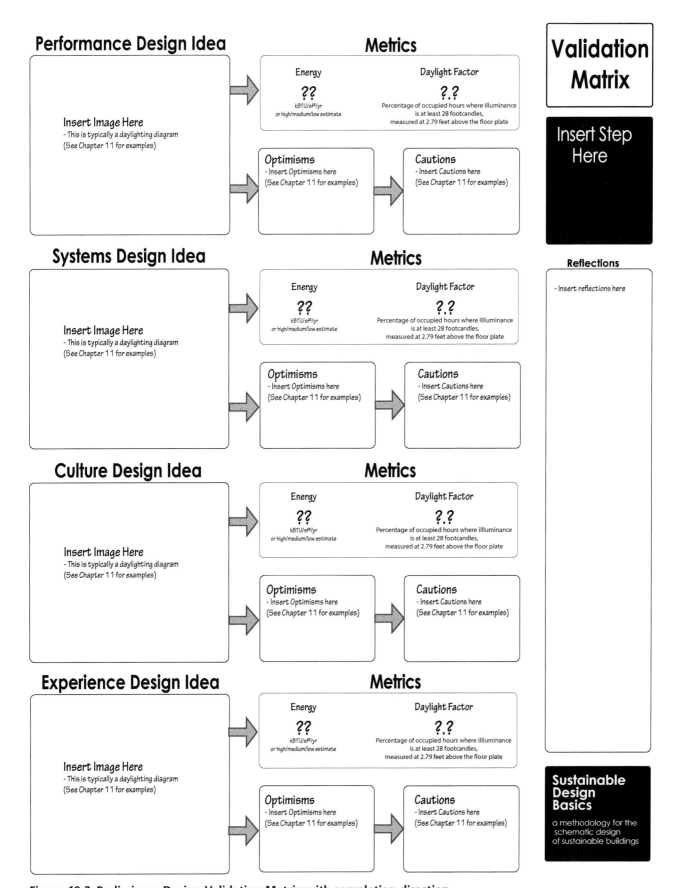

Figure 10.2 Preliminary Design Validation Matrix with completion direction

Source: Rob Fleming

of this is the use of more glass than the recommended window-to-wall ratio. More glass allows for light to enter the building and more views to the outdoors, enhancing the building occupant experience.

The Validation Matrix

The validation matrix, Figure 10.2, is a tool used to assist the design team in evaluating different design ideas during the design process. The validation matrix has application throughout the sustainable design process. In the SDB methodology design explorations are focused through the perspectives of sustainable design: performance, systems, culture, and experience. The validation matrix is configured to compare four different design ideas that are grounded in four perspectives. While this is the recommended use of the validation matrix, another criterion can serve as the basis of organization and evaluation at the discretion of the design team. The process of completing the validation matrix may feel cumbersome or unnecessary to some. Remember that the purpose of the validation matrix format is to ensure that design decisions are based on tangible evidence as much as they are by the more intangible, if more typical, experiential drivers of design.

Design ideas: In the far-left column of the validation matrix, space is provided for an image that represents the design idea that is under evaluation. The design scheme representation may be a simple 3-D model, a floor plan, or a daylight simulation from software.

Performance metrics: The EUI (energy use intensity) for the project is determined through the completion of a simple energy model. Those designers not using software may estimate high, medium, or low to enter as a metric. Health metrics are quantifiable evaluations of light, air, and view. An analysis and square foot calculation of areas on the floor plan will reveal how much of the occupiable space is within 30 feet of a window. Measure the total square footage of the occupiable areas. Measure the total area of space within 30 feet of an operable window and then generate a simple percentage. The metric for ecology is similarly calculated. Subtract the square footage of all impervious surfaces and lawns from the overall square footage of the site to determine the space left to support habitat.

Reflections: "Optimisms" and "cautions" are used to evaluate the metrics. An optimism might be: "This design idea is performing at a higher level than expected," or a caution might be: "This design idea is not getting enough light."

Next steps: In this space, the next steps can be identified to help shape the design process. Here, a recommendation may be made to "combine aspects of two design ideas," or "the experience design idea needs to be tweaked to increase its energy performance."

See a completed validation matrix utilized for the demonstration project in chapter 11 for an example.

Validation Process Accuracy

Validation of a design project can be done in two ways: with software and without. Software allows the design team to gain insights into how the various design ideas are meeting or not meeting the goals.

A Note About Computer-Based Performance Modeling

Computer-based performance modeling is complex. Mistakes that affect the simulation have many causes; inaccurate model construction is one of the most common explanations for model simulation difficulties and output inaccuracies. Also, many environmental factors, such as occupant behavior, cannot be accounted for in performance models. Results from performance modeling, at any stage in the design process, are performance projections or estimates, not actual measurements.

It is not critical for the validation results to be perfect. It is more important to use the numbers to compare the different design ideas. However, care should be taken to ensure that the numbers are not reflecting a significant error in the modeling of the design idea. For example, a single opening anywhere in the envelope of a 3-D model may invalidate the results of the process.

Use the benchmarks derived from case study research to make sure the validation metrics are relatively in order before continuing.

Performance modeling software can simulate and graphically render the effects of daylight, calculate the daylight factor, and calculate the EUI, for each design idea. The validation matrix organizes those metrics values for each of the four design schemes.

Calculations based on the physical properties of the building and site can be used to determine general metrics without the use of software.

The Final Validation Matrices

Table 10.1 shows the first of two final validation matrices. These are different from the validation matrices used for earlier steps in the SDB methodology. These matrices are specific to the final validation used at the end of the project. Table 10.1 provides generic examples of information required to complete the matrix. The project goals matrix focuses on the validating the performance of the final design synthesis against the original project goals determined in step 2 of the SDB process. The project goals established during step 2 included energy use intensity, daylight levels, access to light and air, water efficiency, community engagement, access to views, and engagement of the senses. Table 10.1 lists the project goals and then offers an opportunity to reflect how well the project met the goals. Sometimes a project does not achieve the goals. While disappointing, it is acceptable, especially when the goals themselves were very ambitious.

TABLE 10.1 FINAL VALIDATION MATRIX: PROJECT GOALS

Final Validation Matrix: Project Goals

The Metrics	Metrics	Stated Goal	Predicted Results	Final Evaluation
Energy	**Energy Use Intensity kBTU/S.F./yr**	EUI	EUI	Yes/No/Somewhat
	Building base energy load versus renewable energy generated	**Net Zero?**	**Net Zero?**	Yes/No/Somewhat
Health + Wellness	**Light** Percentage of regularly occupied spaces	XX%	XX%	Yes/No/Somewhat
	Air Percentage of regularly occupied spaces	XX%	XX%	Yes/No/Somewhat
Water	**Water Use** Percentage savings versus water baseline	XX%	XX%	Yes/No/Somewhat
	Stormwater Percentage of rainwater that can be managed on site	XX%	XX%	Yes/No/Somewhat
Ecological Integration	**Habitat** Percentage of landscaped areas covered by native or climate-appropriate plants	XX%	XX%	Yes/No/Somewhat
Culture Goals	**Stakeholder Engagement** (Percentage engaged)	XX%	XX%	Yes/No/Somewhat
	Sense of Community (Walk Score)	?	?	Yes/No/Somewhat
Experience Goals	**Views** (Percentage of regularly occupied spaces with a view to the outdoors)	XX%	XX%	Yes/No/Somewhat

Sustainable Design Basics: a methodology for the schematic design of sustainable buildings

Source: Rob Fleming

Final Validation: Guiding Principles

This task marks the end of the entire SDB methodology. Guiding principles established in step 1 of the process are a response to the interpretation of the client's motivations, the community's perceived concerns, and from larger global movements such as sustainability. The designer can now return to the original guiding principles and reflect on the success of the project. The terms "optimisms" and "cautions" are used to guide the reflections. The last column of the validation matrix offers one last chance to describe some next steps for the project, or the design process (Table 10.2).

These matrices may seem cumbersome and somewhat repetitive, but they do help a designer to remain "intentional" in their work, constantly reflecting and looking for ways to improve. Being "mindful" during the design process is a critical part of the sustainable design because it is so easy to slip back into a more typical mindset that tends to focus on aesthetics as the primary driver of design.

TABLE 10.2 FINAL VALIDATION MATRIX: GUIDING PRINCIPLES

Final Validation Matrix: Guiding Principles				
The Principles	Stated Principle or	Optimism	Caution	Final Evaluation
Performance Guiding Principle	Insert Guiding Principle	Insert Optimism	Insert Caution	Insert Comments
Systems Guiding Principle	Insert Guiding Principle	Insert Optimism	Insert Caution	Insert Comments
	Insert Guiding Principle	Insert Optimism	Insert Caution	Insert Comments
Culture Guiding Principles	Insert Guiding Principle	Insert Optimism	Insert Caution	Insert Comments
	Insert Guiding Principle	Insert Optimism	Insert Caution	Insert Comments
Experience Guiding Principle	Insert Guiding Principle	Insert Optimism	Insert Caution	Insert Comments
	Insert Guiding Principle	Insert Optimism	Insert Caution	Insert Comments

Sustainable Design Basics: a methodology for the schematic design of sustainable buildings

Source: Rob Fleming

STEP 4C: PRESENTING THE PROJECT

Presentation of a sustainable building design must give the audience a holistic sense of the project. This is a more significant challenge than one might expect. Presenters must establish the project context, convey the research and project goals, provide a sense of the design and early decision-making process, communicate the final design itself, and then present the final validation.

Making a Compelling Sustainable Design Presentation

A compelling sustainable design presentation must methodically "make a case" to persuade the audience that the project has successfully met all the goals and objectives of the project. The case must include information about all the steps, so that the audience can understand the process and see how the project design came from a rigorous process.

The Importance of Short Presentations

One of the dangers of presenting a holistic, sustainable design process is that the presentations can get quite long. Holding an audience's attention throughout a long technical presentation is challenging. An audience will only focus for so long. Presentations for sustainable projects contain more numbers and technical details than a standard design project presentation, making it even more difficult for the audience to maintain their focus. The strategies listed below will not only make for a better presentation but will also help to condense the presentation and make it more hard-hitting.

Start with the End Statements and Work Backward

Before finalizing the final presentation, identify the significant successes of the design project. Make sure all the information presented helps the audience see the logical progression of the design process that achieved those successes. This tight focus and progression of information make for a shorter and more compelling presentation. As an example, if the project guiding principles and goals dictate an energy efficiency focus, highlight research and conditions that help to support the goal of energy efficiency, and be sure to emphasize macroclimate information regarding precipitation and sun angles.

Use Highlights and Key Supporting Evidence

So often, presenters will dwell on inconsequential details. It is natural to want to share every decision made during the design process. However, the audience for a design presentation can be quickly overwhelmed with information. The risk of including unimportant detail is especially true in a sustainable design presentation. The strategies discussed as "key takeaways" and relevant information in the following discussions will help to make for a better, more effective presentation.

Key Takeaways

Designers often present vital data such as site inventory and programmatic information early in a presentation. Rarely do they make the connection for the audience regarding the importance of the data and how it influenced the project. In a sustainable design presentation, interpretation of the data is vital in helping the audience understand the significance of the data presented. Providing the audience with "key takeaways" is one way to achieve this. For example, presenting the average temperatures for the macroclimate as part of the overall project context without indicating how those temperatures impact the design is a missed opportunity. If the macroclimate has high humidity and the presentation includes the key takeaway "It will be hard to make passive ventilation work in the design of the building," this makes the connection for the audience between the research and the design strategies. It helps the audience see how the research will, in many ways, determine project goals and design strategies. Another piece of data from the site inventory might include the fact that surrounding buildings are casting deep shadows onto the site. The key takeaway here would be that photovoltaic panels will not be an effective, sustainable strategy for this project.

Matrices and Presentation

The final design, validation, and synthesis matrices are useful parts of the sustainable design process but not intended as a critical part of the presentation. The text and images on the design process and validation matrices are too small for useful presentation images. Therefore, the matrices can be shown to let the audience know more about the process, but the "key takeaways" offer the main points to present to the audience in a clear, bold manner.

The Relevance of Numbers

Another challenge to a successful sustainable design presentation is the inclusion of performance values in a manner that engages the audience. Without context, people generally do not grasp the importance of statistics. When presenting a metric or value, such as 12 EUI, the audience will not know whether or not that is an impressive number. Mentioning the EUI from a case study provides context and can help the audience understand the relevance of the design project's EUI. For example, if the case study project has a EUI of 18 and it was an award-winning sustainable project, then a EUI of 12 is very impressive. Comparing performance values against national averages for a particular building type is also a way to tell the story. For example, contrast the EUI of 12 for the design of an educational building with a national average of a EUI of 61. Now, the audience can start to see the success of the project. The demonstration project presentation in Chapter 14 provides an example of how key takeaways are determined and effectively integrated into a sustainable design presentation.

EUI Countdown

Showing the EUI for each significant step in the process helps the audience to connect the effectiveness of sustainable strategies with energy reductions. As the audience sees the EUI get lower and lower after each step in the process, they can begin to see the impact of each selection of sustainable strategies. Listed below is the breakout of the typical EUI countdown as associated with each step in the sustainable design process.

Preliminary design synthesis	EUI, based on ASHRAE 90.1
Passive design synthesis	EUI, updated
Building envelope synthesis	EUI, updated
Active design synthesis	EUI, updated
Final design synthesis	EUI, finalized and compared against the project goals

During some steps, the EUI may increase, if the team is prioritizing experiential and cultural considerations. For example, sometimes a high visible light transmittance is desirable for windows to create a better quality of daylight in the building. High VLT may reduce the overall EUI of the project. An example of the EUI countdown is available in Chapter 11.

Clarity and visibility are particularly important when showing the EUI countdown. Show the numbers in a large format. An audience cannot see lots of small numbers on a screen or paper. It is critical to enlarge the most noteworthy numbers so that they stand out.

Practicing the Presentation

One of the most difficult but effective strategies for making a compelling presentation is to practice. Most practice sessions will reveal that there is too much information and that the presentation is too long. The design team should immediately remove any unnecessary information and highlight other aspects of the project that did not get as much attention as needed. Having a few volunteers watch the practice presentation is critical as they can offer invaluable feedback. Try to gather a diverse set of volunteers who may receive the presentation in very different ways.

Concluding Comments Regarding a Presentation

The final presentation of a sustainable design project is the last step in the schematic design process for sustainable design. It is more than just showing the final drawings and explaining the project as a finished product. Explaining the process is vital to engaging the presentation audience. A brief narrative illustrating the step-by-step process allows the viewer to understand how the project evolved. This deeper understanding enables a viewer to engage with the design challenge, possibly identifying additional sustainable strategies and design inspirations that may make the project even more effective.

Sample Presentation

Chapter 14 addresses the presentation of the demonstration project. The chapter includes explanations and discussion of the presentation opportunities and general presentation concerns such as format, media, and strategies for verbal presentation, while developing the presentation of the demonstration project. A completed sample presentation is included on the companion website.

11

Demonstration Project

Step 4
**Design
Resolution**

4A Design Synthesis
4B Final DesignValidation
4C Presenting the Project

Step 3
Design

3A Preliminary Design
3B Passive Design
3C Building Envelope
3D Green Materials
 * Beyond the Basics

Step 2
Pre-Planning

2A Research & Case Studies
2B Project Goals
2C Design Criteria
2D Spatial Relationships

Step 1
Context

1A Project Information
1B Guiding Principles
1C Macro / Micro Context
1D Site Inventory & Analysis

Figure 11.0 The four steps of
Sustainable Design Basics
Source: Sharon B. Jaffe

This chapter will illustrate the concepts, principles, calculations, and techniques described in sustainable design basics thus far through a demonstration project. The process starts at the very beginning, as outlined starting in Chapter 3, and will take the reader "beyond the basics" to explore additional sustainable design strategies such as active systems, final validation, and final presentation. The descriptions will be brief, allowing the reader to focus on the steps in the process. Figure 11.1 provides an overview of the SDB methodology. The gray areas represent cognitive aspects of the methodology, the mental activity required during the design process. The white shapes with labels represent the physical product or deliverables of the process. The images and matrices included in this chapter are designed to help the designer navigate through the sustainable design process.

STEP 1: CONTEXT

The role of the designer is to observe, research, and document the project context, and then to synthesize the information and identify the critical research findings that will influence the design.

Step 1A: Project Information

Our Client

The example project used to demonstrate the sustainable design process throughout this text is a career counseling center at a university, an integral part of a medium-sized, state-supported university. It will provide career counseling for alumni and students of all levels. Lecture and seminar-style presentations will present instruction to college and high school educators, who are themselves career counselors. The career counseling center will serve three different campuses and bring internal and external visitors to the site. The university views the career counseling center as an opportunity to engage the local community, strengthening the ties between "town and gown" by offering shared meeting space, and other programs of interest to the broader neighborhood community.

Client Motivation

The University Career Counseling Center is a mission-driven client: an organization that strives to integrate its mission into all aspects of the organization from day-to-day operations to the buildings and structures that it inhabits and builds. A sustainable building employing innovative sustainable strategies and practices is an expression of an organization's purpose and an essential element in an overall public relations and community communications strategy. The site and building will serve as a statement of the university's commitment to the community, sustainability, and social responsibility, promoting enterprise, equity, and education as integral parts of community success. The project design will manifest the spirit of exploration and adventure, maximizing opportunities of the natural site.

Executive Summary

The building will serve as an office and meeting space for the University Career Counseling Center with the projected occupancy of 20. with individual

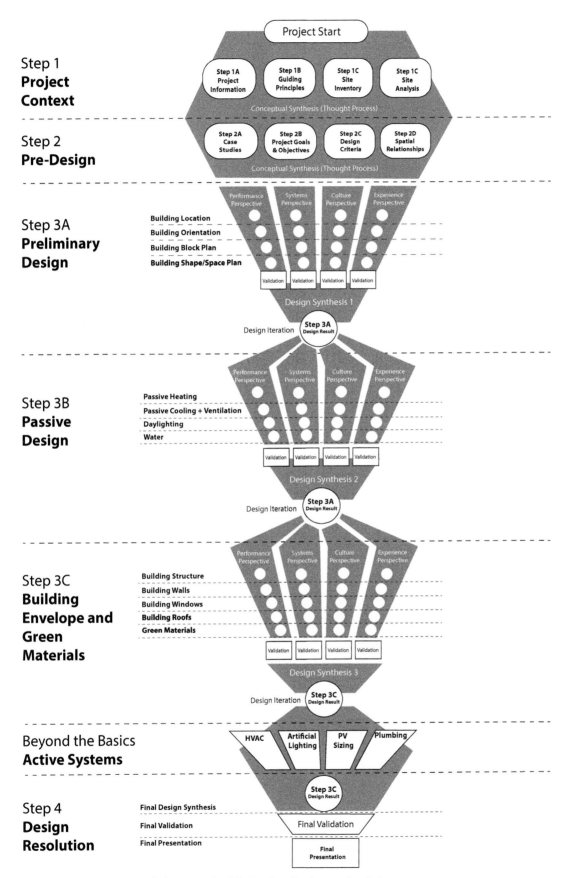

Figure 11.1 Overview of the *Sustainable Design Basics* methodology

Source: Rob Fleming

office and workspaces. It will include individual offices, shared workspace, administrative offices, open cubicles, a large conference room, a "commons" for informal meetings and work. Other necessary support areas will be provided, including restrooms, breakroom, electrical/mechanical rooms, supply rooms, building maintenance facilities, and storage rooms. The large conference space will accommodate 40 occupants and is suitable for large meetings, presentations, and community events. Subdivision of the conference space is required to accommodate smaller seminar gatherings. A small guest apartment is included for visiting scholars. Surface parking for 12 vehicles exists on site.

Building Typology

The career counseling center is predominantly an office building. Auxiliary functions include assembly and residential that are not large enough to warrant the attention of zoning. This site is zoned CMX2.5, which allows an office building use by right. No variances are needed to build this project.

Building Location

In Figure 11.2, maps illustrate and define the project site from multiple scales. Viewing the project at different scales helps a designer place the project into context. Project research is examined at corresponding scales. The site is located on the east coast of the United States, part of the Mid-Atlantic region, in the city of Philadelphia and located in the northwest section of the city.

Step 1B: Guiding Principles

Guiding principles establish the ethical foundations for the project and express the highest aspirations for the design. The four perspectives of integral sustainable design, explained in Chapter 2, organize the guiding principles. The principles are meant to be ambitious; to push design teams to innovate and work through seemingly insurmountable obstacles. The design team and the client, together with stakeholders from the community, collaboratively develop guiding principles for the demonstration project. As organized in the matrix (Table 11.1), guiding principles reflect the client's priorities for the project. Notice that the position of the guiding principle from the performance perspective is primary. Later in the project, performance will drive key design decisions.

Step 1C: Macro and Micro Context:

As described in chapter 3, sustainable designers think across scales to better holistically define the context within which they are designing.

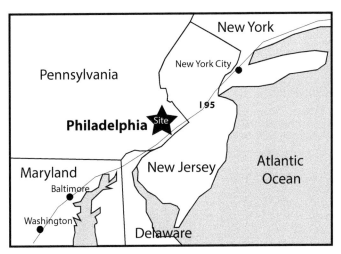
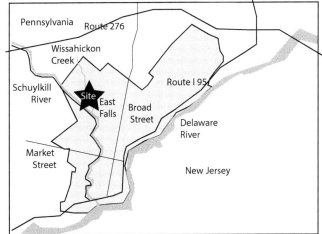
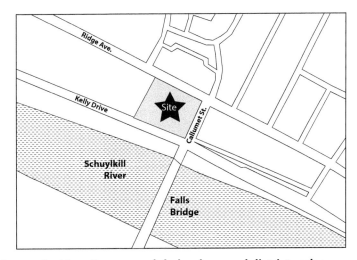

Figure 11.2 Demonstration project location map: global, urban, and district scales

Source: Rob Fleming

TABLE 11.1 GUIDING PRINCIPLES FOR THE DEMONSTRATION PROJECT

Guiding Principles Matrix					
The Four Perspectives	*Objective/Tangible Aspects*		*Subjective/Intangible Aspects*		
	PERFORMANCE	**SYSTEMS**	**CULTURE**		**EXPERIENCE**
Guiding Principles	*Fight climate change by creating the highest energy performing project possible*	*Educate the public about sustainability by showcasing sustainable technologies* *Bring ecology back to the city*	*Become an integral part of a strong sustainable community*	*Celebrate diversity*	*Infuse a sense of beauty in every design decision* *Engage all the senses in the design solution*
Reflections	*This guiding principle is the highest priority for the project*	*Bringing ecology back is the second most important guiding principle*	*This is also a really important principle*	*It will be a challenge to make this visible in the design*	*Biophilic design will be useful here*
	Sustainable Design Basics: a methodology for the schematic design of sustainable buildings				

Source: Rob Fleming

TABLE 11.2 MACROCLIMATE FOR THE DEMONSTRATION PROJECT

Macroclimate Zones					
Climate Group	**Subcategory**	**Characteristic**	**Implication**	**Representative Locations**	**Building Form Expression**
Koppen-Geiger MILD/TEMPERATE	Mediterranean Humid subtropical Marine	Moderate without extremes of temperature and precipitation. Typically, four seasons.	Unpredictable and varied weather. Building structure and systems must accommodate wide variables.	**Philadelphia Pennsylvania**	Maximize solar in winter, minimize solar gain in summer. Rectilinear building form on an east-west axis. Narrow floor plate to facilitate daylight and natural ventilation. High ceilings and windows positioned for cross ventilation.

Source: Sharon Jaffe

Macro Context: Climate

In Table 11.2 Philadelphia is shown as a temperate climate, which means cold, dry winters and hot, humid summers. The challenge presented to designers is to design a building that is efficient through all seasons. Each season requires a different strategy.

Macro Context: Urban

The context for the project site is urban (Table 11.3). Distinct from a dense urban site that has high rises, the site is in an urban neighborhood. Surrounding buildings vary in height from one to four stories with a mix of residential, commercial, and institutional uses.

TABLE 11.3 URBAN CONTEXT FOR THE DEMONSTRATION PROJECT

Settlement Pattern	Definition	Characteristics	Definitions
URBAN	A high-density built environment Commercial, industrial, and cultural center for surrounding areas	Dense development Multi-story buildings Majority nonagricultural workers Limited green space High-density population	Established infrastructure of public utilities, sanitation, roads, bridges, railways Public transit available High level of regulatory oversight for all development

Source: Sharon Jaffe

The urban site asks designers to carefully consider how the building will define and activate the street edge, thereby contributing to the health and wellbeing of the community. When designers do not pay attention to the street edge, the urban context is left with "missing teeth."

Micro Context: Site

The project is located in the East Falls section of Philadelphia as shown in the district scale map. (See Figure 11.3) The site was chosen because of its location near major roads and transportation and the three university campuses it serves.

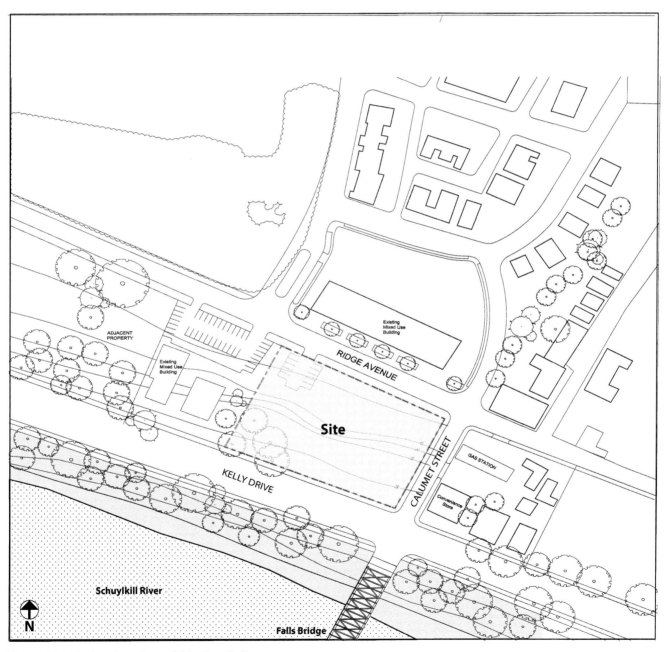

Figure 11.3 Project location within East Falls
Source: Rob Fleming

The site is located between two major urban routes; Kelly Drive connects the city center to the suburbs and is a bustling commuter route, and Ridge Avenue is a busy local commercial street. Parkland is to the west, residential areas to the north, the river to the south, and a business district to the east of the site.

Step 1D: Site Inventory and Analysis

There is always a temptation to start designing the project immediately. However, a patient approach that includes some basic site research generates an awareness of the specific opportunities and challenges on the site. This enhanced awareness will lead to a more integrated project.

General site research is organized by the scale from global to site and by the four perspectives. The highlights of the research are included in the site inventory matrix and the site inventory diagrams. Appendix A contains additional research details supporting the demonstration project.

Site Inventory Matrix

The general site research is often simultaneously too broad and too deep to be applied to the design process in a useful way. It can be overwhelming. The *site inventory matrix* organizes information in a condensed clear manner to communicate the information most relevant to this project.

The macroscale includes concerns of global and urban scale, and microscale encompasses smaller scales of district, site, and building. Notice that in this example, there is limited information regarding the building and interior. In an interior design project that utilizes an existing building, this information would be expanded.

The performance, systems, culture, and experience perspectives organize the research with listings of issues, opportunities, and corresponding design recommendations. Some notable takeaways from the research include the realization that the city uses a combined sewer system. In an extreme storm, a combined sewer system mixes wastewater from buildings with stormwater, all of which flows directly into local rivers. Avoiding heavy stormwater sewer use reduces the chance that sewage will pollute the rivers. Although site design is not the main focus of the demonstration project, it is vital to manage stormwater on site to prevent it from reaching the sewer, and potentially, the river.

Site Elements

The site inventory revealed several site characteristics, both opportunities and constraints, to be addressed in the design. The site inventory matrix (Table 11.4) and diagrams communicate the significant findings of the early design process of step 1.

TABLE 11.4 SITE INVENTORY AND ANALYSIS MATRIX

Site Inventory and Analysis

The Four Perspectives	Objective/Tangible Requirements				Subjective/Intangible Requirements			
	Performance		Systems		Culture		Experience	
	ISSUES	DESIGN DECISIONS	ISSUES	DESIGN DECISIONS	ISSUES	DESIGN DECISIONS	ISSUES	DESIGN DECISIONS
Macro Scale Global, Regional, District	Climate change is a real problem	Fight climate change with an energy efficient building	Greenhouse gas effect is damaging to the planet	Design systems to reduce carbon emissions on site	Disparity in income and equality	Solve it through development of an equality policy	N/A	N/A
	Philadelphia is the 8th largest urban use of energy in the country	Design the project to meet ambitious city energy goals	Combined sewer system is polluting the rivers	Collect 100% of stormwater on site	Kelly Drive is a major urban route. The site has no presence along this road.	Create a landmark visible from Kelly Drive.	Kelly Drive is one of the most beautiful roads in the city	Enhance the beauty of Kelly Drive through the design of the site, especially with the use of trees
	Performance for workers is lessened due to traffic noise	Use building and site elements to reduce noise from coming onto the site	Congested traffic in community and neighborhood	Design parking access to minimize further traffic congestion	East Falls has a wide range of architecturally interesting and culturally vibrant buildings	Design project to continue the architectural traditions of the district	The Schuylkill River and Falls Bridge are key elements of beauty in the district	Take advantage of views of the river and bridge
Micro Scale Neighborhood, Site, Building	Site is subject to flooding	Locate building out of the floodplain	Minimal presence of ecology on site	Establish an ecological community on site by attracting local animals. Use indigenous plants.	Lack of pedestrian activity on the sidewalks	Design project to activate the streets and urban corners	Views of the gas station are not desirable	Block views to the gas station

Sustainable Design Basics: a methodology for the schematic design of sustainable buildings

Source: Rob Fleming

273

Site Inventory Diagrams from the Four Perspectives

The site inventory and analysis diagrams are the synthesis of all the research, presented visually in a simplified diagram to quickly communicate major concerns and opportunities. While there are hundreds of pieces of information collected during the investigation and exploration, the site inventory diagrams are a high-level look at the major aspects that will affect the design. Remember, site inventory is only used to express the reality of the site without considering a specific design. The site analysis, covered in the next section, examines appropriate design approaches. Notice that, once again, the four perspectives organize the different aspects of the research.

Performance Perspective

The site is constrained by two major roadways, each with a congested intersection (Figure 11.4). The topography slopes gently toward the river. Setbacks are required

Site Inventory - Performance Perspective

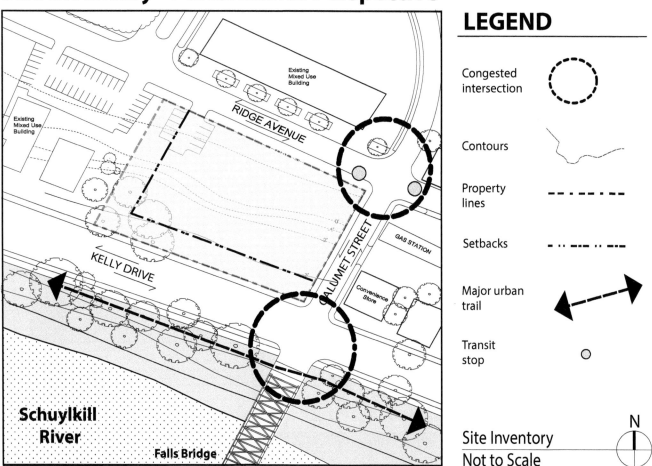

Figure 11.4 Site inventory: performance perspective
Source: Rob Fleming

along two sides of the site, but the commercial corridor edges of this urban site need the building to meet the street edge on the north and east sides of the site. Across Kelly Drive, a river trail for cycling, jogging, and walking connects center city, 4 miles away, to the adjacent Fairmount Park.

Systems Perspective

The systems perspective diagram (Figure 11.5) illustrates excellent solar access to the south, except for an area of trees on the east side of the site. The 100-year floodplain is delineated. Winter winds are from the northwest and summer breezes come from the southwest.

Cultures Perspective

The cultures perspective diagram (Figure 11.6), a historic bridge is highlighted along with two prominent community spaces. The community space on the north side

Site Inventory - Systems Perspective

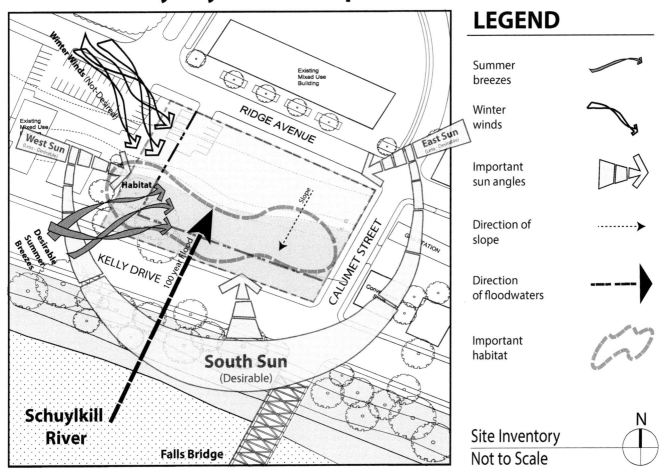

Figure 11.5 Site inventory: systems perspective
Source: Rob Fleming

Site Inventory - Cultures Perspective

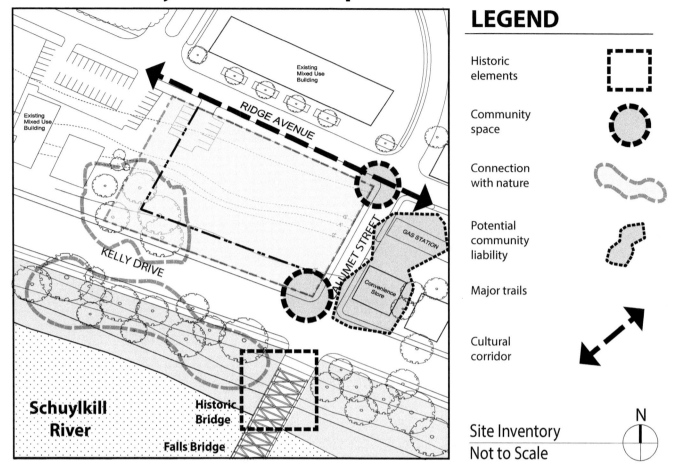

Figure 11.6 Site inventory: cultures perspective

Source: Rob Fleming

connects to a commercial corridor along Ridge Avenue. The other community space connects the site to Kelly Drive, a major urban route through the city. There are many opportunities to connect with nature. Also identified is an eyesore, a gas station across Calumet Street.

Experience Perspective

The experience perspective diagram (Figure 11.7) documents views to and from the site, the beautiful view of the historic Falls Bridge and an undesirable view toward the gas station. The habitat area is defined as an opportunity to collect sounds and smells of nature—a biophilic experience.

Site Analysis: Constraints and Opportunities

The site analysis diagram (Figure 11.8) is a visual transition from the site inventory to the actual design project. The diagram records specific recommendations,

Site Inventory - Experience Perspective

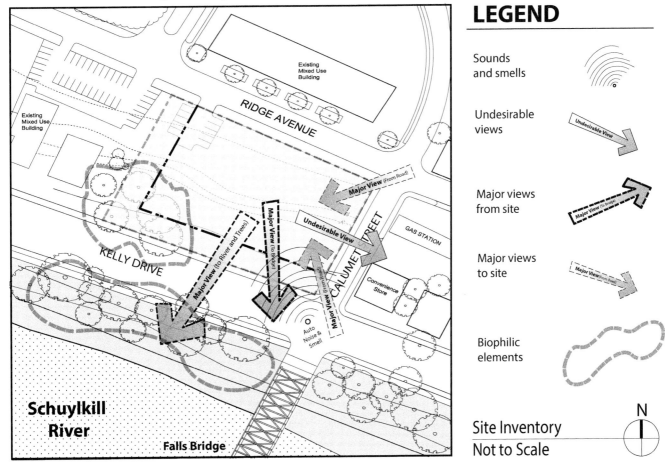

Figure 11.7 Site inventory: experience perspective
Source: Rob Fleming

prioritizing site opportunities and constraints to be addressed that will help focus the design. The major urban northeast corner of the demonstration project should be "activated" in the design to respect the urban street edge and delineate pedestrian and vehicle traffic. Notations to collect sun, optimize views, and collect breezes indicate important design drivers. The corner of Kelly Drive and Calumet Street is identified as a highly visible gateway to the community and an appropriate location for a focal point. "Important movement patterns" identify an existing well-defined street crossing. The floodplain is identified as an area that must be protected from construction.

At this point in the process, step 1 (context) has been completed. However, it is expected that the work in the following tasks will require the return to this step and update the research and analysis as needed.

Site Analysis - All Perspectives

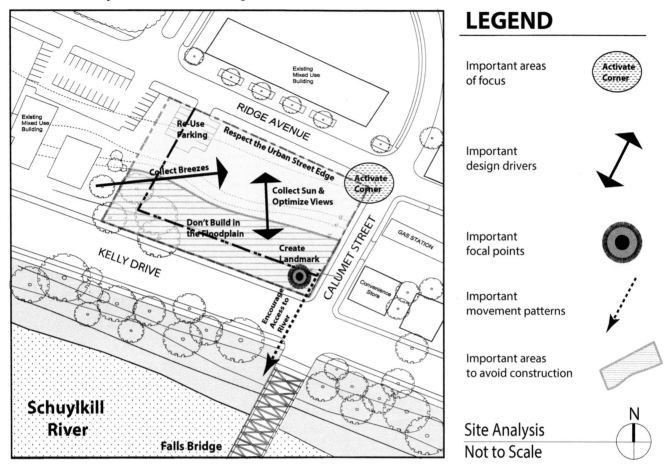

Figure 11.8 Site analysis
Source: Rob Fleming

STEP 2: PRE-PLANNING

Step 2A: Case Study Overview

Case studies of sustainable projects with parallels to the demonstration project provide valuable information relating to the building, site, systems, and more. Analysis of sustainable projects selected for their parallels to the demonstration project provides insight and direction from real-life experiences, ranging from the approach to specific site conditions to metrics achieved in the case study serving as benchmarks.

Commonly, multiple case studies are completed to inform a project before design. In this instance, for the sake of brevity, only two case studies relevant to the demonstration project are included. More information about the case studies is available on the companion website.

Marin County Day School is the first case study; Kern Center at Hampshire College is the second. Both case studies are illustrated with PowerPoint slides. Figure 11.9 is a selection of reduced slides from the case studies of Marin County Day School and Kern Center at Hampshire College.

Basic Research

The case study outline (Table 11.5) indicates the use of multiple scales and multiple perspectives as organizing factors in the case study matrix and the site inventory matrix. Organization by scale is a pattern applied throughout the demonstration project. Case study research is collected and presented in a series of PowerPoint slides. The four perspectives and the various scales organize research topics. The slide layout is flexible; the research is for reference and not for presentation. When a situation requires presentation of case study research, the slides are organized more formally.

Case Study Matrix

The case study matrix organizes and helps a designer to integrate the significant elements of the case study. The format of the case study matrix follows the format used in other steps of the SDB methodology very closely. The systems and strategies identified in the case study project and realized metrics are particularly significant. The design strategies investigated through the case study model suggest potential strategies to reach the performance levels of the project, and the metrics realized by the case study serve as benchmarks and goals for the demonstration project.

TABLE 11.5 CASE STUDY RESEARCH OUTLINE.

1. Title and information about the project			
2. Global scale research			
Performance and Facts: Project location; important statistics such as global temperature rise, sea level rise, loss of biodiversity, etc.	**Systems**: Greenhouse effect, hydronic cycles, global scale climatic drivers such as ocean currents	**Culture**: United Nations sustainable development goals	**Experience**: N/A
3. Regional scale research			
Performance and Facts: Project location; important statistics such as city population	**Systems**: Watershed, biome, ecological issues, technical systems such as transportation	**Culture**: The culture of the region re: food, art, sports, politics, historical events, and places	**Experience**: throughout the city, primarily as related to the project site
4. District scale research			
Performance and Facts: Project location, demographics	**Systems**: Flora and fauna, hydrology, microclimates	**Culture**:The culture of the district: food, art, sports, politics, historical events that shaped the formation of the district	**Experience**: Views around the neighborhood
5. Site-scale research			
Performance and Facts: Site boundaries and any physical elements	**Systems**: Flora and fauna, hydrology, tree canopy, habitat, microclimates on the site (positive or negative)	**Culture**: Historical elements or events that shaped the formation of the district	**Experience**: Views to and from the site
6. Building + interiors scale research			
Performance and Facts: Building basics, plans, sections, elevations, un-rendered factual representations; performance metrics and rating systems	**Systems**: Ecological and technical systems within the building or building envelope assemblies that drive performance	**Culture**: Inclusivity in the design process and the community connectivity of the project	**Experience**: Strategies used to create meaningful experiences in the project

A case study provides important precedents, making it an advantageous pre-planning step. The case study matrix includes a restatement of the overarching goals of the project under study. The goals are similar to guiding principles in that they help the designer keep the big picture in mind. Identify case study project goals from all four perspectives. Case study project goals are measurable, tangible, and define sustainability targets. Generally, the project goals for a case study can be found through research in print or on a website.

Takeaways and Executive Summary

The presentation of a case study as part of an overall final presentation must be short and impactful. The minimum slides required to present the case study include:

1. Project information
2. Case study matrix
3. Case study summary

Thumbnails of the two case studies for the demonstration project are shown in Figure 11.9. The case study matrix is not a practical presentation tool, due to the small size of the text, but is shown to establish that completed research and organized thinking focused on the case study. The matrix also supports the takeaways illustrated in the thumbnails as well considered. The pictures selected for the case study summary correlate to the critical takeaways listed.

Step 2B: Project Goals

The Matrix

The goals matrix organizes project goals by the four perspectives. (See Table 11.7.) The performance column focuses on energy, water, and other measurable metrics. The systems columns address the project's approach to technical and ecological systems. Subjective aspects of culture and experience columns are more difficult to predict, but stating goals is still a valuable process because it focuses one's thinking before design.

The types of targets are organized by row. The top row, guiding principles, records the principles developed earlier in the SDB methodology. Goals and objectives transition from the broad overarching principles to more specific design actions. Notice that each objective relates to the goals and guiding principles. The third row shows metrics, which may be preset by the specific targeted green building rating systems. Targeting a specific green building rating may simplify establishing goals and objectives. However, for the beginning sustainable designer, the sheer number of goals in green rating systems can be overwhelming. It is better to start with a few key metrics, as shown in Table 11.7. Note the metrics used for each perspective. Performance perspective uses energy, light air, and water. As one becomes more familiar with the matrices of the SDB methodology, metrics can be traded out or supplemented. Benchmarks are specific goals that set targets for what can be achieved. Notice that the EUI for the demonstration project is a very ambitious number. It can be identified as ambitious as measured against the standards set by the case studies previously completed, and in comparison to industry standards.

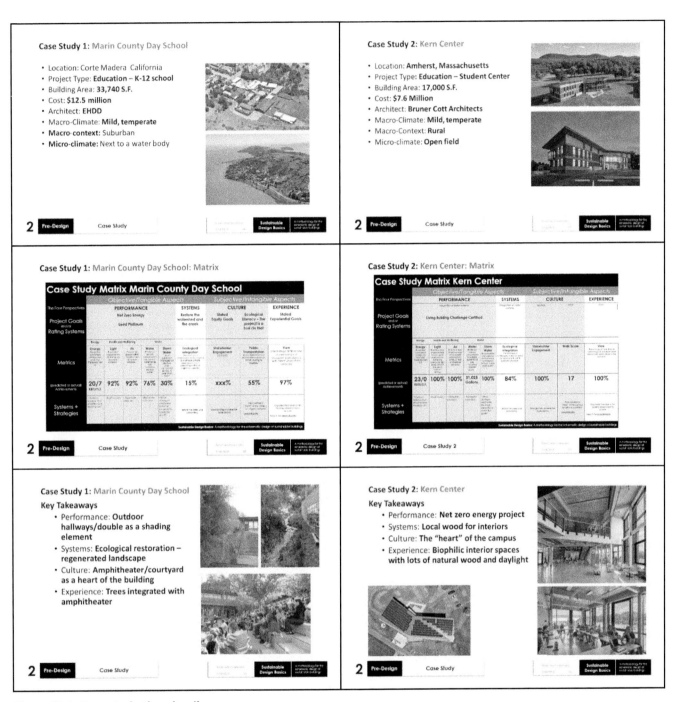

Figure 11.9 Case study thumbnails
Source: AIA

Step 2C: Design Criteria

The criteria matrix shown in Table 11.8 outlines the details required to complete the project space plan. Simple factual information, such as square footage and adjacencies for each area, is indicated under the performance perspective and specialized passive and active system requirements for each space are identified in the systems perspective column. It is not necessary to enter the terms "daylight" and "natural ventilation" for each area space since it is assumed from the metric.

TABLE 11.6 CASE STUDY MATRIX EXAMPLE

Case Study Matrix Kern Center

	Objective/Tangible Aspects						Subjective/Intangible Aspects		
The Four Perspectives	**PERFORMANCE**					**SYSTEMS**	**CULTURE**		**EXPERIENCE**
	Energy	Health and Wellbeing		Water					
	Energy	Light	Air	Water	Stormwater				
Project Goals *and/or* **Rating Systems**	*Living Building Challenge Certified*					Integration of water systems	Meet LBC standards for Just Organization Imperative	Meet LBC standards for Human-Powered Living Imperative	Meet LBC standards for Beauty and Spirit Imperative
Metrics	**Energy** Predicted consumed energy use intensity/predicted net EUI	**Light** Percentage of floor area or percentage of occupant work stations achieving adequate light levels without the use of artificial lighting	**Air** Percentage of floor area or percentage of occupant work stations within 30 feet of operable windows	**Water** Predicted annual consumption of potable water for all uses, including process water	**Stormwater** Percentage of rainwater managed on site from max. anticipated 24-hour, 2-year storm event	**Ecological Integration** Percentage of landscaped areas covered by appropriate plants supporting habitat	**Stakeholder Engagement** Percentage of stakeholders engaged	**Walk Score**	**View** Percentage of floor area or percentage of occupant work stations with direct views of the outdoors
Achievement (Predicted or Actual)	23/0 kBTU/ft²/yr	100%	100%	31,025 Gallons	100%	84%	100%	17	100%
Systems + Strategies	PV array Well-insulated, Good U-value for windows	*High ceilings allow light to enter deeper into the building; reflective materials*	*Operable windows*	*Water reclamation technology*	*Rain gardens*	*Large site with plenty of space for non-lawn landscaping. Future space for food production*	*Design charrettes*		*Window openings allow views to the mountains in the distance*

Sustainable Design Basics: a methodology for the schematic design of sustainable buildings

Source: Rob Fleming

TABLE 11.7 PROJECT GOALS MATRIX

Goals and Objectives Matrix

The Four Perspectives	Objective/Tangible Aspects						Subjective/Intangible Aspects		
	PERFORMANCE					**SYSTEMS**	**CULTURE**	**CULTURE**	**EXPERIENCE**
Guiding Principles	*Fight climate change by creating the highest energy performing project possible*					Integrate the project with the surrounding ecology	Celebrate diversity	Be a vital partner in a strong community	Infuse a sense of beauty in every decision
Stated Project Goals and/or Rating Systems	**Net-Zero Energy**					**Healthy habitat for increased biodiversity**		**Hold public community meetings in conference room**	**Engage all the senses**
Objectives									
	Energy	**Health and Wellbeing**		**Water**		**Site Coverage**			**Views**
	Energy	**Light**	**Air**	**Water**	**Storm Water**	**Ecological Integration**	**Stakeholder Engagement**	**Sense of Community**	**Views**
Metrics	Predicted consumed energy use intensity/ predicted net EUI	Percentage of spaces > 300 lux (28 FC) at 3pm March 21 and/or daylight factor (DF)	Percentage of floor area or percentage of occupant workstations within 30 feet of operable windows	Percentage reduction of water use versus baseline	Percentage of rainwater that can be managed on site from max. anticipated 24-hour, 2-year storm event	Percentage of landscaped areas covered by native or climate-appropriate plants supporting native or migratory animals	Percentage of stakeholders engaged	Walk, transit, bike scores	Percentage of floor area or percentage of occupant workstations with direct views of the outdoors
Benchmarks	20/0 kBTU/ft²/yr	100% **Daylight Factor 2% - 5%**	100%	66%	100%	50%	100%*	72/64/58* Walk, transit, bike scores	100%
Strategies	High-performance building envelope	Thin building plate, high ceiling/ windows/ light shelves	Thin building, operable windows	Collect water from the roof in cisterns	Divert site stormwater to a rain garden	Indigenous plants, limit paving as much as possible	Design charrette	Strategies or policies meet culture achievements	Position workspaces with view to the outdoors.

Sustainable Design Basics: a methodology for the schematic design of sustainable buildings

Source: Rob Fleming

283

TABLE 11.8 CRITERIA MATRIX, INTERIOR

Criteria Matrix: Interior

The Four Perspectives		Objective/Tangible Requirements					Subjective/Intangible Requirements		
Design Criteria		PERFORMANCE				SYSTEMS		CULTURE	EXPERIENCE
Room Name	SQ. FT.	Adjacencies	Acoustics	Furniture Requirements	Active Systems *Specialized heating, cooling, ventilation, plumbing, lighting, equipment only*	Passive Systems *List specialized requirements below*	Privacy	Special Cultural Considerations *Image, brand, sense of community*	Sense of place *Views, smells, textures, colors, taste, sounds, special considerations, spatial sense, other intangibles*
Rm #									
1 Vestibule	80	2	H	Walk-off mats to meet LEED	Supplemental heating		L		
2 Reception	300	1,3,4	H	Reception desk and waiting room chairs for 7 people			L		Welcoming
3 Break Room	175	2,11	H	Counter space, cabinets	Sink, Energy Star refrigerator		M		Bright colors, view to river
4 Copy Room	200	2,8	H	Counter space, cabinets	Copier—consider separate ventilation		M		
5 Restrooms (2)	130	2,8	L	Counters for sinks	Low-flow sinks, dual-flush toilets —rainwater-fed.		H		
6 Apartment	520	-	L	Living room, dining table, 2 chairs, bedroom	Low-flow sinks, dual-flush toilets, mini-split HVAC		H	Sound insulation	View to river
7 Private Office (3@150)	300	2	L	Desk, desk chair, 2 guest chairs, credenza			H	Sound insulation	Views to outdoors

284

#	Space	Sq. Ft.		Priority	Furniture	Equipment	Priority	Notes	Views
8	Open Offices (7 @ 90 sq. ft.)	560	3,4	M	Desk, desk chair, 1 guest chair, systems furniture		M		Views to outdoors
9	Commons	500	8	M	Couches, chairs coffee tables 1 table with chairs		L	"Heart" of the building	Biophilic experiences
10	Large Conference	1000	1,2,3	M	Moveable conference table and chairs—the room can be split in two	A/V	M	Sound insulation	Views to the bridge
11	Small Conference	200	7,2	M	Conference table with chairs	Audio/visual	M	Sound insulation	Views to outdoors
12	Mechanical	50	-	L	-	Electric panel, inverters for solar array	H	Sound insulation	-
13	Storage	50	-		Janitor storage shelves	Mop sink	H		-
	Subtotal Sq. Ft.	4,065					-	-	-
	Circulation @35%	1,423					-	-	-
	Total Sq. Ft.	5,448					-	-	-

Sustainable Design Basics: a methodology for the schematic design of sustainable buildings

Source: Rob Fleming

Desired privacy levels and particular culture and equity aspects of each space are listed in the culture perspective columns. The large conference room and the functional requirements are identified. Finally, the experiential aspects of each area are listed in the experience column.

Step 2D: Spatial Relationships

The relationship diagrams for the demonstration project shown in Figure 11.10 are abstract representations of the adjacencies and relationships between the areas identified in the project program. The diagrams do not represent a building plan, or even a rough bubble or block plan. Notice that solar access is located in one of the diagrams. The systems diagram highlights connections to site elements. The culture diagram emphasizes the relationship to the city and views.

At the end of the demonstration project, it is impossible and not necessary to present everything completed in this task. As before, important takeaways or realizations can be extracted and presented as part of the project overview.

STEP 3: DESIGN

The information, research, and pre-planning work from step 1 (context) and step 2 (pre-planning) have set the groundwork for this step. It is time to design a building. Step 3 comprises some interim steps, some of which require mini steps. The sheer number of variables in the sustainable design process can be overwhelming. Design ideas are developed, step by step, through the four perspectives. Each design idea is examined in the context of the project's guiding principles, and the goals and objectives. Interim steps are analyzed via a validation process to identify the strengths of each design idea. Then design ideas from the four perspectives are synthesized into a single interim design. Each interim step builds on those preceding it. The design process is broken down into a series of actions, limiting the number of design variables so as to not overwhelm the designer.

3A Interim Steps: Preliminary Design
- Mini-Steps: Building location and site Integration, building orientation, building block plan, building shape/space plan, validation, design synthesis

3B Interim Step: Passive Design
- Mini-Steps: Passive heating, passive cooling, daylighting, validation of passive design, design synthesis

3C Interim Step: Building Envelope
- Mini-Steps: Building structure/foundation, walls, windows, roof, validation, design synthesis, green materials

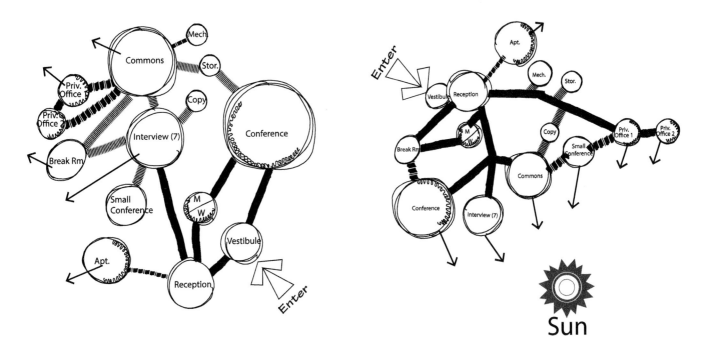

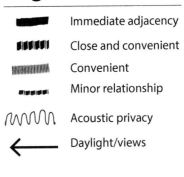

Sun

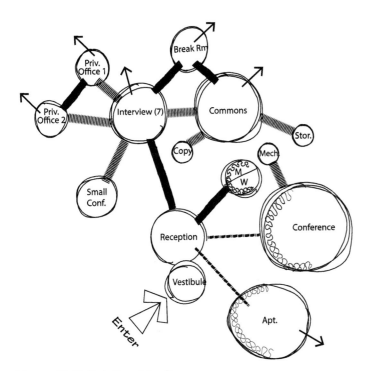

Figure 11.10 Relationship diagrams

Source: Rob Fleming

Legend

▬▬▬	Immediate adjacency
▮▮▮▮▮	Close and convenient
▥▥▥▥	Convenient
▰ ▰ ▰	Minor relationship
∿∿∿∿	Acoustic privacy
←	Daylight/views

Step 3A: Preliminary Design

Building Location and Site Integration

Locating a building on a site is a challenging task that requires the weighing of various driving forces that influence decisions. All of the choices shown in the demonstration project have positive and negative attributes. So what is a designer to do? The overall goal is to integrate the building into the larger site plan, including parking, paths, outdoor elements, and more. Pursuing four different options from four perspectives will help to create a diversity of design ideas. The design matrix (Figure 11.11) is used to organize design ideas and associated thought processes.

Context and Pre-Design Review

It is critical to reference the site analysis from the project context (step 1), to assure design solutions reflect research process conclusions. The macroclimate, micro-climate, and macro context are all entered into the appropriate design matrix boxes. The information entered into the design matrix is simplified, distilled from preceding steps. The design matrix is a reminder to access the research and keep the information foremost in your mind while you are working. The micro-climate information changes for each mini-step because the task at hand is influenced in different ways.

Performance Perspective

The performance design idea locates the building for optimal solar access. The building is located away from the habitat and close to the street, minimizing construction costs, minimizing utility runs from main supplies near the street, and conveniently located in proximity to the existing parking lot.

Systems Perspective

Positioned close to the habitat area but not so close as to disturb the biodiversity on site, this building location allows occupants to connect directly with the local ecology.

Culture Perspective

The building is located tight to the main urban corner of the site to facilitate a connection to the neighborhood. This building location has the potential to increase pedestrian activity, vitality, and safety on the street, thereby strengthening the community.

Experience Perspective

Located in the center of the site, the building may serve as a sculptural object visible from many sides.

Overall Reflections

Building location may seem like a straightforward part of the design process, but the building location is critical to the following steps. The location and orientation

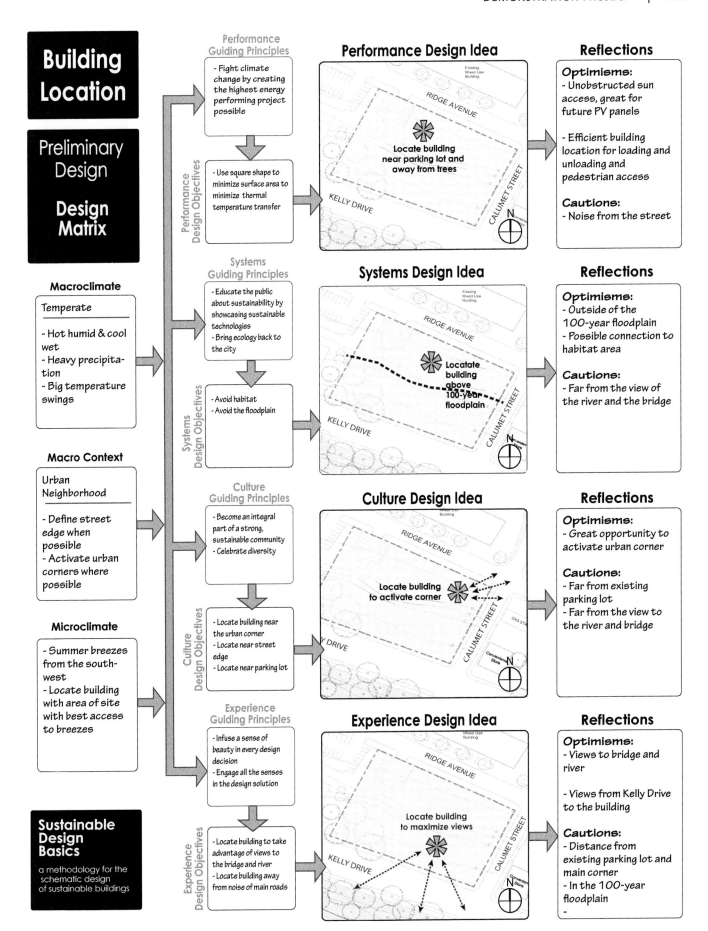

Figure 11.11 Design matrix: building location and site integration

of a building are attributes that once constructed are almost impossible to modify. Since performance was identified as the most important guiding principle, we can look at the four options in the design matrix and start to use the reflections to guide decision making. Keep in mind that the four different design ideas are viewed as distinct ideas until combined during design synthesis later in the SDB methodology. The next step, building orientation, will build directly upon the locations identified in this step.

Building Orientation

Orienting a building is a challenging task that weighs various driving forces such as sun angle, wind direction, view, and the urban context. As per the example of the building location options, (See Figure 11.12) there are many choices, each with its own set of pros and cons. In the design matrix, a simple rectangle is used to represent the building. The simple shape used to indicate orientation is not the final shape, but it helps us to understand that most buildings have a long side and a short side, and those sides react to sun and wind in different ways. (See Figure 11.12) This is not the time to break the building up into smaller buildings and it is critical to resist the urge to propose building shapes at this point.

Context and Pre-Planning Review
It is critical to reference the site analysis from the project context step to make sure that the design solutions reflect the conclusions from the research process. The macroclimate, microclimate, and macro context are all entered in the appropriate boxes of the design matrix. This information is a simplified, boiled down statement of all the research that was carried out in earlier steps.

Performance Perspective
The long side of the building is oriented to face the southern sun providing maximum benefit from solar exposure to the building's interior spaces while minimizing east and west exposures. The southern orientation is also optimal solar exposure for roof-mounted photovoltaic panels.

Systems Perspective
The long side of the building is rotated to face the prevailing southwesterly summer breezes. These breezes often come over the river to provide additional cooling. The rotation of the building goes against the urban context, which is made up of buildings that align with the street.

Culture Perspective
The building is rotated to run parallel to the street to reinforce the urban spatial patterns. The parallel building to the street orientation of the building defines the street spatially while providing activity along the street to make for a safer and more vital urban context.

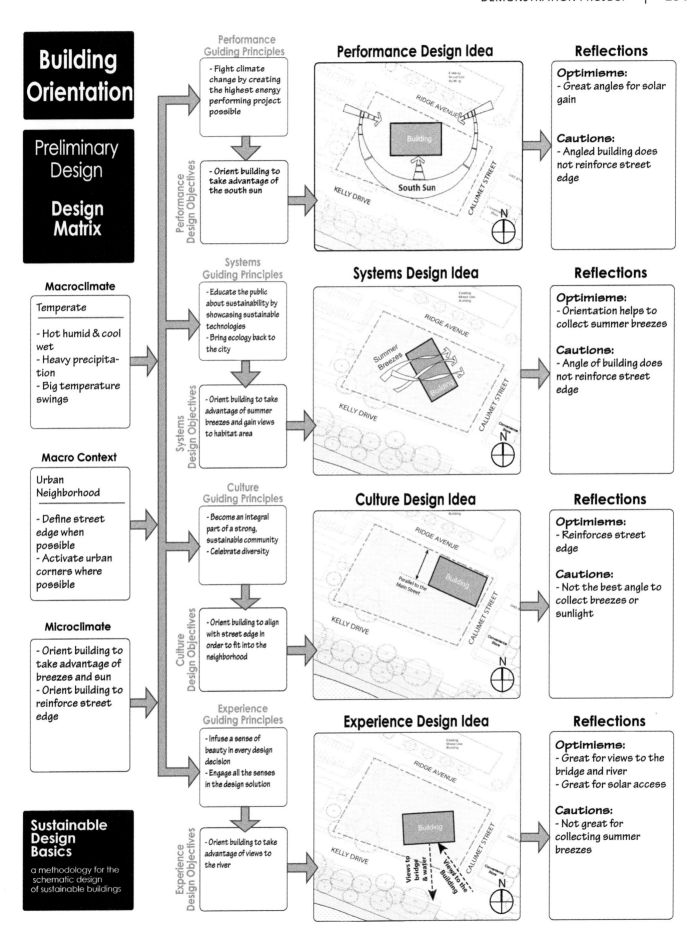

Building Orientation

Preliminary Design

Design Matrix

Macroclimate

Temperate

- Hot humid & cool wet
- Heavy precipitation
- Big temperature swings

Macro Context

Urban Neighborhood

- Define street edge when possible
- Activate urban corners where possible

Microclimate

- Orient building to take advantage of breezes and sun
- Orient building to reinforce street edge

Sustainable Design Basics

a methodology for the schematic design of sustainable buildings

Performance Guiding Principles

- Fight climate change by creating the highest energy performing project possible

Performance Design Objectives

- Orient building to take advantage of the south sun

Performance Design Idea

Reflections

Optimisms:
- Great angles for solar gain

Cautions:
- Angled building does not reinforce street edge

Systems Guiding Principles

- Educate the public about sustainability by showcasing sustainable technologies
- Bring ecology back to the city

Systems Design Objectives

- Orient building to take advantage of summer breezes and gain views to habitat area

Systems Design Idea

Reflections

Optimisms:
- Orientation helps to collect summer breezes

Cautions:
- Angle of building does not reinforce street edge

Culture Guiding Principles

- Become an integral part of a strong, sustainable community
- Celebrate diversity

Culture Design Objectives

- Orient building to align with street edge in order to fit into the neighborhood

Culture Design Idea

Reflections

Optimisms:
- Reinforces street edge

Cautions:
- Not the best angle to collect breezes or sunlight

Experience Guiding Principles

- Infuse a sense of beauty in every design decision
- Engage all the senses in the design solution

Experience Design Objectives

- Orient building to take advantage of views to the river

Experience Design Idea

Reflections

Optimisms:
- Great for views to the bridge and river
- Great for solar access

Cautions:
- Not great for collecting summer breezes

Figure 11.12 Design matrix: building orientation

Experience Perspective

The building is rotated toward the views of the bridge. This rotated orientation will give the building users a dynamic and beautiful view from their desks.

Overall Reflections

Looking at different orientations reveals that every design decision has pros and cons. The guiding principles, developed earlier in the process, will later help to create a hierarchy in the design. For now, it is best to let each of the four design ideas to develop to uncover more opportunities for the design.

Building Block Plans

The design ideas for the building block plans from all four perspectives follow the general locations and orientations from the previous steps. In the design process, it is important to be fluid in thinking and not get locked in to being too literal or too accurate at this early stage. Often design teams return to the first decisions about building location and site design as more information is discovered during the design process. (See Figure 11.13)

Context and Pre-Planning Review

The criteria matrix lists room size and adjacency requirements for the building, providing direction and insight for the development of the building block plan. Relationship diagrams also help organize thinking during this step. Notice that the block plans are pretty rough; that's okay at this stage.

Performance Perspective

Main rooms are positioned to absorb solar gain. Spaces that do not require much daylight are located on the north and west sides of the building. A compact form is proposed to minimize heating costs by exposing less surface area to the elements.

Systems Perspective

The building is subdivided into smaller buildings facilitating natural ventilation, providing space for greenery on the site, and encouraging building users to spend more time outside improving overall health and happiness. Breaking up the building will mean more surface of the buildings exposed to the elements, which may increase the energy required for heating. However, access to daylight and natural ventilation are increased by this approach.

Culture Perspective

This design idea is organized around a corner entry, and the shape developed as a response to the geometry of the building in the neighborhood—a rectangle. The building was moved away from the corner to allow for the creation of a plaza.

Experience Perspective

The building was "stretched out" to afford everyone in the building with great views and access to light and air.

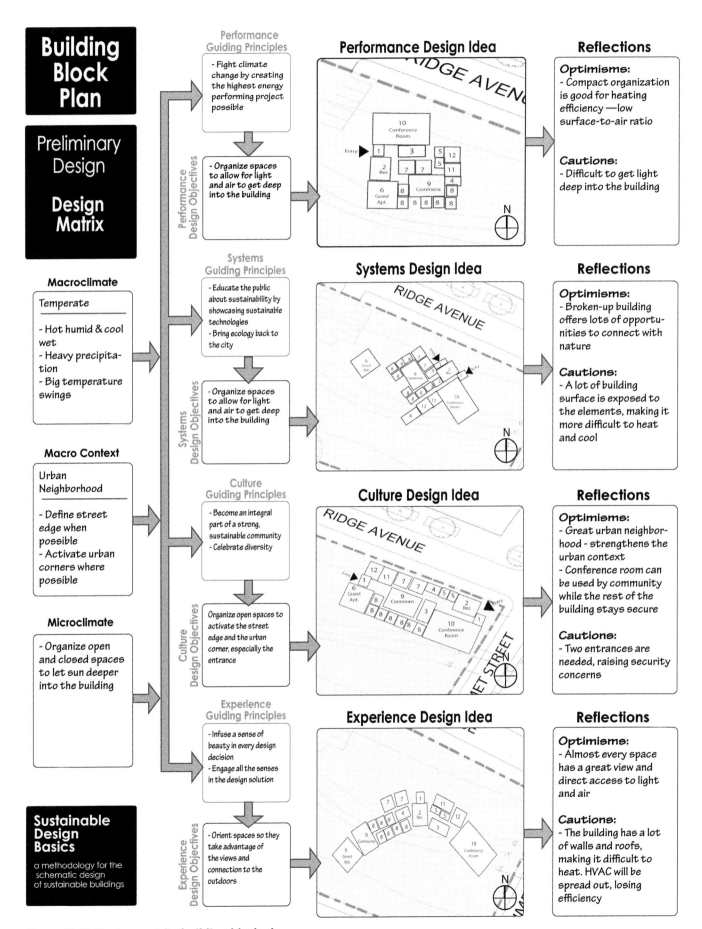

Building Block Plan

Preliminary Design

Design Matrix

Macroclimate

Temperate

- Hot humid & cool wet
- Heavy precipitation
- Big temperature swings

Macro Context

Urban Neighborhood

- Define street edge when possible
- Activate urban corners where possible

Microclimate

- Organize open and closed spaces to let sun deeper into the building

Sustainable Design Basics

a methodology for the schematic design of sustainable buildings

Performance Guiding Principles

- Fight climate change by creating the highest energy performing project possible

Performance Design Objectives

- Organize spaces to allow for light and air to get deep into the building

Systems Guiding Principles

- Educate the public about sustainability by showcasing sustainable technologies
- Bring ecology back to the city

Systems Design Objectives

- Organize spaces to allow for light and air to get deep into the building

Culture Guiding Principles

- Become an integral part of a strong, sustainable community
- Celebrate diversity

Culture Design Objectives

Organize open spaces to activate the street edge and the urban corner, especially the entrance

Experience Guiding Principles

- Infuse a sense of beauty in every design decision
- Engage all the senses in the design solution

Experience Design Objectives

- Orient spaces so they take advantage of the views and connection to the outdoors

Performance Design Idea

Reflections

Optimisms:
- Compact organization is good for heating efficiency —low surface-to-air ratio

Cautions:
- Difficult to get light deep into the building

Systems Design Idea

Reflections

Optimisms:
- Broken-up building offers lots of opportunities to connect with nature

Cautions:
- A lot of building surface is exposed to the elements, making it more difficult to heat and cool

Culture Design Idea

Reflections

Optimisms:
- Great urban neighborhood - strengthens the urban context
- Conference room can be used by community while the rest of the building stays secure

Cautions:
- Two entrances are needed, raising security concerns

Experience Design Idea

Reflections

Optimisms:
- Almost every space has a great view and direct access to light and air

Cautions:
- The building has a lot of walls and roofs, making it difficult to heat. HVAC will be spread out, losing efficiency

Figure 11.13 Design matrix: building block plan

Overall Reflections

The building block plan design ideas demonstrate a wide variety of design possibilities for the project. The variety of valid yet competing design ideas is what makes design such a challenging task. The temptation at this point in the process is to make a shape for the building, but that will occur in the next step.

Building Space Plan and Shape

Developing the building space/shape plan requires a more focused approach to the design, which includes more accuracy and a greater emphasis on circulation through the building and throughout the site. The goal is to complete this set of tasks quickly because all of the design ideas developed are interim ideas on the way to a final design solution. It is also critical not to fall in love with one design idea. (See Figure 11.14)

Context and Pre-Planning Review

The criteria matrix insights are incorporated into the preliminary block plans that inform building shape.

Performance Perspective

The building shape is compact reducing the exposure of roof and walls to the elements making it easier to heat.

Systems Perspective

The space plan of this design idea allows air to pass over and through the open office spaces, facilitating passive cooling in the center of the building.

Culture Perspective

The shape of the building remains a simple rectangle, similar to other buildings in the area. Once again, the open office spaces are positioned toward the south side of the building to allow daylight and air to reach deep into the building.

Experience Perspective

The building shape, curved along the length of the building, creates an interesting form and a courtyard on the south side of the site. The courtyard will create a comfortable buffer against cold northwest winds.

Overall Reflections

Notice that the design ideas from all four perspectives are still relatively basic. It is not necessary to spend too much time perfecting the design ideas at this point. Design synthesis will integrate the different design ideas into a single design idea.

Validation

Using energy modeling and daylighting software, we can begin to predict the performance of the different design ideas. Energy modeling is a critical early task.

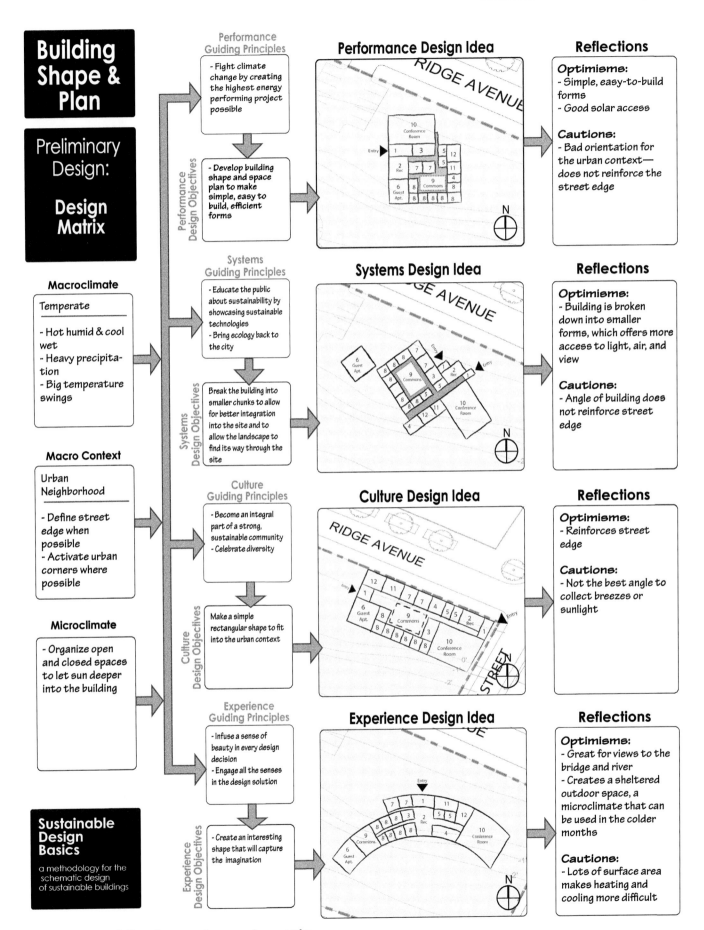

Building Shape & Plan

Preliminary Design: Design Matrix

Macroclimate

Temperate

- Hot humid & cool wet
- Heavy precipitation
- Big temperature swings

Macro Context

Urban Neighborhood

- Define street edge when possible
- Activate urban corners where possible

Microclimate

- Organize open and closed spaces to let sun deeper into the building

Sustainable Design Basics

a methodology for the schematic design of sustainable buildings

Performance Guiding Principles

- Fight climate change by creating the highest energy performing project possible

Performance Design Objectives

- Develop building shape and space plan to make simple, easy to build, efficient forms

Performance Design Idea

Reflections

Optimisms:
- Simple, easy-to-build forms
- Good solar access

Cautions:
- Bad orientation for the urban context—does not reinforce the street edge

Systems Guiding Principles

- Educate the public about sustainability by showcasing sustainable technologies
- Bring ecology back to the city

Systems Design Objectives

Break the building into smaller chunks to allow for better integration into the site and to allow the landscape to find its way through the site

Systems Design Idea

Reflections

Optimisms:
- Building is broken down into smaller forms, which offers more access to light, air, and view

Cautions:
- Angle of building does not reinforce street edge

Culture Guiding Principles

- Become an integral part of a strong, sustainable community
- Celebrate diversity

Culture Design Objectives

Make a simple rectangular shape to fit into the urban context

Culture Design Idea

Reflections

Optimisms:
- Reinforces street edge

Cautions:
- Not the best angle to collect breezes or sunlight

Experience Guiding Principles

- Infuse a sense of beauty in every design decision
- Engage all the senses in the design solution

Experience Design Objectives

- Create an interesting shape that will capture the imagination

Experience Design Idea

Reflections

Optimisms:
- Great for views to the bridge and river
- Creates a sheltered outdoor space, a microclimate that can be used in the colder months

Cautions:
- Lots of surface area makes heating and cooling more difficult

Figure 11.14 Building shape and space plan matrix

It is helpful to get a sense of which of the design ideas is performing better than others. Depending on the priorities set by the guiding principles, one design idea will have more influence than others as the process moves toward design synthesis. (See Figure 11.15)

Because the windows are not yet designed, a generic set of repetitive windows are sprinkled around all sides of the building in an even manner. These are not the final window designs or locations but provide a sense of how the building is daylit.

Validation without Software

Access to fresh air is validated through a quick look at the plan to see how many of the spaces have direct access to light, air, and view. Only regularly occupied spaces such as offices, open office workspaces, and conference rooms are studied. Bathrooms, storage rooms, and mechanical rooms are not regularly occupied. The project goals indicated that 100 percent of workspaces should be within 30 feet of an operable window.

Context and Pre-Design Review

Project goals are critical in this step since we will be comparing the different design ideas against the goals set for the project. It is not necessary for each design idea to meet the goals at this early stage, but they help to serve as a benchmark for how well each design idea meets the goals.

Validation of the Performance Design Idea

The software analysis reveals a tentative EUI from a very crude 3-D model. The results should not be taken too seriously because specific window sizes and locations were completed with simple daylight models without shading. Notice the performance option has a good EUI as compared to the others.

Validation of the Systems Design Idea

Since the building is comprised of separate building sections, the daylighting model shows plenty of daylight potential. Over lighting at this point is not an issue as that will be addressed in the passive design exercise. The EUI is not as successful because the buildings have more perimeter walls exposed to the elements, requiring more energy to heat and cool the building.

Validation of the Culture Design Idea

The culture option shows some significant "optimisms," especially in the engagement of the street and the corner.

Validation of the Experience Design Idea

The experience option has plenty of light because the building is spread out, but its EUI is also not as successful as some of the other design ideas. All of these different ideas have significant positive attributes, but it is important to address tradeoffs in subsequent steps.

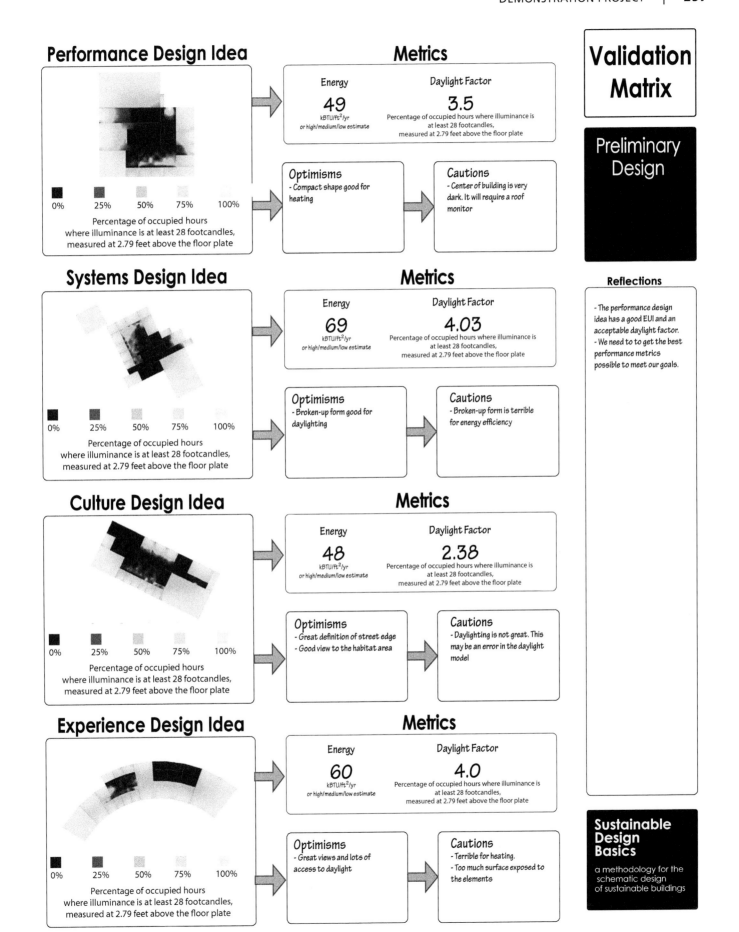

Performance Design Idea

Metrics

Energy

49

kBTU/ft²/yr
or high/medium/low estimate

Daylight Factor

3.5

Percentage of occupied hours where illuminance is
at least 28 footcandles,
measured at 2.79 feet above the floor plate

0%   25%   50%   75%   100%

Percentage of occupied hours
where illuminance is at least 28 footcandles,
measured at 2.79 feet above the floor plate

Optimisms
- Compact shape good for
heating

Cautions
- Center of building is very
dark. It will require a roof
monitor

Systems Design Idea

Metrics

Energy

69

kBTU/ft²/yr
or high/medium/low estimate

Daylight Factor

4.03

Percentage of occupied hours where illuminance is
at least 28 footcandles,
measured at 2.79 feet above the floor plate

0%   25%   50%   75%   100%

Percentage of occupied hours
where illuminance is at least 28 footcandles,
measured at 2.79 feet above the floor plate

Optimisms
- Broken-up form good for
daylighting

Cautions
- Broken-up form is terrible
for energy efficiency

Culture Design Idea

Metrics

Energy

48

kBTU/ft²/yr
or high/medium/low estimate

Daylight Factor

2.38

Percentage of occupied hours where illuminance is
at least 28 footcandles,
measured at 2.79 feet above the floor plate

0%   25%   50%   75%   100%

Percentage of occupied hours
where illuminance is at least 28 footcandles,
measured at 2.79 feet above the floor plate

Optimisms
- Great definition of street edge
- Good view to the habitat area

Cautions
- Daylighting is not great. This
may be an error in the daylight
model

Experience Design Idea

Metrics

Energy

60

kBTU/ft²/yr
or high/medium/low estimate

Daylight Factor

4.0

Percentage of occupied hours where illuminance is
at least 28 footcandles,
measured at 2.79 feet above the floor plate

0%   25%   50%   75%   100%

Percentage of occupied hours
where illuminance is at least 28 footcandles,
measured at 2.79 feet above the floor plate

Optimisms
- Great views and lots of
access to daylight

Cautions
- Terrible for heating.
- Too much surface exposed to
the elements

Validation Matrix

Preliminary Design

Reflections

- The performance design
idea has a good EUI and an
acceptable daylight factor.
- We need to to get the best
performance metrics
possible to meet our goals.

Sustainable Design Basics

a methodology for the
schematic design
of sustainable buildings

Figure 11.15 Demonstration project preliminary design validation

Overall Reflections

The validation matrix provides useful "evidence" upon which to make future design decisions.

Preliminary Design Synthesis

The last step in preliminary design, design synthesis, is the crux of the challenge of design. It is the stage when decisions determine the form of the building. By now a lot has been learned about the project. Research, analysis, and testing of the four different design ideas have been completed. Reflections inform your thinking, and now it is time for all the ideas to be synthesized into a single design idea. The four design ideas from the previous process are "layered on top of each other" to create a composite design idea that takes specific ideas from each of the fours design ideas creating a new design solution. (See Figure 11.16)

Building Design Synthesis

A. The building was "split apart" into multiple forms for site integration, increased air movement throughout the site, and definition of outdoor spaces. This building configuration allows the conference space to be accessed separately by the community and provides the guest suite privacy from the main building.

B. The main building occupied by office spaces is rotated to face due south providing excellent solar access. The determination to prioritize solar exposure is the influence of the performance perspective.

C. The conference room shared with the public is oriented to parallel the street and face an open corner. The corner may serve as open space for the community. The determination to prioritize the community needs is the influence of the culture perspective.

D. The buildings are positioned on a curve reminiscent of the curve proposed from the experience perspective.

Reflections

One important tradeoff is a less energy-efficient building. At this point in the design process, the design has more surface area exposed to the elements versus a square-style building like the performance design idea. One rotation to face the south sun also means that the building tilts toward the main view of the site. The orientation of view and orientation for sun access is a synergy between the performance and experience design ideas. The building layout will allow the conference room to be used by the community in the evenings, along with the restrooms, while securing the rest of the buildings. The synthesized building is not the completed design. Remember that the design process is iterative and it is not unusual to move down a particular path in the process only to discover that a significant design opportunity was missed, which would require restarting the process all over again. The next step will look at opportunities to study the building envelope and to begin to develop a form for the building.

Step 3B: Passive Systems

Now that preliminary design is completed, it is time to look at the passive systems. Remember, it is not unusual to return to previous steps and make changes as the process moves forward.

Design Synthesis

Preliminary Design:

Preliminary Design Synthesis

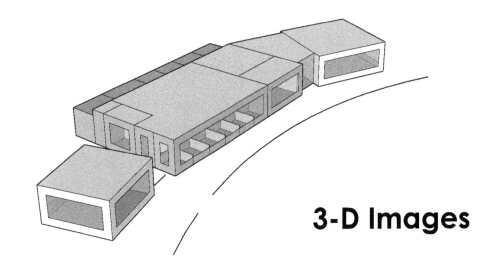

3-D Images

Macroclimate

Temperate

- Hot humid & cool wet
- Heavy precipitation
- Big temperature swings

Macro Context

Urban Neighborhood

- Define street edge when possible
- Activate urban corners where possible

Microclimate

- Organize open and closed spaces to let sun deeper into the building

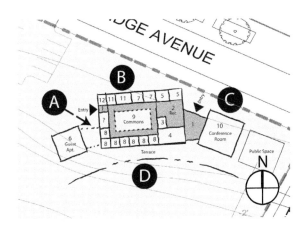

0% 25% 50% 75% 100%

Percentage of occupied hours
where illuminance is at least 28 footcandles,
measured at 2.79 feet above the floor plate

A.) Buildings split apart to better integrate with site
B.) Main building rotated to face south
C.) Conference room defines edge of street and public space on corner
D.) Curved terrace

Reflections

Optimisms:
- Building is broken down into smaller forms, which offers more access to light, air, and view

Cautions:
- Angle of building does not reinforce street edge

Sustainable Design Basics

a methodology for the schematic design of sustainable buildings

Energy Use Intensity (EUI)

51

kBTU/ft^2/yr

Daylight Factor

3.3

Figure 11.16 Preliminary design synthesis

The *SDB* Methodology

In this interim step, the same procedure is followed as the previous interim steps. This time the task will be more laborious as the leap between each mini-step will require more decisions to be made. Also, for this series of mini-steps, the work will be completed in the building section instead of the building plan. This will allow for a better study of the impact of sun, wind, and light on the design ideas. Finally, the order in which the mini-steps are made relates directly to the priorities determined by the macroclimate of a given project. For example, in a cold climate where heating is the priority, passive heating would be the first step. If the project is in a warm or hot climate, passive cooling might be the first mini-step. Guiding principles may also influence the order of the mini-steps. If a client feels very strongly about using daylighting for employee happiness, then the daylight mini-step might be first. For the demonstration project, the cold winters in Philadelphia demand that heating is studied first. However, the summers are quite hot, suggesting that passive cooling is studied second, followed by daylighting. Remember, the goal of the passive systems design is to minimize the need to save energy and fight climate change.

Heating

Now that we have a preliminary plan, it is time to integrate the passive systems into the project. In this phase, site considerations influence passive systems design. (See Figure 11.17)

Context and Pre-Design Review

Always check all of the research before starting passive systems integration. Knowing the direction and angle of the sun, as well as prevailing winter winds, can reveal effective strategies for passive heating.

Performance Perspective

The objective of this design idea is to maximize heating through passive strategies. Direct access to sunlight, especially in winter, helps to heat the building, especially if there are high thermal mass surfaces with the capacity to absorb and store heat. Notice the floor slab is thicker at the edge of the building to absorb heat from the sun and the stone walls in the center of the building will also absorb heat. Thermal mass is a classic passive heating strategy. This design idea gains a lot of heat, which may be a concern during summer months, when too much heat may enter the building. That will be addressed later in the process.

Systems Perspective

The objective of the systems perspective is to bring solar heat gain directly into the center of the building via an atrium to "warm-up" the "commons." The heat will then radiate into other building spaces. Deciduous trees located in the landscape on the south side of the building will shade the building in the summer and allow light and heat into the building in the winter months when the trees lose their leaves. Passively warmed space in the middle of the building will be a great experience during cold winter months, late fall, and early spring, but may be too warm to be comfortable during summer months.

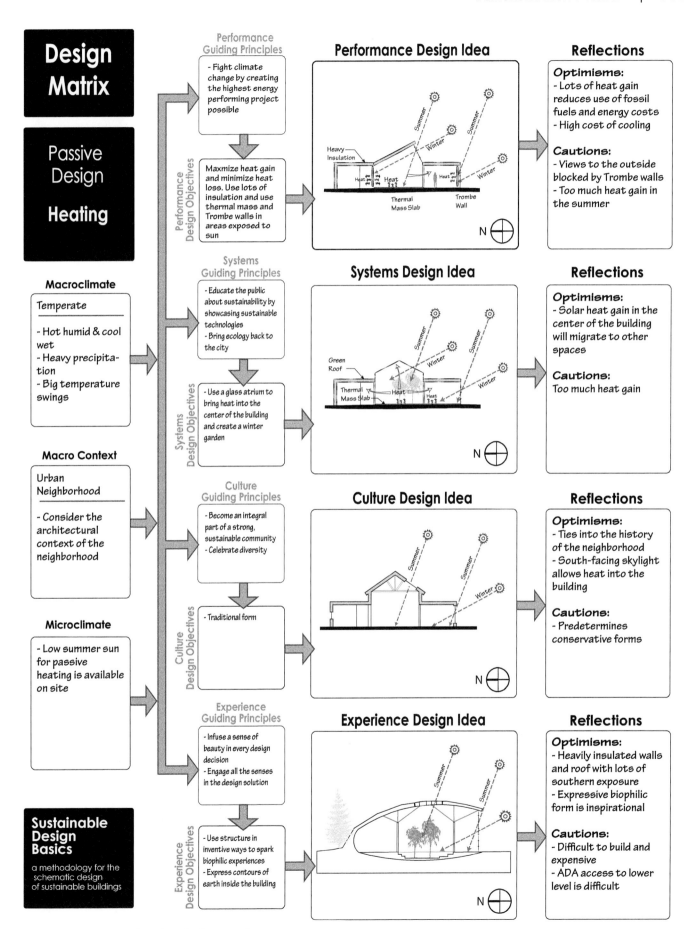

Design Matrix

Passive Design

Heating

Macroclimate

Temperate

- Hot humid & cool wet
- Heavy precipitation
- Big temperature swings

Macro Context

Urban Neighborhood

- Consider the architectural context of the neighborhood

Microclimate

- Low summer sun for passive heating is available on site

Sustainable Design Basics

a methodology for the schematic design of sustainable buildings

Performance Guiding Principles

- Fight climate change by creating the highest energy performing project possible

Performance Design Objectives

Maxmize heat gain and minimize heat loss. Use lots of insulation and use thermal mass and Trombe walls in areas exposed to sun

Performance Design Idea

Heavy Insulation / Heat / Summer / Winter / Summer / Winter / Heat / Thermal Mass Slab / Trombe Wall / N

Reflections

Optimisms:
- Lots of heat gain reduces use of fossil fuels and energy costs
- High cost of cooling

Cautions:
- Views to the outside blocked by Trombe walls
- Too much heat gain in the summer

Systems Guiding Principles

- Educate the public about sustainability by showcasing sustainable technologies
- Bring ecology back to the city

Systems Design Objectives

- Use a glass atrium to bring heat into the center of the building and create a winter garden

Systems Design Idea

Green Roof / Summer / Winter / Summer / Winter / Thermal Mass Slab / Heat / Heat / N

Reflections

Optimisms:
- Solar heat gain in the center of the building will migrate to other spaces

Cautions:
Too much heat gain

Culture Guiding Principles

- Become an integral part of a strong, sustainable community
- Celebrate diversity

Culture Design Objectives

- Traditional form

Culture Design Idea

Summer / Summer / Winter / N

Reflections

Optimisms:
- Ties into the history of the neighborhood
- South-facing skylight allows heat into the building

Cautions:
- Predetermines conservative forms

Experience Guiding Principles

- Infuse a sense of beauty in every design decision
- Engage all the senses in the design solution

Experience Design Objectives

- Use structure in inventive ways to spark biophilic experiences
- Express contours of earth inside the building

Experience Design Idea

Summer / Summer / N

Reflections

Optimisms:
- Heavily insulated walls and roof with lots of southern exposure
- Expressive biophilic form is inspirational

Cautions:
- Difficult to build and expensive
- ADA access to lower level is difficult

Figure 11.17 Passive heating design matrix

Culture Perspective

Getting everyone to have direct access to the warm south side of the building will be a welcome aspect of the design. The proposed sunspace serves as a buffer on the south side of the building, making the overall building easier to heat. However, the sunspace on the south side occupies valuable outdoor space, which could be a concern. The sun-space also blocks views to the river and bridge from inside the building.

Experience Perspective

The curve of the proposed building allows cold winter winds to flow over the building. Soil and plants buffer the north side of the building, shielding the building from the elements. The south side of the building is a tall glass window, which will absorb the sun's heat. The form of the curved roof mimics the undulating site. The site provides a variety of spaces and landscape elements to enliven the user experience. Inside the building, the curved ceiling and stepped floor levels create a feeling of integration between building site and interiors.

Passive Cooling and Natural Ventilation

The ventilation and cooling approaches should be studied separately in the design process but time limitations sometimes force design teams to combine elements that are closely aligned, like cooling and ventilation, to speed up the process. (See Figure 11.18) This mini-step builds directly upon the previous step with each design idea evolving as each passive strategy is applied to the previous design idea.

Context and Pre-Design Review

The knowledge that the summers are humid in Philadelphia should temper expectations of passive cooling effectiveness in this season. However, breezes coming from the southwest and across the river will offer some added air movement in the building.

Performance Perspective

Heating strategies for performance allow excessive heat gain into the building. The goal now is to allow low winter sun into the building when it is most needed and shade high south summer sun when additional heat gain is unwanted. The angled roof is flattened and extended to provide shading. Shading is also added to the south facade.

Systems Perspective

A skylight over the commons will provide beautiful sunlight, but too much heat and glare is gained in the hot summer months. A clerestory window is proposed to replace the skylight. The proposed clerestory is used to accelerate breezes coming in from the southwest side of the site. The south facade was heightened and shaded by deciduous trees. The trees are selected to become tall enough to shade, but not too tall to block light to the solar panels. The deciduous trees help cool the microclimate outdoors, which then helps to cool the building.

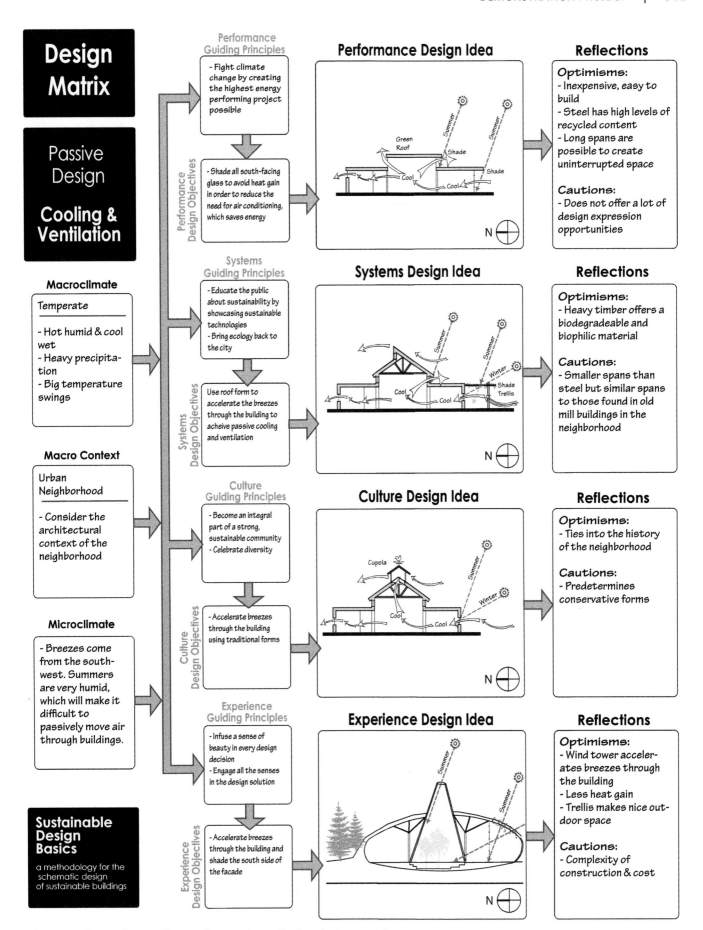

Figure 11.18 Passive cooling and natural ventilation design matrix

Culture Perspective

The buffer space on the south side of the building is a good idea to block cold winds. However, summer heat gain from direct sunlight makes it unusable in the summer, and views toward the bridge and river are blocked from the central office space. The sunspace becomes a trellis with vegetation that shades in the summer and lets the sun into the building in the winter because the leaves will have fallen away in the autumn. Access to outdoor spaces is available at multiple locations. Shade trees are added to allow people to sit outside comfortably. Although the space plan is not shown, all the regularly occupied spaces used for work have direct access to operable windows.

Experience Perspective

Similar to the culture design idea, the objective is to get fresh cool air to pass over people's skin to create comfort. A tower was added to help accelerate the air as it moves from the south facade into the tower. As the tower heats up, fresh cool air is drawn into the tower and accelerated. The more speed the air has, the more it comforts the users. Also, notice that the large glass wall is retained in the design idea with the addition of shading elements to mitigate heat gain.

Daylighting

Daylighting is about more than just saving energy. It is about a healthier environment for the employees, making them happier and more productive.

Context and Pre-Design Review

Daylighting goals are primary drivers of the fenestration design (windows, doors, and clerestories). However, more glass area increases the difficulty in achieving project energy efficiency goals. Competing and conflicting drivers and strategies are the challenge of sustainable design. There are multiple right answers to the design challenge, each with different tradeoffs. (See Figure 11.19)

Performance Perspective

The building revisions for cooling also support daylighting. Adding light shelves to the shading elements is now relatively uncomplicated. Light shelves will bounce daylight further into the building, improving the overall quality of light while saving energy for artificial lighting.

Systems Perspective

A clerestory window aids natural ventilation and passive cooling and is also a useful daylighting element. With a few changes, the clerestory has increased opportunities for reflected light, creating a beautiful daylight center space, perfect for plants to thrive with minimal glare. The objective of natural ventilation makes operable windows mandatory. Operable clerestory windows, and roof monitors will also move air through the building. Operable windows with complex window frames are more visually obtrusive, a tradeoff with the experience perspective. Operable windows also reduce mechanical air conditioning efficiency which is optimized by a closed, sealed building.

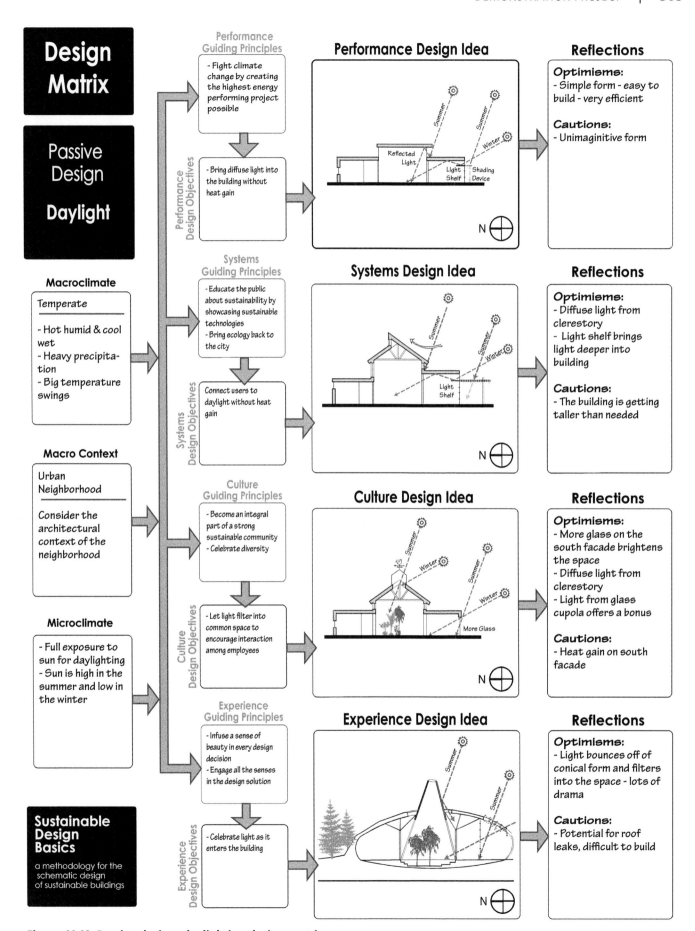

Design Matrix

Passive Design

Daylight

Macroclimate

Temperate

- Hot humid & cool wet
- Heavy precipitation
- Big temperature swings

Macro Context

Urban Neighborhood

Consider the architectural context of the neighborhood

Microclimate

- Full exposure to sun for daylighting
- Sun is high in the summer and low in the winter

Sustainable Design Basics

a methodology for the schematic design of sustainable buildings

---

Performance Design Objectives

Performance Guiding Principles

- Fight climate change by creating the highest energy performing project possible

- Bring diffuse light into the building without heat gain

Performance Design Idea

Reflected Light / Light Shelf / Shading Device

Reflections

Optimisms:
- Simple form - easy to build - very efficient

Cautions:
- Unimaginitive form

Systems Design Objectives

Systems Guiding Principles

- Educate the public about sustainability by showcasing sustainable technologies
- Bring ecology back to the city

Connect users to daylight without heat gain

Systems Design Idea

Light Shelf

Reflections

Optimisms:
- Diffuse light from clerestory
- Light shelf brings light deeper into building

Cautions:
- The building is getting taller than needed

Culture Design Objectives

Culture Guiding Principles

- Become an integral part of a strong sustainable community
- Celebrate diversity

- Let light filter into common space to encourage interaction among employees

Culture Design Idea

More Glass

Reflections

Optimisms:
- More glass on the south facade brightens the space
- Diffuse light from clerestory
- Light from glass cupola offers a bonus

Cautions:
- Heat gain on south facade

Experience Design Objectives

Experience Guiding Principles

- Infuse a sense of beauty in every design decision
- Engage all the senses in the design solution

- Celebrate light as it enters the building

Experience Design Idea

Reflections

Optimisms:
- Light bounces off of conical form and filters into the space - lots of drama

Cautions:
- Potential for roof leaks, difficult to build

Figure 11.19 Passive design: daylighting design matrix

Culture Perspective

The objective of the culture perspective is to "fit" the building into the neighborhood, and the design idea here is to use "punched openings," a term for a window set in a solid wall. The roof has been raised, allowing the top of the trellis to hold a light shelf and bounce light further into the building. The roof design was modified at the center of the building to allow light to enter into the center of the building.

Experience Perspective

The curved roof exposed on the building interior as the ceiling is an excellent shape to direct light into the building. By modifying the shading elements at the south facade, the ceiling will be illuminated with light. The ceiling must be a light color, ideally white, with a high level of reflectivity. The roof around the tower has been cut away to allow daylight to wash down the walls of the tower creating a dramatic effect. For this perspective, floor-to-ceiling glass walls will maximize views and connection to the outdoors.

Validation

Getting a sense of how different design solutions meet the performance goals of the project is always an essential step in the process, although it is not necessary to select the one design idea that has the highest energy performance.

Context and Pre-Design Review

The goals for the project should be reviewed as part of this mini-step to compare the performance of the different design ideas against the goals. (See Figure 11.20)

Performance Perspective

Notice that the performance levels in this design idea are the highest from an energy point of view, but not from a daylighting standpoint. That is not unusual because fewer windows help with heating and cooling, but it certainly hurts the ability of light to penetrate deep into the building. It might be a good idea to take some cues from the other solutions and allow for some more glass, even though that will compromise the overall EUI of the project.

Systems Perspective

This design idea does very well for access to light and air—a critical aspect of the project, and the sizeable sloping roof will help to display the PV panels. Daylighting the common center space and filling it with plants and a water element brings ecology indoors making an excellent space for the building's users.

Culture Perspective

This version of the design achieves the goal of fitting into the neighborhood quite well while still allowing light and air into the building. The flat roofs can also work to support green roofs, a possible synergy for stormwater control and added benefit for heating and cooling.

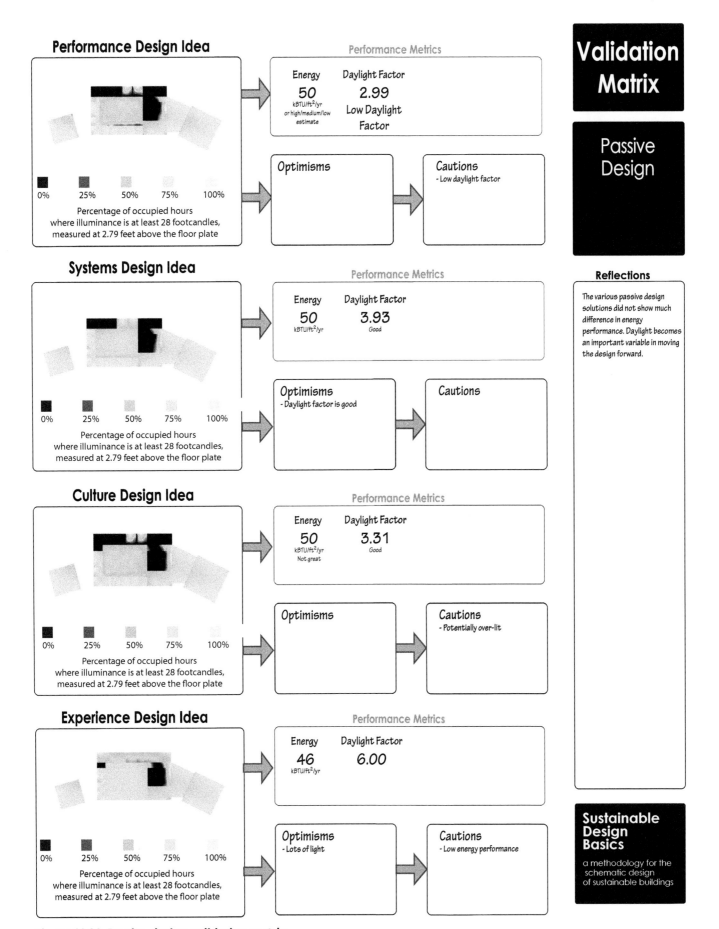

Performance Design Idea

0% 25% 50% 75% 100%

Percentage of occupied hours
where illuminance is at least 28 footcandles,
measured at 2.79 feet above the floor plate

Performance Metrics

Energy
50
kBTU/ft²/yr
or high/medium/low
estimate

Daylight Factor
2.99
Low Daylight
Factor

Optimisms

Cautions
- Low daylight factor

Systems Design Idea

0% 25% 50% 75% 100%

Percentage of occupied hours
where illuminance is at least 28 footcandles,
measured at 2.79 feet above the floor plate

Performance Metrics

Energy
50
kBTU/ft²/yr

Daylight Factor
3.93
Good

Optimisms
- Daylight factor is good

Cautions

Culture Design Idea

0% 25% 50% 75% 100%

Percentage of occupied hours
where illuminance is at least 28 footcandles,
measured at 2.79 feet above the floor plate

Performance Metrics

Energy
50
kBTU/ft²/yr
Not great

Daylight Factor
3.31
Good

Optimisms

Cautions
- Potentially over-lit

Experience Design Idea

0% 25% 50% 75% 100%

Percentage of occupied hours
where illuminance is at least 28 footcandles,
measured at 2.79 feet above the floor plate

Performance Metrics

Energy
46
kBTU/ft²/yr

Daylight Factor
6.00

Optimisms
- Lots of light

Cautions
- Low energy performance

Validation Matrix

Passive Design

Reflections

The various passive design
solutions did not show much
difference in energy
performance. Daylight becomes
an important variable in moving
the design forward.

Sustainable Design Basics

a methodology for the
schematic design
of sustainable buildings

Figure 11.20 Passive design validation matrix

Experience Perspective

This design idea has a lot of visual interest and excitement. The all-glass south wall will allow for a lot of light, air, and a view for the occupants and connects directly to an outdoor space, which has a comfortable climate due to the north winds being blocked. The all-glass wall will be a tradeoff against the performance and culture perspectives but one worth making because of the excellent views of the bridge and river.

Design Synthesis

The design process has already explored many different ideas in a relatively short time frame and through very different points of view. It is amazing how many options in design there are. Most ideas never get used but help to lead to other, better ideas. It is ok to leave ideas undeveloped at this point and focus on committing to a final building form.

Notes for Passive Systems

Figure 11.21 presents a drawing with keyed notes.

- The synthesis of the design detracts slightly from the overall performance of the building, but the tradeoffs result in better indoor and outdoor spaces for the employees' health and well-being.
- The south glass wall will work well for light, air, and view. The light shelf above the pergola will bounce light deep into the building
- The windows on the north side are smaller and "punched," helping the building to "fit" into the neighborhood. The use of outdoor space on the south side will be good for the office community.
- The varying roof heights and shapes make the project more visually appealing. The concept of having a more modern side facing the south side of the site and the views to the bridge is an interesting contrast to the more solid traditional expression on the north side of the building.
- The conference space on the corner is more traditional in a form that strongly relates to the neighborhood.
- Rainwater is collected from the main roof and finds its way to the cisterns near the restrooms.
- The roof extends beyond the north clerestory to gain some more roof area for PV panels.

Step 3C: Building Envelope

Now that the basic plan and massing are determined and the passive systems integrated into the design, it is time to look into the structure and envelope of the building. This is the stage where many key sustainability decisions are made. Thinking about structure early in the process will help later efforts to determine forms and column spacing. It is not critical to make the perfect decision regarding structure, but it is good to think about it. Foundations, slabs, walls, windows, and roof comprises the building envelope and can significantly contribute to the overall performance of the building. Maximizing the energy savings strategies in the envelope means that less energy is needed to heat and cool the building.

Passive Systems

Design Synthesis

Passive Design

Macroclimate

Temperate

- Hot humid & cool wet
- Heavy precipitation
- Big temperature swings

Macro Context

Urban Neighborhood

- Define street edge when possible
- Activate urban corners where possible

Microclimate

- Organize open and closed spaces to let sun deeper into the building

Sustainable Design Basics

a methodology for the schematic design of sustainable buildings

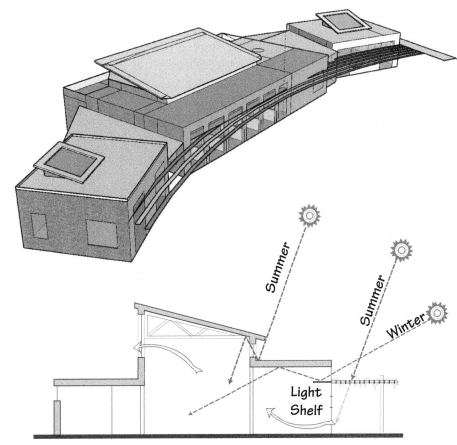

Building Section

Summer

Summer

Winter

Light Shelf

0%	25%	50%	75%	100%

Percentage of occupied hours
where illuminance is at least 28 footcandles,
measured at 2.79 feet above the floor plate

Reflections

Optimisms:
- The daylight is much better balanced in the main center space. The daylight factor is in a good range to meet the project goals

Cautions:
- The EUI is still quite high. Hopefully the optimizations from the building envelope will help

Energy Use Intensity (EUI)

48

kBTU/ft²/yr

Daylight Factor

3.9

Figure 11.21 Passive design: design synthesis

Building Structure and Foundations

Context and Pre-Design Review

In these early steps, the guiding principles were set and ranked to drive some design preferences throughout the process. When considering structure, the embodied energy of the materials is a significant consideration. Steel, concrete, and heavy timber all have different carbon footprints. Also, the different structural spans of each building structure system will affect space planning flexibility, which may either help or hurt the ability to achieve the culture guiding principle. The Design Matrix for building envelope structure guides the analysis and evaluation process for building structure. (See Figure 11.22) It is also at this step in the process when the decision is made to include or exclude a basement. In the case of this project, a basement was rejected due to the possibility of flooding in the future.

Performance Perspective

The performance objectives and design ideas focus on maximizing the volume of space with the minimum structure and finding structural materials with high levels of recycled content. The design idea zeroes in on steel frame structure; that is the most efficient solution because structural steel has a very high level of recycled content. However, the recycling process itself has an energy footprint that negates some of the benefit.

Systems Perspective

The objective for systems is to find an ecologically sensitive structural system. The design idea suggests that heavy timber construction would be an excellent solution for the structure of the building because the material, after a long life, will go back to the soil as it biodegrades. The heavy timber structure will also have a wonderful biophilic effect in the interiors of the building—a nice synergy with the experience perspective.

Culture Perspective

This perspective drives the use of structural systems that mimic the types of structure found in the neighborhood or the city. The neighborhood has a lot of row homes that have exterior bearing wall construction and are about 14 feet wide. The objective is to use the structure of the building to mimic this structural bay size. Using bearing walls 14 feet on center is not typical, but by using a column grid of 14-foot-wide bays the rhythm of the neighborhood's architecture is reflected and acknowledged.

Experience Perspective

The structural system proposed here is concrete, which can be formed into curves. This will allow for an exciting expression of form. The manufacturing of concrete emits millions of tons of carbon dioxide, meaning that this material is not an ideal choice from a performance perspective.

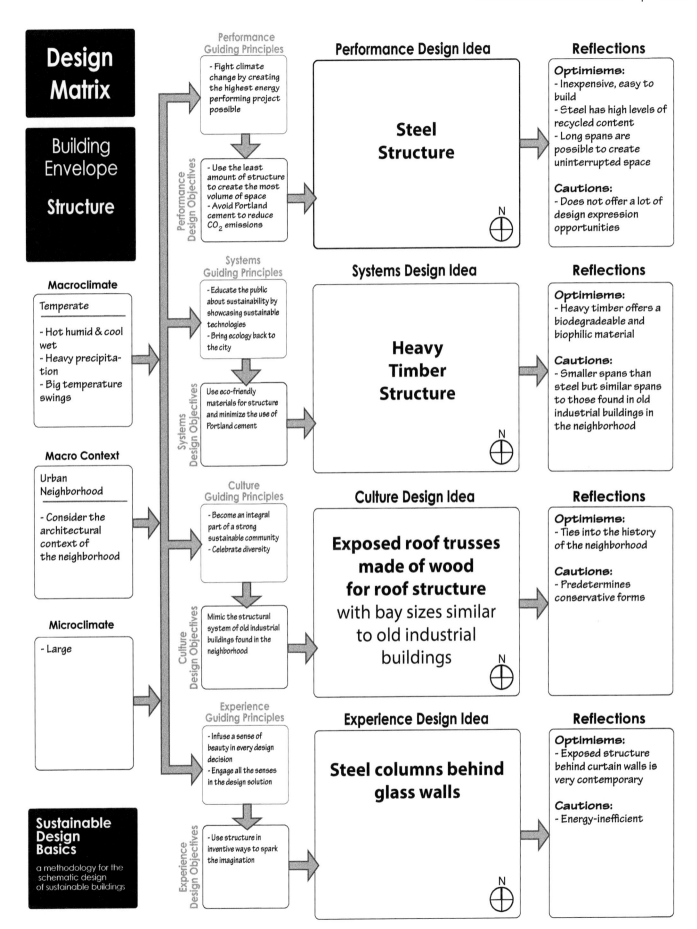

Figure 11.22 Building envelope: building structure design matrix

Walls

The exploration of walls is built on top of the work completed for the structure. This is repeated for each of the four perspectives, leading toward four unique approaches for the building envelope. Walls are important to consider early the design process because of their ability to protect the building from the elements but also because the walls act as one of the main components of the building envelope. See Figure 11.23 for the exploration, analysis and evaluation process for building structure, walls. At this stage, the decision on the wall assembly will greatly impact the energy efficiency of the project. However, if the building is primarily made of glass, the R-value of the solid walls is not very important.

Context and Pre-Design Review

The Project Goals step in the pre-design process set ambitious energy performance targets. Walls help to achieve this with high R-values.

Performance Perspective

The design idea from the performance perspective is a combination of rigid insulation and spray foam insulation proposed for the wall construction. Furthermore, staggered studs are used to protect against thermal bridging. The higher R-value walls are usually thicker, making the building larger on the site or rooms smaller inside the building.

Systems Perspective

In the systems perspective, eco-friendly solutions are typically pursued, such as straw bale or hemp concrete or reclaimed lumber. Straw bale construction is very eco-friendly because it has a very high R-value and very low embodied energy footprint. Great care must be taken because the straw can never get wet, meaning that concrete foundation walls of the building must come up higher than normal and the construction must take place during a dry season.

Culture Perspective

The neighborhood vernacular construction uses brick. Brick is a local material in the Philadelphia region, which reduces the embodied energy of the brick. The objective to "fit" into the neighborhood makes brick a logical choice for the exterior of the building.

Experience Perspective

The objective of this perspective is to improve the experience inside and outside the building. The use of glass allows for views and operable windows to facilitate natural ventilation and plenty of daylight for the building. Notice that this contradicts the culture perspective's objective to use brick. That is another example of the challenging nature of design. The use of glass also requires a tradeoff with the performance perspective, which advocates for solid walls with a lot of insulation.

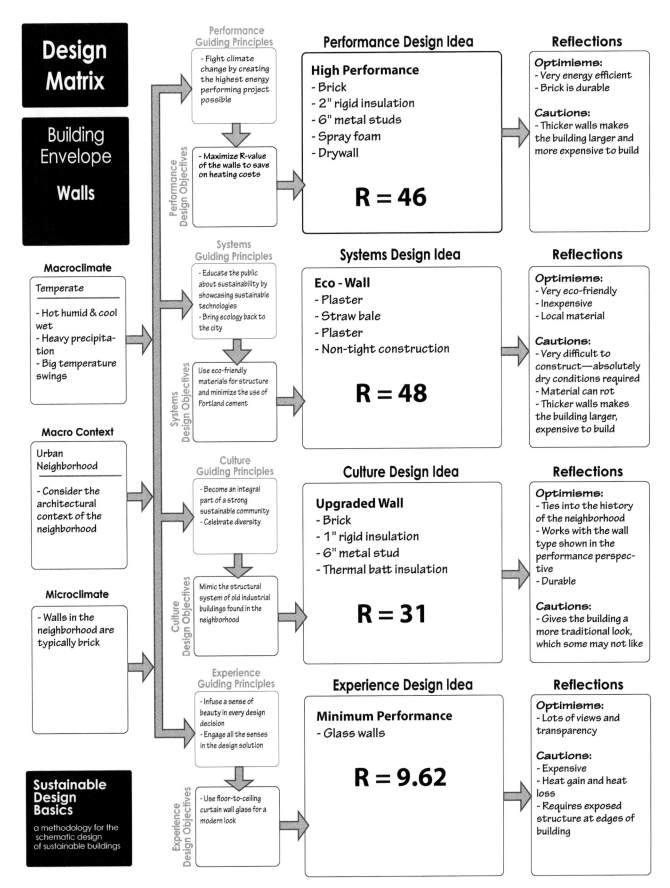

Design Matrix

Building Envelope

Walls

Macroclimate

Temperate

- Hot humid & cool wet
- Heavy precipitation
- Big temperature swings

Macro Context

Urban Neighborhood

- Consider the architectural context of the neighborhood

Microclimate

- Walls in the neighborhood are typically brick

Sustainable Design Basics

a methodology for the schematic design of sustainable buildings

---

Performance Guiding Principles

- Fight climate change by creating the highest energy performing project possible

Performance Design Objectives

- Maximize R-value of the walls to save on heating costs

Performance Design Idea

High Performance
- Brick
- 2" rigid insulation
- 6" metal studs
- Spray foam
- Drywall

R = 46

Reflections

Optimisms:
- Very energy efficient
- Brick is durable

Cautions:
- Thicker walls makes the building larger and more expensive to build

---

Systems Guiding Principles

- Educate the public about sustainability by showcasing sustainable technologies
- Bring ecology back to the city

Systems Design Objectives

Use eco-friendly materials for structure and minimize the use of Portland cement

Systems Design Idea

Eco - Wall
- Plaster
- Straw bale
- Plaster
- Non-tight construction

R = 48

Reflections

Optimisms:
- Very eco-friendly
- Inexpensive
- Local material

Cautions:
- Very difficult to construct—absolutely dry conditions required
- Material can rot
- Thicker walls makes the building larger, expensive to build

---

Culture Guiding Principles

- Become an integral part of a strong sustainable community
- Celebrate diversity

Culture Design Objectives

Mimic the structural system of old industrial buildings found in the neighborhood

Culture Design Idea

Upgraded Wall
- Brick
- 1" rigid insulation
- 6" metal stud
- Thermal batt insulation

R = 31

Reflections

Optimisms:
- Ties into the history of the neighborhood
- Works with the wall type shown in the performance perspective
- Durable

Cautions:
- Gives the building a more traditional look, which some may not like

---

Experience Guiding Principles

- Infuse a sense of beauty in every design decision
- Engage all the senses in the design solution

Experience Design Objectives

- Use floor-to-ceiling curtain wall glass for a modern look

Experience Design Idea

Minimum Performance
- Glass walls

R = 9.62

Reflections

Optimisms:
- Lots of views and transparency

Cautions:
- Expensive
- Heat gain and heat loss
- Requires exposed structure at edges of building

Figure 11.23 Building envelope: walls design matrix

Source: Rob Fleming

Windows

Successful sustainable design requires a thorough exploration of window performance and location. In this step, critical aspects of the window performance are set. The U-value and solar heat gain coefficient are set for each of the four design ideas. The exploration, analysis and evaluation process for building structure windows is detailed in Figure 11.24.

Context and Pre-Design Review

The daylighting goals are one of the primary drivers of the fenestration design (windows, doors, and clerestories). However, the more glass that is used, the harder it will be to meet the energy efficiency goals of the project. This is why design is so tricky, because there are multiple right answers to the design challenge.

Performance Perspective

Use high–U-value windows and glass doors with a good solar heat coefficient (low for Philadelphia's climate) to reduce the impacts of direct sun as it enters the buildings. While we do not address construction cost in our demonstration project, it is good for the reader to know that these kinds of windows may be expensive. Operable windows are not used for this design idea because a "closed" building better supports the HVAC system. Operable windows make it difficult for the HVAC system to provide adequate levels of heating and cooling.

Systems Perspective

It seems obvious, but the objective of natural ventilation means that use of operable windows is critical. Consider using operable clerestories or roof monitors to move air through the building. Operable windows have more complex frames and are less sleek looking, so there is a tradeoff with the experience perspective. Operable windows also reduce the effectiveness of mechanical air conditioning, which functions better in a closed building. Consider the use of a computer system to monitor temperature and humidity to determine when to open and shut the windows.

Culture Perspective

The objective is to fit the building into the neighborhood, and the design idea here is to use "punched openings." Punched openings tend to be smaller windows, which let in less light and air. They tend to work with the performance perspective's goal of maximizing the R-value since the total amount of solid wall is higher than a steel and glass design.

Experience Perspective

The objective of this perspective is to improve the experience inside and outside of the building. The generous use of glass allows for views out of the building and lets light and air into the building. This approach is synergetic with the systems perspective, which wants to connect users to light and air. Notice that this contradicts the culture perspective's objective to use punched openings, which will be a tradeoff.

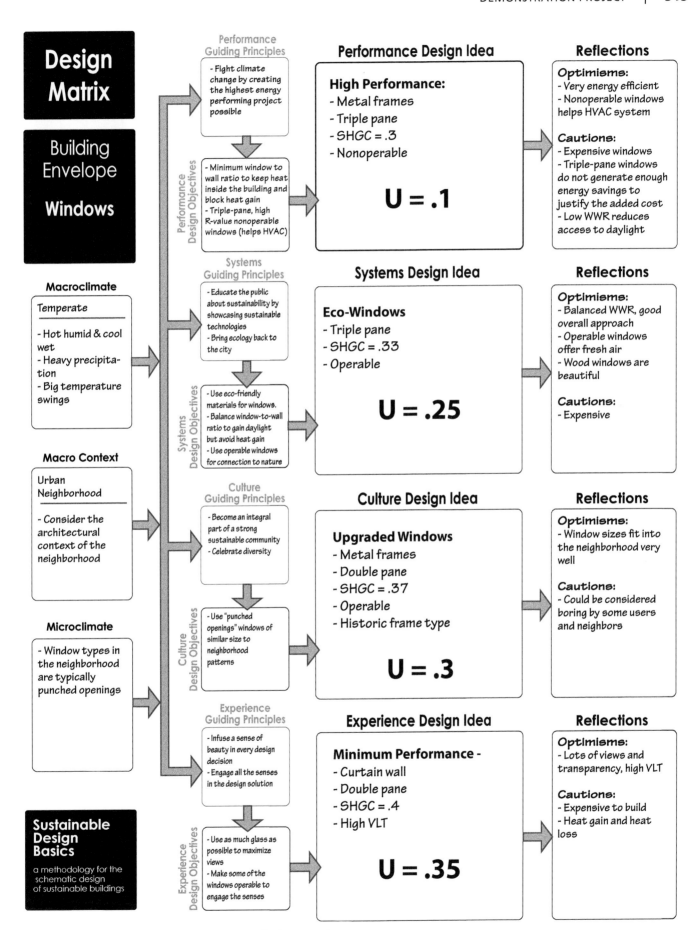

Figure 11.24 Building envelope: windows design matrix

Roofs

The roof is a critical part of the building envelope. Like walls, the roof protects against extreme temperatures and must shed water. The shape of the roof is critical because it helps to define the aesthetic experience of the building form and how the building will or will not "fit" into the local context. (See Figure 11.25)

Context and Pre-Design Review
Goals set for water and solar collection will be pursued in more detail during the active systems design step of the project, but keeping those goals in mind during this stage of design is helpful.

Performance Perspective
Using high R-value roof construction is a must for maximizing energy performance. Depending on the structural system selected, this may mean a thicker roof than usual. Collection of water and sun is critical to meet ambitious performance goals. Sometimes a thicker roof might be a tradeoff with the experience perspective, which may want to have a sleek roof profile for the building.

Systems Perspective
The guiding principle for this perspective encourages the design of the building to be a showcase for sustainable technologies. Therefore, a sloped roof will be best for allowing a green roof to be visible. The use of a green roof is also a good solution to adding habitat, lowering the microclimate, and providing a nice aesthetic if the roof can be made visible. The sloped roof is a tradeoff with the culture perspective, which calls for the use of flat roofs to "fit" the building into its context. Solar arrays make it challenging to consider a green roof, although some hybrid technologies are in use now. The two may be synergetic.

Culture Perspective
A flat roof is proposed to match the architectural context of the neighborhood, which is mostly made up of flat roofs. This is a tradeoff against the systems perspective, which seeks a large sloped roof.

Experience Perspective
The objective here is to use the roof to make a strong visual statement to add beauty and uniqueness to the neighborhood. The proposed design idea is to have roofs of varying heights and forms with a unique design element that is taller and visible from a short distance away from the building. Tall elements can be used to catch daylight and bring daylight into the center of the building. This is synergetic with the systems perspective. PV panels are not always perceived as beautiful, so there is a tradeoff with the systems perspective, which calls for the display of a large sloped roof with PV panels that are visible from the main road.

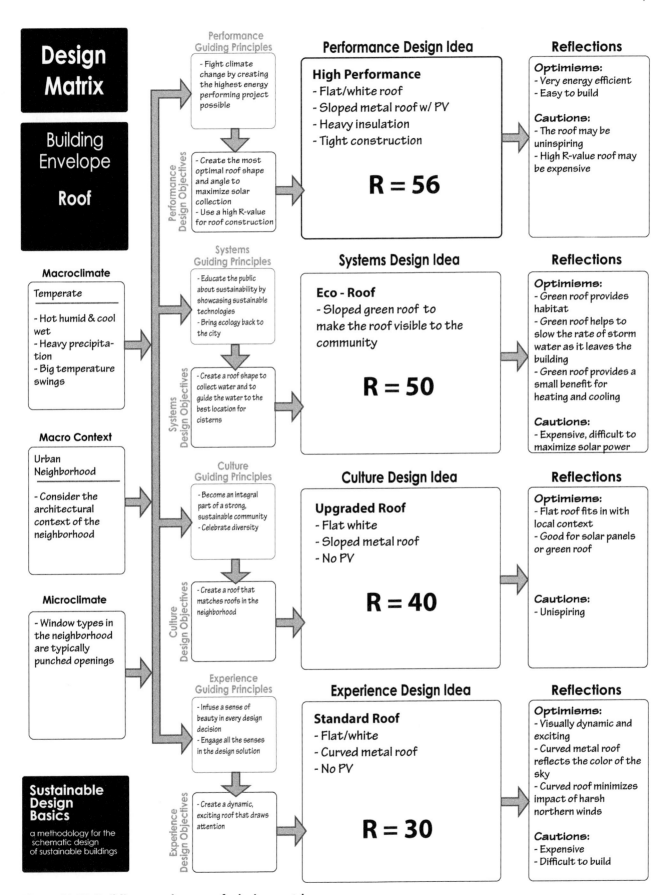

Figure 11.25 Building envelope: roofs design matrix

Source: Rob Fleming

Validation

Getting a sense of how the different design solutions compare to the performance goals of the project and each other is the goal of the validation. It is not necessary to select the one design idea that has the highest energy performance but to look at all the options holistically to discover the best solution. Sometimes a lesser-performing option is selected. The use of software to determine the EUI and daylight levels is the best way to gain this information. Without a computer, the project can still be validated by using the metrics to study how the design differs in respect to access to light air and view. See Figure 11.26 for the validation of the demonstration project building envelope.

Context and Pre-Design Review
The selection of structural systems and wall systems, along with the fenestration (doors and windows) and roofs for the building, all help to achieve the performance metrics and the guiding principles of the project.

Performance Perspective
Notice that the performance in this design idea is the highest from an energy point of view, but not from a daylighting standpoint. That is not unusual. It might be a good idea to take some cues from the other solutions and allow for some more glass, even though that will compromise the overall EUI of the project. Light can be introduced from above the center of the building.

Systems Perspective
This design idea does very well for access to light and air—an essential aspect of the project—and the sizeable sloping roof will help to display the green roof. There are some tradeoffs with the performance perspective because this solution has more glass. A compromise will need to be determined in the next step when the project is synthesized.

Culture Perspective
The use of a flat roof makes sense from this perspective because many of the local buildings also have flat roofs. The client wants the building to reference the existing context, which conflicts with the stated goal of the client to showcase sustainable technologies. This will get resolved in the reflections and the design synthesis that comes next. The punched openings on the north side of the building work well with the performance perspective because there is a lot of solid wall. A high level of insulation in the north wall is appropriate because it is the coldest side of the building, making this an even better synergy. The south side of the building wants to have more glass for view and light—a significant tradeoff.

Experience Perspective
This design idea has a lot of visual interest and excitement. The all-glass south wall will allow for a lot of light, air, and view for the occupants and connects directly to an outdoor space that has a comfortable climate due to the north winds being blocked. The all-glass wall will be a tradeoff against the performance and culture perspectives, but one worth making.

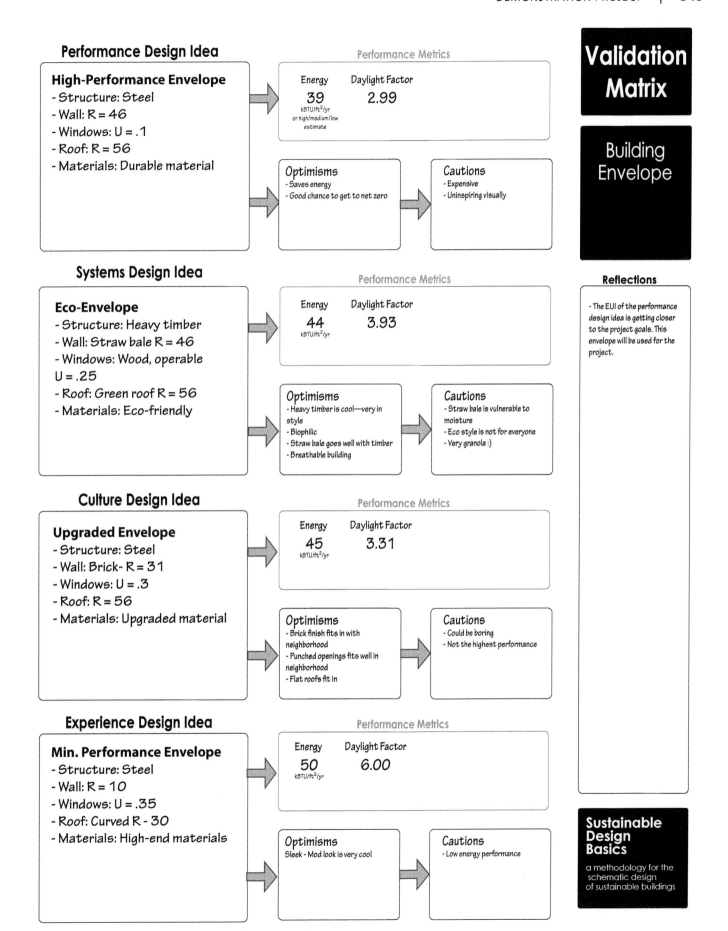

Performance Design Idea

High-Performance Envelope
- Structure: Steel
- Wall: R = 46
- Windows: U = .1
- Roof: R = 56
- Materials: Durable material

Performance Metrics

Energy | Daylight Factor
39 | **2.99**
kBTU/ft²/yr
or high/medium/low
estimate

Optimisms
- Saves energy
- Good chance to get to net zero

Cautions
- Expensive
- Uninspiring visually

Systems Design Idea

Eco-Envelope
- Structure: Heavy timber
- Wall: Straw bale R = 46
- Windows: Wood, operable
U = .25
- Roof: Green roof R = 56
- Materials: Eco-friendly

Performance Metrics

Energy | Daylight Factor
44 | **3.93**
kBTU/ft²/yr

Optimisms
- Heavy timber is cool—very in style
- Biophilic
- Straw bale goes well with timber
- Breathable building

Cautions
- Straw bale is vulnerable to moisture
- Eco style is not for everyone
- Very granola :)

Culture Design Idea

Upgraded Envelope
- Structure: Steel
- Wall: Brick- R = 31
- Windows: U = .3
- Roof: R = 56
- Materials: Upgraded material

Performance Metrics

Energy | Daylight Factor
45 | **3.31**
kBTU/ft²/yr

Optimisms
- Brick finish fits in with neighborhood
- Punched openings fits well in neighborhood
- Flat roofs fit in

Cautions
- Could be boring
- Not the highest performance

Experience Design Idea

Min. Performance Envelope
- Structure: Steel
- Wall: R = 10
- Windows: U = .35
- Roof: Curved R - 30
- Materials: High-end materials

Performance Metrics

Energy | Daylight Factor
50 | **6.00**
kBTU/ft²/yr

Optimisms
Sleek - Mod look is very cool

Cautions
- Low energy performance

Validation Matrix

Building Envelope

Reflections

- The EUI of the performance design idea is getting closer to the project goals. This envelope will be used for the project.

Sustainable Design Basics

a methodology for the schematic design of sustainable buildings

Figure 11.26 Building Envelope: Validation Matrix

Design Synthesis

Building Envelope

Macroclimate

Temperate

- Hot humid & cool wet
- Heavy precipitation
- Big temperature swings

Macro Context

Urban Neighborhood

- Define street edge when possible
- Activate urban corners where possible

Microclimate

- Organize open and closed spaces to let sun deeper into the building

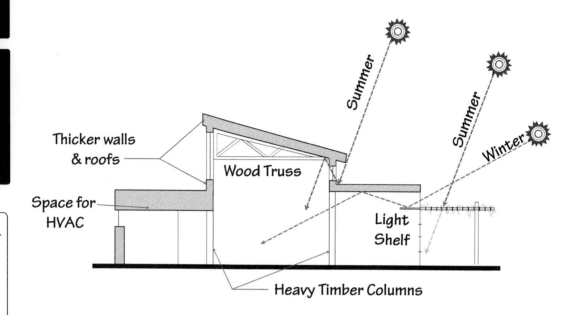

Final Building Envelope Assemblies

- Structure: **Steel Structure + Heavy Timber/Wood Truss**
- Foundation: **Slab on Grade**
- Wall: **R = 46**
- Windows: **U = .1**
- Roof: **R = 56**
- Materials: **Eco-Friendly Materials**

Energy Use Intensity (EUI)

38

kBTU/ft^2/yr

Daylight Factor

3.9

Sustainable Design Basics

a methodology for the schematic design of sustainable buildings

Figure 11.27 Building Envelope: Design Synthesis

Overall Reflections

Recommendations include punched openings and brick walls on the north side to relate to the urban context and open glass walls on the south side.

Design Synthesis

The last action in this step is to update the design to reflect the various design opportunities and recommendations and the validation (Figure 11.27).

Significant observations of the synthesized plan

1. Notice that the main roof is ready for a large array of PV panels, meaning that building has a chance to reach net-zero ready energy as per the performance goals.
2. The all-glass south wall will allow for maximum light, air, and view and will present a contemporary view from the main road.
3. The windows on the north side are smaller and 'punched' helping the building to fit in to the neighborhood. The brick walls also help visually to tie the building into the neighborhood architecture. The use of outdoor space on the south side of the site will be good outside space to share with the community.
4. The varying roof heights and shapes make the project more visually appealing. The concept of having a more modern side facing the views to the bridge is an interesting contrast to the more traditional, more solid expression on the north side of the building.

Now the building has taken definite shape and form, but it is critical not to get locked into the design at this stage and to continue to explore different approaches to the project, which may unlock new solutions that were missed before. It is also possible that the process takes a major step back to the beginning when the building might get moved, or its orientation changed. That is okay. The project is now complete at a "basic" level. The reader may choose to go on to chapter 12, "Beyond the Basics," to explore the active systems of the project. Otherwise, it is time to move on to the final validation and a final presentation of the project in chapters 13 and 14.

12

Beyond the Basics

Step 4
Design Resolution

4A Design Synthesis
4B Final DesignValidation
4C Presenting the Project

Step 3
Design

3A Preliminary Design
3B Passive Design
3C Building Envelope
3D Green Materials
* Beyond the Basics

Step 2
Pre-Planning

2A Research & Case Studies
2B Project Goals
2C Design Criteria
2D Spatial Relationships

Step 1
Context

1A Project Information
1B Guiding Principles
1C Macro / Micro Context
1D Site Inventory & Analysis

Figure 12.0 The four steps of
Sustainable Design Basics
Source: Sharon B. Jaffe

This chapter provides an abbreviated introduction to active systems which includes the integration of technology into the building design. The intent of the chapter is to provide just enough information for a beginner's understanding of the active systems required for a building to reach net-zero energy and to save significant water. It is helpful for the reader to have had a building technology or energy course to better understand the material in this chapter. For those new to design and to building technology, it may be better to skip this chapter and move on to chapter 13. "Beyond the Basics" will build upon the synthesized building design from the previous chapters. This is critical as active systems like HVAC, lighting, and PV power should only be pursued after all the passive design, and building envelope strategies have been addressed. This will yield the best energy efficiency results. The following active systems topics will be introduced in this chapter:

- HVAC efficiency
- Lighting and plug loads efficiency
- PV array sizing and net-zero energy
- Water efficiency

These steps will be followed by the final design synthesis and final validation to test the final metrics detailed in chapter 13. The final presentation, which is used to communicate the essential information about the project, is covered in chapter 14.

ACTIVE SYSTEMS

This book has already covered so much ground in regard to sustainable design that opening a detailed discussion to the design of the active mechanical systems is a difficult task. Engineers are needed at this point to make informed decisions about which HVAC technology is the most efficient selection for a given building. The goal in this section is to acknowledge that a mechanical system must be selected for the energy models to generate results needed for validation.

Software

These next few steps require the use of software to make calculations from the 3-D model of the design resulting from step 3, design. It is important to be sure the model is built perfectly with no hidden openings and with all the surfaces correctly defined. Otherwise, the final results of the energy model will not be accurate or will be impossible to process.

The base energy load for a building is established in energy modeling software by choosing or defining the ASHRAE 90.1 2013 standard. This will yield a code-compliant building and serve as the "baseline" for energy comparisons.

HVAC Efficiency

In all of the steps so far, the mechanical systems have not been altered in the energy modeling software as a means to ensure that all the different design ideas had the same consistent baseline characteristics. This made the design ideas easy to compare. Now that we are beginning to look at developing a net-zero building, the choice of HVAC system matters. Listed below are a few basic strategies:

Alternative technologies such as geo-exchange, passive chilled beams, and radiant floor heating help to save energy. These technologies are not explored in this chapter.

HVAC equipment with higher performance ratings. Traditional air conditioners and heaters come in a variety of efficiency levels with corresponding costs. The better efficiency, the higher the cost.

Better air distribution methods can be used to move air the shortest distance from the air handling units to the spaces being heated or cooled. Limiting the number of bends in the ductwork and the distance conditioned air must travel will increase the efficiency of the unit.

Some basic air distribution terminology is outlined below:

Variable air volume (VAV) systems are located in ceilings as part of the register that delivers heating or cooling and ventilation to a given space. VAV system has the capacity to operate the compressor and fan at variable speeds conserving energy.

Air handling unit (AHU) regulates and circulates air as part of the HVAC system. It can be located on the roof or in a mechanical room with a dedicated source of outside air.

VAV return air packages are rooftop AHUs that supply multi zone heating and cooling and ventilation to the building. This type of system provides some control for the user by zone or area through the use of a thermostat. This is the system that is used in the example building.

VAV outside air central plant is based on the use of larger equipment housed in a mechanical room in the building. It requires access to outside air to work properly. These are used for very large buildings when rooftop units cannot provide enough volume of heating and cooling. A skyscraper, for example, would use this system.

Fan coil units are an option offered in some energy modeling packages. A fan coil unit uses a coil to provide heat or cooling and a fan that moves recirculated air over the coil for distribution, often without ductwork. They are very flexible systems that are useful for buildings that have a lot of different spaces, each requiring individual user control.

Artificial Lighting and Equipment

Artificial lighting energy usage can be reduced by using LED bulbs and efficient lighting ballasts. Indirect lighting on light-colored surfaces with high reflectivity helps to boost light levels. Current trends in lighting do not illuminate the entire space to high levels of functional light but supply additional task lights that can be turned off when not in use. It is now time to begin to model the systems.

Validation of Energy Savings for Artificial Lighting and Power

Energy modeling software uses a variable called *lighting power density* to define the energy needed for lighting. Lighting efficiency is around 1.3 W/ft^2.

Because some improvements can be assumed, the artificial lighting system was changed in the energy model from 1.3 W/ft² to 1 W/ft². The case studies from step 2 all ranged around .5 W/ft² so it is reasonable to assume that this is an acceptable setting. This change can be made in the software, and a model can be run to see the improvement.

Plug Loads (Equipment Power Density)

Plug loads represent the amount of energy of all the equipment used in the building. By using efficient equipment such as Energy Star refrigerators, monitors, and computers, the equipment power density was improved to 1 W/ft², which is considered "good" by the energy modeling software. The EUI improvements from lighting and power density are illustrated in Figure 12.1

Lighting density = .5 W/ft²
Equipment power density = 1 W/ft²
The EUI of the demonstration project is now lowered to 28 kBTU/ft²/yr

PV ARRAY SIZING AND NET-ZERO ENERGY

Calculating Net-Zero Performance

In order to reach net-zero energy, the base energy load of the building, after applying all of the energy-saving strategies, must be matched by the use of renewable energy.

Unlike the previous use of energy modeling, which generated a *relative* comparison between different design ideas, this step features the achievement of an *absolute* or total amount of energy needed to heat, cool, and power the building in a typical year. Keep in mind that the absolute numbers are not precise. An engineer with sophisticated software can make better predictions, but even then, variations in actual use occur. The EUI countdown to this point is shown in Figure 12.2. The term net-zero *ready* is often used to reflect the variability in the occupants use of energy.

Now it is time to leave the "plug-in" software and export the model to the external web interface. It is now possible to use the software to calculate the size of the PV array. Different types of software vary in their ability to provide this function. It is possible to accomplish the PV array sizing task without software. A spreadsheet for this purpose is included on the companion website. Table 12.1 illustrates the PV array sizing function of the software.

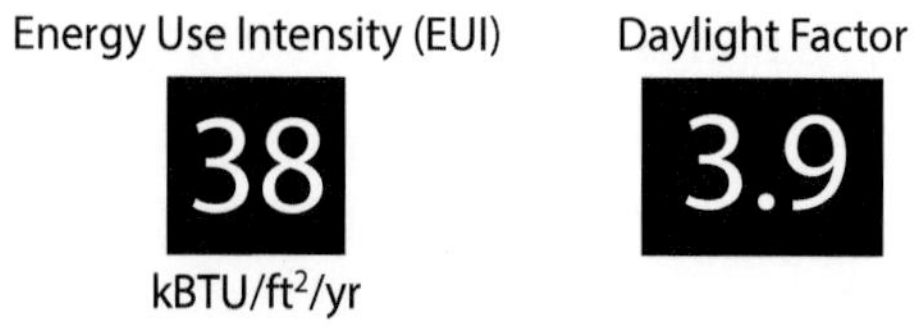

Figure 12.1 EUI after lighting and equipment improvements
Source: Sefaira Software

Energy Use Intensity (EUI)
38
kBTU/ft²/yr

Daylight Factor
3.9

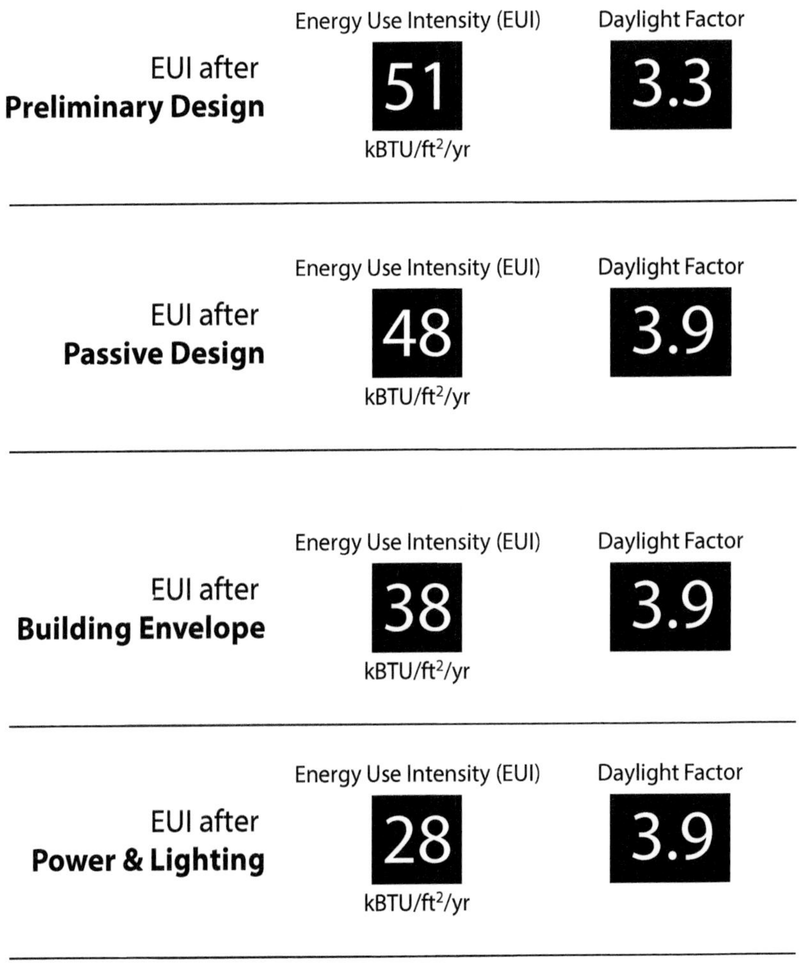

Energy Use Intensity (EUI)　　Daylight Factor

EUI after
Preliminary Design

51

kBTU/ft²/yr

3.3

Energy Use Intensity (EUI)　　Daylight Factor

EUI after
Passive Design

48

kBTU/ft²/yr

3.9

Energy Use Intensity (EUI)　　Daylight Factor

EUI after
Building Envelope

38

kBTU/ft²/yr

3.9

Energy Use Intensity (EUI)　　Daylight Factor

EUI after
Power & Lighting

28

kBTU/ft²/yr

3.9

Figure 12.2 EUI after each step in the demonstration project
Source: Sefaira Software

- The panel efficiency can be used as the default.
- The orientation of the panel installation matters because the software is calculating the number of panels it can fit on the roof; because they are rectangles, the orientation may or may not allow for additional panels.
- The panel tilt angle must be entered. In the example project, the slope of the roof was close to the optimal angle for the use best efficiencies of photovoltaic panels in the Philadelphia latitude. This changes in different latitudes. Chapter 6 discusses the relationship between the angle of the sun and PV panel efficiency.
- The PV panel area should be measured on the angle if using a sloped roof because it takes into account the additional area available of the angled plane of the roof.

TABLE 12.1 BLANK PV ARRAY CALCULATOR

Solar Photovoltaic Panels	Details
PV panel efficiency	X%
PV panel orientation	Angle facing south (180 is typical)
PV panel tilt	X Degrees versus a flat roof
PV panel area	X ft² (of panels)

Source: Sefaira Software

Figure 12.3 EUI before including the PV array

Source: Sefaira Software

EUI after
Power & Lighting

Energy Use Intensity (EUI)

28

kBTU/ft²/yr

Daylight Factor

3.9

The combination of these inputs will calculate the amount of energy the PV array will generate. Notice that before entering the data (see Figure 12.3), the project still has not generated as much power as it needs to reach net-zero. This is the starting point for the PV array sizing. The roof plan in Figure 12.4 illustrates how the PV panels were deployed in the demonstration project. Table 12.2 contains the settings used to define the PV array.

This is the same version of the building with solar added to the main sloped roof.

A EUI of 11 kBTU/ft²/yr (Figure 12.5) does not reach the goal of achieving net-zero energy. Additional solar panels are proposed to reach net-zero energy. Figure 12.6 shows the location of additional PV panels needed to achieve net-zero energy.

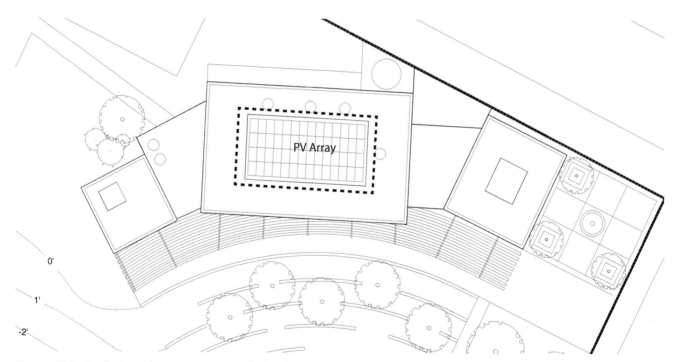

Figure 12.4 Roof plan with PV array area defined

Source: Rob Fleming

TABLE 12.2 SOLAR PHOTOVOLTAIC ARRAY SIZING INFORMATION BASED ON EXAMINATION OF ROOF PLAN

Solar Photovoltaic Panels	Details
PV panel Efficiency	14%
PV panel orientation	180
PV panel tilt	25 degrees
PV panel area	1,440 ft²

Source: Sefaira software

EUI after
**Addition of
PV Panels**

Energy Use Intensity (EUI)

11

kBTU/ft²/yr

Daylight Factor

3.9

**Figure 12.5 EUI of the demonstration
project after PV calculation**
Source: Sefaira Software

Table 12.3 shows the additional ft² area of PV needed to reach net-zero status for the project. More PV could be used on the other roofs, but there was a desire for a green vegetated roof to meet the goals and principles for there was a project. PV optimization was stopped at this point. Notice that blank space was left just in front of the roof monitor on the main building. This space will have a white reflective roof to maintain daylighting levels inside the building. The energy modeling results in Figure 12.7 shows 0 kBTU/ft²/Yr .

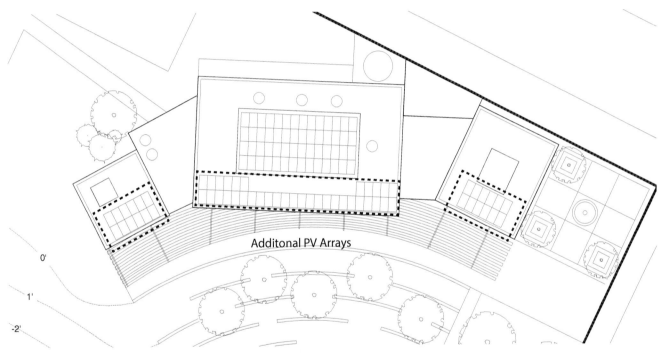

Additonal PV Arrays

0'

1'

-2'

Figure 12.6 Roof plan with additional PV array area defined
Source: Rob Fleming

**TABLE 12.3 SOLAR PHOTOVOLTAIC ARRAY SIZING INFORMATION FOR
THE ADDITIONAL PV PANEL**

Solar Photovoltaic Panels	Details
PV panel efficiency	14%
PV panel orientation	180
PV panel tilt	25 degrees
PV panel area	2,300 ft²

Source: Sefaira Software

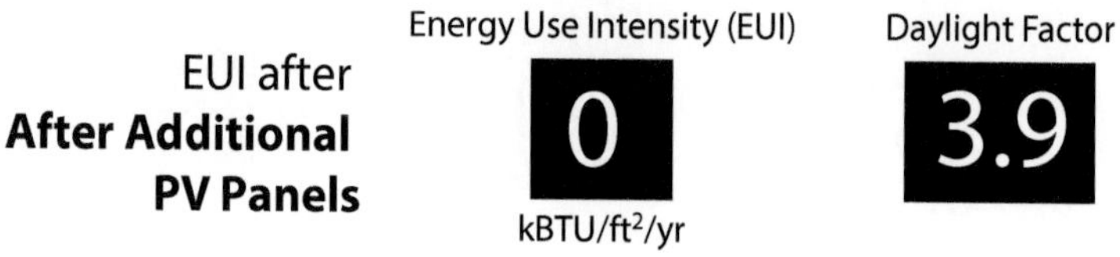

Figure 12.7 EUI of demonstration project after the addition of a second PV array
Source: Sefaira Software

Energy Use Intensity (EUI)

Daylight Factor

EUI after
**After Additional
PV Panels**

0

kBTU/ft²/yr

3.9

In summary, the project is now projected to have a net-zero EUI. Keep in mind that most energy modeling packages provide relatively good estimates, not actual achievement levels.

Building EUI before PV = 28 kBTU/ft²/Yr
PV on sloped main roof 1440 - 11 kBTU/ft²/Yr
Addition PV panels on three roofs 885 S.F. - net-zero 0 kBTU/ft²/Yr

The second array is lying flat, so it may not be as efficient as it could be; the calculations above do not take this into account, to save time and complexity in the process.

Water Savings

Determining water savings requires carefully considered assumptions and a range of calculations, followed by some decisions that affect the design of the building itself. The overall steps are listed below, followed by the details for each step:

- Determine the building's baseline water use with normal fixtures.
- Determine savings based on water efficient fixtures.
- Determine the amount of savings to be gained from rainwater harvesting.
- Additional decisions: Determine if more or less rainwater harvesting is warranted.
- Tabulate final results of all savings.
- Validate water efficiency against the project goals (see chapter 13).
- Communicate the water efficiency metrics in the final presentation (see chapter 14).

Water Baseline
- Determine assumptions:
  o 12 full-time employees (FTE), 160 visitors (10 visitors + 150 guests), 2 residential occupants (1 male, 1 female)
  o The facility is open Monday through Friday = 240 days per year
  o Enter data into a predeveloped spreadsheet (available on companion website)

Water Savings from Water-Efficient Fixtures
- Determine the new flow rates for efficient fixtures and update the spreadsheet used for Table 12.4. Table 12.5 shows the new water use results after the additional of water efficient fixtures.

Rainwater Harvesting
- Determine the catchment area (Figure 12.8):
  o Measure the roof catchment area

Length 75' × width 46' = 3,450 sf

TABLE 12.4 WATER BASELINE FOR THE DEMONSTRATION PROJECT

Water Use Baseline: Demonstration Project

Fixture type	Flow rate	Duration	Default uses per day				
	(gpf/gpm)	(minutes)	FTE	Visitors	Residential	Total water usage per day	
Male	1.6	n/a	1	0.1	0	151.1	Gallons/Day
Female	1.6	n/a	3	0.5	0	481.6	Gallons/Day
Urinal	1		2	0.4	0	103.2	Gallons/Day
Residential (female)	1.6	n/a	0	0	5	8	Gallons/Day
Residential (male)	1.6	n/a	0	0	5	8	Gallons/Day
Lavatory faucet	0.5	0.5	3	0.5	0	150.5	Gallons/Day
Lavatory faucet Residential	2.2	1	0	0	5	22	Gallons/Day
Shower (Residential)	2.5	8	0	0	1	40	Gallons/Day
Kitchen sink							Gallons/Day
Public	2.2	0.25	1	0	0	1.1	Gallons/Day
Residential	2.2	1	0	0	4	17.6	Gallons/Day
						983	**Gallons per day**

Source: Rob Fleming

- Find the yearly amount of rainfall based on your region. This information is readily available on the Internet. Precipitation information for Philadelphia is listed on the companion website. For Philadelphia, 41.45 inches of rain.
- Calculate the amount of rainwater to be collected on the roof for the year:

$$\text{Collected rainwater in gallons} = \text{Area of roof}\,(SF) \times (\text{loss factor}) \times 0.6208\,(\text{gallon})\,\text{conversion.}$$

TABLE 12.5 WATER USE AFTER WATER-EFFICIENT FIXTURES

Water Use Reductions: Demonstration Project

Fixture type	Flow rate	Duration	Default uses per day				
	(gpf/gpm)	(minutes)	FTE	Visitors	Residential	Total water usage per day	
Male	1.28	n/a	1	0.1	0	110.08	Gallons/Day
Female	1.28	n/a	3	0.5	0	385.28	Gallons/Day
Urinal	0.5		2	0.4	0	51.6	Gallons/Day
Residential (female)	1.28	n/a	0	0	5	6.4	Gallons/Day
Residential (male)	1.28	n/a	0	0	5	6.4	Gallons/Day
Lavatory faucet	0.25	0.5	3	0.5	0	75.25	Gallons/Day
Lavatory faucet Residential	0.25	1	0	0	5	2.5	Gallons/Day
Shower (Residential)	1.5	8	0	0	1	24	Gallons/Day
Kitchen sink							Gallons/Day
Public	0.5	0.25	1	0	0	0.25	Gallons/Day
Residential	0.5	1	0	0	4	4	Gallons/Day
						665.76	**Gallons per day**

Source: Rob Fleming

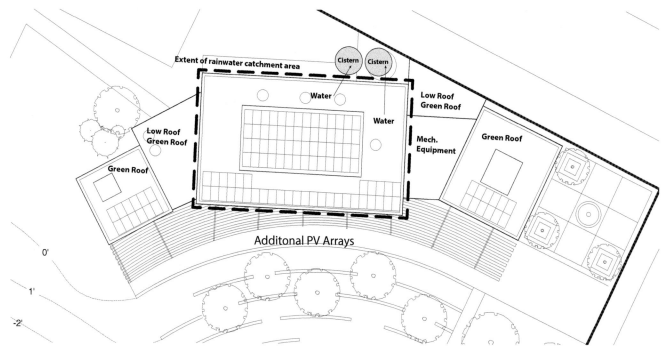

Figure 12.8 Rainwater collection area
Source: Rob Fleming

As part of the equation below, calculate additional loss of water due to evapotranspiration from a green roof (15%). This is water that evaporates into the atmosphere before it can drain off the roof. A loss of 15% was assumed because a large part of the roof is used for photovoltaic panels, which does not experience evapotranspiration.

$$3,450 \times 41.45 \times (41.05 - 41.05 * 0.1) \times .6208 = 79,898 \text{ gallons per year}$$

- The first 15% of rainwater is typically not collected because of sediment and debris. The following equation accounts for this:

$$79,898 - (79,898 * .15) = 67,913 \text{ gallons of rainwater collected each year}$$

- Calculate the size of the cistern to store water:
  - Determine size of cistern; convert from gallons to cubic feet:

$$\text{Cubic feet capacity for the cistern} = \text{total gallons} / 7.48$$

$$67,913 / 7.48 = 9,070 \text{ cubic feet of volume needed to collect all the water for the year}$$

- Decide how many months of water use to collect:
  - Three months was the duration selected for the demonstration project. This will allow the building to function, even in a drought.

$$9,070 / 4 = 2,270 \text{ cubic feet needed to store three-month rainfall on average}$$

TABLE 12.6 CISTERN SIZING CHART

Pi	Radius	Radius squared	Height	Volume	Gallons
3.14	5.5	30.25	14	1,329.79	9,947
	Ft	Ft	Ft	Cubic FT	

Source: Rob Fleming

- Size the cistern (Table 12.6):
  - Check and see what radius of a cistern that fits well on the site

    A 12-foot-high cistern with a 64-inch radius fits on the site in the location that was decided upon during the design process. This size fits between the building and sidewalk, as shown in Figure 12.13.

    The equation shows that the cistern would only account for half of the water needed.

    A second tank of the same size was added to the demonstration project to meet the rainwater harvesting requirements.

$$1,070 + 1,070 = 2,140 \text{ cubic feet which almost matches}$$
$$\text{the } 2,270 \text{ cubic feet needed.}$$

The cisterns could be made a bit taller or wider, but this is close enough for this project. One rainwater harvesting concern that was not considered for this exercise is the cistern sediment that builds up on the bottom of the tank over time. Sediment buildup was not factored into the calculations.

  - Tabulate the results: For this step, the total results need to be tabulated to internally communicate the results to the design team. The presentation of the tabulated results will be even more boiled down and simplified for the public. See Table 12.7 for simplified water savings.

In more advanced and complex sustainable buildings, living machines or other advanced water treatment systems would be used to treat black water (water from toilets) directly on-site for reuse in toilet flushing. Furthermore, the use of indigenous plant types means that no water beyond normal rainfall is required to maintain the landscape features. For this project, the stormwater on site was not addressed.

The next step, which is covered in chapter 13, finalizes the design project and validates the project, determining how well the project meets the pre-established design goals.

TABLE 12.7 FINAL WATER SAVINGS

Water Savings Countdown

Baseline water use	Water Efficient Fixtures	Rain water Harvesting
983	665	383
Gallons per day	Gallons per day	Gallons per day
	33%	61%
	water savings	Total water savings

Source: Rob Fleming

13

Design Resolution

Step 4
Design Resolution

4A Design Synthesis
4B Final DesignValidation
4C Presenting the Project

Step 3
Design

3A Preliminary Design
3B Passive Design
3C Building Envelope
3D Green Materials
 * Beyond the Basics

Step 2
Pre-Planning

2A Research & Case Studies
2B Project Goals
2C Design Criteria
2D Spatial Relationships

Step 1
Context

1A Project Information
1B Guiding Principles
1C Macro / Micro Context
1D Site Inventory & Analysis

Figure 13.0 The four steps of
Sustainable Design Basics
Source: Sharon B Jaffe

Chapter 13 focuses on taking the design process to its logical conclusion, followed by the task of the final validation. Ending the design process is difficult for many designers because there is always the belief that there is more to do.

FINAL DESIGN SYNTHESIS

At this point in the sustainable design methodology, the design is moving toward a more nuanced resolution. Although there is always more to do on a project, there is a need to finish the project to the level within a given time frame. Design projects can last months and even years. This design project is ending at the schematic design level, meaning that the project will be resolved to a certain level of detail that is understood by all stakeholders, professionals, and others who may need to review the design and offer commentary and proposed changes. In a real-life project, the next phases include design development, construction documentation, bidding, construction administration, and project closeout. The design resolution and validation covered in this chapter is considered "complete" for this stage of the process. The term "final" is used here to denote the "final" version of the design at this point in the process.

District Scale

It is crucial to show the project in the context of the larger neighborhood. It offers the opportunity to take a final look at the project in context. A sketch of the aerial view of the project within the urban context is presented as a way to see how the project fits into its site (Figure 13.1). The sketch lacks some details and accuracy because many of the site design ideas came later in the process. For example, the proposed amphitheater is stepped, but in this drawing it looks rather flat. That is acceptable since the time it would take to model the 3-D aspects of the amphitheater would be prohibitive.

Some design additions were added to the project as part of the design resolution. These are shown in the site plan in Figure 13.2.

A. A crosswalk was added to connect the river trail with the site.
B. An observation tower was added to the corner of Calumet Street and Kelly Drive. The tower provides the "landmark element" proposed in the site analysis.
C. The farmer's market helps to activate Ridge Avenue.
D. The wetland helps to meet the project's water goals

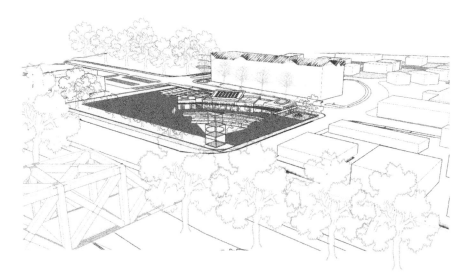

Figure 13.1 Sketch of the aerial view of the demonstration project
Source: Rob Fleming and Rupali Gadagkar

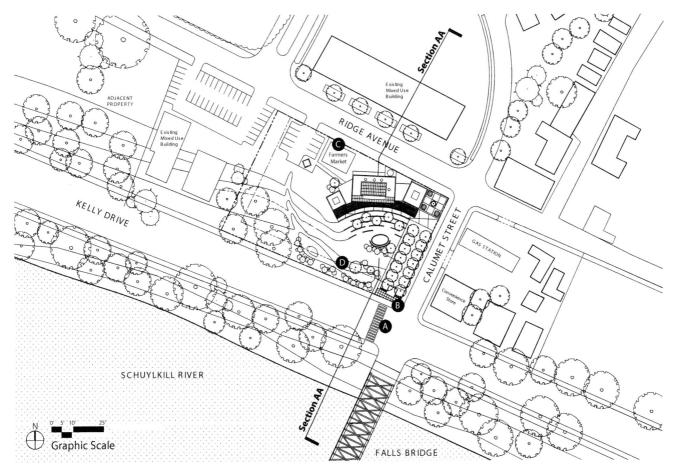

Figure 13.2 Final district plan

Source: Rob Fleming

A section was drawn to study the project one last time in its urban context (Figure 13.3). It is evident that the proposed one-story building is overshadowed by the 4 story building across the street. The section illustrates the following:

A. Existing four-story building
B. The one-story demonstration project
C. The corner tower landmark element now better understood within the urban context
D. Falls Bridge and the river

Site Plan

Although this book does not focus on landscape architecture and site development, the final synthesis includes some thoughts on how the building might integrate with its site. Site design is in itself an entire design project. Ideally, building designers would collaborate with landscape architects to co-develop the project. Figure 13.4 illustrates the following:

A. A wetland was proposed for the low end of the site. It stores and processes rainwater on site.
B. A swale was added to direct water from the parking lot to the wetland.

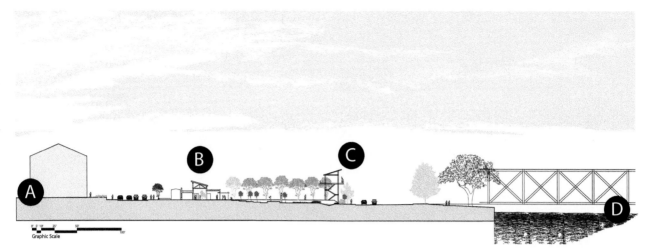

Figure 13.3 District scale site section

Source: Rob Fleming

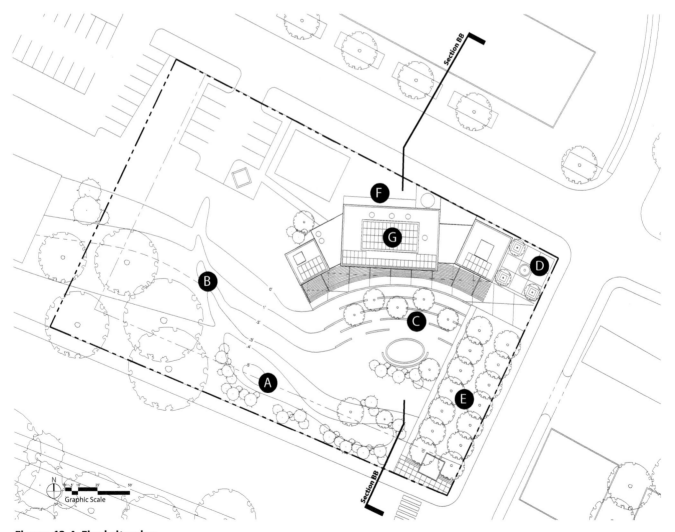

Figure 13.4 Final site plan

Source: Rob Fleming

C. The amphitheater is now further defined with an informal arrangement of stone seating elements and grassy areas. A stage with a backdrop of vegetation was added.

D. A fountain was added to the public space to "engage the senses" and activate the area.

E. An allée of trees (a double row of trees) was added to connect the public square to the landmark element. This space will include tables for chess play and benches.

F. An aromatic shade garden supplements the landscape on the north side of the building.

G. The roof plan shown in Figure 13.4 illustrates the extent of the solar panels, green roof, and roof monitors.

A second section is offered in Figure 13.5 to illustrate some of the details of the site better.

A. The stepped amphitheater is now better defined.

B. The allée of trees remains at the same height as the main corner of the site to allow a smooth progression to the observation tower.

C. Wetland. It is important to note that the site contours and grading were not a focus of this project, but the site section shows stormwater collection.

Final Space Plan/Floor Plan

The final floor plan is a critical part of the design resolution process. Figure 13.6 illustrates some of the key additions to the design. These additions help to achieve the guiding principles or project goals.

A. The open offices were rearranged to allow open space along the south wall. This plan configuration allows passive heat gain via a thicker floor slab at the south edge of the building.

B. The copy room was reduced to allow more room for the reception area.

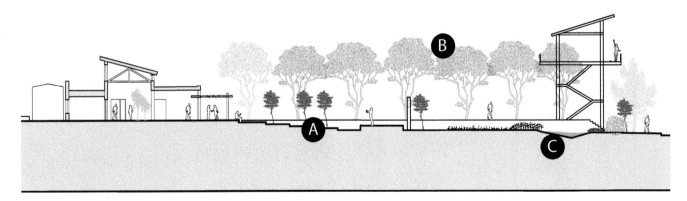

Graphic Scale

Figure 13.5 Final site section
Source: Rob Fleming

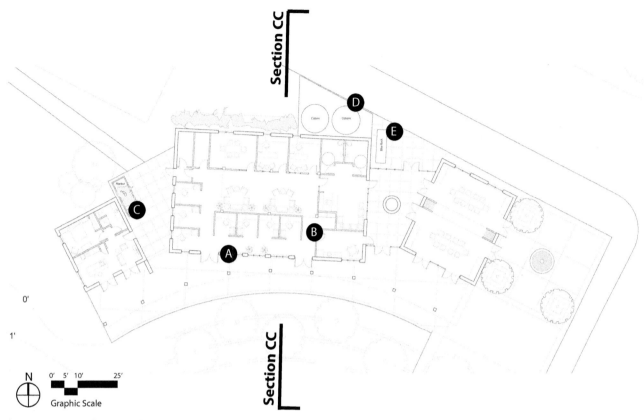

Figure 13.6 Final space plan
Source: Rob Fleming

C. A planter was added to improve the view from the west-facing offices.

D. The cisterns are now sized and located next to the restrooms. They also help to communicate the sustainability commitment of the client, a reflection of the systems guiding principle.

E. A bike rack was added to the entry area.

In the validation of the previous step, it was noted that the overall daylight factor was 2.5, quite low in the desired range of 2–5. In this section, more glass was added to the north side of the building. A new daylight analysis is shown in Figure 13.12 in the final validation step detailed later in this chapter. In Figure 13.7 the following changes to the building section are illustrated.

A. More glass was added to the north side.

B. The parapet for the street side was made higher to help bring more presence to the building.

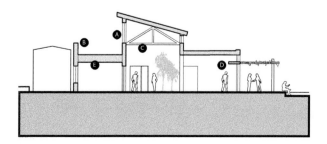

Figure 13.7 Final building section
Source: Rob Fleming

C. The proposed wood truss is further defined.

D. A light shelf was added to bounce light further into the building

E. A lower ceiling facilitates HVAC delivery.

FINAL VALIDATION

The final validation is the penultimate step in the sustainable design methodology. It will provide critical information needed to finish the project and move on to the final presentation. This is the chance to see if the proposed design met the various guiding principles, goals and objectives developed in steps 1 and 2. For example, in the demonstration project, guiding principles were developed to maintain a focus of the overarching goals. A set of specific project goals were established in step 2 to push the design to superior levels of performance (Table 13.1). This chapter presents the final validation process of the demonstration project. Of course, the process can be modified depending on the context of the project. More or less validation can occur.

Energy

The goals for energy efficiency were set at 20 KBTU/ft^2/yr before PV power and 0 after PV power. Based on the last energy models and PV simulations, the EUI results are shown in Figures 13.8 and 13.9. Optimizing the building envelope, location, orientation, and passive and active systems pushed the achieved EUI level to 28. Because the building was broken up into multiple forms, it became difficult to achieve the desired EUI of 20, which then required the use of more PV panels than expected.

Daylight

There are two metrics for daylighting. The first goal is the daylight factor with the goal of between 2% and 5%. The daylight levels reached in the previous step were only at 2.5%. The project was tweaked to generate a better daylight factor of 2.97%. Figure 13.10 shows the new simulation diagram.

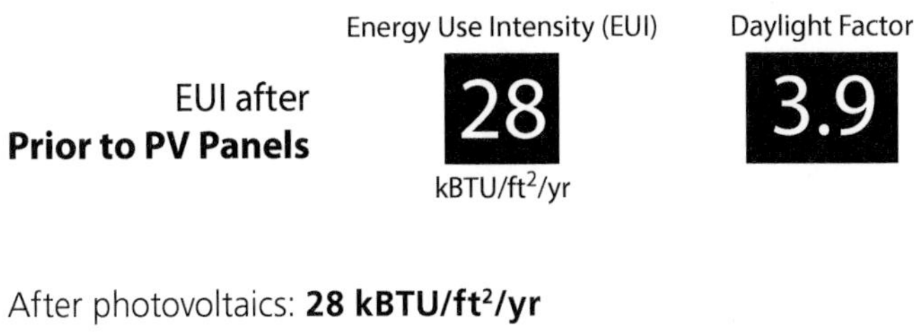

EUI after
Prior to PV Panels

Energy Use Intensity (EUI)

28
kBTU/ft^2/yr

Daylight Factor

3.9

Figure 13.8 Energy modeling results before the addition of photovoltaics
Source: Sefaira Software

After photovoltaics: **28 kBTU/ft^2/yr**

EUI after
After PV Panels

Energy Use Intensity (EUI)

0
kBTU/ft^2/yr

Daylight Factor

3.9

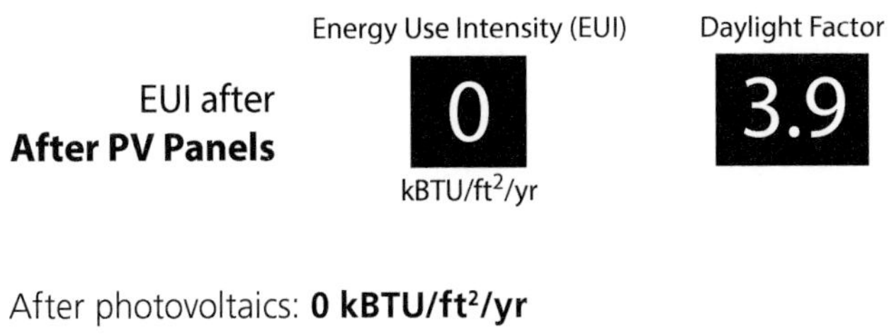

Figure 13.9 Energy modeling results after the addition of photovoltaics
Source: Sefaira Software

After photovoltaics: **0 kBTU/ft^2/yr**

TABLE 13.1 PROJECT GOALS MATRIX

Goals and Objectives Matrix

The Four Perspectives	Objective/Tangible Aspects							Subjective/Intangible Aspects		
	Performance					**Systems**		**Culture**		**Experience**
	Energy	Health and Wellbeing		Water		Site Coverage				
		Light	Air		Stormwater		Ecological Integration	Stakeholder Engagement	Sense of Community	Views
Guiding Principles	*Fight climate change by creating the highest energy performing project possible*					*Integrate the project with the surrounding ecology*		*Celebrate diversity* / *Be a vital partner in a strong community*		*Infuse a sense of beauty in every decision*
Stated Project Goals and/ or Rating Systems	**Net-Zero Energy**					**Healthy habitat for increased biodiversity**		**Hold public community meetings in conference room**		**Engage all the senses**
Metrics	**Energy** Predicted consumed energy use intensity/ predicted net EUI	**Light** Percentage of spaces >300 lux (28 FC) at 3 pm March 21 and/ or daylight factor (DF)	**Air** Percentage of floor area or percentage of occupant work stations within 30 feet of operable windows	**Water** Percentage reduction of water use versus baseline	**Stormwater** Percentage of rainwater that can be managed on site from max. anticipated 24-hour, 2-year storm event:		**Ecological Integration** Percentage of landscaped areas covered by native or climate appropriate plants supporting native or migratory animals	**Stakeholder Engagement** Percentage of stakeholders engaged	**Sense of Community** Walk, transit, bike scores	**Views** Percentage of floor area or percentage of occupant work stations with direct views of the outdoors
Benchmarks	**20/0 kBTU/ft²/yr**	**100% Daylight Factor 2% - 5%**	**100%**	**66%**	**100%**		**50%**	**100%***	**72/64/58*** *Walk, Transit, Bike scores*	**100%**
Strategies	*High performance building envelope*	*Thin building plate, high ceiling/ windows/ light shelves*	*Thin building, operable windows*	*Collect water from the roof in cisterns*	*Divert site stormwater to a rain garden*		*Indigenous plants, limit paving as much as much*	*Design charrette*	*Strategies or policies meet culture achievements*	*Position workspaces with view to the outdoors*

Source: Rob Fleming

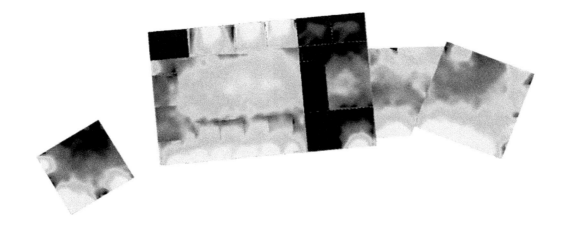

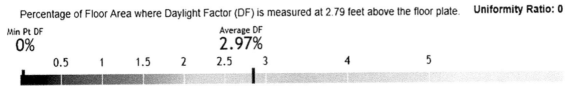

Percentage of Floor Area where Daylight Factor (DF) is measured at 2.79 feet above the floor plate.   **Uniformity Ratio: 0**

Min Pt DF
0%

Average DF
2.97%

0.5   1   1.5   2   2.5   3   4   5

Figure 13.10 Daylight factor
Source: Sefaira Software

The second daylight metric is: "The percentage of spaces that receive greater than 300 lux (28 footcandles) at 3 pm on March 21 on the desktop." The goal was set at 100%. Ten workspaces are numbered and circled. Eight of the ten workspaces reached at least 28 footcandles. The reception area, as marked by the number 10, does not meet the requirement. However, a solotube (skylight) is used to provide additional light to that space. Office space 1 is blocked from west light by the guest apartment, so it fails the metric.

Air

The metric for air is defined in the project goals matrix: percentage of occupant workstations within 30 feet of operable windows. The daylight diagram shown in Figure 13.11 can be used to determine the work spaces in the project. An examination of the floor plan will show if there is an operable window in each of those work spaces is nearby. Of the ten workspaces, only the reception area is not near an operable window. The established goal is for 100% of occupied spaces to be near an operable window; 90% of these spaces met the requirement. The fresh air goal was not achieved, but 90% is still a good score.

Water

The metric for water savings is a percentage reduction of water use, compared to the baseline. In chapter 12, a set of water savings calculations and cistern sizing exercises were conducted to determine the overall water savings on the project. The chart in Table 13.2 illustrates that the project's projected water savings are estimated

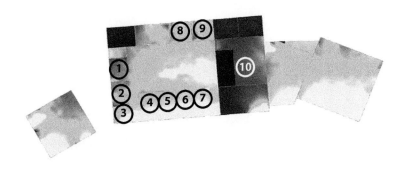

Figure 13.11 Daylighting image from Sefaira, March 21, 3 p.m.

Source: Sefaira Software

Footcandle levels on March 21 at 3PM measured at 2.79 feet above the floor plate

at 61% savings of baseline water. The goal was established at 66%, or two-thirds water savings. The target was not reached because of the desire to keep the cistern size from getting too large. Even so, the cisterns are quite large.

Stormwater

Stormwater was not calculated because site planning was not a focus of the project. The reduction in impervious surfaces coupled with ample area for stormwater capture and management suggests that the goal can be met.

Ecological Integration

The map in Figure 13.12 indicates the extent of the site that was set aside to meet the project goal of "Fifty percent of landscaped areas to be covered by native or climate-appropriate plants supporting native or migratory animals." The drawing in Figure 13.12 is used to determine if the project goal has been met. The square footages were determined by taking measurements of the total area of the site,

TABLE 13.2 WATER SAVINGS VALIDATION

Water Use Per Day			
Total water use before savings	**Water Efficient Fixtures**	**Rain Water Harvesting**	**Totals**
983	**318**	**282**	**383**
Gallons per day	Gallons per day	Gallons per day	Gallons per day
Water Savings Countdown			
Baseline water use	**Water Efficient Fixtures**	**Rain water Harvesting**	
983	665	383	
Gallons per day	Gallons per day	Gallons per day	
	33%	**61%**	
	water savings	Total water savings	

Source: Rob Fleming.

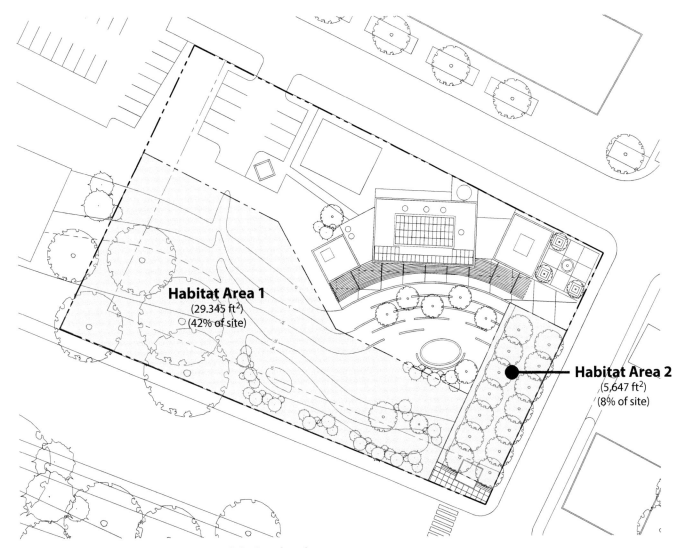

Figure 13.12 Ecological integration validation drawing
Source: Rob Fleming

and the habitat areas of the site in AutoCAD. The area calculations can also be accomplished in SketchUp or whatever software is in use. The validation revealed that the area set aside in the site to be used to meet the goal was only 42%, which is 8% short of the goal. As a response, a second area of the site was identified as having the use of indigenous trees that would attract migrating birds. An additional 8% of site coverage was achieved. The two habitat areas together equal 50% site coverage meeting the project goal. It is quite common to tweak the design of a project to meet project goals.

Equity

For the demonstration project, the metric was: " Percentage of stakeholders engaged." Because this was not an actual project, there was no way to measure community engagement. For the sake of the demonstration project, it is assumed that the full array of stakeholders were engaged in the process. Even then, this is a subjective matrix goal because the definition of the variety of stakeholder varies from project to project. This goal's intent to encourage the use of stakeholder engagement.

Community

Since the site was already selected before design, the walk score, transit score, and bike score were already established. The design of the project does help to encourage these forms of transportation by locating the front door near the corner bus stops, by installing a bike rack near the front door, and by helping to improve the walk experience by activating the main corner of the site. A third-party website was used to calculate the score. The walk score for the project was 72, while transit was 64 and bike was 58. These are all scores that range from good to very good.

Views

The metric for views was set at percentage of regularly occupied spaces with a view to the outdoors. The goal was to achieve a score of 100%. The only regularly occupied space without a view is the reception area, which is blocked by the break room. (a design modification is proposed to add an interior window in the wall between the reception room and the break room to allow a view to the outdoors. See the final floor plan for the proposed change.

Multisensory Engagement

Multisensory engagement is a decidedly more subjective metric that seeks to encourage the design team to consider the senses beyond the visual. The fountain and trees added to the public space on the corner helped to engage vistors. The opening of the south wall of the central office space was a critical step in connecting all users to the site more graciously and directly.

Final Validation Matrix

The final validation matrix in Table 13.3 organizes the validation of aspects of the project developed during steps 1 and 2. The guiding principles themselves can be validated by taking a quick look at the final design resolution to see how well the project expresses these principles. If the design does not entirely reflect all the principles, or if a specific principle is not articulated, it is acceptable, even if less than ideal. The final validation is a time to review the design process and the resulting building design; it is not meant to extend the design process. The final matrix is similar to a worksheet, not a presentation tool. See chapter 14 for information about how to present the validations.

Guiding Principles

Validating the guiding principles is the last step in the demonstration project. It is the most fundamental portion of the validation because it brings the project full circle, from the very beginning to the end. It is not expected that every guiding principle will be flawlessly reflected in the design. Sustainable design features a series of tradeoffs when one goal is sacrificed for another goal that is deemed more important. Table 13.4 offers a condensed overview of the validation of the guiding principles. See Chapter 14 for strategies to present these findings.

TABLE 13.3 FINAL VALIDATION MATRIX

Final Validation – Project Goals and Objectives

The Metrics	Metrics	Stated Goal	Predicted Results	Final Evaluation
Energy	**Energy Use Intensity** Before PV/after PV	20/0 kBTU/ft²/yr	28/0 kBTU/ft²/yr	Yes
Health + Wellness	**Light:** Percentage of regularly occupied spaces	100%	90%	No
	Air: Percentage of regularly occupied spaces	100%	90%	No
Water	**Water Use** Percentage savings	67%	61%	No
	Stormwater Percentage of rainwater that can be managed on site	100%	100%	Yes*
Ecological Integration	**Habitat** Percentage of landscaped areas covered by native or climate-appropriate plants	50%	50%	Yes
Culture Goals	**Stakeholder Engagement** (yes or no)	Yes	Yes*	Assumed to be met
	Sense of Community Walk/Transit/Bike Score	72/64/58	72/64/58*	Already met
Experience Goals	**Views** Percentage of regularly occupied spaces with a view to the outdoors	100%	90%	No
	Senses Engage all the senses in the design solution	Yes	Yes	Yes

Sustainable Design Basics: A methodology for the schematic design of sustainable buildings

Source: Rob Fleming

A. Fight climate change.

Rotation of the central part of the building to face south and the PV panels help to give the building better energy performance and thereby to help fight climate change.

B. Educate the public.

The rainwater cisterns near the front entrance of the building help to tell a story about the building. Information signs have been added to the project at strategic locations, providing opportunities for visitors to learn about the different green strategies of the project.

C. Bring ecology back to the city.

The lower half of the site was reserved for ecology and habitat. The land was placed into a "land trust" to prevent future construction. This part of the site will also better deal with flooding. Instead of locating a wall to prevent flooding, the open area allows a natural, low impact way to accommodate flooding; the area doubles as a park in normal weather conditions. The signage mentioned in

TABLE 13.4 FINAL VALIDATION GUIDING PRINCIPLES MATRIX

Final Validation – Guiding Principles

The Metrics	Stated Principle	Optimisms	Caution	Final Evaluation
Performance Guiding Principle	Fight climate change by creating the highest energy performing project possible	The project met its energy goals	Building users need to maintain good behaviors to keep lighting and plug loads under control	*More PV panels could be added to make the project energy net-positive*
Systems Guiding Principle	*Educate the public about sustainability by showcasing sustainable technologies*	The cistern in the front of the building is very helpful	The green roof was not visible from the street	
	Bring ecology back to the city	The wetland is a great addition to the East Falls neighborhood	Lots of animals will be coming onto the site, which can create issues when intersecting with humans	
Culture Guiding Principles	*Become an integral part of a strong sustainable community*	*The shared conference room is connected to public space on the corner*	*The main entry to the building is not readily visible and does not help to activate the corner of the site*	
	Celebrate diversity	*Gender-neutral bathrooms were used in the project*		
Experience Guiding Principle	*Infuse a sense of beauty in every design decision*	*The building structure is broken up to create more visual interest*	*The one-story building is relatively short compared to the 4 story building across the street*	
	Engage all the senses in the design solution	*The project uses biophilia to activate the*	*Lots of maintenance will be needed to keep the site under control*	*Develop a maintenance plan for the project*

Sustainable Design Basics: A methodology for the schematic design of sustainable buildings

Source: Rob Fleming

the previous guiding principle continues in this area as well to further educate the public.

D. Connect to the community.

The corner plaza and farmers market space become amenities that foster a connection to the community. The conference room will be offered on a limited basis for community meetings and presentations, with the doors to the room unlocked for access to the plaza on the corner. Notice that the reception area, restrooms, and breakout rooms are available to the public at night without compromising the security of the main office space.

E. Infuse a sense of beauty.

An observation tower on the southeast corner of the site offers a sculptural element to the project, which adds visual delight and provides a focal point for views.

F. Engage all the senses.

The rainwater supplies water to the plaza fountain, providing more than visual interest to add soothing sounds. The bench that defines the water feature edge has a smooth texture, encouraging people to sit and listen to the sounds. The gardens that step down from the terrace toward the river offer unique and pleasant smells. Food harvested from the garden affords opportunities for varied tastes. Finally, different types of physical space inside and outside the project offer spatial variety, helping to make a vibrant and enjoyable user experience.

CONCLUSION

For many designers, this process is arduous because it requires a systematic and holistic evaluation of the project after completion. There may be a temptation to redesign the project further to achieve superior results for all the goals and metrics. Redesign is not the intent of final validation; it is not necessary. Ending your project while understanding the "cautions" suggests the "next steps" that would be taken if the project were to go forward. The next steps are listed below but are not illustrated in this book:

1. Develop the form of the building itself to find better proportions and better architectural unity between the three primary forms of the building.
2. Find ways to better activate the street edge along Ridge Avenue..
3. Find ways to make the design more flexible so that it can be expanded in the future. The guest apartment is an excellent function to have, but it blocks the ability to extend the main office building to gain more office space. The guest apartment could be designed to serve as additional office space in the future.
4. Resolve the conflict between the roof monitor over the conference room and the need to split the room into two rooms.

Final Presentation

All of the information contained in the final validation is presented in a condensed format in the final presentation. The next chapter will discuss and illustrate various options and choices for the final presentation. Also explained is how to convey the vast quantities of information of final validation effectively.

14

Demonstration Project: Final Presentation

Figure 14.0 *Sustainable Design Basics,* step 4

Source: Sharon B Jaffe

The slides described below refer to the PowerPoint template found on the companion website (www.wiley.com\go\Jaffesustainable)

The great challenge in developing the final presentation is the need to summarize the process in a streamlined manner so that there is enough time to discuss the final product. It is not necessary to present the entire depth of the project context or the pre-design process. Instead, the best strategy is to quickly show an example of the methodology for each step and then to identify the key takeaways that determined the major design moves of the project. This is much more difficult than it sounds and requires the ability to step back from the project and see it holistically. Examples will be shown in this chapter.

Chapter 10 includes a discussion about some of the key strategies and techniques for an effective sustainable design presentation. This chapter includes sample slides from a final presentation of the demonstration project. The full PowerPoint for the demonstration project is included on the companion website. The text below explains the contents of the final presentation for the demonstration project. Some of the sample slides are shown in large format to give a sense of what the slides look like and how they communicate the essential aspects of the sustainable design project. In other cases, a brief written summary explains the purpose and contents of slides not shown.

STEP 1: PROJECT INTRODUCTION AND CONTEXT

In a sustainable design project, it is essential to give the audience a sense of the project context. That should be accomplished with the minimum number of slides and text. It is crucial not to overwhelm the audience with too much data early in the presentation.

- **Slide: Project Location/Building Use** (not shown): It is important to see the project location with multiple scales.
  - o Maps that illustrate the project location within the global scale, the regional and district scales are included.
  - o Show the building type, the client (if there is one), and the overall size of the project.
- **Slide: Macroclimate and Macro Context** (not shown): When looking at the global scale, it is important to include:
  - o **Temperate climate**
    - o General description of the macroclimate
  - o **Urban Scale:** When looking at the urban or regional scale, it is important to define the macro context. Is it urban, suburban, or rural?
    - o Here generalized information is included about the urban context. This bit of information is what gets used in the design matrices.
- **Slide: District Scale/Micro-Context** (not shown): In this slide, the neighborhood is shown, and the project site is clearly indicated.
- **Slide: Guiding Principles** (Figure 14.1): Here, each principle is shown in text format and is stated aloud by the presenter. A general verbal statement can be made letting the audience know that you will be illustrating how the principles were used in the project later in the presentation.
- **Slide: Site Inventory Matrix** (not shown): The ability to use the entire site inventory matrix as a presentation tool is very difficult. For the demonstration

project, the matrix is shown and briefly described to the audience. The takeaways are what is important to focus on.

- **Slide: Research Major Findings** (not shown): List the key takeaways by the scale of the research. This is a critical task of the designer who must look at all the research and then decide what is most important to share. Looking at some of the major design directions or guiding principles will help make a selection that supports those design directions. This helps to build a continuous story.
- **Slide: Site Inventory Diagram and Takeaways** (Figure 14.2): Here, key takeaways are provided for each perspective. The slide below reflects one of four images, each depicting important site information from different perspectives. The issue/opportunity is shown along with its associated response. By now the audience is gaining a clearer understanding of the intent of the project.
- **Slide: Site Analysis** (not shown): This is the most important part of this part of the presentation because the analysis is a synthesis of the key takeaways from the site inventory maps and takeaways.

Project Information: Guiding Principles

Performance Principle
- *Fight climate change by creating the highest energy performing project possible*

Systems Principles
- *Educate the public about sustainability by showcasing sustainable technologies*
- *Bring ecology back to the city*

Culture Principles
- *Become an integral part of a strong sustainable community*
- *Celebrate diversity*

Experience Principles
- *Infuse a sense of beauty in every design decision*
- *Engage all the senses in the design solution*

Figure 14.1 Guiding principles sample slide
Source: Rob Fleming

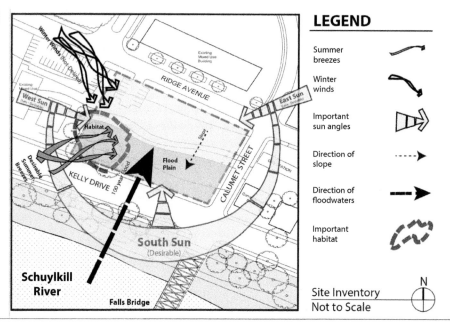

Figure 14.2 Site inventory sample slide

Source: Rob Fleming

STEP 2: PRE-PLANNING

- **Slide: Case Study Intro Page** (not shown): Here the general information about the case study is shown, including the name of the project, the design team, date completed, a location map, and a picture of the project.
- **Slide: Case Study Matrix** (not shown): The matrix is explained in general as a framework for studying the project but is not actually used for presentation. Sometimes presenters will spend a few seconds on this slide to remind the audience that a rigorous process was followed.
- **Slide: Case Study Takeaways** (Figure 14.3): The takeaways are organized by the four perspectives. Each takeaway will include a bulleted sentence along with a picture or statistic. These are typically the sustainable strategies or inspirations from the project that influenced the final design of the project.
- **Slide: Criteria Matrix** (not shown): Include the major spaces and their square footage. It is not a good idea to read all the spaces and their square footage to the audience. Pick out a couple of important spaces and point them out.
- **Slide: Program Key Takeaways:** (Figure 14.4): The takeaways are organized by the four perspectives. Each takeaway will include a bulleted sentence and may include a picture as an example from another project.
- **Slide: Relationship Diagrams** (not shown): Help to communicate the spatial concepts and relationships as derived from the criteria matrix. These are typically shown but not discussed in detail.

Case Study 1: Marin County Day School

Key Takeaways

- Performance:
  Outdoor hallways double as shading elements
- Systems:
  Ecological restoration – regenerated landscape
- Culture:
  Amphitheater/courtyard as a heart of the building
- Experience:
  Trees integrated with amphitheater

Figure 14.3 Case study key takeaways sample slide
Source: Rob Fleming

Design Criteria: Key Takeaways

Performance Strategies
- Make sure all rooms have adequate daylight to complete normal tasks – **30 footcandles on the desktop**

Systems Integration Strategies
- **Operable windows** for regularly occupied spaces

Culture Strategies
- **Shared conference room** with the community – open at night with access to building amenities such as bathrooms and breakout rooms
- **The commons will be the heart of the building** – an informal space to be used in different ways

Experience Strategies
- **Biophilic colors and materials** to heighten experience

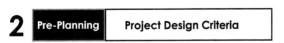

Figure 14.4 Design criteria key takeaways sample slide
Source: Rob Fleming

Design

- **Slide: Validation Matrix** (not shown): Depending on the length of the final presentation, it may be worthwhile to show a few of the validation matrices to underscore the importance of the process.
- **Slide: Preliminary Design** (not shown): It is unreasonable to take an audience through your entire process. Instead, briefly illustrate the steps taken in this part of the process and highlight the design synthesis.
- **Slide: Passive Design** (Figure 14.5) As before, a brief overview of the methods used to study the different opportunities are shown, with the final synthesized project at that point in the process illustrated with some key daylight and EUI statistics.
- **Slide: Building Envelope** (not shown): In this set of slides, major decisions about the structural system, wall type, window type, and roof are presented. Again, the methodology is briefly shown to inform the audience that you went through a process. The summary synthesis slide shows the final decisions about the envelope.
- **Active Design** (not shown): As above, the design synthesis illustrates important information about the HVAC, lighting, PV and other active technologies.
- The totality of the design synthesis slides will paint a strong picture of the design process. The audience can see an evolution of how the design developed. However, it is critical not to dwell on these slides in order to save time for the final drawings.

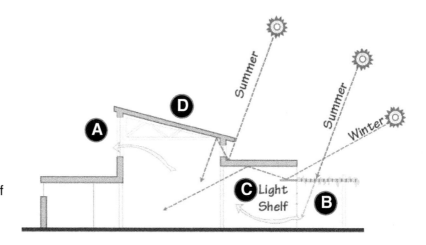

Passive Design:
Design Synthesis

A Passive ventilation

B Shading on the south facade

C Light shelf

D PV panels on south-facing roof

Energy Use Intensity (EUI)

48

kBTU/ft²/yr

Daylight Factor

3.9

Daylight Factor = 3.6

Figure 14.5 Design synthesis sample slide
Source: Rob Fleming

Design Resolution

Presenting the Final Design Drawings

- **Slide: District Plan** (Figure 14.6): In this set of slides, major design decisions as related to the neighborhood are documented. It is good practice to remind the audience how these design moves relate to the project's guiding principles or goals.
- **Slide: District Section** (not shown): This slide shows the project in the context of the slope on the site, any vegetation, and important surrounding buildings that provide a sense of scale.
- **Slide: Site Plan** (not shown): The site plan, which is shown in Chapter 13, is a key drawing. Much of the local ecological and hydrological information and design impacts are illustrated in this drawing. Although site development is not a focus of this book, it is expected that building designers will attempt to reach a higher level of site integration with each project.
- **Slide: Site Section Slide** (Figure 14.7): This "zoomed in" slide indicates major decisions about the immediate site around the building, highlighting level changes, vegetation, and landmarks such as the observation tower.
- **Slide: Floor Plan** (Figure 14.8): The floor plan is shown with some notes that reinforce the project goals and guiding principles.

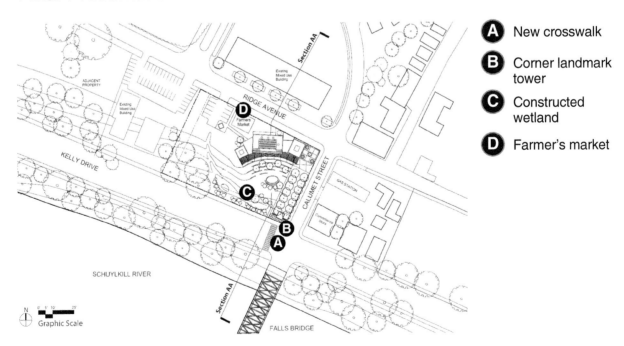

Figure 14.6 District plan sample slide

Source: Rob Fleming

Final Presentation: **Site Section**

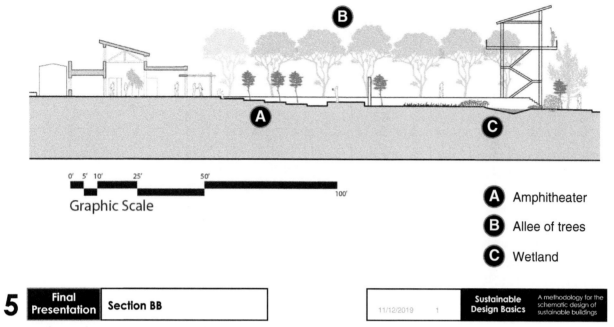

Figure 14.7 Site section sample slide

Source: Rob Fleming

Design Resolution: **Floor Plan**

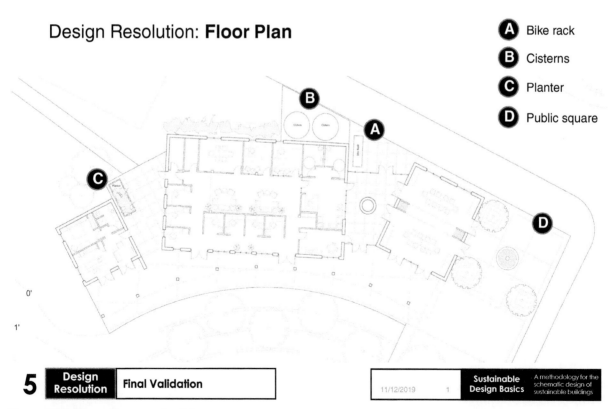

Figure 14.8 Floor plan sample slide

Source: Rob Fleming

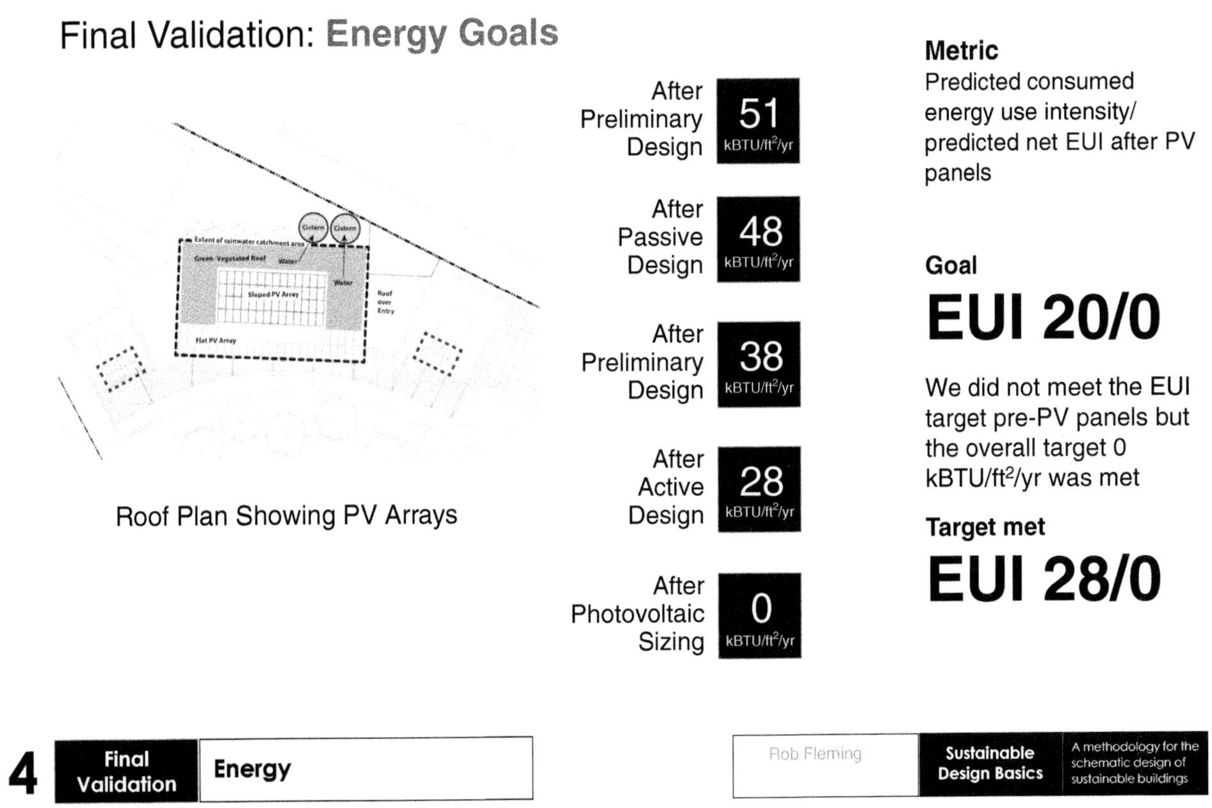

Final Validation: Energy Goals

Roof Plan Showing PV Arrays

After Preliminary Design	51 kBTU/ft²/yr
After Passive Design	48 kBTU/ft²/yr
After Preliminary Design	38 kBTU/ft²/yr
After Active Design	28 kBTU/ft²/yr
After Photovoltaic Sizing	0 kBTU/ft²/yr

Metric
Predicted consumed energy use intensity/ predicted net EUI after PV panels

Goal

EUI 20/0

We did not meet the EUI target pre-PV panels but the overall target 0 kBTU/ft²/yr was met

Target met

EUI 28/0

4 | **Final Validation** | **Energy** | | Rob Fleming | **Sustainable Design Basics** | A methodology for the schematic design of sustainable buildings |

Figure 14.9 EUI countdown sample slide
Source: Rob Fleming

- **Slide: Building Section** (not shown): The building section tells an important story about structure, envelope, and passive strategies. The building section which is shown in Chapter 13 allows the audience to understand the spatial implications of the project.
- **Slide: EUI Countdown** (Figure 14.9): This slide communicates the continuing improvement of the energy performance with each step in the process. It is helpful to see the results of the project goals. This is the heart of the validation. If the goals were not met, the designer has the option of redesigning the project or accepting the deficiencies of the project.
- **Slide: Daylighting** (Figure 14.10): This slide communicates the validation results of the daylighting of the project. Notice that the first metric was not met, but that the overall daylight factor was within the desired range as indicated in the project goals.
- **Slide: Air** (not shown): Just as the daylight was validated at the end of the project, the air, water, and stormwater were studied to see if the project met the goals.
- **Slide: Water** (not shown): Similar to Slide: Air.
- **Slide: Stormwater** (not shown): Similar to Slide: Air.
- **Slide: Ecological Integration** (Figure 14.11): This slide documents the amount of the site that was left to be developed as an ecologically appropriate habitat.
- **Slide: Inclusivity:** (not shown) These slides help to document the intangible goals of the project.

Final Validation: **Daylight Goals**

Footcandle levels on March 21 at 3 p.m. measured at 2.79 feet above the floor plate

| | 19 | 36 | 56 | 74+ |

Metric
Percentage of spaces >300 lux (28 FC) at 3 p.m. March 21 and/or daylight factor (DF)

Goal

100%

8 out of 10 work spaces meet 300 lux at 3 p.m. on March 21

Target not met

80%

| **Metric:** **Daylight Factor** 2-5 | **Metric:** **Daylight Factor** 2.97 Target Met |

5 | **Final Validation** | **Daylight Validation** | | 11/12/2019 | 1 | **Sustainable Design Basics** | A methodology for the schematic design of sustainable buildings |

Figure 14.10 Daylight validation sample slide
Source: Rob Fleming

Final Validation: **Ecological Goals**

Habitat Area 1
(29.345 S.F.)
(42% of site)

Habitat Area 2
(5,647 S.F.)
(8% of site)

Metric
Percentage of landscaped areas covered by native or climate-appropriate plants supporting native or migratory animals

Goal

50%

Total size of site = 69,984
Total habitat area = 34,992

Target met

50%

5 | **Final Validation** | **Ecological Integration** | | 11/12/2019 | 1 | **Sustainable Design Basics** | A methodology for the schematic design of sustainable buildings |

Figure 14.11 Ecological integration sample slide
Source: Rob Fleming

Final Validation: **Guiding Principles**

Stated Principle	Optimisms	Caution	Next Steps
Fight climate change by creating the highest energy performing project possible	**"The project met its energy goals and contributes to fighting climate change"**	Building users need to maintain good behaviors to keep lighting and plug loads under control	**More PV panels could be added to make the project energy net-positive**
Educate the public about sustainability by showcasing sustainable technologies	The cistern in the front of the building is very helpful	**The green roof was not visible from the street**	
Bring ecology back to the city	**"The wetland is a great addition to the East Falls neighborhood"**		
Become an integral part of a strong sustainable community	**"The shared conference room is connected to public space on the corner"**	**"The main entry to the building is not readily visible and does not help to activate the corner of the site"**	
Infuse a sense of beauty in every design decision	*The building structure is broken up to create more visual interest*	*The one-story building is relatively short*	

| Final Validation | Guiding Principles Validation | | Name insert command 11/12/2019   1 | Sustainable Design Basics | A methodology for the schematic design of sustainable buildings |

Figure 14.12 Guiding principles validation sample slide
Source: Rob Fleming

- **Slide: Community** (not shown): Similar to Slide: Inclusivity
- **Slide: Experience** (not shown): Similar to Slide: Inclusivity
- **Slide: Guiding Principles** (Figure 14.12): The project presentation ends with the designer sharing the starting point, the guiding principles, and then validating the project to see how well it expressed and reinforced the guiding principles. It is ill-advised to read every optimism or caution. It is better to pick the most important to focus on.

CONCLUSION

It is helpful for the reader to download the sample PowerPoint from the companion website so that the full extent of the presentation is understood. Final presentations are difficult to organize and deliver. The more practice giving presentations, the more comfortable the presenters become and, by default, the audience becomes more comfortable and more receptive to the information. This is especially true with sustainable design projects where it is sometimes the case that the audience is not supportive, or worse yet combative. Having the design process slides as a backup to answer questions about the process is helpful. PowerPoint allows for slides to be hidden. These can be revealed during the discussion phase of the presentation to help make a specific case in favor of the design. So ends the demonstration project, and with that the primary text of the book. There are a lot more tools provided beyond this chapter including sample exercises, the appendix, and the companion website, which contains the PowerPoints used for this chapter.

15

Exercises

Step 4
**Design
Resolution**

4A Design Synthesis
4B Final DesignValidation
4C Presenting the Project

Step 3
Design

3A Preliminary Design
3B Passive Design
3C Building Envelope
3D Green Materials
 * Beyond the Basics

Step 2
Pre-Planning

2A Research & Case Studies
2B Project Goals
2C Design Criteria
2D Spatial Relationships

Step 1
Context

1A Project Information
1B Guiding Principles
1C Macro / Micro Context
1D Site Inventory & Analysis

Figure 15.0 The four steps of
Sustainable Design Basics
Source: Sharon B Jaffe

SUSTAINABLE BUILDING DESIGN EXERCISES

The design exercises in this chapter follow the same pattern as the *Sustainable Design Basics* demonstration project. However, some of the basic research, a building program, and other details are provided to facilitate the process. All of the materials needed to complete the exercises, including blank matrices in a variety of formats, are included on the companion website. Additional building types and programs can be used instead of the provided buildings and programs.

The variables are:
Choice 1: Client
Choice 2: Site selection and macro climate
Choice 3: Macro context (settlement pattern)
Choice 4: New or existing building

Choice 1: Client

The type of client will become the primary driver of the design as defined by the guiding principles. A set of guiding principles is provided below with the list of client types.

The details for each client can be found later in this chapter and on the companion website. Each client comes with a particular point of view, mission, and vision. Each client requires office space and requires a special function that is used to interface with the public in different ways, and the special function is different for each client. Although the same set of guiding principles applies to all clients (Table 15.1), each client emphasizes one principle over the others, as shown below. This is important to understand, because many designers impose their own values on a design project even when it is at odds with the stated goals of the client.

The program of the building is similar to the University Career Counseling Center, which was used in the demonstration project. A criteria matrix is included and is discussed later in this chapter. It is also included on the companion website so that it can be altered for a custom project.

Choice 2: Site Location and Macroclimate

The site selection will yield radically different environmental conditions, different terrain, and different architectural contexts. Each of the locations features a very different climate and should therefore offer a different set of challenges. Site information is provided later in this chapter and on the companion website.

TABLE 15.1 BUILDING PROGRAM OPTIONS

	Client Type	Perspective/Emphasis	Guiding Principles: Client's Specific Emphasis
A.	**Brokerage Firm** Office space and cigar bar	Performance	*Design the most energy-efficient project possible*
B.	**Audubon Society** Office space and nature interpretive space	Systems	*Integrate the project with the surrounding ecology.*
C.	**Social Services Agency** Office space and nature interpretive space	Culture and equity	*Be a vital partner in a strong community.*
D.	**Arts Organization** Office space and gallery	Experience	*Infuse a sense of beauty into every decision.*

Choose a location
a. Miami, Florida (hot, humid)
b. New London, Connecticut (warm, temperate, continental)
c. Phoenix, Arizona (dry, arid)
d. Breckenridge, Colorado (polar, subarctic)

Choice 3: Macro Context (Settlement Pattern)

The choice of the context impacts the design of the project, especially the building setbacks, views, and the influence of surrounding buildings types.

Choose a context:
a. Urban
b. Suburban
c. Rural

Choice 4: New Building or Existing Building

The choice of a new structure or the renovation of an existing structure adds to the variety of the exercises. The same criteria matrix applies to the project.

Choose a project type:
a. New building
b. Existing building

Design professionals who typically focus on new construction should be encouraged to explore the design of a project by using an existing building shell, and designers without experience with new construction should be encouraged to work with a new building. It is important for young designers to leave their comfort zone and work from a new point of view. It makes them better teammates for group projects because they have empathy for the other disciplines.

Detailed information about the site context is discussed later in this chapter. It is also included on the companion website so that it can be altered for a custom project.

CHOICE 1: CLIENT DETAILS

The criteria matrix shown in Table 15.2 lays out the requirements for the whole design program. The program is similar to that used for the demonstration project, but the guest apartment has been removed. The "commons area" from the demonstration project has been changed for each of the different programs for the exercises.

Client A: Green Brokerage Firm

The Green Brokerage Firm is a company that helps people find and invest in green and sustainable technologies and companies. The firm is comprised of typical office space with open and closed offices, a reception area, a small conference room, and a break-out room.

TABLE 15.2 GENERIC CRITERIA MATRIX

Criteria Matrix: Interiors

				PERFORMANCE		SYSTEMS			CULTURE	EXPERIENCE
The Four Perspectives / Design Criteria						Objective/Tangible Requirements			Subjective/Intangible Requirements	
Rm #	Room Name	SQ. FT.	Adjacencies	Acoustics	Furniture Requirements	Active Systems — Specialized heating, cooling, ventilation, plumbing, lighting, equipment only	Passive Systems — List specialized requirements below	Privacy	Special Cultural Considerations — Image, brand, sense of community	Sense of place — Views, smells, colors, taste, textures, sounds, Special considerations, Spatial sense, other intangibles
1	Vestibule	80	2	H	Walk-off mats to meet LEED	Supplemntal heating		L		-
2	Reception	300	1,3,4	H	Reception desk and waiting room chairs for 7 people		Daylight	L		- Welcoming
3	Breakroom	175	2,10	H	Counter space, cabinets	Sink, EnergyStar refridgerator	Daylight + natural ventilation	M		- Bright colors, View to River
4	Copy Room	200	2,8	H	Counter space, cabinets	Copier		M		-
5	Restrooms (2)	130	2,8	L	Counters for sinks	Low-flow sinks, dual-flush toilets - rainwater-fed.	Daylight + natural ventilation special	H	Sound insulation	
6	Private Office (2@150)	300	2	L	Desk, desk chair, 2 guest chairs, credenza	Plumbing, HVAC, lighting, equipment	Daylight + natural ventilation special	H	Sound insulation	- Views to outdoors
7	Open Offices (7 @ 80 sq. ft.)	560	3,4	M	Desk, desk chair, 1 guest chairs, systems furniture	Plumbing, HVAC, lighting, equipment	Daylight + natural ventilation special	M	Low partitions high enough to block sounds	- Views to outdoors
8	Flex Space	500	8			See Client-Specific Requirements				"
9	Small Conference Room	200	7,2	M	Conference table with chairs	Audiovisual	Daylight + natural ventilation special	M	Sound insulation	- Views to outdoors
10	Special Function (varies)	1000	2,3,5			See Client-Specific Requirements				
11	Mechanical	50	-	L	-	Electric panel, inverters for solar array		H	Sound insulation	-
12	Storage	50	-		Janitor storage shelves			H		-
	Subtotal Sq. Ft.	3,545							-	-
	Circulation @35%	1,240				-	-		-	-
	Total Sq. Ft.	4,785				-	-			-

Special Function: Cigar Bar

The project includes a 1,000-square-foot bar, which includes informal seating areas, a small wet bar, and display area for cigars. The space must be connected to the main building so that restrooms can be accessed. The special function can have its own entrance, or it can share an entrance with the office space. It can share a vestibule. The office space needs to be secured in the evening.

Client-Specific Requirements

The requirements below will help to guide the design. Depending on your level of design experience, you may not be able to meet every requirement perfectly. That is acceptable.

- The client has sophisticated computer equipment that runs 24/7 and requires uninterrupted power.
- The client will own and control all utilities for the building.
- The client is interested in net-zero buildings.
- The client has determined that adding two more paying tenants (2,000 feet of total lease space) can offset a good portion of the mortgage costs.

Guiding Principles

The client has decided that energy efficiency is the most important design principle because they are most concerned with fighting climate change. The other guiding principles are still in effect and should influence the design as well.

- **Design the most energy-efficient project possible**.
- Integrate the project with the surrounding ecology.
- Be a vital partner in a strong community.
- Infuse a sense of beauty into every decision.

Client B: The Audubon Society

The Audubon Society is a nonprofit advocacy group that works on behalf of the natural world to protect local ecologies. The Audubon Society space is comprised of typical office space with open and closed offices, a reception area, a small conference room, and a break-out room.

Special Function: Nature Interpretive Space

The project includes a 1,000-square-foot nature interpretive space, which includes informal seating areas, a wall with environmental graphics, and some three-dimensional exhibits that illustrate the local ecology. The space must be connected to the main building so that restrooms can be accessed. The special function can have its own entrance, or it can share an entrance with the office space. It can share a vestibule. The office space needs to be secured in the evening.

Client-Specific Requirements

The requirements below will help to guide the design. Depending on your level of design experience, you may not be able to meet every requirement perfectly. That is acceptable.

- The client wants an outdoor classroom.
- A member gave money for a memorial garden in her mother's name.
- They were awarded a $50,000 grant for a demonstration water project as part of the new building.
- The program director uses a wheelchair.

Guiding Principles

The client has decided that integrating the project with the surrounding ecology is the most important design principle because they are most concerned with respecting the natural environment. The other guiding principles are still in effect and should influence the design as well.

- Design the most energy-efficient project possible.
- **Integrate the project with the surrounding ecology.**
- Be a vital partner in a strong community.
- Infuse a sense of beauty into every decision.

Client C: Intercultural Family Services, Inc.

Intercultural Family Services, Inc., is a non-profit advocacy group that works on behalf of citizens who are in distress. This social services agency spatial requirements include typical office space with open and closed offices, a reception area, a small conference room, and a break-out room.

Special Function: Training Space

The project includes a 1,000-square-foot multipurpose space that is primarily used as a job training space to provide valuable knowledge and skills for those in need. The special function must be able to access the restrooms in the main building. The special function may have its own entrance, or it can share an entrance with the office space. It may also share a vestibule. The office space must have the ability to be secured independent of the special function space.

Client-Specific Requirements

The requirements below will help to guide the design. Depending on your level of design experience, you may not be able to meet every requirement perfectly. That is acceptable.

- The client wants their building to be an accessible community resource.
- Most of their clients come with children and family members.

- Many of their clients have disabilities, and some have limited English language skills.
- Because client dignity and privacy are very important, the client wants to add three private family meeting rooms.

Guiding Principles

The client has decided that being a vital partner in the community is the most important design principle because they are most concerned with supporting the community. The other guiding principles are still in effect and should influence the design as well.

- Design the most energy-efficient project possible.
- Integrate the project with the surrounding ecology.
- **Be a vital partner in a strong community.**
- Infuse a sense of beauty into every decision.

Client D: Art Alliance

The Art Alliance is a non-profit advocacy group that promotes the adoption of the arts and arts-based education in the local community. The Art Alliance is comprised of typical office spaces with open and closed offices, a reception area, a small conference room, and a break-out room.

Special Function: Art Gallery

The project includes a 1,000-square-foot gallery, featuring display walls for paintings as well as pedestals for sculptures, and a small informal seating area. The space must be connected to the main building for restroom access. The special function can have its own entrance, or it can share an entrance with the office space. It can share a vestibule. The office space needs to be secured in the evening.

Client-Specific Requirements

The requirements below will help to guide the design. Depending on your level of design experience, you may not be able to meet every requirement perfectly. That is acceptable.

- The program runs evening and afterschool art classes for students in grades 6–12. Two classes usually run concurrently.
- The art alliance received funding to create a computer lab.
- The client wants a performance space.

The client has decided that infusing every decision with a sense of beauty is the most important design principle because they are most concerned promoting beauty in the community, so the building itself should exemplify the standard of beauty that is promoted by the organization. The other guiding principles are still in effect and should influence the design as well.

- Design the most energy-efficient project possible.
- Integrate the project with the surrounding ecology.
- Be a vital partner in a strong community.
- **Infuse a sense of beauty into every decision**.

CHOICE 2: SITE SELECTION AND MACRO CLIMATE

The site selection for the exercise will have a "generic" site configuration (Figure 15.1), as well as actual locations in real places within the selected region (Table 15.3). Links are provided for each of these locations in the companion website. Even if the generic site is chosen, the links will provide a good sense of the architectural and ecological contexts for the project. The actual sites have a different configuration

Sustainable Design Basics: Site Plan

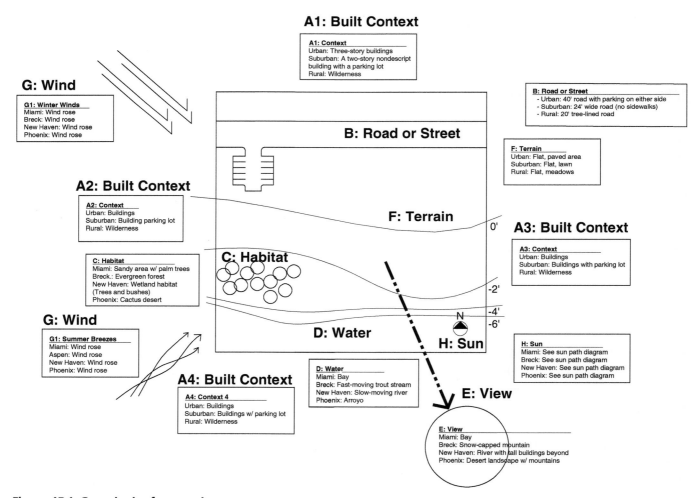

Figure 15.1 Generic site for exercises

Source: Rob Fleming

TABLE 15.3 SPECIFIC SITES IN DIFFERENT CLIMATES.

SITE A: MIAMI, FLORIDA (HOT AND HUMID)

Urban Site	Suburban Site	Rural Site
A beachfront property just off the main strip of art deco buildings	Suburban beachfront site	Beachfront site north of Miami
Location: **25°48'33.5"N** **80°07'21.1"W**	Location: **25°57'30.3"N** **80°07'09.8"W**	Location: **26°02'16.9"N** **80°06'50.7"W**

SITE B: NEW LONDON, CONNECTICUT (WARM, TEMPERATE, CONTINENTAL)

Urban Site	Suburban Site	Rural Site
Existing warehouse to the left and parking lots to the right. Views to a harbor and bay to the south.	View to the ocean on the south and scattered buildings to the north south and west. A road to the north allows access to the site	Heavily wooded area overlooking a lake. There is a country road to the north that allows access to the site.
Location: **41°21'01.6"N** **72°05'52.4"W**	Location: **41°18'03.3"N** **72°07'57.0"W**	Location: **41°26'28.5"N** **72°12'19.9"W**

SITE C: BRECKENRIDGE, COLORADO (CONTINENTAL, SUBARCTIC)

Urban Site	Suburban Site	Rural Site
Urban site near the center of town	Forested suburban site	Mountaintop site
Location: **39°28'31.5"N** **106°02'38.5"W**	Location: **39°47'61.01"N** **106°03'04.67"W**	Location: **39°49'00.99"N** **106°00'30.69"W**

Site D: PHOENIX, ARIZONA (SUBTROPICAL DESERT)

Urban Site	Suburban Site	Rural Site
Urban, industrial site	Scottsdale suburbs, near Taliesin West Scottsdale, Arizona, is a suburban community to the north of Phoenix. It is a community of typical suburban homes.	Desert site north of Phoenix
Location: **33°26'40.8"N** **112°05'07.1"W**	Location: **33°36'14.9"N** **111°50'14.0"W**	Location: **33°44'27.0"N** **111°41'46.4"W**

Source: Rob Fleming

than the generic site shown below. The zoning and building code for each site must be throughly researched. Chapter 3 contains important information that will help to understand the differences between each climate.

CHOICE 3: MACRO CONTEXT DETAILS

The settlement patterns of a particular site are a strong driver of design decisions. The choice between urban, suburban or rural contexts will include many factors including architectural context, infrastructure, major amenities and other variables. In the generic site, (Figure 15.1), these elements are noted. In the specific sites, google maps and google earth can be used to study the context of the area. It is important to remember that the suburban, urban and rural contexts are simplifications of the context of a particular site. and that all contexts are different and may contain a mix of urban and suburban or a mix of rural and suburban. The purpose of the types it help guide thinking around some basic design approaches that make sense within that context. Feel free to develop a more nuanced and sophisticated description of the context for your site. Chapter 3 contains important information that will help to understand the differences between each climate.

CHOICE 4: NEW BUILDING OR EXISTING BUILDING

Option A: New Construction

The type of new construction is defined in the design process during the building envelope step in the process. Here are some ground rules:

- The new building must fit within the specified setbacks.
- The new building will be one story tall and there will be no basement.
- The building may be broken into smaller buildings.
- All new construction must meet ADA requirements.

Option B: Existing Building

The existing building (Figure 15.2) is a 1926 industrial building. The location and orientation of the existing building is indicated on the site plans shown in dashed lines, with the front of the building indicated. Respect property boundaries and local zoning and building codes, including building setbacks. The existing building can be modified within these parameters:

- Clerestories, roof monitors, and skylights may be added.
- Windows and doors may be added or removed.
- Columns may not be removed.
- No spaces may be added to the form of the building.
- The building cannot be moved on the site.

The existing building was originally built in 1926 as a gas station and mechanic garage with double brick walls with no insulation. The original windows were steel frame with single pane glass. There is a structural steel grid, with the roof being supported with decorative metal trusses, bearing on the exterior walls. There are no interior bearing walls.

The floor is reinforced concrete, 12 inches thick, designed to support the heavy machinery. The plate height at the exterior walls is 18 feet. The roof has a 6/12 slope. The windows are 10 feet 6 inches high, with a sill height of 2 feet 6 inches. The building has a ground floor at the rear section of the building with a 10-foot ceiling height. The original garage doors have been filled in with a large window for retail and entrance doors to accommodate the possibility of three separate tenants.

Existing building facts
- Originally built in 1926 as a gas station and mechanic garage.
- Structural steel grid as shown. No interior bearing walls.

 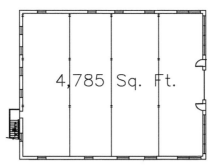 

Figure 15.2 Existing building drawings
Source: Saglinda Roberts

- Exterior walls are double-layer brick with air space with a plate height of 18 feet.
- Floors are reinforced concrete, 1 foot thick, designed to support the weight of machinery.
- Full ground floor for half of floor plan; other areas considered crawl space with approximately 6 feet of head room.
- Ground floor has 10-foot ceiling height, with 11-foot floor to floor and concrete masonry unit walls.
- Roof is 6/12 slope currently with asphalt shingles supported with decorative metal trusses.
- Original windows were steel frame with single-pane glass, replaced with low-E double-hung windows. Windows are 10 feet 6 inches high and have sill height of 2 feet 6 inches.
- Garage doors in front of the building were replaced with large display windows and entrance door, along with a central entrance to the building, making it easy to have three separate tenants.

EXERCISES

The steps listed here are explained in an abbreviated format below. The detailed assignments and video tutorials are available on the companion website. Additional documents needed to complete the exercises are available on the companion website. It is important to remember not to skip any steps.

- Blank matrices
- Site plans of the various sites in various digital formats
- Blank PowerPoint final presentation template

Step 1: Context
- Complete Step 1A: Project Information.
- Complete Step 1B: Guiding Principles. (If this has already been completed. Feel free to alter the principles or add new ones. Enter them into the Guiding Principles matrix.)
- Complete Step 1C: Macro Context and Micro Context.
- Complete Step 1D: Site Inventory and Analysis.

Step 2: Pre-Planning

- Complete Step 2A: Research and Case Studies.
- Complete Step 2B: Project Goals.
- Complete Step 2C: Design Criteria.
- Complete Step 2D: Spatial Relationships.

Step 3: Design

- Complete Step 3A: Preliminary Design.
  - Location, orientation, block plan, space/shape plan, validation, design synthesis
- Complete Step 3B: Passive Design.
  - Passive heating, cooling, and ventilation, daylighting, water conservation, validation, design synthesis
- Complete Step 3C: Building Envelope.
  - Structure/foundation, walls, windows, roof, validation, design synthesis
- Complete Step 3D: Green Materials.
- Complete Step 3E: Beyond the Basics: Active Systems (Optional).
  - Power, artificial lighting, plumbing, PV panel sizing

Step 4: Design Resolution

- Complete Step 4A: Design Synthesis.
- Complete Step 4B: Final Design Validation.
- Complete Step 4C: Presenting the Project.

Typically, designers will jump to design part of the project without much consideration of the context and climate. The purpose of this book is to introduce a new sense of rigor in the design process in order to reach a net-zero design solution.

APPENDIX A

Demonstration Project Program, Climate, and Context Resources

STEP 1A: PROJECT INTRODUCTION

University Career Counseling Center Program Requirements

The University Career Counseling Center (UCCC) is meant to become an integral part of a medium-size state-supported university and will provide curriculum and career counseling for all levels of students and graduates seeking employment opportunities. It plays a primary role in each of the institution's programs and also serves the university's other three branches in other parts of the state. The UCCC will conduct seminar-type instruction for college and high school educators and councilors with the conference spaces being available for community or private events.

The bulk of the center's traffic is from the consistent flow of students to the director, assistant director and the interview councilors will see multiple visitors each day either in pairs or alone. Several times each week groups ranging from 6 to 40 people come for conferences, training, lectures, group counseling, community events or private meetings during the day or at night. There is a need for a kitchen area to serve as a break room and for preparation or warming for any catered functions. The kitchen and restrooms need to be accessible during non-business hours or without having to access the business spaces. There are frequent out of town visitor for business and private functions that require having a one-bedroom apartment on site.

Special Requirements
- The general atmosphere should reflect and emulate real-world professional experience.
- Exterior views, daylight, and natural elements are to be optimized.

- All areas of the facility and site are to be designed with universal design principles and be compliant with ADA standards.
- The director's office, conference room, and guest apartments require acoustic privacy
- The guest apartment should have a residential quality and avoid the chain hotel feel. The guest apartment should have a private entrance.
- The director, assistant director, and administrative assistant work closely together. Locate the interview stations with convenient access the reception area.

Vestibule
1. Walk off mats
2. Independent heating/cooling system
3. Serve the office and conference area

Reception area
1. The reception station shall include an uninterrupted work surface of at least 12 sq. ft.; a transaction surface for visitors, 40" AFF; a flat screen monitor, keyboard tray, and a small desktop printer; two box/file drawer pedestals; a small console telephone; and a task chair.
2. Immediately adjacent to the station, 12 lin. ft. of lateral files, and a fax machine (18" w × 16" d × 9" h) must be accommodated.
3. Guest seating for five to six visitors.
4. Wall-hung literature rack (40" w × 60" h × 5" d), easily accessible by visitors.

Interview stations (seven at approx. 80 sq. ft. each)
1. Stations shall be created through the use of systems furniture work surfaces, acoustic partition panels, and storage elements; panel height shall not exceed 65".
2. Primary work surface and return shall provide a combined surface of 18 to 20 sq. ft. per station.
3. Provide two box/file drawer pedestals; a minimum of 4 lin. ft. of overhead storage bin; and a flat screen monitor, keyboard tray, and a small desktop printer per station.
4. One operational task chair and one guest chair per station.
5. A minimum of 75 lin. ft. of lateral files shall be accessible to all four stations.
6. Without creating "offices," each station should use acoustic partition panels to create a sense of separateness and privacy from the other stations.

Private office (2 at approx. 150 sq. ft.)
1. A comfortable, no-frills, executive office, consistent with institutional standards.
2. An executive desk 6' long with credenza. Work area is to accommodate a flat screen monitor, keyboard, and a small desktop printer.
3. An executive swivel-tilt desk chair and two guest pull-up chairs.
4. Minimum of 20 lin. ft. of book/artifact shelving, 12" d.

Small conference room (approx. 150 sq. ft.)
1. Table and chairs for four
2. Tackable surface wall
3. Whiteboard wall

Copy room/work area (approx. 200 sq. ft.)

1. Freestanding copier (44″ w × 27″ d × 38" h), requiring 54" w space.
2. Storage cabinet, 36″ w x 18" d × 78″ h.
3. Min. 6 lin. ft. of lateral files.

Commons; informal meeting space (approx. 500 sq. ft.)

1. Comfortable lounge seating
2. Proximity to interview stations
3. Central location to offices
4. Daylighting
5. Views and natural elements

Seminar room (approx. 1000 sq. ft.)

1. Multipurpose presentation, conference, and encounter activities, with flexible arrangement potential. Possible subdivision into 2 distinct spaces with moveable partitions.
2. Provide direct access from entrance vestibule when the space is one room or divided.
3. Provide access to outdoor areas.
4. Provide classroom seating for 20, conference or seminar seating for 12 at one central table, or (through the use of a folding partition) two small conference rooms, each to seat at least six at a central table.
5. Beverage serving surface, plus paper and pencil storage below it; this should be available when the room is set up as one large space or as two small spaces.
6. Provide storage for tables and chairs that are not in use.
7. Projection screens or large format monitors for use when the room is set as one or when divided into two separate conference rooms
8. Visuals board placed for use when the room is set as one large space.
9. Tackable wall surface, min. 8 lin. ft. located for use when the room is set as one large space.
10. Acoustic privacy
11. Proved daylighting and views and incorporate room darkening for presentations when required

Public restrooms (2, total approx. 130 sq. ft.)

1. Unisex private bathrooms
2. Toilet, sink, changing table in each
3. ADA-compliant
4. Accessible to office areas and conference space. Access during non-office hours is required.

Kitchen area for daily staff use and support of seminar room activities.

1. Provide a minimum of 15 sq. ft. of work counter (not including sink) plus base and overhead cabinets.
2. Provide a double-burner commercial coffee urn, sink, under-cabinet microwave, 30′full-size refrigerator.

Break room (approx. 175 sq. ft.)

1. For daily staff use and support of seminar room activities.

Mechanical room (approx. 150 sq. ft.)
1. Hot water heater, heating system, electric panel
2. Conditioned, interior building location

Storage (approx. 200 sq. ft.)
1. Janitors Sink
2. High capacity, heavyweight shelving

One-bedroom apartment (approx. 520 sq. ft.)
1. Living area: comfortable lounge seating for four or five, coffee table for informal serving, and entertainment center (TV, VCR, music) with book/artifacts shelving.
2. Dining area: minimal in size; can be part of living area or kitchen; table surface to double as desk/work surface.
3. Kitchen: small but serviceable for occasional food preparation, with sink, small four-burner range/oven (20″ to 24″ w), and adequate countertop space and cabinets.
4. Separate bedroom for a queen-size bed, night table, and lamp, 3 to 4 lin. ft. of closet space, drawer storage, and space for a luggage rack.
5. Bathroom: basic but comfortable apartment bathroom, with lavatory, toilet, and tub or stall shower, plus small linen closet or cabinet.

Building site requirements
1. Parking lot
2. Entry plaza and public greenspace area
3. Exterior event and working space
4. Views
5. Water management and harvesting
6. Daylighting and shading strategies
7. Land and indigenous species restoration

STEP 1C MACRO AND MICRO CONTEXT

Regional Scale Information, Philadelphia, PA 19129
- The city of Philadelphia was founded in 1682 by William Penn on land peacefully ceded by the Lenape.
- Designed to incorporate green space within the integrated residential and commercial areas of the city.
- Originally settled by those seeking religious freedom. It grew into a leading political and economic center in the nineteenth and twentieth centuries.
- It was the first capital of the United States between 1790 and 1800. Was the seat of power during the Revolutionary War. Independence Hall is the site of the signing of the Declaration of Independence.
- Many areas still have a shared sewer and stormwater management system, which can cause contamination during heavy storms.
- Stormwater management is now a serious concern.
- Located along the Delaware River and the southeastern corner of Pennsylvania.
- Known as the "City of Brotherly Love."

- Extensive park system that runs from center city to the outer reaches of the surrounding suburbs.
- Many sustainable initiatives are sponsored by local and city government agencies.
- Member of the Biophilic Cities Project.

District Scale Information, East Falls, Philadelphia 19129
4300-38 Ridge Avenue
Corner of Ridge Avenue and Calumet Street

Performance Perspective

Location
Coordinates 40.009866, latitude -75.19666 longitude
Population: 14,401

Demographics
- Caucasian: 72.06%
- African American: 19.98%
- Asian: 4.79%
- Hispanic -2.58%
- Median age for males: 30.2
- Median age for women: 33
- 51.3% of households are families

Education Statistics
- 51% college graduates
- 23% college graduates with advanced degree
- 13.4% currently enrolled in college

Residential Property Ownership:
- 52% Rentals
- 38% Owned
- 64% of properties row or attached homes

Transportation
- 19.4% ride train or public transportation
- 58.4% drive individual vehicles
- 8.5% carpool
- Average number of vehicles per household: 1.4

Safety
Above-average safety rating

Environmental Context
- Historically an industrial community that was known for textiles and pharmaceutical manufacturing
- Recently redeveloped urban community known for education, medical and technical developments
- Shops and restaurants

Systems Perspective

Adjacent to Fairmount and Wissahickon Park with extensive wildlife habitat

Adjacent to Schuylkill River and Schuylkill Heritage Trail that runs from the East Falls Bridge east to the Philadelphia Museum of Art, and west toward and beyond the Montgomery County line.

Part of Wissahickon watershed, with extensive watershed protections

In 100-year flood zone

Close connection to surrounding community parks and wildlife corridors

Technical:
- Infrastructure
- Utilities
- Communications
- Transit
- Roadways

Good air flow from the river and surrounding hills

Excellent access to public transportation, regional railroad and bus system.

No existing vegetation and limited natural features on the building site due to previous development.

Cultures Perspective

Originally a Native American settlement of the Lena Lenape.

East Falls community name is derived from its location east of the Falls of the Schuylkill. Construction of river dams submerged the original falls after 1822.

Historically served as industrial center, which influences the form of the existing structures.

Community celebrates a rich history of the area and seeks to preserve it along with its close ties to the river.

Largely a residential community adjacent to Fairmount Park.

Surrounding communities include Manayunk and Roxborough to the northwest, Germantown to the northeast, Tioga to the east, Allegheny West to the south and Bala and Parkside to the southwest.

A recent resurgence of the area, with multiple new housing and retail spaces along with many new restaurants.

Local historic bridges, particularly the Falls River Bridge, adjacent to the site, are cultural landmarks for the community.

Art and Community Opportunities
- Community theater
- Art centers
- Artist and glass-blowing studios
- Two recreation centers
- Library provides programming for toddlers, students, seniors
- Universities within proximity to the site: Jefferson University, Drexel University College of Medicine

Annual Events and Traditions
- International Pro Bike Race viewing
- Philadelphia Marathon
- Dance on the Falls Bridge

Resident demographics: Highly educated, middle-income community. Residents are very active in community and city politics.

Kelly Drive runs adjacent to the Schuylkill River from East Falls to Center City Philadelphia. The drive is named to honor John B. Kelly Jr., an East Falls resident, Philadelphia councilman, son of John B. Kelly (3x Olympic rower and gold medalist) and brother to the American actress Grace Kelly, later to become Princess Grace of Monaco. The Kelly family lived in the East Falls neighborhood in the 1960s.

Experience Perspective

The beauty and natural elements of the river, Fairmont Park and the Heritage Trail are prominent features in the neighborhood.

Strong historic aesthetic of the existing structures in the neighborhood. Sense of history and connection to past is valued.

Park-adjacent location inspires physical activity on local recreation trails and access to the river for fishing and boating.

Multiple historic bridges, natural beauty of the adjacent river and park, and urban village-like charm contribute to the neighborhood character.

Natural beauty from the river, bridges, and green space along the river.
- Favorable views from the south side and north corner of the site.
- Unfavorable view on Calumet, and adjacent building on the west.
- Multiple bridges lend a sculptural and industrial feel to the area.

Exceptional views toward the river and bridges. Optimal views towards East Falls Bridge, Schuylkill River and Philadelphia skyline.

High energy, commercial corridor due to pedestrian, retail, and restaurant activity and local and commuter vehicle traffic.

While the surrounding community is rich in aesthetic, historic, or natural features, the current site is enclosed with metal cyclone fencing. It is an existing asphalt parking lot with a one-story masonry block building that feels disconnected from nature.

Kelly Drive and Ridge Avenue constrain the site and are heavily traveled commuter roads. Rush hour traffic produces noise and unpleasant traffic odors that can be distracting.

Project Information

Site Scale, 4300-38 Ridge Avenue, Philadelphia 19129
Coordinates: 40.009866 latitude, -75.19666 longitude
Corner of Ridge Avenue and Calumet Street, Philadelphia PA 19129.
Lot size: 73,370 sq. ft. or 1.6-acre site
Sidewalks on two sides, Kelly Drive and Ridge Avenue
Currently a large vacant lot with areas of concrete paving a small masonry structure

Zoning = CMX-3, commercial mixed-use district (mixed use: community commercial and residential)

- Maximum occupied area: intermediate 79%, corner 80%
- Minimum rront yard depth: not applicable
- Minimum side yard: 8 ft. if used for building with dwelling units
- Minimum rear yard: not applicable
- Maximum floor area ratio (FAR): 500% up to an additional 300% with bonuses

Part of the site is in a 100-year flood zone.

Adjacent to recreational trail, river, and park.

Views of the waterways, parks and wildlife corridors on the southeastern and southwestern sides.

Technical: infrastructure, utilities, communications, close to transportation.

Adjacent to Kelly Drive, with 40,000 vehicles during rush hour.

Ecosystem restoration of the site required.

STEP 1D SITE INVENTORY AND ANALYSIS

Site Conditions

Performance Perspective

Temperate climate: moderate seasonality with hot, humid summers, mild winters, and year-round precipitation

Annual rainfall: 4.4 inches per year; number of wet days: 121; percentage of sunny to cloudy daylight hours: 60(40)

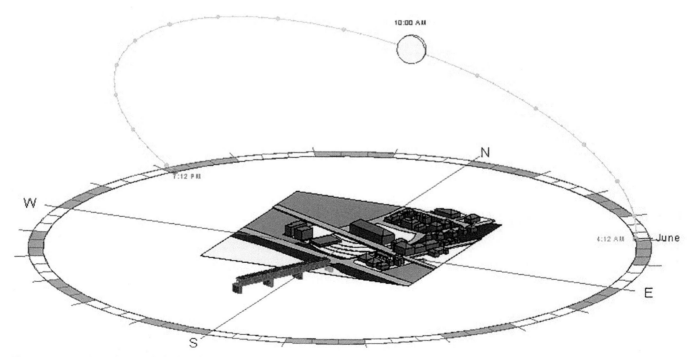

Figure A.1 Solar Chart, Philadelphia Pennsylvania

Illustration created by authors with Revit Autoivedesk software

Annual snowfall: 23 Inches

Annual temperatures: average high 64.7 F | average low: 47 F

Strong sunlight potential on the southern and southwestern sides

Site Information

- Topography
    - Mildly sloping terrain partially in 100-year flood plain.
    - Soil composition
    - Clay soil polluted from earlier chemical manufacturing building site.
- Water
    - The selected site is adjacent to the Schuylkill river.
    - Water travels SE across site from Ridge Avenue towards the river or Kelly Drive
- Vegetation
    - Deciduous forest biome: Alleghany Ridge Piedmont, Atlantic Coastal Plain
- Restoration on site required from past construction/uses

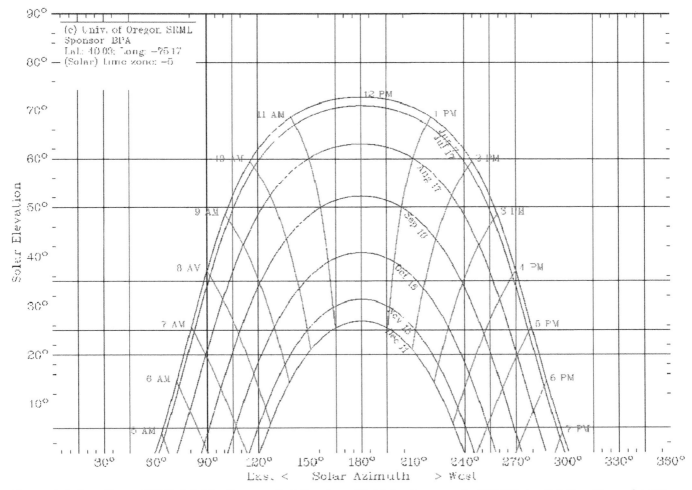

Figure A.2 Sun Chart of Philadelphia, Summer Solstice: June 21; highest sun angle: 74°. Winter Solstice: December 21; highest sun angle, 26°. Water slopes primarily in the SW direction across the site from Ridge Avenue, toward the Schuylkill River.

Created by authors with software from University of Oregon. Solar Radiation Monitoring Laboratory, Sun Path Chart Program: http://solardat. uoregon.edu/SunChartProgram.html

Winter cold winds blow from west/northwest (December)

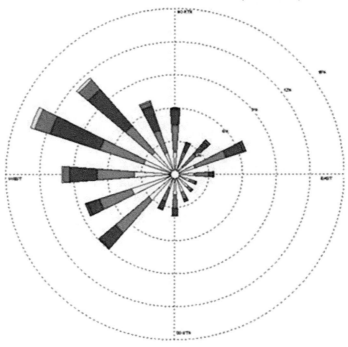

Summer warm winds blow from southwest to northeast (July)

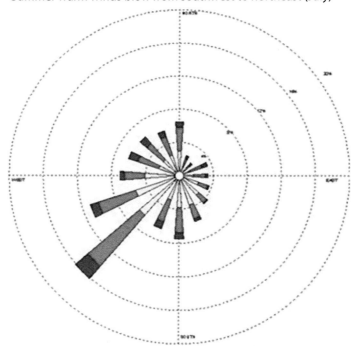

Figure A.3 Wind Rose, Philadelphia PA 19129. Summer wind direction: southwest; average speed 8.2 mph; prevalent from southwest. Winter wind direction: northwest; average speed 10.8 mph; prevalent from northwest

Source: National Resource Conservation Service, National Water and Climate Center. https://www.wcc.nrcs.usda.gov/ftpref/downloads/climate/windrose/pennsylvania/philadelphia/

Systems Perspective

Part of the Delaware River Watershed. Water from storms can enter the Delaware watershed via streams, culverts, underground piping or site drainage from open land or roadways. Water on the site runs diagonally to the southwest.

Philadelphia has a large majority of the city with combined sewer and stormwater management. Mitigating storm water has ecological and monetary advantages.

The site is between Fairmount and Wissahickon parks, which act as bio-diverse habitat. East Falls joins these two areas. Site restoration of Flora and Fauna should be a priority to mitigate changes from past development.

Part of the site is located in a 100-year flood zone.

Transportation: Surrounded on three sides by heavy traffic, both vehicular and pedestrian. Close access to buses and trains for ready public transportation.

- Heavy vehicle traffic on Kelly Avenue on the south side of the site.
- Road noise should be mitigated for occupants.
- Green space should be located away from heavy traffic for safety.
- Clear traffic signals and crossing areas need to be delineated for safety.

Great potential for passive airflow, solar gain, shading, and photovoltaic harvesting. Assess existing site conditions and incorporate into new building configuration.

Cultures Perspective

Historically, the land of the site was previously occupied by the Lenape Native American Tribe before the formation of Philadelphia in 1682.

In colonial times, East Falls was the highest point on the river navigable by boats. It was a transfer point to the Native American path and colonial roadways.

In the 1700s East Falls was farmland. During the Revolutionary War it was headquarters for General George Washington and there were several battles on both sides of the river.

In 1859 the East Falls Bridge was built. In 1872 the Fairmount Park Commission was established.

From the early 1800s to the 1940s it was mostly industrial multistory brick buildings.

Many historic buildings remain all over the city. With factories, churches, and industrial buildings still present in the East Falls area. The site is believed to have been part residential and part industrial.

In the late 1950s, the Philadelphia Redevelopment Authority included a new clause in its development contract requiring all building projects to allocate a minimum of one percent of the total construction budget to public art.

In 1984 the Department of Recreation created the Mural Arts Program, an extension of the city's Anti-Graffiti Network. The program is intended to beautify neighborhoods and also provide an outlet for graffiti artists. Today Philadelphia has more public art than any other American city.

East Falls is currently undergoing redevelopment, elevating its local status relative to nearby Manayunk and other local shopping districts in the Philadelphia area.

The Schuylkill River and East Falls Bridge are landmarks that see a lot of recreational activity. Parks and recreational trails run alongside the edge of the Schuylkill River, creating a lively community

The East Falls Community Council (EFCC) represents and advocates for the residents. The East Falls Development Corporation promotes community-based economic development and organizes events throughout the year, such as the East Falls Bridge Dance.

The subject site is adjacent to residential and commercial properties, each with requirements for community connection.

Experience Perspective

Natural beauty from the river, bridges, and green space along the river.
- Favorable views from the south side and north corner of the site.
- Unfavorable view of Calumet, and adjacent building on the west.
- Multiple bridges lend a sculptural and industrial feel to the area.

Exceptional views toward the river and bridges. Optimal views toward East Falls Bridge, Schuylkill River and Philadelphia skyline.

High-energy commercial corridor with pedestrian, retail, and restaurant activity and local and commuter vehicle traffic.

Current site void of aesthetic, historic, or natural features that are prevalent in other areas of the exiting neighborhood. Site feels disconnected from nature.

Noisy with unpleasant odors from heavy motor traffic. Can be distracting.

APPENDIX B

Forms and Matrices

TABLE B.1 PROJECT INFORMATION.

Project Information

Client Name:	
Project Type:	
Site Location:	
Climate Zone:	
Heating or Cooling Dominated:	
Notes:	

Sustainable Design Basics: A methodology for the schematic design of sustainable buildings

TABLE B.2 GUIDING PRINCIPLES MATRIX.

Guiding Principles Matrix					
The Four Perspectives	*Objective/Tangible Aspects*		*Subjective/Intangible Aspects*		
	Performance	**Systems**	**Culture**		**Experience**
Guiding Principle					
Reflections					

Sustainable Design Basics: A methodology for the schematic design of sustainable buildings

Guiding Principles are fundamental truths.
- They are aspirational and inspirational, often expressed as "*I believe*" statements

Project Goals are the desired achievements that are the result of design decisions.
- *They are specific, measurable, actionable, relevant, and time-based.*

TABLE B.3 SITE INVENTORY AND ANALYSIS MATRIX.

Site Inventory and Analysis Matrix

The Four Perspectives	Objective/Tangible Requirements				Subjective/Intangible Requirements			
	Performance		*Systems*		*Culture*		*Experience*	
	Issues	Design Decisions	Issues	Design Decisions	Issues	Design Decisions	Issues	Design Decisions
Macro Scale Global, Regional, and District								
Micro Scale Neighborhood, Site, Building								

Sustainable Design Basics: A methodology for the schematic design of sustainable buildings

TABLE B.4 CASE STUDY MATRIX.

Case Study Matrix

The Four Perspectives	Objective/Tangible Requirements		Subjective/Tangible Requirements	
	Performance	**Systems**	**Culture**	**Experience**
Project Goals & Objectives				
Benchmark				
Metric Category				
Metric				
Metric Performance				
Systems				
Strategies				

Sustainable Design Basics: A methodology for the schematic design of sustainable buildings

BENCHMARK OPTIONS: There are a number of relevant benchmarks to use

Building Codes: choose the most recent

Energy Codes: based on ASHRAE/ANSI standards

EnergyStar: Building energy, water, and waste usage

ASHRAE Standards: 90.1, 62.1, etc. – mostly energy and IAQ specific

Rating Systems: Based on accepted high-performance standards, rating systems by themselves are general benchmarks

- LEED
- Living Building Challenge
- Breeam
- Passive House
- Well Building Standard

METRIC OPTIONS Projects are not limited to these below. Choose metrics appropriate for your project

PERFORMANCE	SYSTEMS	CULTURE	EXPERIENCE
Energy: EUI; kBTU/sf	**Rainwater**: % captured Gals/yr.	**WalkScore**: WalkScore rating	**Views**: % of spaces with views to exterior
Carbon: mtCO2e	Gals. Used	**Transit Accessibility**: # of transit options	
Electricity: kWh/yr.	**Stormwater**: % managed Gals/yr.	**ADA Accessibility**: % of spaces	**Comfort**: % of spaces within comfort parameters
Energy: MMBtu/yr.	Cu.ft/yr.	Accessible	
Lighting: LPD; W/sf.	**Solar**: kWh/yr.	**Inclusivity**: Inclusivity rating	**Acoustics**: % of spaces within acoustic parameter
IAQ: CFM; Cu.ft/min.	**Wind**: kWh/yr.	**Economy**: Cost per sf.	
Water: Potable Gals annually	**Daylight**: % of reg. occupied	**Engagement**: # of stakeholders	**Materials**: % Redlist materials used
	Space daylit	engaged if the design process	
	Ventilation: % of spaces		**Materials**: % recycled, reused salvaged materials
	naturally ventilated		
	Habitat: % of site that supports		**Waste**: % of construction waste recycled
	Habitat		
	Perviousness: % of coverage		**Waste**: % of waste generated annually
	Pervious/impervious		

Inclusivity Rating:

Open to all people – regardless of:	Limited to people – based on:
Race, Age, Orientation, Education, Economics, Affiliation, Location	Race, Age, Orientation, Education, Economics, Affiliation, Location
10	0

TABLE B.5 GOALS AND OBJECTIVES MATRIX.

Goals and Objectives Matrix

The Four Perspectives	*Objective/Tangible Aspects*			*Subjective/Intangible Aspects*			
	PERFORMANCE			**SYSTEMS**	**CULTURE**		**EXPERIENCE**
					Equity Goals	Culture Goals	
Guiding Principles							
Project Goals							
Project Objectives							
Metric Category	Energy	Health and Wellbeing	Water				
Metric							
Benchmarks							
Strategies							

Sustainable Design Basics: A methodology for the schematic design of sustainable buildings

Guiding Principles are fundamental truths
- *They are aspirational and inspirational, often expressed as "I believe" statements*

Project Goals are those things you want to achieve.
- *They are the things that are achievable in the design.*

Project Objectives are actions you want to achieve as a result of design decisions
- *They are specific, measurable, actionable, relevant, and time-based*

Metrics are how you measure achievement of goals
- *They are a standard of measurement used to compare actions*

TABLE B.6 CRITERIA MATRIX: BUILDING INTERIOR.

Criteria Matrix Interiors

The Four Perspectives / Design Criteria		Objective/Tangible Requirements						Subjective/Intangible Requirements			
		PERFORMANCE				SYSTEMS		CULTURE		EXPERIENCE	
Rm #	Room Name	Sq. Ft.	Adjacencies	Acoustics	Furniture Requirements	Active Systems — Specialized heating, cooling, ventilation, plumbing, lighting, equipment only	Passive Systems — List specialized requirements below	Privacy — Need for privacy high/medium/low	Special Cultural Considerations — Image, brand, sense of community	Sense of place — Views, smells, textures, colors, taste, sounds, Special considerations Spatial sense, other intangibles	
1											
2											
3											
4											
5											
6											
7											
8											
9											
10											
11											
12											
Subtotal Sq. Ft.											
Circulation @35%											
Total Sq. Ft											

Sustainable Design Basics: A methodology for the schematic design of sustainable building

TABLE B.7 CRITERIA MATRIX BUILDING AND SITE.

Criteria Matrix Building and Site

		Objective/Tangible Requirements							Subjective/Intangible Requirements						
		PERFORMANCE				**SYSTEMS**		**CULTURE**			**EXPERIENCE**				
The Four Perspectives Design Criteria		SQ. FT.	Adjacencies	Acoustic Levels	Outdoor Furniture Requirements	Infrastructure	Ecological Systems _Habitat, stormwater, plant communities_	Safety Level	Special Cultural Considerations	Image, brand, sense of community, relationship to nature	Sense of place _Views, smells, textures, colors, taste, sounds_	Special considerations _Spatial sense, other intangibles_			
A #	Area														
1															
2															
3															
4															
5															
6															
7															
8															
9															
10															
11															
12															
Subtotal Sq. Ft.															
Total Sq. Ft.															

Sustainable Design Basics: A methodology for the schematic design of sustainable buildings

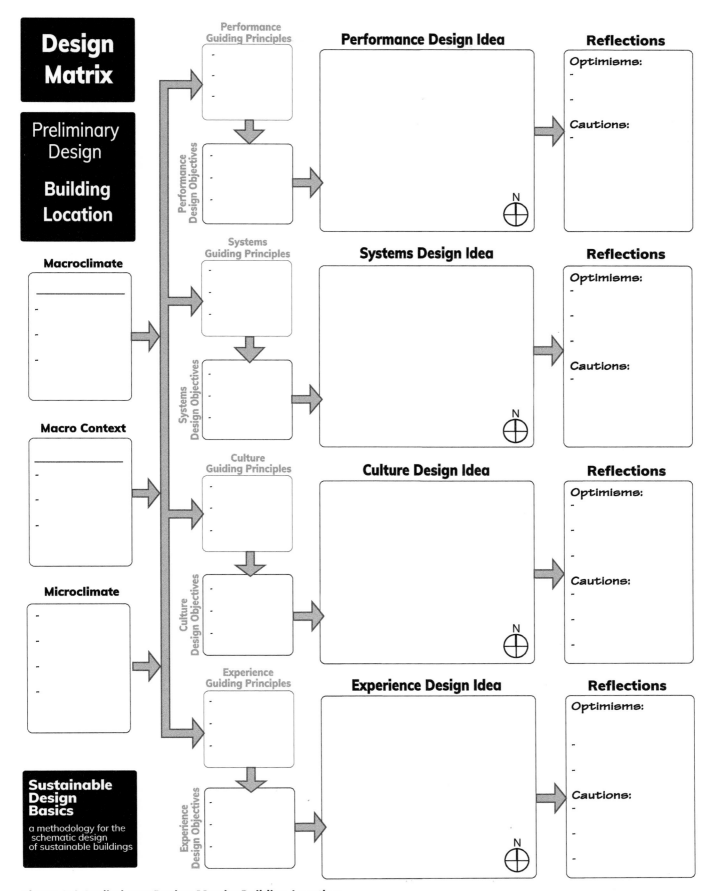

Figure B.1 Preliminary Design Matrix: Building Location

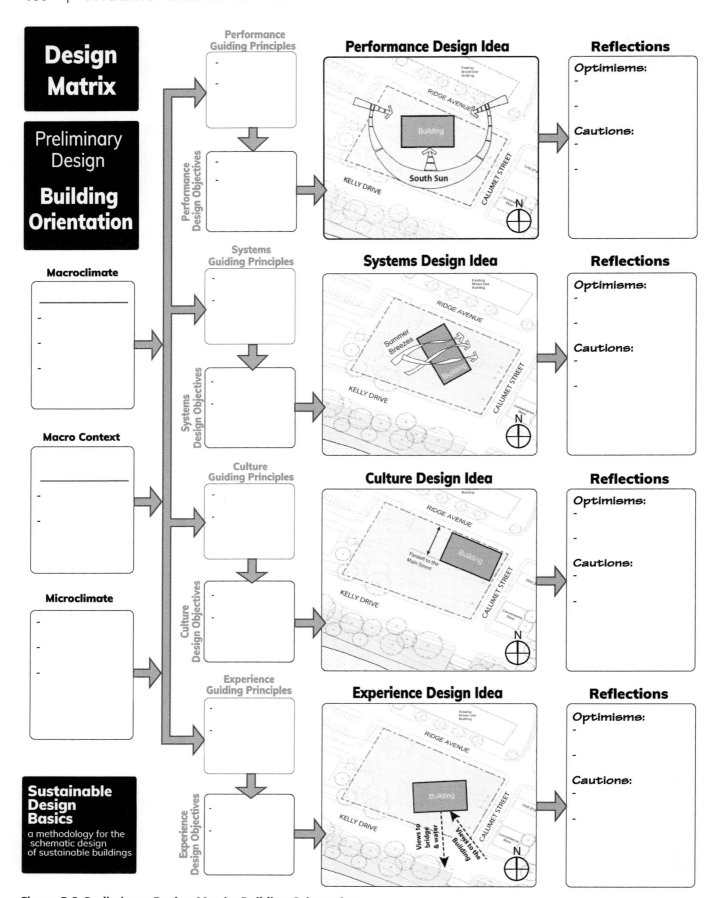

Figure B.2 Preliminary Design Matrix: Building Orientation

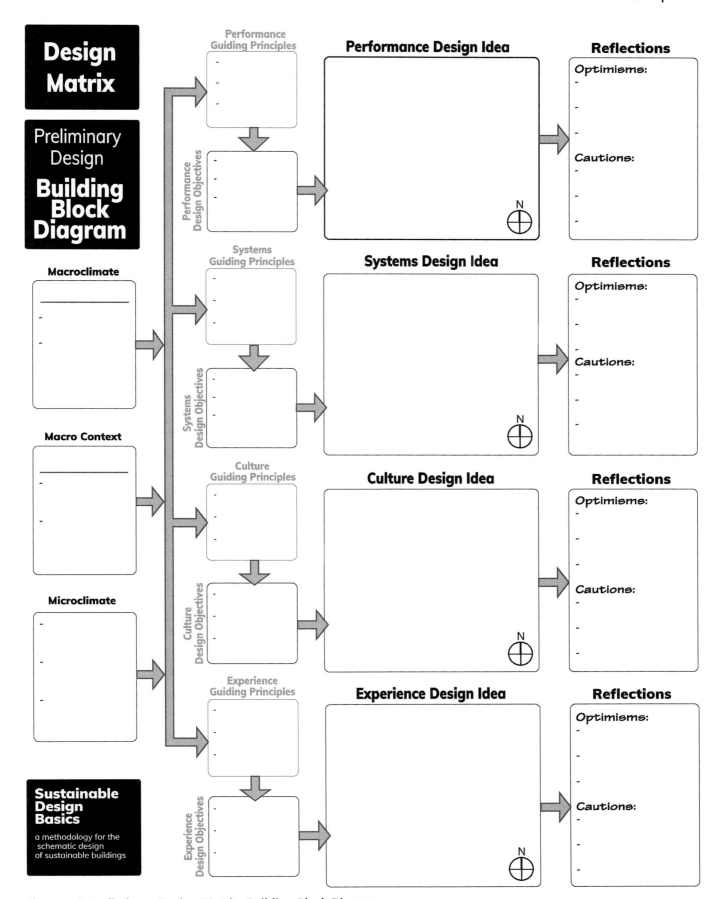

Figure B.3 Preliminary Design Matrix: Building Block Diagram

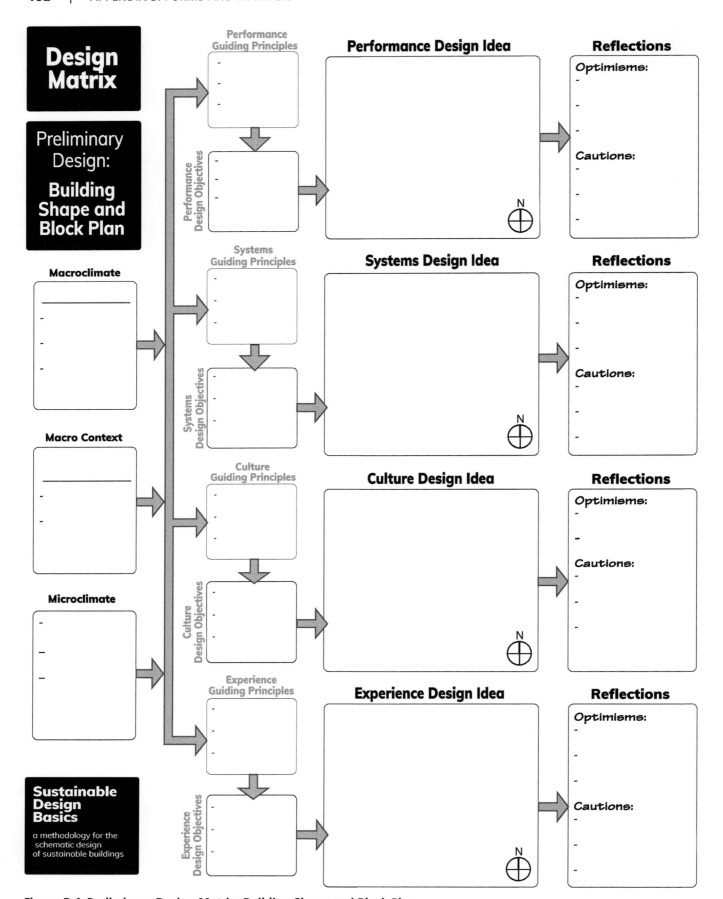

Figure B.4 Preliminary Design Matrix: Building Shape and Block Plan

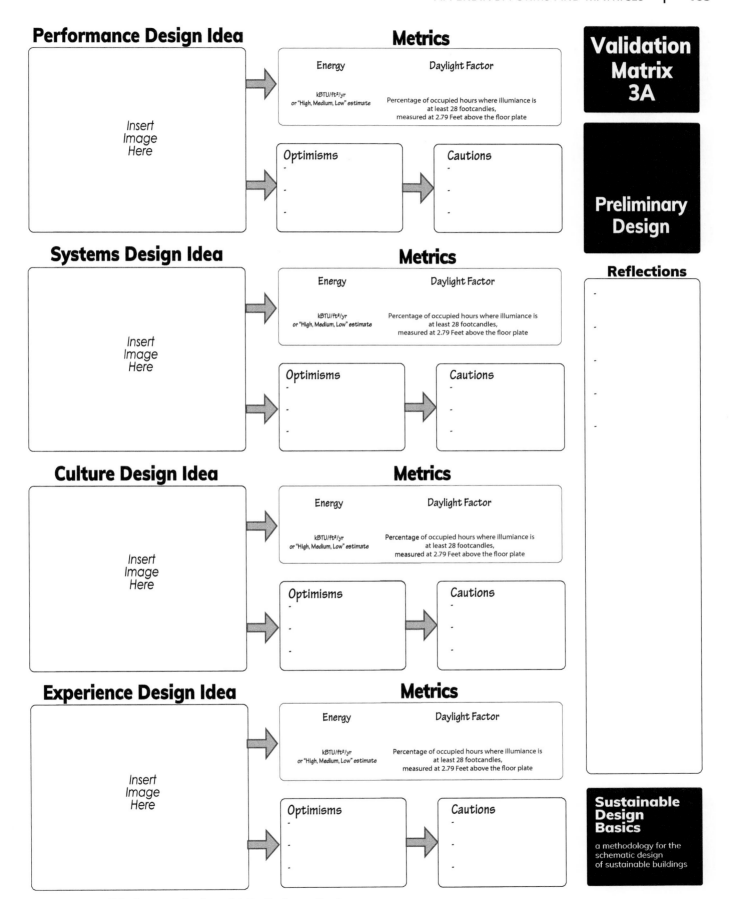

Figure B.5 Validation Matrix: Step 3A Preliminary Design

Design Synthesis 3A

Preliminary Design

Preliminary Design Synthesis

3-D Image(s)

2-D Image(s)

N

Macroclimate

Macro Context

Microclimate

Daylight Study

Reflections

Optimisms:
-
-
-

Cautions:
-
-
-

Sustainable Design Basics

a methodology for the schematic design of sustainable buildings

Energy Use Intensity (EUI)

kBTU/ft²/yr

Daylight Factor

Figure B.6 Design Synthesis: Step 3A Preliminary Design

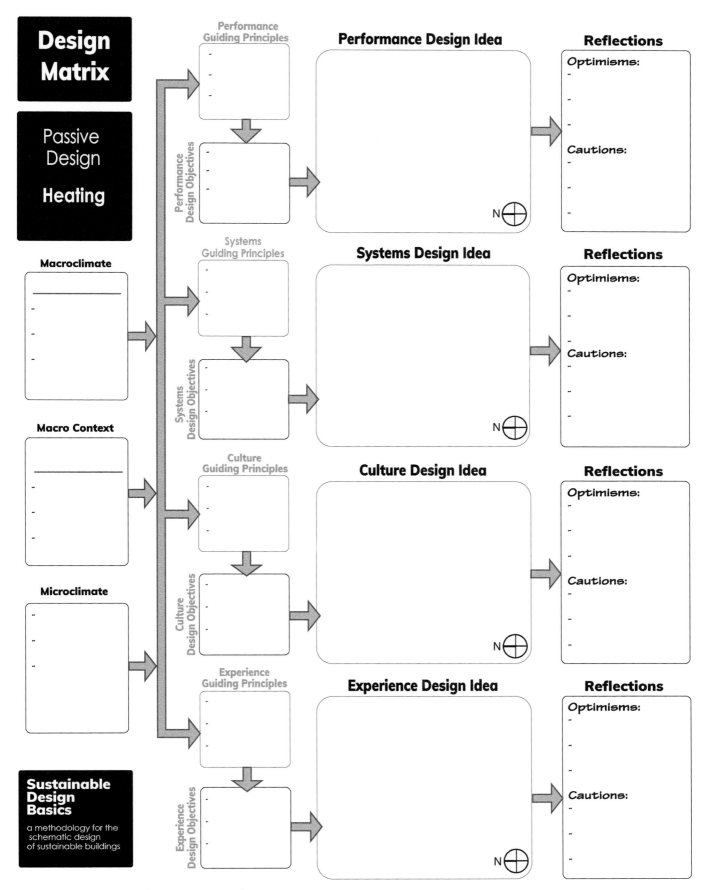

Figure B.7 Passive Design Matrix: Heating

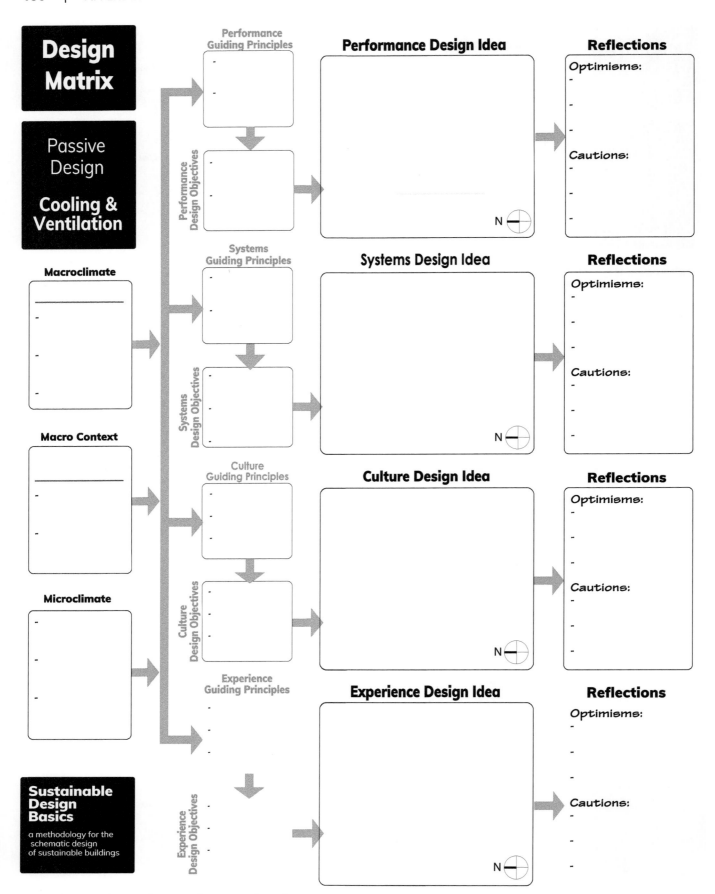

Figure B.8 Passive Design Matrix: Natural Cooling and Ventilation

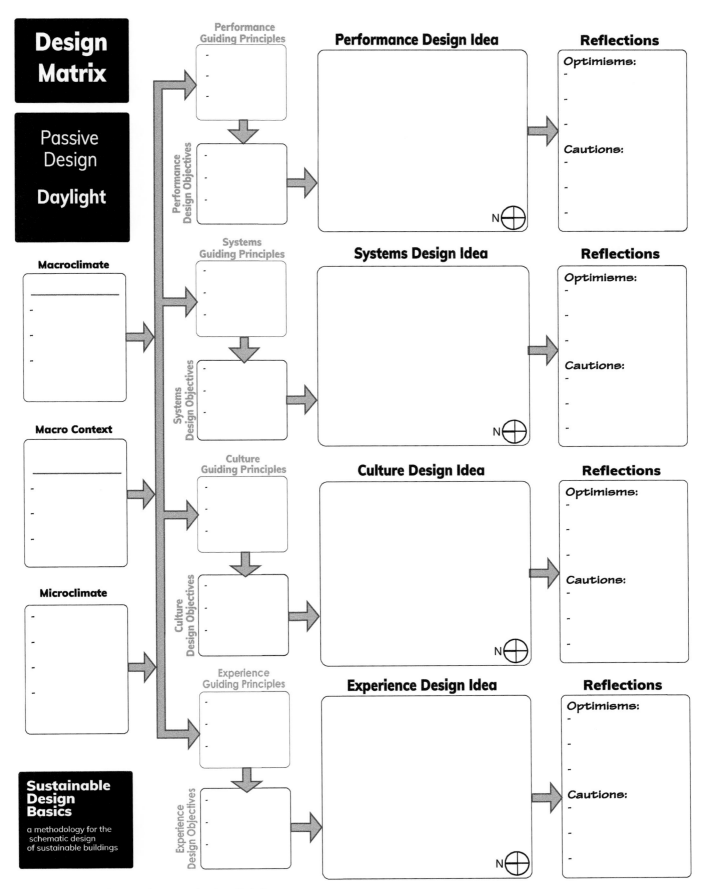

Figure B.9 Passive Design Matrix: Daylighting

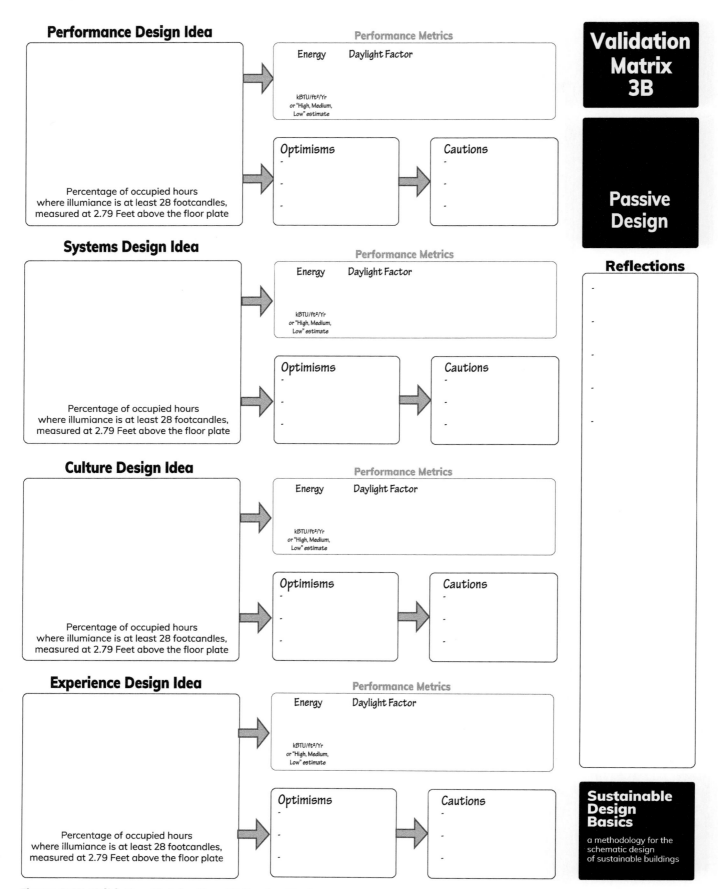

Figure B.10 Validation Matrix: Step 3B Passive Design

Design Synthesis 3B

Passive Design

Passive Design Synthesis

3-D Image(s)

2-D Image(s)

N

Daylight Study

Reflections

Optimisms:
-

-

-

Cautions:
-

-

-

Macroclimate

_____
-

-

-

Macro Context

_____
-

-

Microclimate

-

-

-

Sustainable Design Basics

a methodology for the schematic design of sustainable buildings

Energy Use Intensity (EUI)

kBTU/ft²/yr

Daylight Factor

Figure B.11 Design Synthesis: Step 3B Passive Design

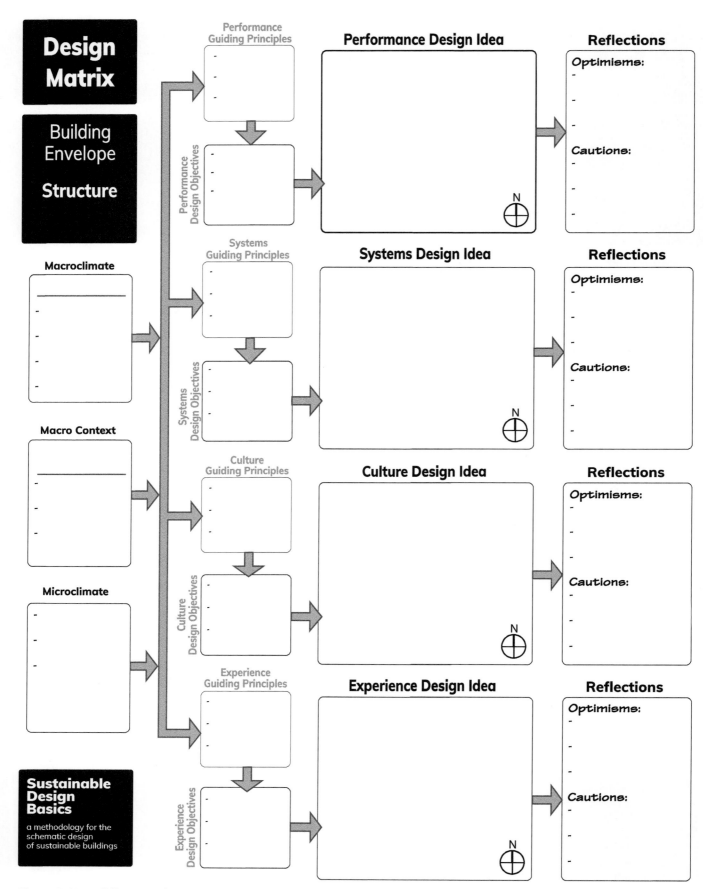

Figure B.12 Building Envelope Design Matrix: Structure

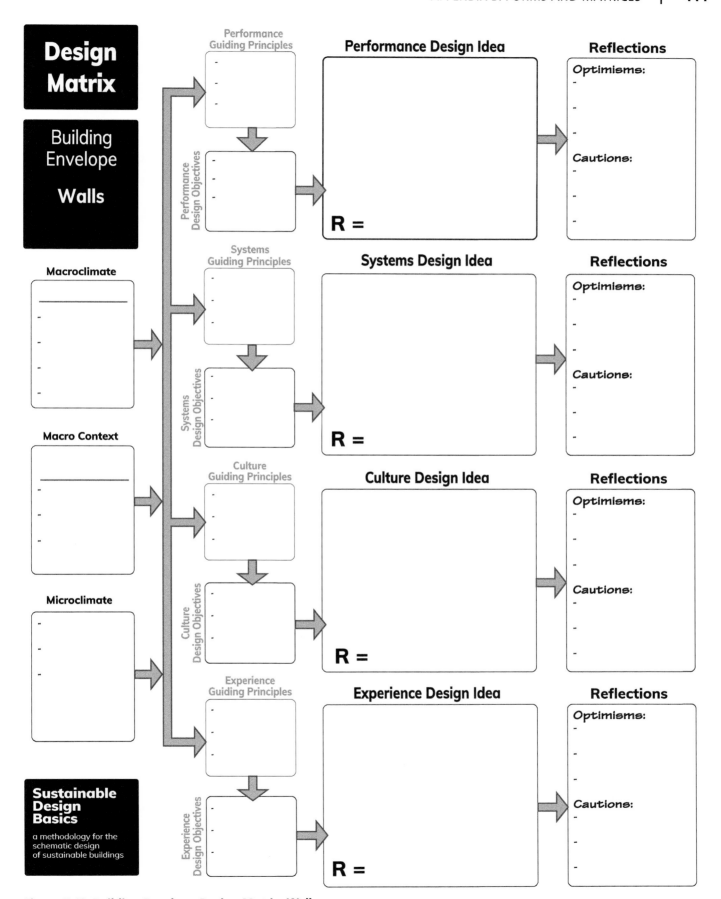

Figure B.13 Building Envelope Design Matrix: Walls

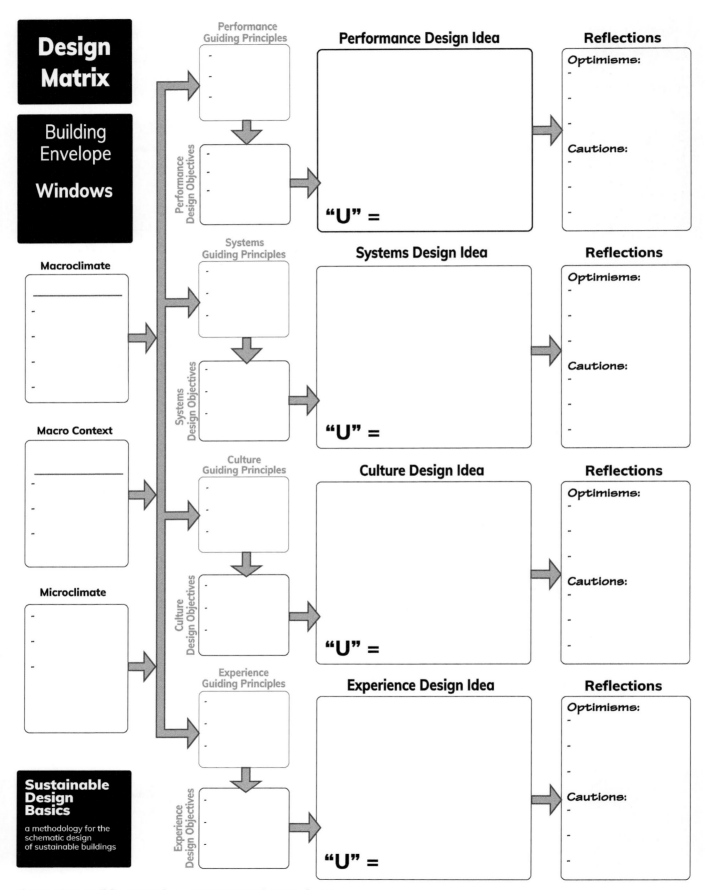

Figure B.14 Building Envelope Design Matrix: Windows

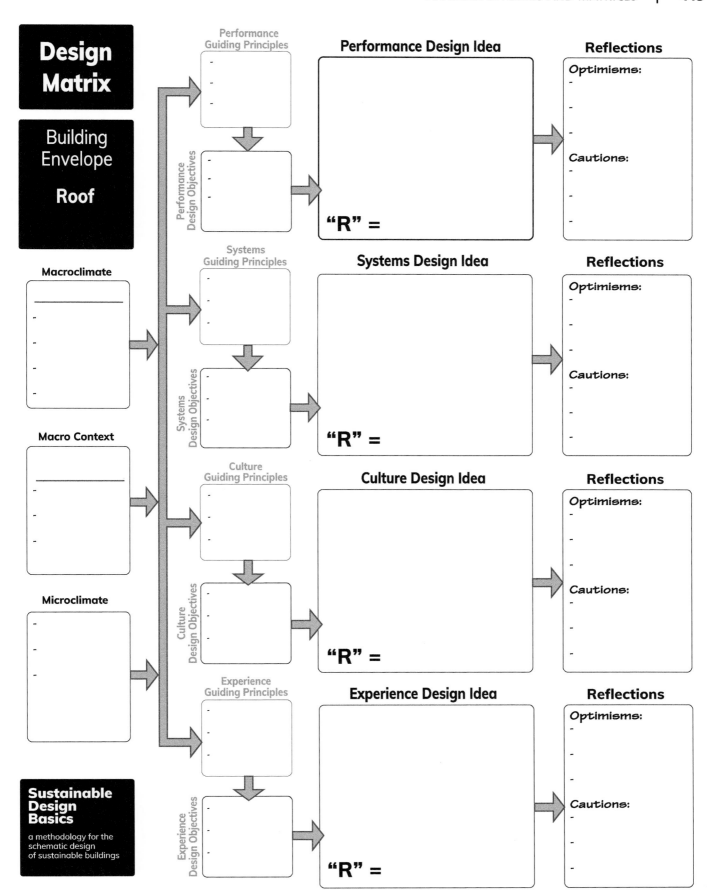

Figure B.15 Building Envelope Design Matrix: Roof

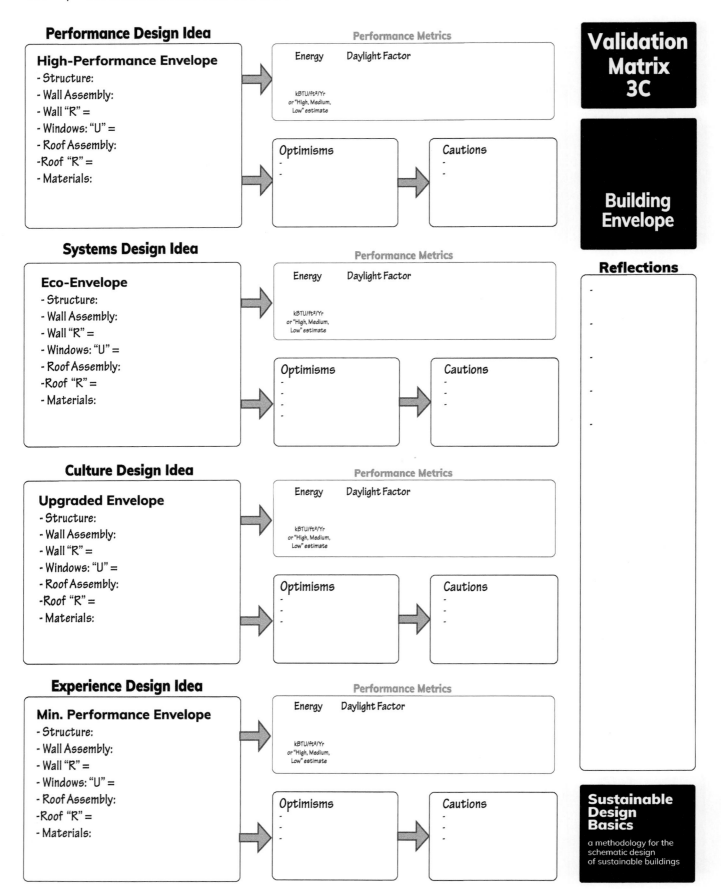

Performance Design Idea

High-Performance Envelope
- Structure:
- Wall Assembly:
- Wall "R" =
- Windows: "U" =
- Roof Assembly:
- Roof "R" =
- Materials:

Performance Metrics

Energy   Daylight Factor

kBTU/ft²/Yr
or "High, Medium,
Low" estimate

Optimisms
-
-

Cautions
-
-

Systems Design Idea

Eco-Envelope
- Structure:
- Wall Assembly:
- Wall "R" =
- Windows: "U" =
- Roof Assembly:
- Roof "R" =
- Materials:

Performance Metrics

Energy   Daylight Factor

kBTU/ft²/Yr
or "High, Medium,
Low" estimate

Optimisms
-
-
-

Cautions
-
-

Culture Design Idea

Upgraded Envelope
- Structure:
- Wall Assembly:
- Wall "R" =
- Windows: "U" =
- Roof Assembly:
- Roof "R" =
- Materials:

Performance Metrics

Energy   Daylight Factor

kBTU/ft²/Yr
or "High, Medium,
Low" estimate

Optimisms
-
-
-

Cautions
-
-

Experience Design Idea

Min. Performance Envelope
- Structure:
- Wall Assembly:
- Wall "R" =
- Windows: "U" =
- Roof Assembly:
- Roof "R" =
- Materials:

Performance Metrics

Energy   Daylight Factor

kBTU/ft²/Yr
or "High, Medium,
Low" estimate

Optimisms
-
-

Cautions
-
-

Validation Matrix 3C

Building Envelope

Reflections
-
-
-
-

Sustainable Design Basics

a methodology for the schematic design of sustainable buildings

Figure B.16 Validation Matrix: Step 3C Building Envelope

Design Synthesis 3C

Building Envelope

Macroclimate

- _____
- -
- -
- -

Macro Context

- _____
- -
- -

Microclimate

- -
- -
- -

Building Plan and/or Section

Final Building Envelope Assemblies

- Structure:
- Foundation:
- Wall: 'R' =
- Windows: 'U' =
- Roof: 'R' =
- Materials:

Reflections

Optimisms:
-

-

-

Cautions:
-

-

-

Sustainable Design Basics

a methodology for the schematic design of sustainable buildings

Energy Use Intensity (EUI)

kBTU/ft²/yr

Daylight Factor

Figure B.17 Design Synthesis: Step 3C Building Envelope

TABLE B.8 VALIDATION MATRIX: FINAL DESIGN, GOALS AND OBJECTIVES.

Final Validation – Project Goals and Objectives

	Metrics	Stated Goal	Predicted Results	Final Evaluation
Energy	**Energy Use Intensity**			
	Building base energy load versus renewable energy generated			
Health + Wellness	**Light:** Percentage of regularly occupied spaces			
	Air: Percentage of regularly occupied spaces			
Water	**Water Use** % savings			
	Stormwater Percentage of rainwater that can be managed on site			
Ecological Integration	**Habitat** Percentage of landscaped areas covered by native or climate-appropriate plants supporting native or migratory animals			
Culture Goals	**Stakeholder Engagement (yes or no)**			
	Sense of Community Walk Score			
Experience Goals	**Views** Percentage of regularly occupied spaces with a view to the outdoors			

Sustainable Design Basics: A methodology for the schematic design of sustainable buildings

TABLE B.9 VALIDATION MATRIX: FINAL DESIGN, GUIDING PRINCIPLES.

Final Validation – Guiding Principles

	Stated Principle	Optimism	Caution	Final Evaluation
Site Analysis				
Design Criteria				
Performance Guiding Principle				
Systems Guiding Principle				
Culture Guiding Principles				
Experience Guiding Principle				

Sustainable Design Basics: A methodology for the schematic design of sustainable buildings

APPENDIX C

Energy Modeling Software

NOTES ABOUT ENERGY AND DAYLIGHTING SIMULATION

Energy modeling is the process of computer analysis to determine energy consumption, utility bills, or efficiencies in sustainable strategies. It also is used to predict savings and provide a rationale for using sustainable or renewable resources like photovoltaic panels, wind turbines, hydronic heating, geothermal heating systems, or higher efficiency appliances, windows and insulation. Energy modeling can also predict annual energy costs, CO_2 emissions, and aid in photovoltaic calculations as well as some rating system points/qualifiers.

Energy modeling can be used by anyone in the design or maintenance process, and starts with creating a virtual or computerized model of the building. The more accurate the model is in conveying wall construction and R-values, window types, and any shading or daylighting strategies the more accurate the predictions will be. The geographic location and the position of the building on the site are of paramount importance, along with the building occupancy rate (number of hours it will be in operation daily), in determining the energy a building will use over time.

The model simulates all the conditions within the building, usually over one year. It looks at the weather and daylighting's effect on the building as well as the energy used for heating, air conditioning, plug loads, water usage, lights, hot water, occupancy rates or any other factors necessary for successful building operation.

Energy modeling can be done during any phase of the design but is most effective when initiated during the schematic design phase to support the generation of general massing model options. Building configuration and site placement greatly influence energy efficiency, and the hardest to change after construction is completed. Modeling done in the later stages can evaluate and help drive decisions related to wall construction, roof construction, windows, building components, HVAC systems, renewable resource harvesting, plug loads, lighting, and so on. Most modeling software enables designers to make comparison studies based on changes in strategies, construction methods, or mechanical specifications. Performance modeling's greatest benefit is the ability to compare different building design scenarios.

The information and results from performance modeling, at any stage in the design process, are performance projections or estimates; they do not reflect actual achievement. Although simulations can be very accurate, many environmental factors cannot be accounted for; occupant behavior is the biggest unpredictable variable. As a result, some rating systems, like the Living Building Challenge, require a full year of monitoring and reporting before finalizing a building's certification or rating.

Energy modeling done during the final stages of building design or construction serves as validation confirming that the strategies planned or employed will meet the proposed projections for energy efficiency. Often, validation and energy modeling are requirements for rating systems or government funding. Other reasons to pursue energy modeling may be:

- Create higher performing buildings and resource efficient design
- Enhance the speed and quality of information and workflow between professionals and stakeholders
- Facilitate better integration among team members
- Provide rapid feedback on the energy performance of design decisions
- Save energy and money
- Reduce carbon footprint
- Meet performance goals early on in the design process
- Establish clear strategies that meet sustainability or rating system goals
- Source for graphics and quantitative information to drive design decisions and provide the rationale

Computer-based performance modeling is complex, and mistakes that affect the simulation have many causes: inaccurate model construction is one of the most common explanations for model simulation difficulties and output inaccuracies. Regardless of the selected software, it is essential that the virtual model be as accurate as possible, and that the software used for the building model and energy modeling are compatible.

There are a lot of energy modeling software packages currently available, each with advantages and disadvantages. Software is a tool of design and not discussed as part of the design process in this textbook. Choice of software is based on user preference. Building performance software and associated technology are ever-changing. Seek advice from current software users. Specialized consultants, consulting engineers, or expert web-based forums are important resources to make an informed selection of software. This summary of the prominent software packages currently used in the design built environment professions is intended as a brief overview to start you on your search.

SEFAIRA

Sefaira* (https://sefaira.com) is a software platform aimed at architects, engineers, and sustainability consultants that is available on a subscription basis with a free 30-day trial. Subscriptions are available at varying levels based on need and intended use. The software company provides students and faculty free software as part of the company's educational outreach program. Sefaira's website has a large number of resources for architects, designers, and educators, including white papers, case studies, ebooks, and a current topics blog. Features include:

- Models are based on Revit or SketchUp
- Uses EnergyPlus and Radiance whole building simulation program
- A wide range of input and category options
- Runs full hourly annual simulations
- Energy
  - Use
  - Cost
  - CO_2
  - Renewable energy
- Daylighting
  - Annual or date + time
  - Daylight factor
  - Direct sunlight
- Thermal comfort
  - Air temperatures
  - PMV
  - Operative temperature
- HVAC sizing
  - EnergyPlus sizing reports
  - Peak heating and cooling loads
  - Mechanical system sizing
- Can evaluate:
  - Massing
  - Layout
  - Natural ventilation
  - Envelope options
- Comparison with ASHRAE standard
- Graphic analysis available

RHINO ARCHITECTURAL SOFTWARE

Rhino (www.rhino3d.com) is a 3D modeling tool mostly used by architects, industrial designers, and jewelry designers. It allows 3D design and rendering without the time required to learn CAD or other architectural drafting software. It produces very realistic, clean, easily animated architectural renderings for presentation or analysis. Files can be exported directly to 3D printers or other types of manufacturing or modeling

---

* Sefaira is utilized for SDB textbook examples because of its 30-day free trial and because it works with SketchUp, which is free; this does not mean that this is the best combination.

machines. The renderings are realistic and clean and easily animated for presentation or analysis. The company provides deeply discounted full commercial software to students and educators with the ability to upgrade in the future.

Rhino requires the DIVA-Solemma LLC plug-in: (http://solemma.net/Diva.html).

The plug-in provides the ability to conduct energy modeling and simulation through Rhino for a single building, urban landscapes, or groups of buildings. The software can understand, calculate, and design off of the synergies that occur when multiple buildings are present. Includes a large variety of analysis tools to predict and drive the design of interior spaces to understand the amount of melatonin that is expected to reach the eye of an occupant based on their position within the space, time of day, sky conditions, colors, and materials properties and the effect on reflected light reflects. Findings are represented with graphs, charts, and renderings for analysis and presentations.

Types of calculations and analysis available include:

- Sun path diagrams with shadows in real-time by latitude and for specific dates.
- Radiation maps. Solar exposure renderings, calculate PV potential, can do simulations by season, annual or point in time.
- Radiance renderings. Accurate renderings in color or black and white of daylighting and its effects over time within a building.
- Glare analysis by points in time or an entire year.
- Animated renderings show daylighting throughout a day or year.
- Dynamic shading simulates arbitrary use of independently operated window shades by percentage of occupied hours shades are open.
- Radiance and EnergyPlus are both open source and validated energy modeling and daylighting engines.
- Spatial energy load visualization provides visualization of buildings by mass, thermal layers or spatial load to help identify energy loads and potential savings.
- Airflow network simulations simulate natural airflow through exterior or interior spaces based on wind direction, wind pressure, buoyancy effects, and surface orientation. It does not simulate thermal stratification within a thermal zone.
- Urban energy modeling provides the ability to run energy models and analyze energy performance to understand synergies or areas of concern present at the urban or site scale.

Adaptive Lighting for Alertness (ALFA) Plug-inThe ALFA plug-in (https://solemma.net/alfa.htm) is meant to assess and design for circadian rhythm benefits within the built environment. The tool can analyze and direct-design by predicting the amount of actual daylight that strikes the occupants' eyes based on their position within the space. It is also able to calculate WELL circadian lighting credits.

OPEN STUDIO

Open Studio (www.openstudio.net) is a free open-source cross-platform software for energy modeling using Energy Plus and Radiance for daylighting analysis that supports Windows and Mac. It was developed by the National Renewable Energy

Laboratory and the United States Department of Energy. It is meant to be used by all design and facility management professionals, developers, or owners. Building models can be in SketchUp or Revit.

Types of calculations and analysis available are:

- Models building envelope loads, schedules, loads and HVAC.
- Parametric analysis tool – shows the results of applying multiple combinations of sustainable strategies and allows EDAPT or energy design assistance program tracker.
- Supports import of gbXML and IFC for geometry creation.
- Models the energy performance of the envelope, heating loads, and HVAC.
- Results viewer enables browsing, plotting, and comparing simulation output data, especially time series.

Available as either an application suite used by designers and a development suite for software developers and researchers.

The development suite can be accessed directly with the ability to customize programs by accessing the software's coding. Tutorials and a brief video overview of how Open Studio works are available on the website.

IES (INTEGRATED ENVIRONMENTAL SOLUTIONS)

IES (www.iesve.com/software) is a corporation that develops energy modeling software for use by the general public as well as consults in all the building and sustainable industries. Their goal is to reduce energy usage and costs with integrated building performance analytics. There is an extensive range of software modeling packages for architects, engineers, project managers, owners, developers, and contractors. The company's software products have won awards for innovation. The website has a full spectrum of integrated, in-depth software tools available for design, project management, digital engineering, and simulation. Full license fees are based on the programs or packages selected, and free trials are available. Student software is available at 50 Pounds Sterling or approximates $65.00 US.

The engineering suite includes multiple applications to evaluate the following:

- Airflow
- Daylight simulation and lighting design
- Life cycle analysis
- Solar Shading
- Whole building energy simulation
- Renewable energy design and optimization
- Climate analysis and weather
- HVAC system and sizing optimization
- Egress analysis
- UK + Ireland regulations, and global compliance requirements
- LEED

The architectural suite includes multiple applications to evaluate the following:

- Climate integration
- Resource availability
- Renewable potential
- Energy tradeoffs
- Passive strategies
- Solar Shading
- Glazing percentages
- Water reduction
- Building massing and form
- Material characteristics
- Solar orientation
- Occupant comfort
- LEED/BREAM potential
- Detailed daylighting

The software is compatible with Revit, SketchUp, and other BIM packages so the building model can be imported from these programs or can be modeled directly in IESVE programs. Training programs and technical support are included with the full license purchase along with video tutorials on the page for each program. Student licenses are directed to online and YouTube tutorials.

IES Consultation services include:

- BIM4 analysis
- Energy master planning
- Design
- Building regulations
- LEED
- Green rating systems
- CFD
- Building operation.

IES virtual environmental software validation packages have been assessed against regional and global standards, including ASHRAE, the California Energy Code, the EU, and the UK. For more info see their website, www.iesve.com/software/software-validation.

EQUEST

Equest (https://energydesignresources.com/resources/software-tools/equest.aspx) is a free energy modeling software that can be used at any stage of the building development. It provides complex calculation and analysis without extensive engineering or modeling experience or knowledge. The software leads the user through the modeling process with step-by-step prompts that are part of the program. The default inputs are based on California Title 24 building energy code. With internet connectivity, the program has access to over 1000 weather data files from North America. Equest only runs on Windows and is not available for Mac, OSX, IOS, or Android.

The software performs an hourly simulation for the building for one year, calculating the heating and cooling loads based on wall construction, window, percentage and quality of glass, people loads, plug in loads, and ventilation. It also tabulates projected energy use for lighting, plug loads, heating, cooling, ventilation, plumbing, and other mechanical systems. . It is capable of modeling at three different levels of complexity: schematic, design development, and energy efficiency. Simulations are available for energy cost estimating, daylighting and lighting system control, and implementation of common energy efficiency measures. The results are shown in a variety of graphic forms. Multiple simulations can also be viewed in graph form as well.

REVIT GREEN BUILDING STUDIO BY AUTODESK

Green Building Studio (https://gbs.autodesk.com/GBS) is a cloud-based energy simulation software that also powers Revit's whole building energy analysis tools. As an integrated product to Revit, Green Building Studio software allows energy analytical models can be based on detailed architectural models. It uses DOE-2a proven and validated simulation engine to provide energy use, water use, and carbon emissions.

The dynamic whole-building simulation engine is capable of estimating building energy and operating costs based on the effects and interactions of building form, materials, systems, usage, and climate. Simulations automatically account for all the buildings systems, adding defaults and assumptions based on building type and location to reduce variable or unknown conditions. The software automatically evaluates potential energy savings, losses, and strategies that will have the greatest impact. Simulations can be run on your choice of conceptual massing elements, room or space elements, or building elements, such as the thermal properties of walls, roofs, or floors.

Climate and weather data can be accessed by geographic location or for existing buildings by accessing historical weather data collected through a service called 3Tier automatically. For buildings within the United States, an ENERGY STAR score is estimated. The software is also able to estimate LEED points for glazing and water credits along with ways to improve daylighting and water use. Autodesk has student and educational software licenses for all its products and 30 days free trial for Green Building Studio. Video tutorials and available through Autodesk and YouTube.

APPENDIX D

Abbreviations and Acronyms

ACH	Air changes per hour
ADA	Americans with Disabilities Act
AHU	Air handling unit
AIA	American Institute of Architects
AL	air leakage
ANSI	American National Standards Institute
ASHRAE	American Society of Heating, Refrigerating, and Air Conditioning Engineers
ASE	annual sun exposure
ASTM	American Society for Testing Materials
AWEA	American Wind Energy Association
BEES	Building for Environmental and Economic Sustainability
BIFMA	Business and Institutional Furniture Manufacturer Association
BIM	Building information modeling
BOD	basis of design
BOMA	Building Owners and Managers Association International
BREEAM	Building Research Establishment Environmental Assessment Method
BTU	British thermal units
C2C	Cradle 2 Cradle
CBE	Center for the Built Environment
CBECS	commercial buildings energy consumption survey
CBDM	climate-based daylight modeling
CEC	California Energy Commission
CFCs	chlorofluorocarbons

CFM	cubic feet per minute
CO	carbon monoxide
CO_2	carbon dioxide
CPT	carpet
CR	condensation resistance
CRI	Color rendering index
CRRC	Cool Roof Rating Council Standard
CSI	Construction Specifications Institute
dB	decibel
DF	daylight factor
DOE	U.S. Department of Energy
DSF	double-skin facade
EA	effective aperture
ECMs	energy conservation measures
EER	energy efficiency rating
EF	energy factor
EMCS	energy management control system
EPA	Environmental Protection Agency
EPD	environmental product declaration
EPP	environmentally preferred products
EPS	expanded polystyrene insulation
fc	footcandle
FSC	Forest Stewardship Council
ft	foot
GPF	gallons per flush
GPM	gallons per minute
GBI	Green Building Initiative
GBCI	Green Building Certification Institute
GHG	greenhouse gas
GSF	gross square feet
EUI	energy use intensity
HBN	Healthy Building Network
HCFC	hydrochlorofluorocarbon
HERS	home energy rating system
HPD	health product declaration
HVAC	heating, ventilation, and air conditioning
IAQ	indoor air quality
IBC	International Building Code
IDP	integrative design process
IECC	International Energy Conservation Code
IES	Illuminating Engineering Society
IESNA	Illuminating Engineering Society of North America
IEQ	indoor environmental auality
IFMA	International Facility Management Association

IgCC	International Green Construction Code
ILFI	International Living Future Institute
IMC	International Mechanical Code
ISO	International Organization of Standardization
kW	kilowatt
kWh	kilowatt hour
KWH	kilowatt hours
KW/H	kilowatt hours
LBC	Living Building Challenge
LCA	life cycle assessment
LCCA	life cycle cost assessment
LEED	Leadership in Energy and Environmental Design
LEED BD + C	Leadership in Energy and Environmental Design Building Design + Construction
LEED ID + C	Leadership in Energy and Environmental Design Interior Design + Construction
LEED v4	Leadership in Energy and Environmental Design Version 4
LPD	lighting power density
LRV	light reflectance value
lx	lux
MEP	mechanical, electrical, and plumbing
MERV	minimum efficiency reporting value
MSDS	material safety data sheet
MRT	mean radiant temperature
NAHB	National Association of Home Builders
NALFA	North American Laminate Floor Association
NFRC	National Fenestration Rating Council
NGO	nongovernment organizations
NSF	National Science Foundation
OECD	Organization for Economic Co-operation and Development
F	obstruction factor
OPR	owner project requirements
PCR	product category rules
PHIUS	Passive House Institute U.S.
PMV	predicted mean vote
PPD	predicted percentage dissatisfied index
PV	photovoltaic
RH	relative humidity
ROI	return on investment
R-Value	A measure of a material's resistance to heat flow
SCAQMD	South Coast Air Quality Management District
SDB	Sustainable Design Basics
SDS	safety data sheet
SFI	Sustainable Forestry Initiative

SHGC	solar heat gain coefficient
SIP	structural insulated panels
SMaRT	sustainable materials rating technology
SRI	solar reflectance index
UBC	Uniform Building Code
UL	Underwriters Laboratory
USDA	United States Department of Agriculture
USGBC	United States Green Building Council
UV	ultraviolet
VAV	variable air volume
VOC	volatile organic compounds
VT	visual transmittance
VLT	visual light transmittance
W	watts
WBDG	Whole Building Design Guide
WUI	water use index
WWR	window-to-wall ratio

APPENDIX E

Green Building Standards, Codes and Rating Systems

THE ROLE OF CODES AND STANDARDS

Appendix "E" is intended to provide a general overview of the sustainability standards, certifications, and green building rating systems, currently available. The applicable or appropriate standard, system, or certification, is dependent on project sustainability goals. Codes whether local, regional, national or international are requirements of design and construction of the built environment.

THE ROLE OF RATING SYSTEMS

Green Building Rating systems are voluntary. Programs, certifications, and rating systems, for green products and materials, are profiled in greater detail in Chapter 9 Green Materials. While designing, building, and certifying a sustainable building to a specific green building standard may add modest incremental costs to the initial capital costs. Generally, increased initial costs are offset by increased building and system efficiencies, reduced operational costs, and overall durability and longevity of the facility. Further, Green properties have been gaining in popularity with the public, increasing the marketing and public relations value of green properties as demand for these properties continues to increase.

GREEN BUILDING STANDARDS, CODES AND RATING SYSTEMS

The following is a brief overview of the major standards, codes and rating systems that focus on sustainable design methodology and strategies.

Standards and Rating systems

Architecture 2030: https://architecture2030.org/

Focused on reducing greenhouse gas emissions and carbon footprint of the built environment. Architecture 2030 Provides education, design + planning strategies, policy engagement, and collaborative opportunities aimed at the professions in the building sector.

BREEAM (Building Research Establishment Environmental Assessment Method): https://www.breeam.com/

Third party international certification to assess environmental, social and economic sustainability of masterplans, infrastructure, and buildings.

CASBEE (Comprehensive Assessment System for Built Environment Efficiency): http://www.ibec.or.jp/CASBEE/english/overviewE.htm

A streamlined rating system specifically designed to address the specific sustainability issues in Japan and Asian countries. The rating system is meant to apply to residential and commercial buildings, new construction and renovation projects.

Comprehensive Procurement Guidelines (CPG) Program: https://www.epa.gov/smm/comprehensive-procurement-guideline-cpg-program

Environmental Protection Agency's (EPA) Sustainable Materials Management initiative that promotes a systems approach to reducing materials use and the associated environmental impacts over the materials' entire life cycle. It promotes the use of materials recovery and reuse in the manufacturing of new products.

Cradle to Cradle: http://www.c2c-centre.com/home

Promotes a holistic and regenerative design approach to products, materials that include social, industrial and business models. It seeks to improve the quality of products, their design, waste streams, and the end of life disposal. Based on five principles: value materials for safe and continuous cycling through manufacturing and consumption process | Maintain flows of biological and technical nutrients | 100% renewable energy | Regard water as a precious resource | celebrate people and natural systems.

ECOLOGO: https://industries.ul.com/environment/certificationvalidation-marks/ecologo-product-certification

Third-party, multi-attribute, life-cycle based certification for products, services, cleaning materials, office products, electronics, building materials, and packaging. Certification requires scientific testing, auditing and is part of Underwriter's Laboratory (UL).

Energy Star: https://www.energystar.gov/

Is a government-backed program. The Energy Star symbol signifies energy efficiency which is part of the EPA (Environmental Protection Agency). The symbol provides a credible and simple way for consumers to make informed choices on appliances, products, homes, and help building owners with sustainable management strategies.

Environmental Product Declarations (EPD): https://www.environdec.com/

Standardized, third-party verified documents that communicate the results of a product's life cycle assessment (LCA), including all relevant performance information. EPDs also include information on mechanical, safety, human health, and any other issues that are of particular importance for that product.

Fitwel: https://fitwel.org/

Certification system focused on optimizing buildings to support human health for multi-family residential and Multi-tenant workplaces.

Forest Stewardship Council (FSC) – https://us.fsc.org/en-us

A non-profit organization that set out to create a voluntary, market-based approach to regulate the responsible and sustainable management of forests. Regulations relating to the growing, harvesting, and certification of forests. FSC also certifies the chain of resources to assure that wood used in construction, furniture and finishes are growing in an ecologically responsible way.

GreenBlue: http://greenblue.org/

A non-profit corporation whose mission is to foster the creation of a resilient system of commerce based on the principles of sustainable material management. They look at the packaging, chemical composition, large scale composting, recycling, and forest management.

GREENGUARD: http://greenguard.org/en/index.aspx

A third-party certification party that is a division of Underwriters Laboratory (UL) that assesses and certifies Building Materials, Furniture, and Furnishings; Electronic Equipment; Cleaning and Maintenance Products; Medical Devices for Breathing Gas Pathways. Certification is based on a set of standards to evaluate the chemical composition, off-gassing, and leaching of chemicals during use. Certified products will have a GREENGUARD label.

Green Globe: http://www.greenglobes.com/home.asp

Canada based green building rating assessment, guidance, and certification program for the design, construction, and operation of high-performance interiors and buildings.

Green Seal: http://www.greenseal.org/

Green Seal is a non-profit environmental standard development and certification organization. Its services are used by product manufacturers and other services providers. Certification is based on a list of Green Seal standards covering performance, health, and sustainability criteria.

Green Squared: https://greensquaredcertified.com/

Multi-standard, third-party certification that deals specifically with the tile industry and tile installation. Green Squared certification verifies products which are in conformance with ANSI A138.1.

ICC 700 National Green Building Standard: https://www.epa.gov/smartgrowth/icc-700-2012-2012-national-green-building-standard-icc-700

Certification and rating system aimed at designing and specification involved with residential construction and the planning of subdivisions.

Leadership Energy and Environmental Design (LEED): https://new.usgbc.org/leed

The LEED system is a green building rating system established by the U.S. Green Building Council (USGBC). It is a certification process based on third-party verification of a comprehensive list of green building strategies. It is a point-based system that allows buildings to achieve a different level of rating depending on the number of green building strategies used. Each of the rating systems has a credit category that covers: Materials and resources | Water Efficiency | Indoor Environmental Quality | Sustainable Sites. Within each of the categories, there are specific goals. Each goal reviews the intent along with any requirements. Project members can choose the goals that are most applicable to each project.

Living Building Challenge (LBC) - https://living-future.org/lbc/

A holistic and integrative third-party green rating system. Seven performance categories called "Petals" comprise the overall system. Petals include Place | Water | Energy | Health + Happiness | Materials | Equity | Beauty. Living Building Certification requires all imperatives be met for the specific project typology. A building can be Petal certified by achieving at least 3 of the seven petals.

Net Zero (NZEB): https://living-future.org/net-zero/

One hundred percent of the building's energy needs on a net annual basis must be supplied by on-site renewable energy. No combustion is allowed. Certification is based on actual, not modeled, performance.

Passivhaus/ PHUS: http://www.passivehouse.com/

Passive Haus focuses on reducing energy consumption through high insulation and an airtight building envelope. The performance standard is an absolute, requiring adherence to stringent energy performance requirements. Elements of the envelope construction are Super Insulation | High-performance windows | Air tightness | Thermal bridging | Air exchange using a Heat Recovery Ventilator (HRV). Because of the tight envelope, air exchange is critical. The type of materials used and their chemical composition is also extremely important.

SB Tool: http://www.iisbe.org/sbmethod

A multi-national generic framework for rating the sustainable performance of buildings and projects. It may also be used as a toolkit that assists local organizations to develop local SBTool rating systems.

Sustainable Materials Rating Technology (SMaRT): http://mts.sustainable-products.com/SMaRT_product_standard.html

A standard and certification system for products that incorporate life cycle assessment, environmental performance, social performance, and business benefits into its evaluation and certification process.

The United States Environmental Protection Agency (EPA): https://www.epa.gov/

Agency of the United States Federal government established with the stated mission of protecting human health and the environment be creating policies and regulating: the extraction and use of natural resources, economic growth, energy, transportation, agriculture, industry, and international trade and areas that affect human health.

Well Building: https://v2.wellcertified.com/v2.1/en/overview

A performance-based system for measuring, certifying, and monitoring features of the built environment that impact human health and wellbeing, through the air, water, nourishment, light, fitness, comfort, and mind. Founded on medical research that explores the connection between the buildings and the health and wellness of its occupants. WELL v2 is founded on the following principles: Equitable | Global | Evidence-based | Technically robust | Customer-focused | Resilient. Managed and administered by the International WELL Building Institute (IWBI)

Codes

American Society of Heating, Refrigeration, and Air-Conditioning Engineers' ANSI/ASHRAE/USGBC/IES - Standard 189.1-2011.

ASHRAE 52.2 - Standardized method of testing building ventilation filters for removal efficiency by particle size.

ASHRAE 55 - Standard describing thermal and humidity conditions for human occupancy of buildings

ASHRAE 62 - Standard that defines minimum levels of ventilation performance for acceptable indoor air quality

ASHRAE 192 - Standard for measuring air-change effectiveness

ASTM E408 - Standard of inspection-meter test methods for normal emittance of surfaces

ASTM E903 - Standard of an integrated-sphered test method for solar absorptance, reflectance, and transmittance

IBC (International Building Code) - https://www.iccsafe.org/codes-tech-support/codes/2018-i-codes/ibc/

Foundation for all international building codes that are standard for construction and codes in most areas of the world. Promotes health and safety by addressing the design and installation of materials and construction practices.

IECC (International Energy Conservation Code) – https://www.iccsafe.org/codes-tech-support/codes/2018-i-codes/iecc/

Examines the design of energy efficient structures by addressing the construction of building envelopes, and the components of mechanical systems, lighting, and power systems. The code deals with commercial and residential structures

IgCC (International Green Construction Code) - https://www.iccsafe.org/codes-tech-support/codes/2018-i-codes/igcc/

A collaboration of industry members working together to develop model codes and sustainable strategies to promote safety, sustainability, affordability, and resilience. The website outlines a broad range of educational resources, new events, and strategies.

Dedicated to developing model codes and standards used in the design, build and compliance process to construct safe, sustainable, affordable and resilient structures.

NIOSH (National Institution for Occupational Safety and Health): https://www.cdc.gov/niosh/index.htm

Part of the Center for Disease Control (CDC) and helps to ensure safe and healthful working conditions by providing research, information, education, and training in the field of occupational safety and health. NIOSH provides national and world leadership to prevent work-related illness, injury, disability, and death by gathering information, conducting scientific research, and translating the knowledge gained into products and services.

OSHA (Occupational Safety and Health Administration): https://www.osha.gov/law-regs.html

Creates laws, regulations, and codes with detailed requirements for materials, chemical exposure and work environments. The intention is to provide safe working conditions. The regulations cover construction, maritime, and agriculture industries and other general business types along with state-specific mandates for worker safety.

Standard for the Design of High-Performance Green Buildings Except Low-Rise Residential Buildings - (ASHRAE 189.1), 2011 edition

National Association of Home Builders (NAHB): https://www.nahb.org/

Latest information on sustainable and traditional building strategies and requirements.

Local Zoning and building codes – It is critical that local zoning ordinances are consulted before any project begins to assure compliance with any sustainable or standard building codes or standards. Local zoning can differ at the community level, so finding and checking with the projects specific code is imperative.

Green Product Directories

Products, manufacturers, and rating systems are always evolving, so it is best to access the latest version. Below are just a few resources to help with specifying materials for the built environment that reduce embodied energy, toxicity, off-gassing, and manufactured responsibly.

Comprehensive Procurement Guide (CPG): www.epa.gov/smm/comprehensive-procurement-guideline-cpg-program

Component of the EPA's Sustainable Materials Management initiative to promotes the reduction of material use and associated impact over the products life-cycle. The site profiles 62 products regarding recycling, recovery, and reuse.

Cradle to Cradle (C2C – Centre): www.c2c-centre.com/home

Webbased database with a directory of products, companies, and buildings that comply with the C2C

Centre rating system.

Declare. https://living-future.org/declare/

A transparency platform and product database website. Manufacturers are encouraged to submit information to the database to aid in the process of achieving the Materials Pedal. Each project in the database is assigned a label that profiles; components including Red List Items or EPA's Contaminants of Concern (COC), End-of-life options; Location of extraction; VOC Information and if the product is LBC compliant with Red List.

ECO- Specifier Global: http://www.ecospecifier.com/

International database with educational resources and material composition. Search Materials by project type, use, or rating system compliance

EPD (Environmental Product Declaration) Registry: http://www.environdec.com/EPD-Search/

An International database that provides life-cycle information for product comparison. Information is independently verified and registered. Submission of declarations are voluntary.

GreenSpec: http://www.greenspec.co.uk/

Independent government-funded agency to promote sustainable building products, materials and construction techniques in the UK. Edited by practicing architects and specifiers.

International Living Future Institute: https://living-future.org/

Parent organization to Living Building Challenge, Living Product Challenge, Living Community Challenge, Just, Declare, and Reveal. Non-profit organization that is dedicated to creating communities that are socially just, culturally rich, and ecologically restorative. Site profiles programs and initiatives to reach these goals.

Just. https://living-future.org/just/

A voluntary disclosure tool for organizations or businesses to disclose their operations, including how they treat their employees and where they make financial and community investments. The participating organization is scored in a range from 1–3, in six categories related to social justice: Worker Benefits, safety, Stewardship,

Diversity, Equity, and Local Benefits.

Level by BIFMA: http://www.levelcertified.org/

Level is a sustainability certification focused on commercial office furniture based on the social and ecological impacts of furniture products on the built environment. Sponsored by Business and Institutional Furniture Manufacturers Association

MSDS Online Database: www.msdsonline.com/msds-search/

Important for Living Building Challenge Materials Pedal Research. The chemical composition of any product or systems component can be searched with the CAS or Chemical Abstracts Service number. A CAS# is a unique identifier assigned to every chemical substance in open scientific literature. All MSDS are required to list the CAS#s for all their components or ingredients.

Oikos Green Building Library: www.eerl.org/index.php?P=FullRecord&ID=1308

Environmental and energy resource library providing resources on sustainable design and construction strategies. Provides access to an extensive library, case studies and bookstore.

Stanford Library: http://library.stanford.edu/guides/green-building-resources

Database for online and print resources related to all aspects of green and sustainable design and construction.

Perkins + Will Material Transparency Website: https://transparency.perkinswill.com/about#usingthelist

Resource for Health Product Declarations (HPDs), database of generic products, and product database using filters for certifications and other transparency documentation. The website also includes case studies for various project types and information on government agencies.

Perkins + Will Precautionary List: https://transparency.perkinswill.com/lists/precautionary-list

Information on the health and safety of materials or products based on chemical composition or health-related claims. Products are searchable by materials, CSI specification, or Hazards. The main goal is to provide transparency in material usage that affects indoor air quality and human health.

Reveal. https://living-future.org/reveal/

A verification system that creates a "label" for each building based on energy performance encompassing three separate metrics: energy use intensity, the zero-energy performance index, and reduction in energy use from baseline. Based on 12-month verifiable energy consumption and also indicates compliance with Architecture 2030.

UL Spot: https://spot.ul.com/

A sustainable product database that allows searches based on Manufacturer's Brands, Certification types, LEED credits, Master Format, or Product types. Source for design professionals, retailers, manufacturers or purchasing professionals.

Well Building: https://v2.wellcertified.com/v2.1/en/overview

WELL v2 is founded on the following principles: equitable, global, evidence-based, technically robust, customer-focused, and resilient.

Bibliography

Below are the texts, articles, and websites that have been foundational in the formation of the process and methodology presented in this textbook. While it is not an all-inclusive list, the listed books are an excellent place to begin learning more about sustainability topics.

2020 Vision Workgroup. 2009. *Sustainable Material Management: The Road Ahead*. EPA 530-R-09-009 (June). Available at www.epa.gov/sites/production/files/2015- 09/documents/vision2.pdf.

Acaroglu, L. 2017. "Tools for Systems Thinkers." (September 7). Retrieved from Disruptive Design at https://medium.com/disruptive-design/tools-for-systems-thinkers-the-6-fundamental-concepts-of-systems-thinking-379cdac3dc6a

Alker, J., ed. 2014. *Health, Wellbeing & Productivity in Offices*. Retrieved from World Green Building Council website: www.ukgbc.org/sites/default/files/Health%2520Wellbeing%2520and%2520Productivity%2520in%2520Offices%2520-%2520The%2520next%2520chapter%2520for%2520green%2520building%2520Full%2520Report_0.pdf

Allen, Edward. 2005. *How Buildings Work: The Natural Order of Architecture* (3rd ed.). New York: Oxford University Press.

Allen, Edward, and Joseph Iano. 2017. *The Architect's Studio Companion: Rules of Thumb for Preliminary Design* (6th ed.). Hoboken, NJ: John Wiley & Sons.

Alter, L. 2008. "Renovation Uses Twice as Much Labor, Half as Much Material as New Construction." Retrieved from Treehugger.com website: www.treehugger.com/sustainable-product-design/renovation-uses-twice-as-much-labor-half-as-much-material-as-new-construction.html

———. 2008.. "The Greenest Brick is the One That's Already in the Wall" (December 19). Retrieved from Treehugger.com website: www.treehugger.com/sustainable-product-design/the-greenest-brick-is-the-one-thats-already-in-the-wall.html

ASLA. (n.d.). "The Sustainable Sites initiative: SITES." Retrieved from The American Society of Landscape Architects website, January 6, 2020, www.asla.org/sites/.

Bayer, Charles. 2010. *AIA Guide to Building Life Cycle Assessment in Practice. Russel Gentry (ed).*, Sarabhi Joshi (trans). New York: The American Institute of Architects.

Binggeli, C. 2014. *Materials for Interior Environments.* Hoboken, New Jersey: John Wiley & Sons.

Boubekri, M., I. N. Cheung, K. J. Reid, C. H. Wang, and P. C. Zee. 2014. "Impact of Windows and Daylight Exposure on Overall Health and Sleep Quality of Office Workers: A Case-Control Pilot Study." *Journal of Clinical Sleep Medicine* 10(6): 603–611.

Brand, Stewart. 1994. *How Buildings Learn: What Happens after They're Built.* New York: Viking.

Brown, Lester R. 2009. *Plan B 4.0: Mobilizing to Save Civilization.* New York: W. W. Norton & Co.

Brown, G. Z. and Mark DeKay. 2001. *Sun, Wind & Light: Architectural Design Strategies.* New York: John Wiley and Sons.

Brundtland Commission. 1987. *Our Common Future: Report of the World Commission on Environment and Development.* Oslo: World Commission on Environment and Development.

Buchanan, Peter. 2012. "The Big Rethink: Integral Theory." *Architectural Review* (February 29) 1/25-25/25.

Buchanan, Peter and Architectural League of New York. 2005. *Ten Shades of Green: Architecture and the Natural World.* New York: Architectural League of New York.

Ching, Francis, D. K., and I. M. Shapiro. 2014. *Green Building Illustrated.* Hoboken, NJ: John Wiley and Sons.

Cowan, C., E. Barella, M. K. Watson, and R. Anderson. 2017. "Validating Content of a Sustainable Design Rubric Using Established Frameworks." In *Thinking Globally, Acting Locally: The Role of Engineering Education towards Attaining UN Sustainable Development Goals.* Columbus, OH: American Society For Engineering Education.

Crawley, E., B. Cameron, and D. Selva D. 2015. *Systems Architecture: Strategy and Product Development for Complex Systems.* Hoboken, NJ: Pearson Higher Education.

DeKay, M. 2014. "The Four Sustainable Design Perspectives." 30th Passive and Low Energy Architecture Conference (PLEA 2014) (December 16–18). Ahmedabad, India.

Devaney, K. 2015. "An Integral Approach to Systems Engineering." *INCOSE International* (October 29) https://doi.org/10.1002/j.2334-5837.2015.00100.x.

Edwards, Andres R. and David W. Orr. 2005. *The Sustainability Revolution: Portrait of a Paradigm Shift.* Gabriola Island, BC: New Society Publishers.

Elefante, C. 2012. "Proof that the Greenest Building is the One Already Standing Released in New Report from Preservation Green Lab" (January 24). Retrieved from Treehugger.com website: www.treehugger.com/green-architecture/proof-greenest-building-one-already-standing-released-new-report-preservation-green-lab.html

Fleming, Rob. 2013. *Design Education for a Sustainable Future.* New York: Routledge.

Fleming, Rob and Christopher Pastore. 2002. "Transcendent Sustainable Design: The Role of Aesthetics." Association of Collegiate Schools of Architecture.

Fleming, Rob and Saglinda H. Roberts. 2019. *Sustainable Design for the Built Environment*. New York: Routledge.

Ford, B. 2017. "Harnessing the Power of Natural Light." Work Design Magazine website https://workdesign.com/2017/05/harnessing-power-natural-light/

Friedman, Avi. 2017. *Designing Sustainable Communities*. London: Bloomsbury Visual Arts.

Froeschle, L. M. 1999. Environmental Assessment and Specification of Green Materials. *The Construction Specifier* (October): 53.

Goodbun, Jon, Jeremy Till, and Deljana Iossifova. 2012. *Scarcity: Architecture in an Age of Depleting Resources*. London: John Wiley and Sons.

Gould van Praag et al, C. D. 2017. *Mind-wandering and alterations to default mode network connectivity when listening to naturalistic versus artificial sounds*. Science.

Grondzik, Walter T., and Alison G. Kwok.2019. *Mechanical and Electrical Equipment for Buildings* (13th ed.). Hoboken, NJ: John Wiley and Sons.

Hammer, M. S., T. K. Swinburn, andd R. L. Neitzel. 2017. "Environmental Noise Pollution in the United States: Developing an Effective Public Health Response." *Environmental Health Perspectives* (122)2: 115–119.

Héroux, M. E., & et al. 2015. "Quantifying the Health Impacts of Ambient Air Pollutants: Recommendations of a WHO/Europe Project." *International Journal of Public Health*, 619–627.

Hosey, Lance. ed. 2012. *The Shape of Green: Aesthetics, Ecology and Design* (2nd ed.). Washington, DC: Island Press.

Iano, E. A., & Iano, J. 2017. *The Architect's Studio Companion* (6th ed.). Hoboken, NJ: John Wiley and Sons.

Institute of Medicine (US). 2001. *Rebuilding the Unity of Health and the Environment: A New Vision of Environmental Health for the 21st Century*. Washington, DC: National Academies Press.

Indigenous Corporate Training. "What is the Seventh Generation Principle." Indigenous Corporate Training, Inc., accessed 7/28, 2018, www.ictinc.ca/blog/seventh-generation-principle.

Iwaro, J., A. Mwasha, and P. Narinesingh. 2017. "Validation of Integrated Performance Model for Sustainable Envelope Performance Assessment and Design." *International Journal of Low-Carbon Technologies* 12(2): 189–207.

Karlen, M., & Fleming, R. 2016. *Space Planning Basics*. *4th*. Hoboken, NJ: Wiley.

Karlen, M., J. R. Benya, and C. Spangler. 2012. *Lighting Design Basics*. Hoboken, NJ: John Wiley and Sos.

Kellert, Stephen R., Judith Heerwagen, Martin Mador. 2008. *Biophilic Design: The Theory, Science, and Practice of Bringing Buildings to Life*. Hoboken, NJ: John Wiley and Sons.

Kellert, Stephen R. and Elizabeth F. Calabrese. 2015. *The Practice of Biophilic Design*. Retrieved from biophilic-design.com: https://4eb001d0-b89e-44ef-8a43-a66d-4e82feb3.filesusr.com/ugd/21459d_81ccb84caf6d4bee8195f9b5af92d8f4.pdf.

Kellert, Stephen R. *Building for Life Designing and Understanding the Human-Nature Connection*. Washington, DC: Island Press.

Kenzer, Marie. 1999. "Healthy Cities: A Guide to the Literature." *Environment and Urbanization* 11 (1): 201.

Kibert, C. J. 2007. *Sustainable Construction; Green Building Design and Delivery* (2nd ed.). Hoboken, NJ: John Wiley and Sons.

Klepeis, N. E., W. C. Nelson, W. R. Ott, J. P. Robinson, A. M. Tsang, P. Switzer, W. H. Engelmann et al. 2011. "The National Human Activity Pattern Survey (NHAPS): A Resource for Assessing Exposure to Environmental Pollutants." *Journal of Exposure Analysis and Environmental Epidemiology*, 231–52.

Kwok, Alison G., and Walter T. Grondzik. 2011. *The Green Studio Handbook: Environmental Strategies for Schematic Design.* (2nd ed.). Burlington, MA: Architectural Press.

Lechner, N. 2014. *Heating, Cooling, Lighting: Sustainable Methods for Architects* (3rd ed.). Hoboken, NJ:John Wiley and Sons.

Lelieveld, J., J. S. Evans,, D. Giannadaki, and A. Pozzer. 2015. "The Contribution of Outdoor Air Pollution Sources to Premature Mortality on a Global Scale." *Nature* 525, 367–371.

Leung, Dennis Y. C. 2015. "Outdoor-Indoor Air Pollution in Urban Environment: Challenges and Opportunity." *Frontiers in Environmental Science.*

Loftness, V., & et al. 2017. "Elements That Contribute to Healthy Building Design." *Environmental Health Perspectives*, 965–970. www.ncbi.nlm.nih.gov/pmc/articles/PMC1892106/

Lopez Barnett, Dianna, William D. Browning. 1995. *A Primer on Sustainable Building.* SnowmassCO: Rocky Mountain Institute.

Luscomb, Richard. 2017. "How Climate Change could Turn US Real Estate Prices Upside Down." *The Guardian*: July 28.

McDonough, William. 1993. "A Centennial Sermon Design, Ecology Ethics and the Making of Things." The Cathedral of St John the Devine.

———. 1992. The Hannover Principles Design for Sustainability. Charlottesville, VA: William McDonough & Partners.

McDonough, William and Michael Braungart. 2013. *The Upcycle: Beyond Sustainability—Designing for Abundance.* New York: North Point Press.

McDonough, William and Michael Braungart . 2002. *Cradle to Cradle: Remaking the Way we Make Things.* New York: North Point Press.

McHarg, Ian. 1971. *Design with Nature.* Garden City, NY: Natural History Press.

Monat, J. P., and T. S. Gannon. 2015. "What is Systems Thinking? A Review of Selected Literature Plus Recommendations." *American Journal of Systems Science* 11–26.

Montzka, S. A. 2018. "Hydrochlorofluorocarbon measurements in the Chloro-fluorocarbon Alternatives Measurement Project." Retrieved from Earth System Research Laboratory: www.esrl.noaa.gov/gmd/hats/about/hcfc.html

Morfeld, P., and T. C. Erren. 2016. "Premature Deaths Attributed to Ambient Air Pollutants: Let Us Interpret the Robins–Greenland Theorem Correctly." (July 22). *International Journal of Public Health* 62 (July 22): 337–338. Retrieved from Springer Link: https://link.springer.com/article/10.1007%2Fs00038-016-0865-1

Nesheim, M. C., M. Oria, and P. Tsai Yih. 2015. *A Framework for Assessing Effects of the Food System.* Washington, DC: National Academies Press.

NOAA. (n.d.). Ranking of Cities Based On % Annual Possible Sunshine in Descending Order From Most To Least Average Possible Sunshine Retrieved from https://www1.ncdc.noaa.gov/pub/data/ccd-data/pctposrank.txt.

NREL. U.S. Lifecycle Inventory Data Base. National Renewable Energy Laboratory, accessed January 7, 2020, www.nrel.gov/lci/.

OECD. 2015. *Material Resources, Productivity and the Environment.* Paris: OECD.

Office of Energy Efficiency & Renewable Energy. 2015. *Guide to Determining Climate Regions by County.* Volume 7.3 of Building America Best Practices Series. Retrieved from Office Of Energy Efficiency & Renewable Energy: www.energy. gov/sites/prod/files/2015/10/f27/ba_climate_region_guide_7.3.pdf

Peel, M. C., B. L. Finlayson, and T. A. McMahon. 2007. Updated world map of the Köppen-Geiger Climate Classification, *Hydrology and Earth System Sciences* 11, 1633–164. Available at www.hydrol-earth-syst-sci.net/11/1633/2007/hess-11-1633-2007.html

Penn, Ivan. 2018. "California Will Require Solar Power for New Homes." *New York Times* (May 9). Retrieved January 6, 2020 from www.nytimes.com/2018/05/09/business/energy-environment/california-solar-power.html.

Pignataro, M. A., G. Lobaccaro, and G. Zani. 2014. Digital and Physical Models for the Validation of Sustainable Design Strategies. *Automation in Construction* 39 (April): 1–14. https://doi.org/10.1016/j.autcon.2013.11.006

Quirk, Vanessa. 2014. "The BIG U: BIG's New York City's Vision for "Rebuild by Design" Retrieved from Archdaily website January 6, 2020, www.archdaily.com/493406/the-big-u-big-s-new-york-city-vision-for-rebuild-by-design. appaport, Nina. 2016. *Vertical Urban Cities.* New York: Actar.

Raworth, Kate. 2012. A Safe and Just Space for Humanity Can We Live Within the Doughnut?: Oxfam.

Register, Richard. 1993. *Ecocity Berkeley: Building Cities for a Healthy Future.* Berkeley, CA: North Atlantic Books.

Roberts, Saglinda H. 2013. "The Implications of Integral Theory on Sustainable Design." Master's thesis,Philadelphia University/Thomas Jefferson University.

Roberts, Saglinda H. and Rob Fleming. 2017. "Structural Sustainability." In *Special Structural Topics,* Paul W. McMullin, Jonathan S. Price, and Sarah Simchuk, eds. New York: Routledge.

Schelmetic, Tracy. 2012. "Titanium Dioxide Coats Buildings, Structures to Help Them Stand Up to Smog Monster" (May 22). Retrieved from Thomas for Industry website: https://news.thomasnet.com/imt/2012/05/22/titanium-dioxide-coats-buildings-structures-to-help-them-stand-up-to-smog-monster#

Singh, Amanjeet, Matt Syal, Sue C. Grady, and Sinem Korkmaz. 2010. "Effects of Green Buildings on Employee Health and Productivity." *American Journal of Public Health* 100 (9): 1665–1668.

Skidmore, Owings and Merrill, Inc. 2015. "Intelligent Densities | Vertical Communities." London, NLA Breakfast Talk July 2015: NLA London's Center for the Built Environment.

Smith, Martin. 2015. "Building Cities Like Forests" (June 2). Retrieved from The Modern Ape website. January 6, 2020, http://themodernape.com/2015/06/02/building-cities-like-forests-when-biomimicry-meets-urban-design/.

Sommer, Robert. 1983. *Social Design: Creating Buildings with People in Mind.* Englewood Cliffs, NJ: Prentice-Hall.

Soufiane, F., M. Said, and A. Atef. 2015. "Sustainable Urban Design of Historical City Centers." *Energy Procedia* 1633–1644.

———. 2015. *Sustainable Urban Design of Historical City Centers.* Energy Procedia 74 (August): 301–307. https://doi.org/10.1016/j.egypro.2015.07.612

Sternberg, Esther M. 2010. *Healing Spaces: The Science of Place and Well-being.* Cambridge, MA: Belknap.

Tan, Sho Yen. 2012. "The Practice of Integrated Design: The Case Study of Khoo Teck Puat Hospital, Singapore." Master's thesis, Universitiy of Nottingham. Retrieved from www.academia.edu/6425550/The_Practice_of_Integrated_Design_The_Case_Study_of_Khoo_Teck_Puat_Hospital_Singapore.

Turner, M. D., D. K. Henze, S. L. Capps, et al. 2015. "Premature Deaths Attributed to Source-Specific BC Emissions in Six Urban U.S. Regions." *Environmental Research Letters* 10: 11.

U.S. Department of the Interior | U.S. Geological Survey. 2018. The Water Cycle: Water Storage in the Atmosphere. (H. Perlman, ed.). (April 19) Retrieved February 3, 2019, from The USGS Water Science School: https://water.usgs.gov/edu/water-cycleatmosphere.html

US General Services Administration. 2012. *Circulation: Defining and Planning* (May 11), Retrieved From U.S. General Services Administration: https://www.gsa.gov/cdnstatic/Circulation_-_Defining_and_Planning_%28May_2012%29.pdf

US Environmental Protection Agency. (n.d.). *Air Quality - National Summary.* Retrieved from EPA: www.epa.gov/air-trends/air-quality-national-summary

_____ "Overview of Greenhouse Gases." (n.d.). US Environmental Protection Agency, last modified April 11, 2018, accessed January 7, 2020, www.epa.gov/ghgemissions/overview-greenhouse-gases.

_____ (n.d.). "Particulate Matter (PM10) Trends." Retrieved from the EPA website: www.epa.gov/air-trends/particulate-matter-pm10-trends

_____ "Stormwater Management and Green Infrastructure Research." (n.d.). United States Environmental Protection Agency, accessed January 7, 2020, www.epa.gov/water-research/stormwater-management-and-green-infrastructure-research.

Urban Land Institute. "Brock Environmental Center." Accessed January 3, 2020, http://returnsonresilience.uli.org/case/brock-environmental-center/.

Wilson, Alex. 2015. "The Brock Environmental Center: A Pinnacle of Sustainability—and Resilience." Retrieved from Resilient Design Institute website, accessed January 6, 2020, www.resilientdesign.org/the-brock-environmental-center-a-pinnacle-of-sustainability-and-resilience/.

Wines, James, and Philip Jodidio. 2000. *Green Architecture.* New York: Taschen.

WEBSITES, CALCULATORS, AND ONLINE TOOLS

ClearDarkSky. www.cleardarksky.com

Climate Change & Infectious Diseases Group World Maps of Köppen-Geiger Climate Classification. http://koeppen-geiger.vu-wien.ac.at/

Energy Design Tools. Software overview: www.energy-design-tools.aud.ucla.edu/

Marsh, A. J., http://andrewmarsh.com/:

National Trust for Historic Preservation Preservation Leadership Forum Research & Policy Lab, https://forum.savingplaces.org/act/research-policy-lab?_ga=2.46118817.48947571.1501688782-1692506511.1501688782

Passive House Alliance, www.phius.org/home-page.

SunEarthTools.com. http://sunearthtools.com

Sustainable Sources, Green Building Databases and Design Resources. Retrieved from Sustainable Sources website: http://sustainablesources.com/resources/green-building-databases-design-resources/Univeristy of Oregon Solar Radiation Monitoring Laboratory sun path chart program, http://solardat.uoregon.edu/SunChartProgram.html.

National Oceanic and Atmospheric Administration Solar Calculator. https://www.
esrl.noaa.gov/gmd/grad/solcalc/

National Renewable Energy Laboratory. Solar maps, www.nrel.gov/gis/solar.html.

U.S. Department of Energy (DOE)/NREL/ALLIANCE, https://maps.nrel.gov/re-atlas

U.S. Green Building Council. "About USGBC," https://new.usgbc.org/about.

The United States Naval Observatory (USNO) Sun or Moon Altitude/Azimuth Table,
http://aa.usno.navy.mil/data/docs/AltAz.php

Sun angle calculator from Sustainable By Design website: https://susdesign.
com/sunangle/

SunCalc sun path calculator, www.suncalc.org

Lawrence Berkeley National Laboratory Radiance download. http://radsite.lbl.gov/
radiance/download.html

Index

Page numbers followed by *f* and *t* refer to figures and tables, respectively.